the Unofficial Guide® Color Companion to Walt Disney World®

4th Edition

Bo... ..., and Brian McNichols

Please note that prices fluctuate in the course of time and that travel information changes under the impact of many factors that influence the travel industry. We therefore suggest that you write or call ahead for confirmation when making your travel plans. Every effort has been made to ensure the accuracy of information throughout this book, and the contents of this publication are believed to be correct at the time of printing. Nevertheless, the publishers cannot accept responsibility for errors or omissions, for changes in details given in this guide, or for the consequences of any reliance on the information provided by the same. Assessments of attractions and so forth are based on the authors' own experience; therefore, descriptions given in this guide necessarily contain an element of subjective opinion, which may not reflect the publisher's opinion or dictate a reader's own experience on another occasion. Readers are invited to write the publisher with ideas, comments, and suggestions for future editions.

Published by:
AdventureKEEN
2204 First Ave. S, Ste. 102
Birmingham, AL 35233

Cover design by Scott McGrew
Interior design by Steveco International

For information on our other products and services or to obtain technical support, please contact us from within the United States at 888-604-4537 or by fax at 205-326-1012.

AdventureKEEN, LLC also publishes its books in a variety of electronic formats. Some content that appears in print may not be available in electronic formats.

ISBN 978-1-62809-054-3; eISBN 978-1-62809-055-0

Distributed by Publishers Group West

Manufactured in the United States of America

5 4 3 2 1

CONTENTS

LIST OF MAPS

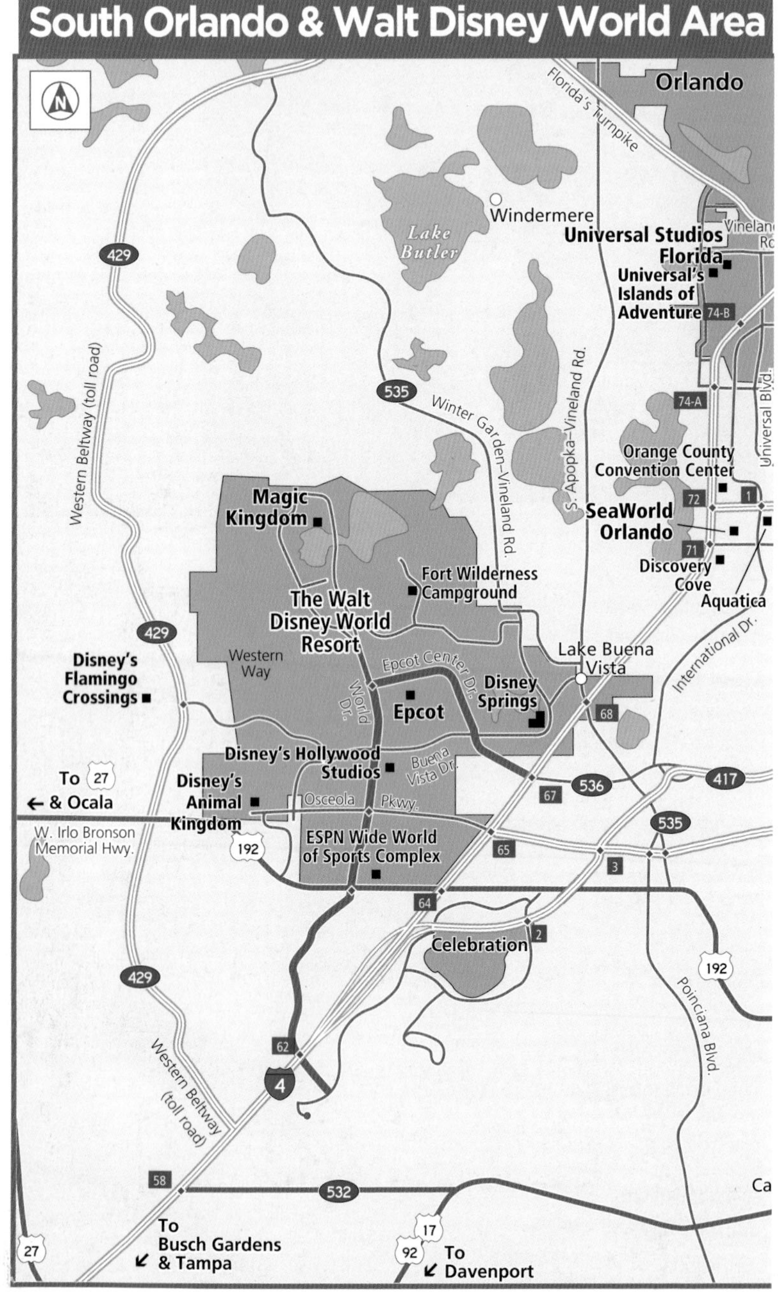
South Orlando & Walt Disney World Area
N
Orlando
Florida's Turnpike
Windermere
Lake Butler
429
Universal Studios Florida
Universal's Islands of Adventure
Vineland Rd.
74-B
74-A
Universal Blvd.
535
Winter Garden–Vineland Rd.
S. Apopka–Vineland Rd.
Western Beltway (toll road)
Orange County Convention Center
72
1
SeaWorld Orlando
71
Discovery Cove
Aquatica
Magic Kingdom
Fort Wilderness Campground
The Walt Disney World Resort
Western Way
Disney's Flamingo Crossings
Lake Buena Vista
International Dr.
Epcot Center Dr.
World Dr.
Epcot
Disney Springs
68
Disney's Hollywood Studios
Buena Vista Dr.
To 27 & Ocala
Disney's Animal Kingdom
Osceola Pkwy.
67
536
417
535
W. Irlo Bronson Memorial Hwy.
192
ESPN Wide World of Sports Complex
65
3
64
2
Celebration
192
Poinciana Blvd.
429
62
4
Western Beltway (toll road)
58
532
Ca
To Busch Gardens & Tampa
17
92
To Davenport
27

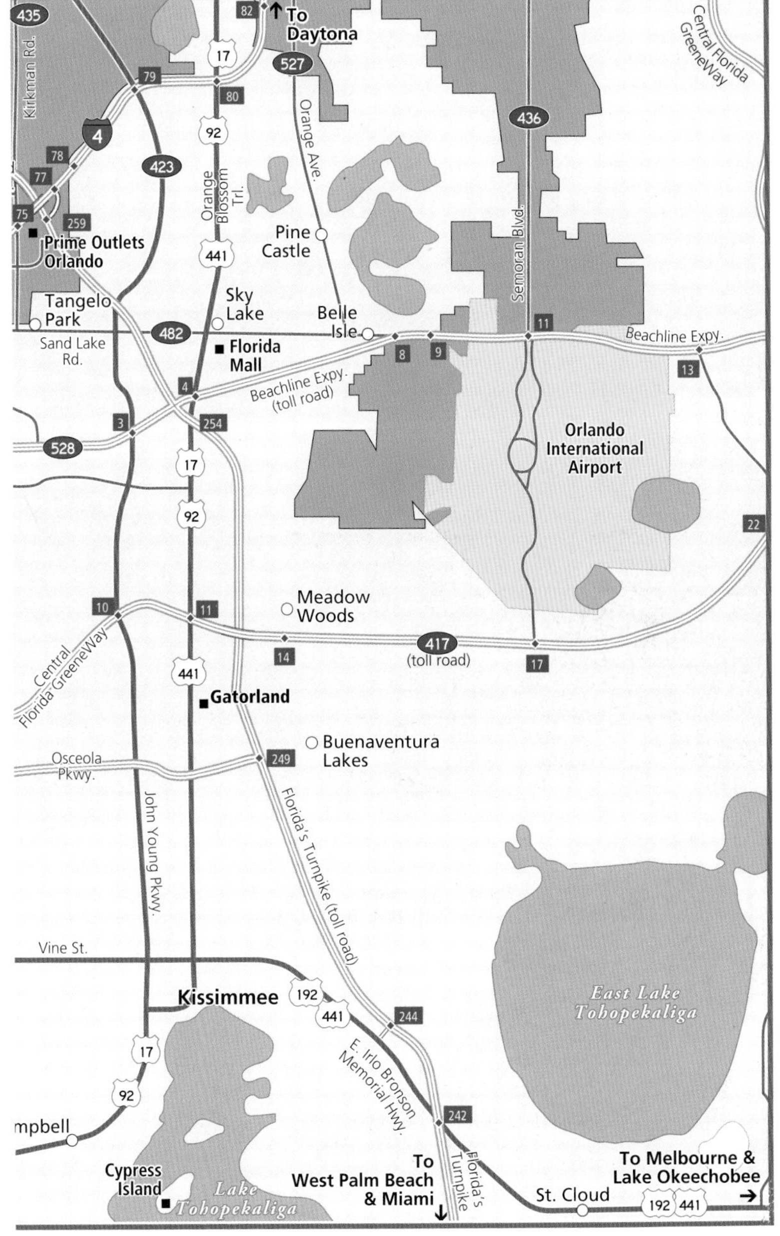

435
Kirkman Rd.
82
To Daytona
17
527
79
80
Orange Ave.
Central Florida GreeneWay
4
92
436
78
423
77
Orange Blossom Trl.
75
259
Prime Outlets Orlando
Pine Castle
441
Semoran Blvd.
Tangelo Park
Sky Lake
Belle Isle
11
482
Beachline Expy.
Sand Lake Rd.
Florida Mall
8
9
13
4
Beachline Expy. (toll road)
3
254
Orlando International Airport
528
17
92
22
Meadow Woods
10
11
14
417
(toll road)
17
Central Florida GreeneWay
441
Gatorland
Buenaventura Lakes
Osceola Pkwy.
249
Florida's Turnpike (toll road)
John Young Pkwy.
Vine St.
East Lake Tohopekaliga
Kissimmee
192
441
244
17
E. Irlo Bronson Memorial Hwy.
92
242
mpbell
To West Palm Beach & Miami
Florida's Turnpike
To Melbourne & Lake Okeechobee
Cypress Island
Lake Tohopekaliga
St. Cloud
192
441

Walt Disney World

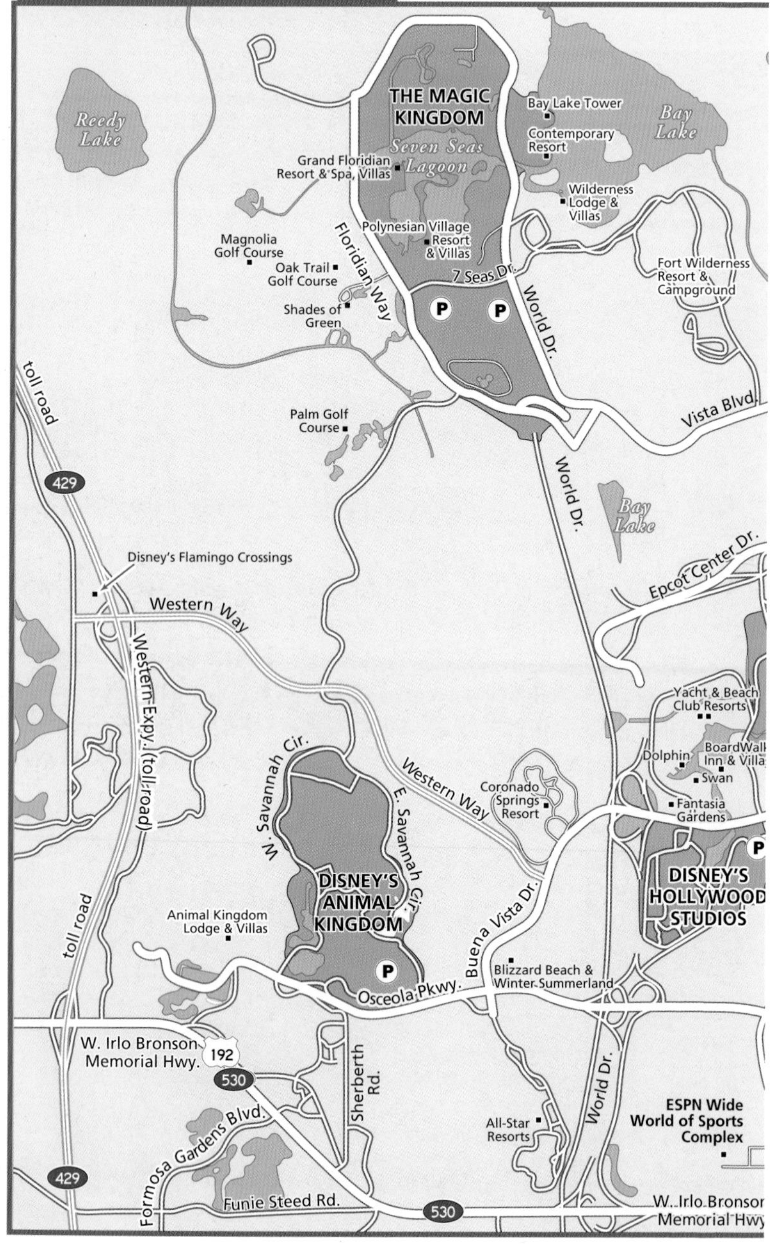

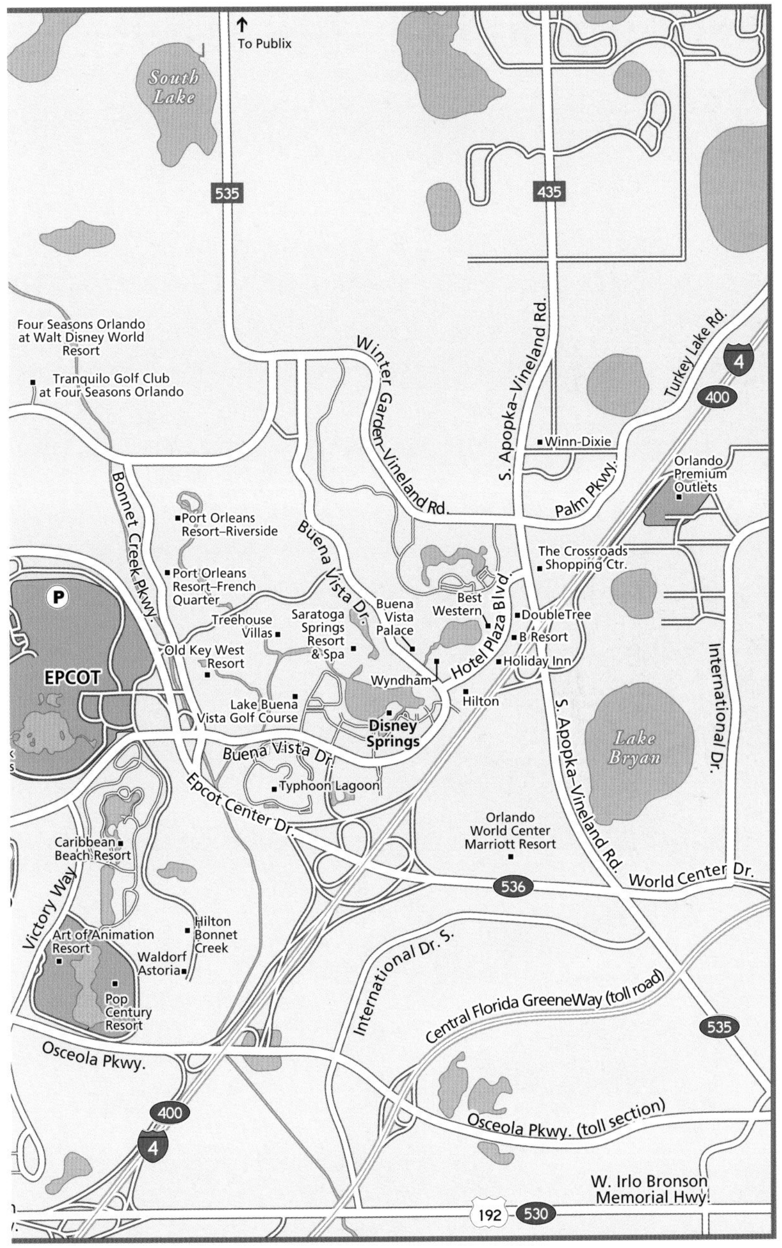

To Publix
South Lake
535
435
Four Seasons Orlando at Walt Disney World Resort
Tranquilo Golf Club at Four Seasons Orlando
Winter Garden–Vineland Rd.
S. Apopka–Vineland Rd.
Turkey Lake Rd.
4
400
Winn-Dixie
Palm Pkwy.
Orlando Premium Outlets
Bonnet Creek Pkwy.
Port Orleans Resort–Riverside
Buena Vista Dr.
The Crossroads Shopping Ctr.
Port Orleans Resort–French Quarter
P
Treehouse Villas
Saratoga Springs Resort & Spa
Buena Vista Palace
Best Western
Hotel Plaza Blvd.
DoubleTree
B Resort
Old Key West Resort
Holiday Inn
International Dr.
EPCOT
Wyndham
Hilton
Lake Buena Vista Golf Course
Disney Springs
S. Apopka–Vineland Rd.
Lake Bryan
Buena Vista Dr.
Typhoon Lagoon
Epcot Center Dr.
Orlando World Center Marriott Resort
Caribbean Beach Resort
536
World Center Dr.
Victory Way
Art of Animation Resort
Hilton Bonnet Creek
Waldorf Astoria
International Dr. S.
Central Florida GreeneWay (toll road)
Pop Century Resort
535
Osceola Pkwy.
400
4
Osceola Pkwy. (toll section)
W. Irlo Bronson Memorial Hwy.
192
530

DECLARATION OF INDEPENDENCE

The authors and researchers of this guide specifically and categorically declare that they are and always have been **TOTALLY INDEPENDENT** of the Walt Disney Company, Inc.; of Disneyland, Inc.; of Walt Disney World, Inc.; and of any and all other members of the Disney corporate family not listed. The material in this guide has not been reviewed, edited, or approved by the Walt Disney Company, Inc.; Disneyland, Inc.; or Walt Disney World, Inc.

In this guide, we represent and serve you. If a restaurant serves bad food, or a gift item is overpriced, or a ride isn't worth the wait, we say so, and in the process we hope to make your visit more fun and rewarding.

AND UNTO ALL
OF PENSY
MADE IN

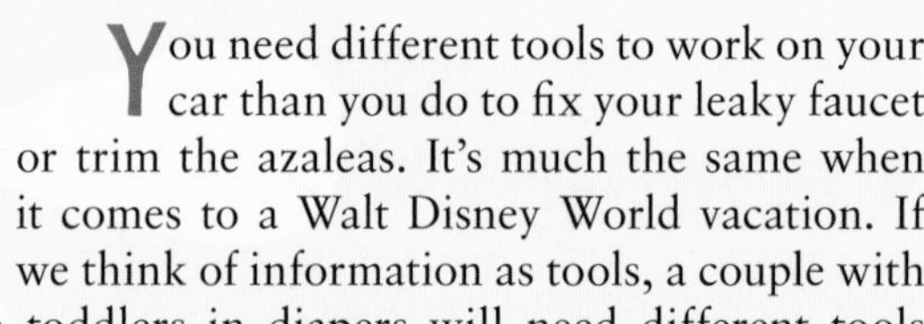

YOUR UNOFFICIAL TOOLBOX

You need different tools to work on your car than you do to fix your leaky faucet or trim the azaleas. It's much the same when it comes to a Walt Disney World vacation. If we think of information as tools, a couple with two toddlers in diapers will need different tools than a party of seniors going to the Epcot Flower and Garden Festival. Likewise, adults touring without children as well as families with kids of varying ages both require their own special tools.

To meet the various needs of our readers, we have created one very comprehensive (and rather porky) guide, *The Unofficial Guide to Walt Disney World.* At about 850 pages, we call this guide the **Big Book.** The Big Book contains the detailed information anyone traveling to Walt Disney World needs to have a super vacation. It's our cornerstone guide.

As thorough as we try to make *The Unofficial Guide to Walt Disney World,* there isn't sufficient space for all the tips and valuable information that may be important and useful to certain readers. Thus, we've developed five additional Disney World and Orlando-area guides, each designed to work in conjunction with the Big Book. All provide information tailored to specific vacationers. Although some tips from the Big Book (such as arriving early at the theme parks) are echoed in these guides, most of the information is unique. You could think of the Big Book as a vacuum cleaner and the other guides as specialized attachments that certain users might need for a particular job (back to tools, you see).

So here's what is in the toolbox:

The Unofficial Guide to Walt Disney World with Kids, by Bob Sehlinger and Liliane J. Opsomer with Len Testa, presents planning and touring tips for a family vacation, along with more than 20 special touring plans for families that are not published anywhere else.

Beyond Disney: The Unofficial Guide to SeaWorld, Universal Orlando, & the Best of Central Florida, by Bob Sehlinger and Seth Kubersky, is a guide to non-Disney attractions, restaurants, outdoor recreation, and nightlife in Orlando and central Florida.

The Unofficial Guide to Universal Orlando by Seth Kubersky gives an in-depth look at Universal Studios and Universal Islands of Adventure, including The Wizarding World of Harry Potter. Check out this title for tips on touring and detailed information about the Universal-area hotels, dining, and attractions.

The Unofficial Guide to Disney Cruise Line, by Len Testa, with Erin Foster, Laurel Stewart, and Ritchey Halphen, covers Disney at sea, whether you're extending your Walt Disney World experience with a land/sea vacation or traveling the Disney Cruise Line in Europe, Alaska, or other parts of the world. Learn everything there is to know about all four Disney ships and their ports of call.

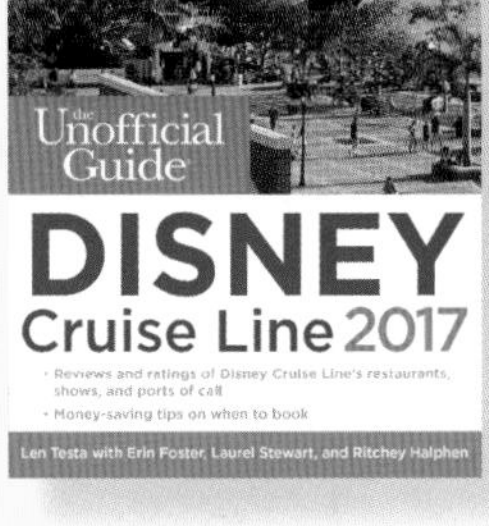

This guide, *The Unofficial Guide Color Companion to Walt Disney World,* is a full-color visual feast that proves a picture *is* worth 1,000 words. You can read everything you need to know about Disney's Wilderness Lodge Resort in the Big Book, but in the *Color Companion* you can *see* the guest rooms, the pool, and the magnificent lobby. For the first time, photos will illustrate how long the lines are at different times of day, how drenched riders get on Splash Mountain, and how the parks are decked out for various holidays. The *Color Companion* will whet your appetite for Disney fun, picture all the attractions, serve as a keepsake, and as always, help make your vacation more enjoyable. Most of all, the *Color Companion* is for fun.

ABOUT THIS BOOK

1. It Really Is a Companion While there's some information that's better communicated in prose, other information is best presented photographically. For example, photos of rooms or the pool at a Disney hotel are better than verbal descriptions. Our 850-plus-page *Unofficial Guide to Walt Disney World* is the most comprehensive guidebook in print to Disney's Orlando empire. However, when it comes to visualizing something, there's just no substitute for a good photo. So, to cover all the bases, we offer this companion guide. There's more than enough information here to plan your entire Disney vacation, but if you want to dig deeper, using the *Color Companion* in conjunction with *The Unofficial Guide to Walt Disney World* gives you the whole enchilada.

2. This Guide Has a Sense of Humor There is a plentiful assortment of dry, plodding travel guides for readers who would prefer to know how many rivets there are in a flying elephant than to have a good chuckle. As for us, we're all about providing excellent information *and* having some fun. No useful information was sacrificed to make room for humor in the *Companion*. We nailed down the essential content first and then added artistic and humorous elements to make the *Companion* a zippier and more enjoyable read. So, if you can tolerate a little irreverence, parody, and general wackiness, the *Color Companion* will serve you well.

3. Sometimes We'll Pull Your Leg We might describe a fantasy resort that's 100 feet underground with rock-chiseled furniture and an occasional mole in the guestrooms, or an octopus sandwich with tentacles everywhere and malevolent eyes peeking from between the buns. We're pretty good at this, and sometimes we might fool you for a minute, but to make sure you don't call Disney reservations and attempt to book a room, or try to order the octopus sandwich at the theme park, we've included this little icon to signal that we've taken a brief break from reality.

4. It's in the Genes The humor in this guide is totally consistent with the humor in *The Unofficial Guide to Walt Disney World*. In fact, most of the humorous elements in *Color Companion* originally appeared in the Big Book, though not in photographic form.

THE PIT DIPPER

What it is **Ferris wheel refreshment.** Scope and scale **Minor attraction, major hygiene booster.** When to go **When folks start giving you a 20-foot radius.** Authors' rating **Beats a shower any day; ★★★★.** Duration of ride **Varies, depending on if the fish are biting.** Average wait in line per 100 people ahead of you **35 minutes (estimated).** Loading speed **Slow.**

Walking around in the blistering Florida heat can make those armpits mighty ripe. Give yourself and everyone around you a break by riding The Pit Dipper, the world's first Ferris wheel that goes underwater. As the wheel turns, you'll splash down like an astronaut, be propelled to a depth of 15 feet, and shoot across 40 horizontal feet underwater. Then up you'll come in a huge wet eruption like a humpback whale in a feeding frenzy. If you have a Florida fishing license, you can rent a net and try to snag a big one while you're down there. By the time you unload, you'll be one of the best-smelling people in the park. Nose plugs are available on request.

THE UNOFFICIAL TEAM

It takes a big team to create an Unofficial Guide. Allow us to introduce our crew, except for our dining critic, who shall remain anonymous, and our on-site researchers who, as you can see, shall remain kinda anonymous:

★ BOB SEHLINGER Author and publisher

★ LEN TESTA Coauthor and webmaster

★ ERIN FOSTER Coauthor

★ BRIAN MCNICHOLS Coauthor

★ FRED HAZELTON Statistician

★ TRAVIS BRYANT theunofficialguides.com webmaster

★ SARAH KELLETH touringplans.com webmaster, Lines developer

★ KAREN TURNBOW, PhD Child psychologist

★ JIM HILL Entertainment reporter

★ LARRY OLMSTED Golf expert

★ LAUREL STEWART Fact-checking supervisor

Data Collectors

Rob Sutton, *supervisor*
Chantale Brazeau
Guy Garguilo
Shane Grizzard
Lillian Macko
Richard Macko
Kristen Mitchell
Cliff Myers
Jeff "Fred" Reisdorf
Darcie Vance
Rich Vosburgh
Kelly Whitman

Hotel Inspectors

Ritchey Halphen
Kristen Helmstetter
Lillian Macko
Richard Macko
Darcie Vance

Contributing Writers

Rich Bernato
Liliane J. Opsomer
Sue Pisaturo
Laurel Stewart
Darcie Vance
Mary Waring
Deb Wills

Editorial and Production

Molly B. Merkle, *production manager*
Holly Cross, Ritchey Halphen, and Amber Kaye Henderson, *managing editors*
Dan Downing, *photo coordinator*
Stephen Sullivan, *design and layout*
Steve Jones, Scott McGrew, and Travis Bryant, *chief creative guys*
Ann Cassar, *indexer*
Scott McGrew, Steve Jones, and Cassandra Poertner, *cartographers*

MORE KUDOS

The Unofficial Guides have always been a team effort. Our heartfelt appreciation goes to the dozens of Unofficial Guide readers who provided photos for *The Unofficial Guide Color Companion to Walt Disney World*.

Many thanks to Sam Gennawey for providing the interesting "Disney Design" sidebars in our parks chapters. Sam is an urban planner in Pasadena, California. His past projects include designs for Walt Disney World. In his spare time, Sam has authored three books on the history and design of theme parks: *The Disneyland Story: The Unofficial Guide to the Evolution of Walt Disney's Dream, Walt and the Promise of Progress City*, and *Universal vs. Disney: The Unofficial Guide to American Theme Parks' Greatest Rivalry*. Visit Sam's blog at samlanddisney.blogspot.com.

Thanks to Sara Moore for her logistic support of the research team; to Carol Damsky, Larry Bleiberg, and Lisa Schultz Smith for their good humor and creative contributions; to Jol Silversmith for his keen proofreading skills; and to intellectual property counsels Andrew Norwood and Deirdre Silver.

THE PHOTOGRAPHERS

The work of the following photographers has come together as a symphony of color and excitement in this all-color *Unofficial Guide*.

Gail Mooney If our photographers create a visual symphony, Gail Mooney is our first chair violin. Co-partner of Kelly/Mooney Productions in the NYC area, she has more than 30 years of experience in still photography. Her work has appeared regularly in *National Geographic*, *Smithsonian*, *Islands*, and *Travel & Leisure*, among many other publications. She has published books on Martha's Vineyard and Nantucket, Provence, and *Down on the Delta* about the Delta blues musicians. She is also a documentary videographer.

Richard Macko Unofficial Guide Research Team photographer Richard Macko recently moved from Orlando to Raleigh, North Carolina. A retired newspaper executive, he frequently worked at Walt Disney World on a shoot or research project. He and his wife, Lillian (also an Unofficial Guide researcher), have two married sons and three young grandchildren.

Liliane J. Opsomer Liliane was born in Belgium, lived in New York for 25 years, and now resides in Birmingham, Alabama. She is passionate about travel, Disney, and Hobbits. Liliane is the coauthor of *The Unofficial Guide to Walt Disney World with Kids* and visits the parks several times each year.

Tom Bricker After becoming engaged to his princess, Sarah, on the beach of Disney's Polynesian Resort in 2007, Tom's childhood love for Disney was rekindled. Tom and Sarah now visit the Disney parks several times per year. In addition to the *Unofficial Guide*, Tom's Disney photography has appeared in *Popular Photography* magazine, *Celebrations* magazine, and numerous other publications. Visit disneytouristblog.com for more of Tom's photos and musings on the parks.

Samantha Decker Samantha is a French teacher and photographer from Saratoga Springs, New York. Her love of photography first developed through admiring photos taken by other amateur photographers at Walt Disney World, and she never grows tired of capturing the many details of the happiest place on earth. You can read her blog at samanthadeckerphoto.com.

Cory Disbrow Cory is a lifelong Disney and theme park fan, having visited the Orlando parks ever since he was a young child. Theme parks were his inspiration for learning photography, which has become a serious hobby and passion. He made the move from New Jersey with his wife, Samantha, to the Orlando area in 2012 to be closer to the theme park world. You can find more of his work at his website, disneyphotographyblog.com, as well as his weekly news column, "Dateline Disney World," over at micechat.com.

Matt Pasant Matt's first trip to Walt Disney World was in 1992 and forever sparked a passion in the magic of Disney. For many years he has sought to share the memories of Disney through his photography. Matt now enjoys trips to Walt Disney World with his wife, Aubrey, and their children, Allison and Brandon.

Joe Penniston Although he lives in Iowa, Joe Penniston's heart lies in Walt Disney World. With wife Bridget and daughters Olivia, Anna, and Norah, the Pennistons are always looking forward to their next Disney trip. When not visiting WDW, Joe enjoys practicing all aspects of photography—from initial capture to final edit. For more of Joe's work, visit flickr.com/expressmonorail.

Stefan Zwanzger Born in Germany, Stefan became an entrepreneur at age 19 and now dedicates all his energy to thethemeparkguy.com. Stefan lives in a different country every other year, with Bratislava, Dubai, London, Stockholm, and Abu Dhabi being his latest residential encounters. His favorite theme park in the world is Tokyo DisneySea.

Other Contributing Photographers (listed alphabetically)

J. David Adams
Amber Alexandria
AllAroundOrlando.net
Theo Amditis
Kara Bacon
Nick Barese
Jeff Bergman
Mike Billick
Brendan Bowen
Daniel M. Brace
Derek Burgan
Steve Burns
Brian Carey
Dave Cass
Mona Collentine
Chris Cornwell
Kirk Damato
Leo DeCandia
Corey Dorsey
Dennis Dunkman
Ron Duphily Jr.
Jon Fiedler
Luis Garcia
Tim Gerdes
Brandon Glover
Malanie Gorrasi
Paul Gowder
Vanessa L. Guzan
Samantha Jo Hendricks
Kris Jaus
Randall Keller
Vic Kesse
Brett Kiger
Leslie Krzan
Reto Kurmann
Curtis Lannom
Marine Le Bras
Marc Lorenzo
Diane Luba
Ritzy McCarthy
Don McLaughlin
Peter Morrey
Chad Oneil Myers
Greg Nutt
Linda O'Keefe
Dave Oranchak
Jay B. Parker
Andrew Petersen
Matthew Pock
Jeremy Randall
Alan Rappaport
Bri Sabin
Thomas Damgaard Sabo
Matthew Sanchez
Victoria Shingleton
Mike Sperduto
Neil Staeck
Don Sullivan
Rob Sutton
Annette Thompson
George Trovato
Unofficial Guide Readers
Andrea Updyke
Diane Watkins
Larry White Jr.
Darren Wittko
Alice Wojtaszek

Note: For a complete list of photo credits, see page 373.

INTRODUCTION

WHEN YOU WISH UPON A STAR . .

When the Magic Kingdom opened its doors in 1971, it was the only theme park on the vast acreage that Walt Disney cagily acquired near the sleepy central Florida city of Orlando. Since then, there have been more than 50 million Disney Parks guests annually. Tourists from all corners of the globe travel to Walt Disney World to participate in the most successful amusement concept in history: part playground, part schoolroom, and part sugarplum fairy. Many of them bring their children, of course; many have been coming since they themselves were children.

What these multigenerational, multinational, and multicultural visitors all have in common is a lack of self-consciousness, a sense of playfulness, and perhaps also a sense of relief in escaping what seems to be an increasingly dark and complex real world for the instant gratifications of the Magic Kingdom and its sister parks. Other resorts may bill themselves as "antidotes to civilization," but Disney World offers an antidote to incivility; a respite from violence, squalor, hunger, and environmental depredation; and even a sort of inoculation against aging. Like Peter Pan, the international citizens of Disney World never really grow up. In many ways, it is Walt Disney's greatest gift, as close to eternal youth as we will ever get. Ponce de León may have failed to find his fountain of youth in Florida, but only because he was in the right place at the wrong time.

FROM WHENCE IT CAME

The vastness of Walt Disney World was no happy accident. Disney had made one mistake building his first kingdom—not building a big enough "moat" around it—and he wasn't about to make such a mistake with the second one. "One thing I learned from Disneyland," Walt Disney once groused, "was to control the environment." Almost as soon as Disneyland opened in 1955, motel operators, fast-food franchises, and tacky souvenir shops tried to camp as close to the castle door as possible. The entrance to the Anaheim park is on Harbor Boulevard, and that jerry-built, neon-splattered strip became the company's version of the Alamo: "Never again!"

After watching what happened to the periphery of Disneyland once the get-rich-quick jackals moved in, Walt Disney was determined that the next time he began such an endeavor, he would control the visual horizon in every direction, no matter how much land it took. The illusion, the controlled perspective, would not blur even at the

edges. That has remained one of the most remarkable aspects of Walt Disney World today. Despite its (now) urbanized location, Walt Disney World seems to exist entirely apart from any city. Once inside the perimeter, no concrete skyscrapers, no truck exhaust, no billboards, and no power lines interrupt the perfect sky.

An unblemished vista wasn't the only consideration, of course: Disney wanted to hold enough territory to exercise total control over development in the practical sense as well. For one thing, in Disneyland's first decade the merchants in the area just outside the park bled off an incredible amount of the entertainment dollars that would otherwise have been spent inside. By one estimate, the exploiters made twice the money Disney did. Dealing with Anaheim's local utilities cost him a fortune as well: He had to pay for installing power lines a second time in order to have them buried underground.

So, for Disney, aesthetics and economics went hand in hand. That meant finding a large enough tract of undeveloped, or at least minimally developed,

land that at the same time would be accessible—under Disney's own terms—to the millions of people he needed to attract. The site needed to be in a fairly warm climate, so it could operate year-round. That eliminated such early suggestions as Niagara Falls, Baltimore, and Washington, D.C.

It was the beauty of the area itself—the mixture of pasture, orange groves, forest, and marsh—that finally sold Walt Disney on his future kingdom. In 1964, when Disney had his pilots swing the corporate Gulfstream over the pine swamps of central Florida, he pointed out a spot about 15 miles south of Orlando where an unfinished expressway (soon to be the Florida Turnpike) was scraping toward I-4. Then Disney caught a glimpse of a little island in the blue of Bay Lake. "Great," he pronounced. "Buy it." (That island is now the abandoned Discovery Island, working its way back to the natural state it was in when Walt first admired it.)

Disney also quickly dispensed with the Harbor Boulevard problem. When at one meeting early in the planning stages his brother Roy, the financial fall guy, objected to buying yet more land, saying, "We already own about 12,500 acres," Walt shot back: "Two questions: Is the price right? Do we have the money?"

"Yes to both," his brother conceded.

"OK," Walt said, ending the discussion. "How would you like to own 10,000 acres next to Disneyland right now?"

But even that didn't quite satisfy Walt. "If he could have," one of his key staffers said later, "he would have bought 50,000 acres."

YOUNG AT HEART

Walt Disney died on December 15, 1966, which means that the vast majority of park guests don't really remember him, or only know a video ghost. But that doesn't mean he isn't visible: To a great extent, the "character" of Disney World reflects the personality of Walt Disney himself. Even in his 50s, when Walt started work on the original Disneyland, he was building it as much for himself—for if there was ever a man who cherished his inner child, it was he—as for his children.

What a man cherishes, he hopes to preserve and pass to his children. It was the settings and stories, the fairy tales, and young people's adventures that he remembered from his own childhood, such as *Kidnapped, The Adventures of Tom Sawyer, The Wind in the Willows, Peter Pan, The Jungle Book, Just So Stories, Tarzan of the Apes, The Arabian Nights, 20,000 Leagues Under the Sea,* and Howard Pyle's rousing versions of *The Adventures of Robin Hood* and *The Story of King Arthur and His Knights,* that Walt re-created in the original Adventureland, Fantasyland, and Tomorrowland, as well as in his first movies.

When Walt was still a toddler, the Wright brothers made the dream of flight a reality, in a clumsy-winged box far less graceful than Dumbo the Flying Elephant. When Walt was in his mid-20s, Charles Lindbergh made the first nonstop solo Atlantic air crossing and inspired the very first Mickey Mouse cartoon, *Plane Crazy.* (It was the first Mickey cartoon made, though it wasn't released until after the better-known *Steamboat Willie,* in which Mickey's alter ego echoed Mark Twain as much as it played on the contemporary popularity of Edna Ferber's *Show Boat.*) In fact, as Walt himself not only scripted Mickey's adventures but also provided his actual voice until 1946, one can plausibly argue that all of Mickey's roles reenacted Walt's own childhood fantasies.

Walt Disney's first full-length feature was a version of *Snow White and the Seven Dwarfs,* a fairy tale he'd seen in a silent version in his early teens. Pyotr Tchaikovsky's *Nutcracker* and *Sleeping Beauty* ballets were instantly classics, and he remembered them too. All these images, all these national obsessions, romances, and heroes, and in particular all the explorers and inventors—everything except the plagues and the wars—reappear in the part of Walt's amusement park that was closest to his own vision: the Magic Kingdom. The symbols of various other countries that appear in It's a Small World—which foreshadow many of the icons at the World Showcase—are straight out of early newsreels that featured the Eiffel Tower, the Sphinx, the Acropolis, the Taj Mahal, and Big Ben.

Walt grew up in the age of such inventors as Thomas Edison and Alexander Graham Bell and photographers George Eastman and Eadweard Muybridge. He grew up in a time when the medical research of Walter Reed, Louis Pasteur, and their colleagues seemed to promise a future free of disease. Because of this, he remained fascinated by and absolutely confident of the advances of science and technology. Like Muybridge and Eastman, he pushed camera technology forward; like Karl Benz and Bell, he dreamed of impulsive travel and instantaneous communication. These images and ideas pop up again and again throughout the Disney kingdom.

The three-part *Men in Space* series that began airing as a Disneyland TV show in the mid-1950s, and that featured such eminent scientists as Wernher von Braun, was so forward-looking—and so convincing—that it helped push the Pentagon into backing the space program. Walt's original vision for Epcot, the Experimental Prototype Community of Tomorrow, was of the sort of technological utopia Jules Verne would have welcomed. And for many of the original Disney generation—those uncynical post–World War II baby boomers who could remember iceboxes and operator-assisted telephones—the rapid transformation of American culture was just as magical as it seemed to Disney. Even the phrase "Atomic Age" conjured notions of progress rather than debate.

So, though the actual Epcot is not a living city but a sort of permanent world exposition, it nevertheless echoes the unquestioning faith Disney's generation placed in the captains of industry. "Progress equals prosperity" is the credo; dreams, especially the American dream, can come true if you're young at heart.

Walt Disney and Wernher von Braun at the Redstone Arsenal in 1954.

And the young at heart, like Super Bowl quarterbacks and Olympic heroines, go to Walt Disney World, where they are joined by their children, grandchildren, and thousands of their peers in a mini-nation. For the 20-somethings who throng to Disney World, the continual barrage of music, lights, lasers, and special effects provides a three-dimensional ambience that's as stimulating as a computer game. For the 30- and 40-somethings, the movie references that make up the Disney vocabulary are as familiar as their real-life friends. For older visitors, the international pavilions of Epcot's World Showcase and the safaris of Animal Kingdom are as close to foreign travel as possible without need of a passport. For the self-indulgent, a few days at the resorts can supply the delights of three or four holidays in one: beach time, wilderness hiking, club hopping, chore-free dining, sports, spa services, and shopping.

None of this is purely coincidental. So broad a potential audience doesn't go unnoticed, or unexploited. Neither does the ever-greater proportion of disposable income and increased leisure time of young and old alike. Self-fulfillment is no longer considered selfish; it's spiritual. It may require years to achieve. The Disney Company is notoriously clever at creating both demand and supply, and over the past decade it has deliberately targeted middle-aged professionals (supplying business services in the hotels and offering management and efficiency seminars to companies), sports fans (purchasing ESPN and constructing the huge Wide World of Sports complex), active retirees (offering part- and full-time jobs to seniors as well as emphasizing golfing vacations), young lovers (constructing a fairy tale wedding pavilion and offering a wide range of fantasy ceremonies), and trend-savvy yuppies (offering expensive restaurants and wine bars). It was ahead of the curve on taking special notice of military personnel, working with the Department of Defense to establish a whole resort (Shades of Green) for armed service members and their families.

Under former CEO Michael Eisner, who, during his 20-year reign, used his own very broad interests as the litmus test for Disney programs, the company went from being amenable to all age groups to specifically targeting each age group. Disney's marketing has become hyper-focused under current CEO Bob Iger, leveraging technology from mobile phone apps to RFID-enabled wristbands for theme park admission, so that sales pitches can be refined to the *n*th degree. And what will these theme park guests see? New themed lands based on the *Star Wars* and Pixar films are in the works for Disney's Hollywood Studios, and an *Avatar*-themed area is being developed for Disney's Animal Kingdom park. The company's acquisition of the Marvel universe may also influence future park construction. While those are in development, Disney continues to cater to high spenders with a variety of special events, ranging from after-hours parties with food, alcohol, and entertainment to quickly arranged diversions based on the latest hit film. We hope you liked *Frozen*.

OK, I'LL BITE. HOW BIG IS IT?

It was almost kismet—Kismet, Florida. But even then, it might not have been big enough for Walt Disney's dreams. Walt Disney World comprises more than 25,000 acres, or 43 square miles, which include four major theme parks, two water parks, 40 hotels, a campground, more than 100 restaurants, convention venues, shopping districts, a nature preserve, highways, and an interconnected series of lakes, streams, canals, and other waterways. Disney's 43 square miles is almost the size of Boston, about twice the size of Manhattan, and about 55 times the size of Monaco. Grace Kelly would have been queen of a larger and wealthier kingdom if she'd married Uncle Walt instead of Prince Rainier.

For another frame of reference, keep in mind that a standard American football field, including the end zones, is about 1.32 acres. The Magic Kingdom is 107 acres, or about 81 football fields. Disney's Hollywood Studios is 137 acres, or 103 football fields.

Epcot is about 300 acres, or about 227 football fields, or almost three Magic Kingdoms. Disney's Animal Kingdom is 500 acres, or more than 378 football fields, or almost five Magic Kingdoms. It's no wonder your feet are tired at the end of a day at the parks.

Walt Disney World has more than 70,000 employees, or cast members, making it the largest single-site employer in the United States. Keeping the costumes of those cast members clean requires the equivalent of 16,000 loads of laundry a day and the dry-cleaning of 30,000 garments daily. Mickey Mouse alone has 130 different sets of duds, ranging from a scuba wet suit to a tux. (Minnie boasts more than 100 outfits.) Each year, Disney restaurants serve 10 million burgers, 7 million hot dogs, 75 million Cokes, 9 million pounds of fries, and more than 150 tons of popcorn. In the state of Florida, only Miami and Jacksonville have bus systems larger than Disney World's.

A QUICK TRIP AROUND THE MAJOR THEME PARKS

MAGIC KINGDOM

When people think of Walt Disney World, most think of the Magic Kingdom, which opened in 1971. The Magic Kingdom consists of adventures, rides, and shows featuring Disney cartoon characters, as well as, of course, Cinderella Castle. This park is only one element of Disney World, but it remains the heart.

The Magic Kingdom is subdivided into six lands arranged around a central hub. First encountered is Main Street, U.S.A., which connects the Magic Kingdom entrance with the hub. Clockwise around the hub are Adventureland, Frontierland, Liberty Square, Fantasyland, and Tomorrowland. Each land will be detailed later, including lots of photos of Fantasyland's recently completed major expansion (the largest in the park's history).

Three properties (the Contemporary and Bay Lake Tower, the Grand Floridian Resort and Villas, and the Polynesian Village Resort and Villas) are near the Magic Kingdom and directly connected to it by monorail. Two more properties (Fort Wilderness and the Wilderness Lodge, Villas, and Cabins) are nearby, with Magic Kingdom access via boat and bus. Additionally, the military-only hotel, Shades of Green, is near the Magic Kingdom and is accessible by bus.

EPCOT

Opened in October 1982, Epcot is twice as big as the Magic Kingdom and comparable in scope. It has two major areas: Future World consists of pavilions that exhibit human creativity and technological advancement; World Showcase, arranged around a 40-acre lagoon, presents the architectural, social, and cultural heritages of almost a dozen nations, including Mexico, Norway, China, Germany, Italy, United States, Japan, Morocco, France, United Kingdom, and Canada. Each country is represented by replicas of its famous landmarks and settings. Epcot is more educational than the Magic Kingdom and has been characterized as a permanent world's fair.

Epcot is massive. A single lap around the World Showcase area is more than a mile, and the overall area of Epcot is greater than that of the Magic Kingdom and Disney's Hollywood Studios combined. Plan to take more than a single day to explore all of Epcot; the size and scope are time-consuming, even for good walkers. Also remember that Future World opens earlier and (with a few exceptions) closes earlier than the World Showcase, so plan your time accordingly. Look for the Tip Board near the entrances.

The Epcot resort hotels—Disney's Beach Club Resort and Villas, Disney's Yacht Club, Disney's BoardWalk Inn and Villas Resort, the Walt Disney World Swan, and the Walt Disney World Dolphin—are within a 5- to 15-minute walk of the International Gateway (backdoor) entrance to the theme park. A walkway connects these resorts to Disney's Hollywood Studios. The hotels are also linked to Epcot and Disney's Hollywood Studios by canal. Epcot is connected to the Magic Kingdom and nearby hotels by monorail.

© Disney

ANIMAL KINGDOM

About five times the size of the Magic Kingdom, Animal Kingdom combines zoological exhibits with rides, shows, and live entertainment. The park is arranged somewhat like the Magic Kingdom, in a hub-and-spoke configuration. A lush tropical rain forest serves as Main Street, funneling visitors to Discovery Island, the park's hub. Dominated by the park's central icon, the 14-story-tall, hand-carved Tree of Life, Discovery Island offers services, shopping, and dining. From there, guests can access the themed areas: Africa, Asia, and DinoLand U.S.A. Discovery Island, Africa, and DinoLand U.S.A. opened in 1998, followed by Asia in 1999. Africa, the largest themed area at 100 acres, features free-roaming herds in a re-creation of the Serengeti Plain. Guests tour in open-air safari vehicles. A new land, based on James Cameron's *Avatar* film franchise, opens in 2017.

Disney's Animal Kingdom is accessible to the other theme parks and resorts by bus or car. There is no boat or monorail access. The closest hotel to the Animal Kingdom theme park is Disney's Animal Kingdom Lodge and Villas, which also offers views of live animals. The All-Star resorts and the Coronado Springs resort are the next closest hotels.

DISNEY'S HOLLYWOOD STUDIOS

Opened in 1989 and about the size of the Magic Kingdom, Disney's Hollywood Studios is a theme park in flux. Originally conceived as a hybrid homage to cinema and a working film studio, Disney's Hollywood Studios is now on its way to becoming a more traditional theme park, with disparate, unrelated lands, albeit all based on motion picture entities. While some elements of the old Studios remain, notably the centerpiece Great Movie Ride, which is an overview of film classics, newer additions will change the tone of the park considerably. In late 2015, Disney announced the development of a dedicated Star Wars land, as well as an entire area themed to the Pixar film universe. We're interested to see how the Studios evolves over the next few years as these and other transitions come to fruition.

Disney's Hollywood Studios is accessible via bus and car from the Magic Kingdom and Animal Kingdom. A boat transportation system serves the canal area between the Studios and Epcot. Additionally, ambitious guests may walk to the Studios from Epcot and the Epcot-area resort hotels.

CROSSROADS
OF THE WORLD

DISNEY-SPEAK POCKET TRANSLATOR

It may come as a surprise to many, but Walt Disney World has its own somewhat peculiar language. See the following chart for some terms you are likely to bump into.

DISNEY-SPEAK	ENGLISH DEFINITION
Adventure	Ride
Attraction	Ride or theater show
Attraction host	Ride operator
Audience	Crowd
Backstage	Behind the scenes, out of view of customers
Bullpen	Queuing area
Cast member	Employee
Character	Disney character impersonated by an employee
Costume	Work attire or uniform
Dark ride	Indoor ride
Day guest	Any customer not staying at a Disney resort
Face character	A character who does not wear a head-covering costume (Snow White, Cinderella, Jasmine, and the like)
FastPass+	Timed reservation system for rides and other attractions
General public	Same as day guest
Greeter	Employee positioned at an attraction entrance
Guest	Customer
Hidden Mickeys	Frontal silhouette of Mickey's head worked subtly into the design of buildings, railings, vehicles, golf greens, attractions, and just about anything else
Onstage	In full view of customers
Preshow	Entertainment at an attraction prior to the feature presentation
Resort guest	A customer staying at a Disney resort
Role	A cast member's job
Soft opening	Opening a park or attraction before its stated opening date
Standby Line	Waiting area for an attraction. Use this if you don't have a FastPass+
Transitional experience	An element of the queuing area and/or preshow that provides a story line or information essential to understanding the attraction

Backstage

PHOTOS AND COMMENTS FROM READERS

Many who use *The Unofficial Guide Color Companion to Walt Disney World* write us to comment or share their own photos of their Disney World visits. Their comments and photos are frequently incorporated into revised editions of the Unofficial Guides. If you write us or send a photo, rest assured that we won't release your name and address to any mailing-list companies, direct-mail advertisers, or other third parties. Unless you instruct us otherwise, we'll assume that you don't object to being quoted or having your photo appear in *The Unofficial Guide Color Companion to Walt Disney World*. If you're up for having your comments or photos appear in the guide, please be sure to tell us your hometown.

How to Contact the Authors
Bob Sehlinger and Len Testa
The Unofficial Guide Color Companion to Walt Disney World
2204 First Ave. S., Suite 102
Birmingham, AL 35233
unofficialguides@menasharidge.com
facebook.com/theunofficialguides, twitter.com/theugseries

When you write, put your address on both your letter and envelope; the two sometimes get separated. It's also a good idea to include your phone number. If you e-mail us, please tell us where you're from. Remember, as travel writers, we're often out of the office for long periods of time, so forgive us if our response is slow. Unofficial Guide e-mail isn't forwarded to us when we're traveling, but we'll respond as soon as possible after we return.

Online Reader Survey
Our website hosts a questionnaire you can use to express opinions about your Walt Disney World visit. Access it here: touringplans.com/walt-disney-world/survey. The questionnaire lets every member of your party, regardless of age, tell us what he or she thinks about attractions, hotels, restaurants, and more.

PART 1

PRACTICAL STUFF

PLANNING BEFORE YOU LEAVE HOME

There's certainly no scarcity of information on Walt Disney World. There are almost 7,000 books in print (according to Amazon.com), hundreds of dedicated websites and blogs, numerous videos and DVDs, and a growing phalanx of podcasts pertaining to this well-known destination. We've boiled down the best sources of information on Walt Disney World to a manageable few, each described in this chapter.

In addition to this guide, we recommend the following resources:

1. *THE UNOFFICIAL GUIDE TO WALT DISNEY WORLD* by Bob Sehlinger and Len Testa is the most comprehensive guide to Walt Disney World in print and contains field-tested touring plans that can save you more than 4 hours a day standing in line. We update the Big Book's Kindle edition about once per month. The *Color Companion* is designed to work in conjunction with *The Unofficial Guide to Walt Disney World.*

2. *THE WALT DISNEY TRAVEL COMPANY FLORIDA VACATIONS BROCHURE* AND DVD These cover Walt Disney World in its entirety, list rates for all Disney resort hotels and campgrounds, and describe Disney World package vacations. They're available from most travel agents, by calling the Walt Disney Travel Company at ☎ 407-828-8101 or 407-934-7639, or by visiting disneyvacations.com. Be prepared to hold if you inquire by phone.

3. *THE DISNEY CRUISE LINE BROCHURE* AND DVD This brochure provides details on vacation packages that combine a cruise on the Disney Cruise Line with a stay at Walt Disney World. Disney Cruise Line also offers a free DVD that tells all you need to know about Disney cruises and then some. To obtain a copy, call ☎ 800-951-3532 or order online at disneycruise.disney.go.com/cruise-planning-tools.

4. *THE UNOFFICIAL GUIDE TO WALT DISNEY WORLD* WEBSITES Our website, touringplans.com, offers daily updates on what's going on in Walt Disney World, Universal Orlando, and the Disney Cruise Line, plus more than 140 customizable touring plans and a mobile application showing actual wait times for every attraction in every park, among other features. The site is described more fully later in this chapter. Our other website, theUnofficialGuides.com, is dedicated to news about our guidebooks, and Unofficial Guide authors contribute to its blog. Here, you can sign up for the "Unofficial Guide Newsletter," which contains even more travel tips and special offers.

5. VISIT ORLANDO VACATION PLANNING KIT If you're considering lodging outside Disney World or if you think you might patronize out-of-the-World attractions and restaurants, obtain the free *Orlando Official Visitors Guide.* On the website check out Visit Orlando Deals, which includes discounts for hotels, restaurants, ground transportation, shopping malls, dinner theaters, and non-Disney theme parks and attractions. To order the guide, call ☎ 800-643-9492. For more information and materials, call ☎ 407-363-5872 Monday–Friday, 8:30 a.m.–6:30 p.m. Eastern time, or go to visitorlando.com.

6. *HOTELCOUPONS.COM FLORIDA GUIDE* Another good source of discounts on lodging, restaurants, and attractions statewide is the *HotelCoupons.com Florida Guide.* You can sign up at hotelcoupons.com to have a free monthly guide sent to you by e-mail, or you can view the guide online. If you prefer a hard copy over a digital version, you can request one by calling ☎ 800-222-3948 Monday–Friday, 8 a.m.–5 p.m. Eastern time. The guide is free, but you pay $4 for handling ($6 if it's shipped to Canada).

7. *KISSIMMEE VISITOR'S GUIDE* This full-color guide is one of the most complete resources available and is of particular interest to those who intend to lodge outside Walt Disney World. The guide features ads for hotels, rental houses, time-shares, and condominiums, as well as a directory of attractions, restaurants, special events, and other useful info. For a copy, call the Kissimmee Convention and Visitors Bureau at ☎ 800-333-5477 or 407-742-8200, view it online at experiencekissimmee.com, or download the Kissimmee Travel Guide app for your tablet or smartphone.

8. *GUIDEBOOK FOR GUESTS WITH DISABILITIES* Available at Guest Relations when entering the theme/water parks, at resort front desks, and wheelchair-rental areas (listed in each theme park chapter). More-limited information is available at disney world.disney.go.com/faq/guests-with-disabilities.

Request information as far in advance as possible and allow 4 weeks for delivery. Follow up if you haven't received your materials within 6 weeks.

Walt Disney World on the Web: Our Recommended Sites

Searching online for Disney information is like navigating an immense maze for a very small piece of cheese: there's a lot of information available, but you may find a lot of dead-ends before getting what you want. Our picks follow.

BEST OFFICIAL THEME-PARK SITE Disney revamped its website (disneyworld.com) to support its MyMagic+ program (more on that later). A lot of work has gone into the Disney website. You can make hotel, dining, and recreation reservations; buy admission; and get park hours, attraction information, and much more.

BEST Q&A Site Who knew? Walt Disney World has a Mom's Panel all chosen from among 10,000-plus applicants. The panelists have a website (disneyworldmoms.com) where they offer tips and discuss how to plan a Disney World vacation. Several panelists have specialized experience in areas such as group travel, Disney Cruise Line, runDisney, and Disney Vacation Club; some also speak Spanish, French, and Portuguese. The parents are unpaid and are free to speak their minds.

BEST GENERAL UNOFFICIAL WALT DISNEY WORLD WEBSITE We highly recommend Deb Wills's allears.net to friends who want to make a trip to Disney World. Updated several times a week, the site includes breaking news, tons of photos, Disney restaurant menus, resort and ticket information, tips for guests with special needs, and more. We also check wdwmagic.com for news and happenings around Walt Disney World.

BEST MONEY-SAVING SITE MouseSavers (mousesavers.com) keeps an updated list of discounts for use at Disney resorts. Discounts are separated into categories such as "For the general public" and "For residents of certain states." Anyone who calls or books online can use a current discount. Savings can be considerable—up to 40% in many cases. MouseSavers also has discounts for rental cars and non-Disney hotels in the area.

BEST WALT DISNEY WORLD PREVIEW SITE If you want to see what a particular attraction is like, touringplans.com offers free videos or photos of every attraction. Videos of indoor ("dark") rides are sometimes inferior to those of outdoor rides due to poor lighting, but even the videos and photos of indoor rides generally provide a good sense of what the attraction is about. YouTube.com is also an excellent place to find videos of Disney and other Central Florida attractions.

SOCIAL MEDIA Facebook, Twitter, and Instagram are popular places for Disney fans to gather online and share comments, tips, and photos. Following fellow Disney-philes as they share their in-park experiences can make you feel like you're there, even as you're stuck in a cubicle at work. For Disney World's official social-media outlets, visit facebook.com/waltdisneyworld, twitter.com/waltdisneyworld, and instagram.com/waltdisneyworld. Disney Parks also has an official blog covering news from the worldwide theme parks, Disney Cruise Line, and Adventures by Disney. Find them at disneyparks.disney.go.com/blog. For additional news and insights, visit our Facebook page: facebook.com/The UnofficialGuides.

BEST SITE FOR GUESTS WITH FOOD ALLERGIES At allergyeats.com/disney, you put in your allergies and your park, and it shows you where and what you can eat. For official information from Disney, e-mail specialdiets@disneyworld.com or visit tinyurl.com/wdwspecialdiets.

Walt Disney World Main Information Number

When you call the main information number, ☎ 407-824-4321, you will be offered a menu of options for recorded information on theme-park operating hours, recreation areas, shopping, entertainment complexes, tickets and admissions, resort reservations, and directions by highway and from the airport. If you are using a rotary telephone, your call will be forwarded to a Disney information representative. If you are using a touch-tone phone and have a question not covered by recorded information, press eight (8) at any time to speak to a Disney representative.

Important Walt Disney World Telephone Numbers

General Information	☎ 407-824-4321 *or* 407-824-2222
General Information for the Hearing-Impaired (TTY)	☎ 407-827-5141
Accommodations/Reservations	☎ 407-934-7639
Blizzard Beach Information	☎ 407-560-3400
Convention Information	☎ 321-939-7129
Dining Advance Reservations	☎ 407-939-3463
Disabled Guests Special Requests	☎ 407-939-7807
Golf Reservations and Information	☎ 407-WDW-GOLF (939-4653)
Guided-Tour Information	☎ 407-WDW-TOUR (939-8687)
Lost and Found	☎ 407-824-4245
Merchandise Guest Services Department	☎ 407-363-6200
Outdoor Recreation Reservations and Info	☎ 407-939-1929
Resort Dining	☎ 407-939-3463
Security	☎ 407-560-7959 (routine) or ☎ 407-560-1990 (urgent)
Tennis Reservations/Lessons	☎ 321-228-1146
Ticket Inquiries	☎ 407-939-7679
Typhoon Lagoon Information	☎ 407-560-4120
Walt Disney Travel Company	☎ 407-939-6244
Weather Information	☎ 407-827-4545
Wrecker Service (or call Security after hours; see above)	☎ 407-824-0976

WHEN TO GO TO WALT DISNEY WORLD

Selecting the Time of Year for Your Visit

Walt Disney World between mid-June and mid-August is rough. You can count on large summer crowds as well as Florida's trademark heat and humidity. Avoid these dates if you can. Ditto for Memorial Day weekend at the beginning of the summer and Labor Day weekend at the end. Other holiday periods (Thanksgiving, Christmas, Easter, Halloween, spring break, and so on) are extremely crowded, but the heat is not as bad.

The least busy time historically is from Labor Day in September through the beginning of October. Next slowest are the weeks in mid-January after the Martin Luther King Jr. holiday weekend up to Presidents' Day in February (except when the Walt Disney World Marathon runs after MLK Day). The weeks after Thanksgiving and before Christmas are less crowded than average, as is mid-April–mid-May, after spring break and before Memorial Day.

Late February, March, and early April are dicey. Crowds ebb and flow according to spring-break schedules and the timing of Presidents' Day weekend. Besides being asphalt-melting hot, July brings throngs of South American tourists on their winter holiday. Though crowds have grown in September and October as a result of promotions aimed at families without school-age children and the international market, these months continue to be good for touring.

The basic rule of thumb is that Disney World is more crowded when school is out and less crowded when kids are in school. However, Disney has become increasingly adept at loading slow periods of the year with special events, conventions, food festivals, and the like. Discounts on rooms and dining during slower periods also figure in. In fall 2015 we thought the large crowds were an anomaly, but they persisted into winter and spring. The bottom line is that the World can be packed at any time, and you need to dig a little deeper than merely the time of year to pinpoint the least-crowded dates.

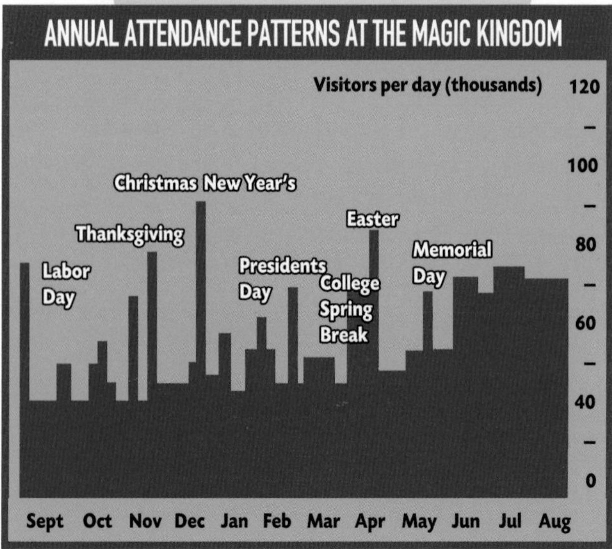

The Downside of Off-Season Touring

Though we strongly recommend going to Disney World in the fall, winter, or spring, there are a few trade-offs. The parks often close early during the off-season, either because of low crowds or special events such as the Halloween and Christmas parties at the Magic Kingdom. This drastically reduces touring hours. Even when crowds are small, it's difficult to see big parks such as the Magic Kingdom between 9 a.m. and 7 p.m. Early closing also usually means no evening parades or fireworks. And because these are slow times, some rides and attractions may be closed. Finally, Central Florida temperatures fluctuate wildly during late fall, winter, and early spring; daytime highs in the 40s and 50s aren't uncommon.

Given the choice, however, smaller crowds, bargain prices, and stress-free touring are worth risking cold weather or closed attractions. Touring in fall and other "off" periods is so much easier that our research team, at the risk of being blasphemous, would advise taking children out of school for a Disney World visit.

Lastly, don't forget August. Kids go back to school pretty early in Florida (and in a lot of other places too). This makes mid- to late August a good time to visit Walt Disney World for families who can't vacation during the off-season.

Crowd Conditions and the Best and Worst Parks to Visit for Each Day of the Year

We receive thousands of e-mails and letters inquiring about crowd conditions on specific dates throughout the year. Readers also want to know which park is best to visit on each day of their stay. To make things easier for you (and us!), we provide at touringplans.com a calendar covering the next year (click "Crowd Calendar" on the home page). For each date, we offer a crowd-level index based on a scale of 1–10, with 1 being least crowded and 10 being most crowded. Our calendar takes into account all holidays, special events, and more. All you have to do is look up the days of your intended visit on the calendar. Our online Crowd Calendar explains why we rate the parks a specific way on a specific day, including how we weigh the various factors listed above. The site also shows you our predictions versus actual crowd levels for past days, so you can see how we fared with our predictions. This information is also available through our Lines app for your tablet or smartphone. To support our research, there is a small charge to access the calendar.

Extra Magic Hours

Extra Magic Hours (EMHs) are a perk for families staying at a Walt Disney World resort, including the Swan, Dolphin, and Shades of Green. On selected days of the week, Disney resort guests are able to enter a Disney theme park 1 hour earlier or stay in a selected theme park about 2 hours later than the official park-operating hours. Theme park visitors not staying at a Disney resort may stay in the park for Extra Magic Hour evenings, but they can't experience any rides, attractions, or shows. In other words, they can shop and eat.

▶**UNOFFICIAL TIP** If you're going to get up early for one morning Extra Magic Hour session during your vacation, make sure it's for the Magic Kingdom.

Summer and Holidays

The upside to visiting Disney World among teeming hordes of vacationers is that Disney puts on an incredible array of first-rate live entertainment and events to compensate for the packed parks.

Shows, parades, concerts, and pageantry continue throughout the day. In the evening, so much is going on that you have to make tough choices. Concerts, parades, light shows, fireworks, and dance productions occur almost continuously. Disney also provides colorful decorations for most holidays, plus special parades and live entertainment for Christmas, New Year's, Easter, and Fourth of July, among others.

If you visit on a nonholiday midsummer day, plan to arrive at the turnstile 30–40 minutes before the stated opening on a non–Extra Magic Hour morning day. If you visit during a major holiday period, arrive 1 hour before. To save time in the morning, buy your admission in advance. Also, consider bringing your own stroller or wheelchair instead of renting one of Disney's.

Hit your favorite rides early using one of our touring plans, and then go back to your hotel for lunch, a swim, and perhaps a nap. If you're interested in the special parades and shows, return to the park in the late afternoon or early evening. Assume that unless you use FastPass+ (see pages 40–42), early morning will be the only time you can experience the attractions without long waits. Finally, don't wait until the last minute in the evening to leave the park—the exodus at closing is truly mind-boggling. Above all, bring your sense of humor, and pay attention to your group's morale.

MAKING THE MOST OF YOUR TIME AND MONEY

Allocating Money

How much you spend depends on how long you stay at Walt Disney World. But even if you visit only for an afternoon, be prepared to drop a bundle. This section will give you some sense of what you can expect to pay for admission, as well as which admission option will best meet your needs.

Walt Disney World Admission Options

Disney offers a number of different admission options in order to accommodate various vacation needs. These range from the humble 1-Day Base Ticket, good for a single day's entry into one Disney World theme park, to the blinged-out Platinum Plus Annual Pass, good for 365 days of admission into every Disney World theme park and water park, Disney's Oak Trail golf course, and ESPN Wide World of Sports complex, plus Memory Maker photography downloads.

The number of ticket options available makes it difficult to sort out which option represents the least expensive way to see and do everything you want. The average family staying for a week at an off-World hotel and planning a couple of activities outside the theme parks has about a dozen different ticket options to consider.

Ticket selection is complicated enough that we wrote a computer program to make it easier to understand. Visit the touringplans.com home page, click the "Save Money" button, and try our Ticket Calculator tool. It aggregates ticket prices from Disney and a number of online ticket vendors. Answer a few questions relating to the size of your party and the parks you intend to visit, and the calculator will identify your four cheapest ticket options. It will also show you how much you'll save. That said, the following section explains how Disney tickets and various add-ons work, so you'll know which kinds of tickets to price.

Magic Your Way

Disney calls its customizable ticket options "Magic Your Way." The simplest option, visiting one theme park for one day, is called a 1-Day Base Ticket, but be careful: You'll need a different 1-Day Base Ticket to visit the Magic Kingdom than you will to visit the other major parks. Other features, such as the ability to visit more than one theme park in a single day ("park hopping") or the inclusion of admission to Disney's minor venues (Typhoon Lagoon, Blizzard Beach, ESPN Wide World of Sports, minigolf, and the like), are available as add-ons to the Base Ticket.

In early 2016 Disney introduced seasonal, demand-based pricing for single-day admission to its theme parks. Each day of the year is now classified into one of three seasons—value (least-attended days), regular (average attendance), or peak (days of heaviest attendance, typically holidays)—according to how busy Disney thinks its parks will be on that day. The cost to enter the park depends on the season.

Disney has a calendar of the next 8–11 months, showing each day's seasonal classification. If you want to visit one Disney World theme park for 1 day, first, determine which theme park you want to visit. Next, determine the exact date on which you plan to visit. Then look up the park and date on Disney's calendar to see the price.

Multiday ticket pricing is still uniform across the calendar year; there is no seasonal distinction for tickets of 2 or more days. The more days of admission you buy, the lower the cost per day. For example, if you buy an adult 5-Day Base Ticket for $362.10 (tax included), each day costs $72.42, compared with $103–$121 a day for a 1-day pass to Epcot, the Studios, or Animal Kingdom and $112–$132 for the Magic Kingdom. Tickets can be purchased from 1 up to 10 days and admit you to exactly one theme park per day; you can reenter your chosen park as many times as you like on that day.

Disney says its tickets expire within 14 days of the first day of use. In practice, they really mean 13 days after the first day of use. If, say, you purchase a 4-Day Base Ticket on June 1 and use it that day for admission to the Magic Kingdom, you'll be able to visit a single Disney theme park on any of your three remaining days from June 2 through June 14. After that, the ticket expires and any unused days will be lost.

Base Ticket Add-on Options

Three add-on options are offered with the Magic Your Way Ticket, each at an additional cost.

PARK HOPPER This add-on lets you visit more than one theme park per day. The cost is $43–$53 (tax included) on top of the price of a 1-Day Base Ticket and a flat $58.58 on 2- and 3-Day Base Tickets—exorbitant for 1 or 2 days but more affordable the longer your stay. As an add-on to a 7-Day Base Ticket, the flat fee works out to $10.50 per day for park-hopping privileges. If you want to visit the Magic Kingdom in the morning and eat at Epcot in the evening, this is the feature to request. Park hopping is not necessary for all guests; good planners visiting for a short stay may not need it. However, the added flexibility of park hopping can be helpful for those planning longer visits, allowing you the ability to switch parks due to weather conditions or changes in the mood of your party.

WATER PARK FUN & MORE (WPF&M) This option gives you a certain number of visits to a non-theme-park venue based on the length of your ticket. The locations covered in the WPF&M add-on include Blizzard Beach, Typhoon Lagoon, ESPN Wide World of Sports, Disney's Oak Trail golf course, and Winter Summerland and Fantasia Gardens mini-golf courses for rounds prior to 4 p.m. Cost is $68.16 (including tax) regardless of the number of days of your Base Ticket. With 1- and 2-Day Base Tickets, guests are allowed two admissions to these venues. For longer Base Tickets, the number of admissions is the same as your number of Base Ticket days. For example, if you have a 6-Day Base Ticket and purchase the WPF&M add-on, you will receive 6 admissions. You have the same 14-day window to use all theme park admissions and all WPF&M admissions associated with your ticket.

You are not able to buy, say, an 8-Day Base Ticket with 3 or 4 WPF&M admissions. Any admissions not used during your 14-day span will be forfeited. You can, however, buy separate single admissions to any of the locations included in the WPF&M add-on. If you're only going to a water park once, this will be your least expensive option. Single-day adult water park admissions are $61.77 (including tax), or just under the WPF&M price. Mini-golf costs $14 (plus tax) for adults. The WPF&M add-on makes the most sense for guests planning a longer visit to Walt Disney World with substantial time away from the theme parks. Disney also offers a Park Hopper–WPF&M combo for $101.18 (including tax) per adult. If you plan to both park hop and make multiple water park visits, this option will provide savings.

You can add the Park Hopper and WPF&M options to your Base Ticket at any time before or during your visit, but be aware that Disney does not prorate the cost, so you'll pay the full add-on rate regardless of when you buy the option.

MEMORY MAKER Memory Maker is Disney's name for the photos taken in the theme parks, water parks, and resorts by their official photographers, along with the on-ride photos taken during some attractions. These include things like official photos at character greeting locations and the picture taken during the big drop on Splash Mountain. Guests may add the ability to download all of these photos for $149 if purchased at least three days in advance of their trip, or for $199 if purchased for immediate use. These prices remain the same regardless of the number of days of your stay or the number of guests in your immediate party. If you do purchase Memory Maker, you can increase its value by asking all members of your party to pose for as many Memory Maker pictures as possible.

Annual Passes

A Walt Disney World Platinum Annual Pass provides unlimited use of the four major theme parks for one year during normal operating hours. A Platinum Plus Annual Pass adds the unlimited use of Blizzard Beach, Typhoon Lagoon, ESPN Wide World of Sports Complex, and Disney's Oak Trail golf course. Both versions of the pass also include complimentary theme park parking and Disney Memory Maker downloads, as well as some room, food, and merchandise discount offers. Annual Passes do not include access to special events such as Mickey's Very Merry Christmas Party, Mickey's Not-So-Scary Halloween Party, or Night of Joy. Platinum passes cost $797.69 (including tax), while Platinum Plus passes cost $882.89. There is no child-level pricing for these passes; the rate is the same for all guests ages 3 and up.

How to Get the Most from Magic Your Way

First, be realistic about what you want out of your vacation. A seven-day theme park ticket with seven WPF&M admissions might seem like a great idea when you're snowbound in February and planning your trip. But actually trying to visit all those parks in a week in July might end up feeling more like Navy SEAL training. If you're going to visit only one water park, or ESPN Wide World of Sports, you're almost always better off purchasing that admission separately rather than in the WPF&M option. If you plan to visit two or more WPF&M venues, you're better off buying the add-on.

Anticipating Price Increases

Disney usually raises prices every 8–12 months, with the last few increases having gone into effect just before the crowds arrived: the latest ticket price hikes came in February 2016 and February 2015. Price increases have generally run about 5% per year, but specific ticket categories are frequently bumped at a significantly higher rate. If you're constructing a budget for a distant trip, assume at least a 5% increase.

Where to Purchase Magic Your Way Tickets

You can buy your admission passes on arrival at Walt Disney World or purchase them in advance; however, be aware that if you want to take advantage of advance FastPass+ selections (see page 31), you'll need advance tickets. Admission passes are available at Walt Disney World resorts and theme parks. Passes are also available at some non-Disney hotels and certain Walt Disney World–area grocery stores, and from independent ticket brokers. Offers of free or heavily discounted tickets abound, but they generally require you to attend a time-share sales presentation. Tickets are also available at Disney Stores and at disneyworld.com.

If you're trying to minimize costs, consider using an online ticket wholesaler, such as officialticketcenter.com, parksavers.com, or mapleleaftickets.com, especially for trips with five or more days in the parks. All tickets sold are brand-new, and the savings can range from $4 to more than $60, depending on the ticket and options chosen. All three companies offer discounts on tickets for almost all Central Florida attractions, including Disney World, Universal Orlando, and SeaWorld. Discounts for the major theme parks range from about 6% to 12%. Tickets for other attractions are more deeply discounted.

Avoid purchasing tickets from unknown vendors on sites such as eBay or Craigslist. Once used, Disney World park tickets are not transferrable. The risk of finding an unscrupulous seller is high.

For Additional Information on Passes

If you have a question or concern regarding admissions that can be addressed only through a person-to-person conversation, call ☎ 407-939-7679 or e-mail ticket .inquiries@disneyworld.com. If you call, be aware that you may spend considerable time on hold; if you e-mail, be aware that it can take up to three days to get a response. In contrast, the ticket section of the Disney World website—disneyworld. disney.go.com/tickets—is surprisingly straightforward in showing how ticket prices break down.

Disney's MyMagic+, MagicBands, and FastPass+

Disney has rolled out a set of high-tech enhancements to its theme park and hotel experience. If you haven't been to Walt Disney World for several years, many aspects of your experience, and some of your touring strategies, will feel quite different.

The centerpiece of these technological initiatives, officially known as MyMagic+, is a rubber wristband, known as the MagicBand. MagicBands include an embedded computer chip and RFID (Radio Frequency Identification) technology. Depending on your situation, the MagicBand may function as your Disney World resort hotel room key, your park admission ticket, a charging mechanism for food and merchandise purchases, a photograph locator, and a locator for ride and restaurant reservations.

Disney has also overhauled its FastPass ride priority system. The old in-park kiosks and paper "tickets" are completely gone. The new system, known as FastPass+, is entirely electronic. Guests can now make FastPass+ selections online.

Disney has also revamped its website (disneyworld.com) and mobile app (My Disney Experience), which now function as the "glue" binding all the technology together. It's all but imperative that you have a disneyworld.com account to get the most from your park experience. Much of a Disney World vacation experience must now be planned at home well in advance of your trip; because of this we're covering the basics of Disney's website and app in this section. We're providing navigational instructions here; however, Disney web designers change direction faster than hypercaffeinated squirrels in traffic, so you'll likely find that things are different than described and you may have to hunt around for some of the features. Full coverage of MagicBands starts on page 32; details on the FastPass+ system start on page 40.

My Disney Experience at DisneyWorld.com

The most important tool you'll need to manage your Walt Disney World experience is, not surprisingly, the My Disney Experience tool on the disneyworld.com website. To use this tool, you'll need to register on the password-protected website by providing your e-mail address and other biographical information. Some portions of the My Disney Experience tool are only available if you have a Disney World hotel reservation confirmation number, a Disney World theme park ticket confirmation number, or a credit card number available to input.

GETTING STARTED In the upper-right corner of the disneyworld.com home page, click on **My Disney Experience** to access the welcome page. Click **Create An Account** if you don't already have one. After that, check **My Reservations and Tickets.** If you have any hotel or ticket confirmation numbers, input those prior to taking any further steps. Then click on the **My Family & Friends** link and enter the names and ages of everyone traveling with you, even babies. You'll need this information when you make dining reservations and FastPass+ selections.

Back on the My Disney Experience page, click **My Itinerary** in the top right corner of the page. A calendar will then appear—if you have a Disney-hotel reservation, the calendar should display those dates of travel. If not, you'll need to manually enter your reservation number, and then select your travel dates using the calendar.

For each day of your trip, the website will display operating hours for the theme and water parks. Select the theme park you'll be visiting on a particular day; if you're visiting more than one, select the one at which you want to make reservations now.

MAKING FASTPASS+ RESERVATIONS Click the **FastPass+** link from the menu on the right side of your screen. Next, select one of your displayed travel dates, and then indicate which members of your group will be with you and which park you'll be visiting on that date. At press time, you could make advance FastPass+ reservations for just one park per day—this may change, however.

Now you'll see a list of your chosen park's participating FastPass+ attractions. Select the ones you'd like to reserve; if an attraction is grayed out, the attraction may be closed that day for maintenance, or all the FastPass+ selections for that day have been taken by other guests. Pending availability, you can tinker with your FastPass+ selections as often as you like before, or even during, your vacation.

You'll need to repeat these steps for every day for which you want to use FastPass+ in the theme parks. If you're unsure of the attractions or times of day for which you should use FastPass+, our touring plan software can make recommendations that will minimize your time in line. See touringplans.com for details.

MAKING DINING RESERVATIONS Click the **My Itinerary** link, then click the **Reserve Dining** link. (You may have to reenter your travel dates.) A list of every Disney World eatery will be displayed. Use the filtering criteria at the top of the page to narrow the list.

Once you've settled on a restaurant, click the restaurant's name to check availability for your dining time and the number of people in your party. If space is available and you want to make a reservation, you'll need to indicate which members of your party will be joining you. If you want to make other dining reservations, you'll need to repeat this process for every reservation. You will be required to input a credit or debit card number to secure every dining reservation; see page 127 for details on cancellation policies and fees.

Once you've made your initial set of FastPass+ and dining reservations, you'll be able to view and edit them (along with your hotel reservation) in the **My Reservation and Tickets** section of My Disney Experience.

My Disney Experience Mobile App

Along with the website, Disney offers a companion app for iOS and Android devices. It includes park hours, attraction operating hours and descriptions, restaurant hours and descriptions, the ability to make FastPass+ and dining reservations online, GPS-based directions, and more. My Disney Experience is optimized for the latest phones and tablets, so some features may not be available on all devices.

Magic Bands

With MyMagic+, Disney introduced MagicBands—reusable rubber wristbands—as a sort of wearable theme park ticket. Small and reusable across trips, a MagicBand is imprinted with your first name, an ID number, and some legalese, along with a Mickey logo. A tiny RFID chip embedded in the wristband holds your ticket and travel information.

Each RFID chip sends a unique serial number over short distances via radio waves. When you purchase theme park admission, Disney's computers will store that serial number, along with your ticket information. To enter a theme park, you'll touch your MagicBand to an RFID reader instead of going through a turnstile. The RFID reader will collect your MagicBand's serial number, compare your biometric information, and verify with Disney's computer systems that you have the correct admission to enter the park.

Disney hotel guests get a MagicBand by default but may request a plastic Key to the World (KTTW) Card instead. If you're staying off-site or you bought your admission through a third party, you can upgrade to a MagicBand for a fee; otherwise you get a credit card–size laminated ticket. Like the MagicBand, the two card options use RFID.

Each member of your family gets his or her own MagicBand, each with a unique serial number. Along with the wristband, each family member will be asked to select a four-digit personal-identification number (PIN) for purchases—more on that below. The wristbands are resizable and waterproof, and they have ventilation holes for cooling. Disney hotel guests may choose from eight colors included with their room reservation: red, blue, green, yellow, orange, pink, purple, or gray. Choose your basic band and name personalization on the **My Disney Experience** section of the Disney website. Off-site guests can purchase any of the basic colors. Any guest may buy additional MagicBands in decorative or commemorative styles for about $20–$25.

▶ **UNOFFICIAL TIP** Old non-RFID tickets must be converted to the new medium before you can enter the theme parks or use FastPass+. You can get this done only at Guest Relations, just outside each park.

ALLOCATING TIME

Which Park to See First?

This question is less academic than it appears, especially if your party includes children or teens. Children who see the Magic Kingdom first may expect the same type of fantasy entertainment at the other parks. At Epcot, they may be disappointed by the educational orientation and serious tone. (Some adults may feel this too. Buy them a drink and move on.) Disney's Hollywood Studios is currently a slow park, with many attractions closed in preparation for the development of the new Star Wars and Pixar areas. The remaining DHS attractions are primarily family-friendly stage shows, with a few thrill rides. The Animal Kingdom can be hit or miss because live animals can't be programmed to entertain on cue.

First-time visitors should see Epcot first; you will be able to enjoy it fully without having been preconditioned to think of Disney entertainment as solely fantasy or adventure in nature. See the Animal Kingdom second. Like Epcot, it's educational, but its live animals provide a change of pace. Next, see Disney's Hollywood Studios, which helps all ages make a fluid transition from the educational Epcot and Animal Kingdom to the fanciful Magic Kingdom. Also, because Disney's Hollywood Studios is smaller, you won't walk as much or stay as long. Save the Magic Kingdom for last.

OK, what do we do next? (This is why you need a plan.)

Disney Touring Tips
from Cinderella:
1. Timing is everything.
2. Wear the right shoes.
3. Believe in the magic.
4. Have a ball.

Operating Hours

The Disney World website publishes preliminary park hours 180 days in advance, but schedule adjustments can happen at any time, including the day of your visit. Check disneyworld.com, the My Disney Experience app, or call ☎ 407-824-4321 for the exact hours before you arrive. Off-season, parks may be open as few as 8 hours (9 a.m.–5 p.m.). At busy times (particularly holidays), they may operate 8 a.m.–2 a.m.

Official Opening versus Real Opening

When you call, you're given official hours. On many days, the parks open earlier. If the official hours are 9 a.m.–9 p.m., for instance, Main Street in the Magic Kingdom might open at 8:30 a.m. and the remainder of the park at 9 a.m.

Disney surveys local hotel reservations, estimates how many visitors to expect on a given day, and opens the theme parks early to avoid bottlenecks at parking facilities and ticket windows and to absorb crowds as they arrive.

Rides and attractions shut down at approximately the official closing time. Main Street in the Magic Kingdom remains open 30 minutes to an hour after the rest of the park has closed. Also remember that morning or evening Extra Magic Hours (see page 25) can impact the park hours for guests staying at Disney resort hotels.

The Cardinal Rules For Successful Touring

Even the most time-effective touring plan won't allow you to cover two or more major theme parks in one day. Plan to allocate at least an entire day to each park (an exception to this rule is when the parks close at different times, allowing you to tour one park until closing and then proceed to another park).

One-Day Touring

A comprehensive one-day tour of the Magic Kingdom, the Animal Kingdom, Epcot, or Disney's Hollywood Studios is possible but requires knowledge of the park, good planning, and plenty of energy and endurance. One-day touring doesn't leave much time for sit-down meals, prolonged browsing in shops, or lengthy breaks. One-day touring can be fun and rewarding, but allocating two days per park, especially for the Magic Kingdom and Epcot, is always preferable. Successful touring of any of the Disney parks hinges on three rules:

1. Determine in Advance What You Really Want to See

To help you set your touring priorities, we describe the theme parks and every attraction in detail in this book. In each description, we include the authors' evaluation of the attraction and the opinions of Disney World guests expressed as star ratings. Five stars is the highest rating. Finally, because attractions range from midway-type rides and horse-drawn trolleys to high-tech extravaganzas, we have developed a hierarchy of categories to pinpoint an attraction's magnitude:

Super-Headliners

These are the best attractions the theme park has to offer. They are mind-boggling in size, scope, and imagination and represent the cutting edge of attraction technology and design.

The Tower of Terror at Disney's Hollywood Studios is one of the park's super-headliner attractions. To house the ride, Disney built a 1930s-style hotel—complete with gardens, lobby, and gift shop—almost 200 feet tall. Inside are some of Disney's most sophisticated special effects. And, of course, the hotel's elevators go up, down, backward, and forward.

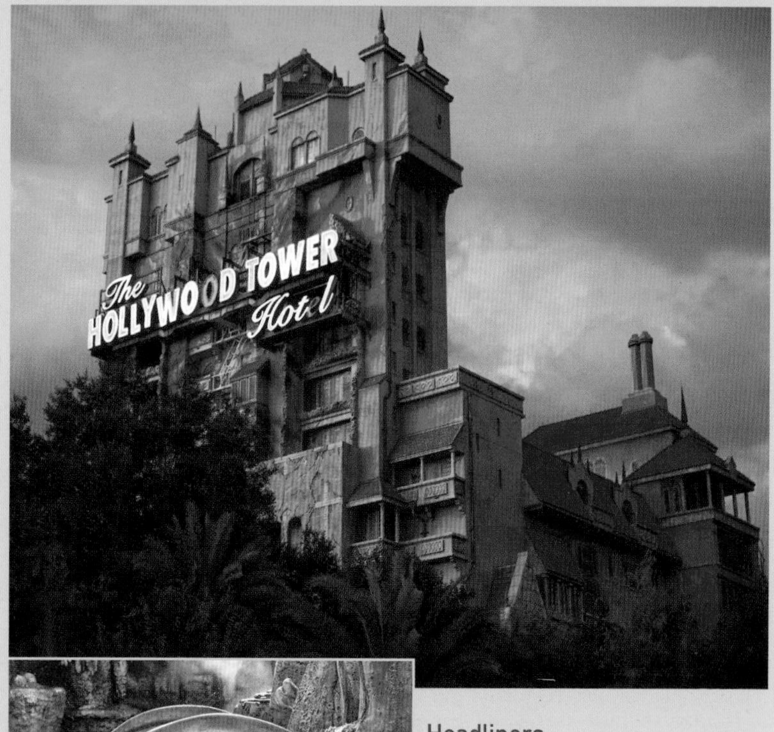

Headliners

These full-blown multimillion-dollar themed adventures and theater presentations are modern in technology and design and employ a full range of special effects.

Big Thunder Mountain Railroad in Frontierland is one of several headliner attractions in the Magic Kingdom. This mellow roller coaster is a visual feast, though you have to feast fast. After writing about Big Thunder for more than 20 years, we still discover new details every time we ride.

Major Attractions

These are themed adventures on a more modest scale but which incorporate state-of-the-art technologies, or they are larger-scale attractions of older design.

Seven Dwarfs Mine Train is a mild roller coaster designed for older grade-school children ready for something more than Dumbo. There are no loops, inversions, or rolls in the track, and no massive hills or steep drops. The Mine Train's trick is that your ride vehicle's seats swing side to side, and Disney has designed a curvy track with steep turns.

Minor Attractions

These are midway-type rides, small "dark" rides (such as cars on a track, zigzagging through the dark), small theater presentations, transportation rides, and walk-through attractions.

Enchanted Tales with Belle is an elaborate set-up for what is essentially a short photo op with Belle. What makes *Enchanted Tales* unique is the detail Disney has put into the waiting areas: each of them is heavily themed and involves substantial guest participation.

Diversions

Exhibits, both passive and interactive, such as playgrounds, video arcades, street theater, and transportation rides.

Main Street Vehicles transport visitors from one end of Main Street to the other in vintage style. In addition to the omnibus pictured here, guests can hop aboard jitneys, old-timey fire engines, and horse-drawn street cars.

UNOFFICIAL TIP Meeting characters, posing for photos, and collecting autographs can burn hours of touring time.

2. Arrive Early! Arrive Early! Arrive Early!

Theme parks don't begin the day in gridlock. In fact, they usually don't hit their peak attendance until about 1 or 2 p.m. Guests arrive from the time the gates open and continuously throughout the day. As the day wears on, waits of more than an hour become common at the most popular attractions. But by that time, those who arrived early will have all the big attractions in the rearview mirror.

Arriving early is the single most important key to efficient touring and avoiding long lines. First thing in the morning, there are no lines and fewer people. The same four rides you experience in 1 hour in early morning can take as long as 3 hours after 10:30 a.m. Eat breakfast before you arrive; don't waste prime touring time sitting in a restaurant.

The earlier a park opens, the greater your advantage. This is because most vacationers won't rise early and get to a park before it opens. Fewer people are willing to make an 8 a.m. opening than a 9 a.m. opening. If you visit during midsummer, arrive at the turnstile 30–40 minutes before opening. During holiday periods, arrive 45–60 minutes early.

Many readers share their experiences about getting to the parks before opening. From a 13-year-old girl from Bloomington, Indiana:

> **If you want to ride anything with a short wait, you have to get up in the morning! If this is a sacrifice you aren't willing to make, reconsider a Disney World vacation. Most people say they will then be exhausted, but if [you] take a break at the hot part of the day, you'll be fine.**

3. Avoid Bottlenecks

In this guide we provide detailed information on all rides and performances, enabling you to estimate how long you may have to wait in line and allowing you to compare rides for their capacity to accommodate large crowds. In our sister guide, *The Unofficial Guide to Walt Disney World* (whose Kindle edition is revised about once per month), we provide touring plans for the Magic Kingdom, the Animal Kingdom, Epcot, Disney's Hollywood Studios, and Disney's water parks to help you avoid bottlenecks. The step-by-step plans are scientifically derived and field-tested and can save more than 4 hours of time in line in a single day. The touring plans in *The Unofficial Guide to Walt Disney World* are the most time-efficient plans available anywhere.

9AM
11AM
1PM

FastPass+

Disney introduced its FastPass ride reservation system in 1999 as a way to moderate high wait times at some of Disney's headliner attractions. A new version of the system, called FastPass+, completely replaced the old one in January 2014. Whereas the old system printed your reservation times on small slips of paper dispensed from ATM-like kiosks next to each attraction, the new FastPass+ system is entirely electronic: you must use a computer, mobile device, or in-park terminal to make and modify FastPass+ reservations, and you must use your RFID-enabled MagicBand, Key to the World Card, or day-guest card to redeem the reservation. As before, FastPass+ is free of charge to all Walt Disney World guests.

FastPass+ doesn't eliminate the need to arrive early at a theme park. Because each park offers a limited number of FastPass+ attractions, you still have to make an early start if you want to avoid long lines at non-FastPass+ attractions. Plus, a limited supply of FastPasses is available for each attraction on any day. If you don't reserve in advance and you arrive at your park of choice after noon, you might find no more spots available for your favorites.

Making a FastPass+ Reservation

Anyone with an upcoming stay at a Walt Disney World hotel can make FastPass+ reservations up to 60 days in advance at disneyworld.com and through the My Disney Experience app; Annual Pass holders staying off-property may reserve up to 30 days in advance, as may day guests with a valid ticket. Set aside at least 30 minutes to complete the booking process.

If you buy your admission the day you arrive at the park or you want to change your previous FastPass+ selections once you're inside, you can do so using the mobile app or in-park computer terminals.

Returning to Ride

Each FastPass+ reservation lasts for an hour, and Disney officially enforces the ride return time. Thus, if you make a FastPass+ reservation to ride Space Mountain at 7:30 p.m., you have until 8:30 p.m. to either use it or change it to something else. Just like a restaurant reservation, your FastPass+ may be canceled if you don't show up on time. In practice, however, we've found that you can usually be up to 15 minutes late to use your reservation.

When you return to Space Mountain at the designated time, you'll be directed to a FastPass+ return line. Before you enter the line, you'll need to validate your reservation by touching your MagicBand or RFID ticket to a reader at the FastPass+ return entrance. Then you'll proceed with minimal waiting to the attraction's pre-show or boarding area.

If technical problems cause an attraction to be closed during your return time, Disney will automatically adjust your FastPass+ reservation in one of three ways:

1. If it's early in the day, Disney will offer you the chance to return to the attraction at any point in the day after it reopens.

2. Alternatively, Disney may let you choose another FastPass+ attraction in the same park, on the same day.

3. If it's late in the day, Disney will automatically give you another selection good for any FastPass+ attraction at any park the following day.

If you encounter a closed ride for which you have a FastPass+, your first step should be to check the My Disney Experience app or an in-park kiosk. This will tell you which of the replacement options you've been offered.

DISNEY
FASTPASS+
ENTRANCE
STAND-BY
ENTRANCE
WAIT TIME
MINUTES
SPACESHIP EARTH
SPACESHIP EARTH
CAUTION
Those who are made uncomfortable by enclosed, dark spaces should not ride.
Supervise children at all times.
Must Transfer

FastPass+ Rules

Disney has put rules in place to prevent guests from obtaining certain combinations of FastPass+ reservations before they get to the parks:

RULE #1: **You can obtain additional FastPass+ reservations once you use your preselected Fastpasses.** You are allowed to make anywhere from one to three FastPass+ selections prior to your visit. Once you use all of the preselected reservations, you may choose additional Fastpasses from any currently available FastPass+ reservations via the My Disney Experience app or an in-park kiosk.

It's generally a bad idea to make advance FastPass+ reservations for any of the evening parades or fireworks because you won't be able to get any more reservations while you're in the park. We suggest checking around 4 p.m. to see if any reservations are available for the fireworks and parades. If they are and you're done with the headliner attractions, grab a FastPass+. The exception to this rule is if you're making FastPass+ selections for your arrival day when you're getting to Walt Disney World in the afternoon; this might be an ideal time to get a FP+ for an evening parade or show.

RULE #2: **FastPass+ reservation times can't overlap;** Disney's computer system doesn't allow it. If you have a FastPass+ reservation for 2–3 p.m., you can't make another reservation later than 1 p.m. or earlier than 3 p.m. in the same park. When offering FastPass+ times, Disney may also take into account any dining reservations or other activities in your account, not allowing you FastPass+ selections that pose a conflict.

FASTPASS+ TIERS Disney also prohibits guests from using FastPass+ on all of a park's headliner attractions. The practice, known informally as FastPass+ tiers, was in effect only at Epcot and Disney's Hollywood Studios at press time but may possibly be extended to all four parks eventually.

At Epcot, by way of example, the FastPass+ attractions are divided into the following two tiers:

TIER A (*Choose* 1)	TIER B (*Choose* 2)
• Frozen Ever After	• Disney & Pixar Short Film Festival
• *IllumiNations*	• Journey Into Imagination with Figment
• Soarin'	• Living with the Land
• Test Track	• Meet Disney Pals at the Epcot Character Spot
	• Mission: SPACE (Green or Orange)
	• Spaceship Earth
	• The Seas with Nemo & Friends
	• *Turtle Talk with Crush*

FastPass+ lets you choose only one attraction from Tier A and two from Tier B. Note that Tier A comprises the attractions with the longest lines. The introduction of a new Soarin' film and the addition of the Frozen Ever After attraction likely means that most guests will choose between those two rides for their Tier A selection. Disney periodically tinkers with attraction tier placement, so check before making final plans. Also note that few of the attractions in Tier B actually require a FastPass+ for most of the year.

Again, though, the tiers don't apply beyond your first three advance FastPass+ reservations—any reservations you make beyond the first three when you're in the parks are totally up to you.

Louisiana oysterman Spud LeBlanc has three pieces of advice he gives everyone. Number one is to stop and smell the roses at Walt Disney World. We agree. There's so much to savor and appreciate, but you'll miss it, Spud says, "if you run around like a beagle chasing a coon." What are Spud's other two bits of advice? Never buy a car from anyone wearing white shoes, and don't drive no ugly truck.

FastPass+ University

Is this you?

Having problems with FastPass+? Spent hours on your computer and still didn't get what you wanted, or maybe you're bogged down simply trying to understand the system? You might be the perfect candidate for FastPass+ University!

We'll start you off with the Frustration Maze. Here you'll learn how to manage anger and handle aggravation. If you're unable to find your way out, we'll bring you pizza and sodas and an umbrella if necessary. By the time you complete the maze, the frustration of dealing with FastPass+ will seem inconsequential. Just mellow out and enjoy a latte while you slog through making your FastPass+ reservations.

Next, it's off to the date-counting classroom where you'll be shown how to count days backwards in order to determine the correct date to go online to make your reservations. You'll find that counting backwards 30, 60, or even 180 days (for some restaurants) is not as hard as it sounds. Watch out for leap year!

Optional: Attend a round table discussion about why Disney scrapped a simple FastPass system that worked great and that everyone loved and replaced it with a baffling system that drives folks bat-poop nuts. Also covered is why there are now long lines for attractions you could previously walk onto.

Then attend a series of classes, workshops, and labs where our experienced instructors will lead you through the rigors of the FastPass+ process. We'll help you figure out what, when, and where you want to eat and which park you'd like to visit 90 days in advance.

FastPass+ made simple

Disney World Vacation Planning Chart

- 13 years in advance: Set up Disney Vacation Fund
- 10 years in advance: Identify genetic markers of potential spouses predisposed to enjoy a Disney vacation. Create a dating app to sort candidates.
- 8 years in advance: Woo and marry Disney-loving partner.
- 7 years in advance: First child comes along. Decorate his/her room with tasteful Disney decor. (Winnie the Pooh and Friends in muted pastels works well.)
- 6 years in advance: Set up college savings fund.
- 5 years in advance: Teach child to talk. First words should be, "These are not the droids you're looking for."
- 4 years in advance: Second child comes along. Install large-screen monitors in nursery to run a continuous loop of Disney programming 24/7.
- 2 years in advance: Buy *Unofficial Guide* and subscribe to touringplans.com and Lines to begin assessment of crowd and wait time trends.
- 1 year in advance: Book hotel using touringplans.com room finder app. Start a rigorous walking program. Mantra: tired kids will not hold me back.
- 9 months in advance: Cash in Disney vacation fund.
- 8 months in advance: Also cash in college savings fund to cover Disney price increases.
- 180 days in advance: Make dining reservations.
- 90 days in advance: Begin psychotherapy.
- 60 days in advance: Make FastPass+ selections.
- 40 days in advance: Add Aunt Mary to your group. Change all of your dining reservations and FastPass+ selections. Buy stock in Xanax.
- Zero day: Enjoy!
- Zero day + 14: Research your state's bankruptcy laws.

SPECIAL TIPS FOR SPECIAL PEOPLE

Walt Disney World for Singles

Walt Disney World is great for singles. It is a safe, clean, and low-pressure environment. If you're looking for a place to relax without being hit on, Disney World is perfect. Bars, lounges, and nightclubs are the most laid-back and friendly you're likely to find anywhere. In many, you can hang out and not even be asked to buy a drink (or asked to let someone buy a drink for you). Parking lots are well lit and constantly patrolled. For women alone, safety and comfort are unsurpassed.

There's also no need to while away the evening hours alone in your hotel room. Between the BoardWalk and Disney Springs, nightlife options abound. If you drink more than you should and are a Disney resort guest, Disney buses will return you safely to your hotel.

Walt Disney World for Couples

Weddings, Commitment Ceremonies, and Vow Renewals

So many couples tie the knot or honeymoon in the World that Disney has a dedicated department to help arrange the day of your dreams. Disney's Fairy Tale Weddings & Honeymoons (☎ 321-939-4610; disneyweddings.com) offers a range of ceremony venues and services, plus honeymoon planning and registries.

Couples wishing to get hitched at Walt Disney World can choose from an array of packages, starting at about $2,500 for a simple ceremony with a handful of guests on up to hundreds of thousands of dollars for an elaborate ceremony and reception for hundreds. Depending on your needs and your budget, Disney can provide transportation, lodging, music, flowers, photography, food, and more.

To marry at Walt Disney World, you need a license, issued at any Florida courthouse; additional requirements may also apply. The officiant and marriage license are not included in any package, but Disney can provide you with a list of recommendations, or you can provide your own. A wonderful resource for planning a Disney wedding is *Passporter's Disney Weddings & Honeymoons* by Carrie Hayward (available in print via Amazon.com or as an ebook at passporter.com/weddings.asp). Hayward also has more information available at disneyweddingpodcast.com.

Romantic Getaways

Disney World is a favorite getaway for couples, but not all Disney hotels are equally romantic. Some are too family-oriented; others swarm with convention-goers. For romantic (though expensive) lodging, we recommend Animal Kingdom Lodge & Villas; Bay Lake Tower at the Contemporary; the Polynesian Village Resort; Wilderness Lodge & Boulder Ridge Villas; the Grand Floridian Resort, Spa, & Villas; BoardWalk Inn & Villas; and the Yacht & Beach Club Resorts. The Alligator Bayou section at Port Orleans Riverside, a Moderate Disney resort, also has secluded rooms.

© Jeff Bergman

Quiet, Romantic Places To Eat

Restaurants with good food and a couple-friendly ambience are rare in the theme parks. Only a handful of dining locales satisfy both requirements: Coral Reef Restaurant, an alfresco table at Tutto Italia, the terrace at the Rose & Crown, and the upstairs tables at the France Pavilion's Monsieur Paul, all in Epcot; and the corner booths at The Hollywood Brown Derby in the Studios. Waterfront dining (though not necessarily quiet or romantic) is available at Paddlefish, Paradiso 37, and Portobello at Disney Springs and Narcoossee's at the Grand Floridian.

While quiet romance can be difficult to find in the parks, there are a number of special and romantic dining venues in the Disney hotels. Victoria & Albert's at the Grand Floridian is the World's showcase gourmet restaurant; expect to pay big bucks. Other good choices for couples include Artist Point at Wilderness Lodge, Yachtsman Steakhouse at the Yacht Club, Shula's at the Dolphin, Jiko—The Cooking Place at Animal Kingdom Lodge, and Flying Fish at the BoardWalk.

Eating later in the evening and choosing a restaurant we've mentioned will improve your chances for intimate dining; nevertheless, children—well behaved or otherwise—are everywhere at Walt Disney World, and there's no way to escape them.

RESERVED FOR
"Breaker 5, breaker 5, this is the Red Rattlesnake. We got ourselves a convoy!"

Walt Disney World for Seniors

Most seniors we interview enjoy Disney World much more when they tour with folks their own age. If, however, you're considering going to Disney World with your grandchildren, we recommend an orientation visit without them first. If you know firsthand what to expect, it's much easier to establish limits, maintain control, and set a comfortable pace when you visit with the youngsters.

Because seniors are a varied and willing lot, there aren't any attractions we would suggest they avoid. For seniors, as with other Disney visitors, personal taste is more important than age. We hate to see mature visitors pass up an exceptional attraction such as Splash Mountain because younger visitors call it a thrill ride. Splash Mountain, a full-blown adventure, gets its appeal more from music and visual effects than the thrill of the ride. Because you must choose among attractions that might interest you, we provide facts to help you make informed decisions.

Getting Around

Many seniors like to walk, but a 7-hour visit to a theme park includes 4–10 miles on foot. If you're not up to that, let someone push you in a rented wheelchair. The theme parks also offer fun-to-drive electric convenience vehicles (ECVs). You can rent a chair at the Magic Kingdom in the morning, return it, go to Epcot, present your deposit slip, and get another chair at no additional charge. If you'll need a wheelchair or ECV for the entirety of your trip, or for use at your hotel, a better (and cheaper) option will be to rent this equipment from an off-site vendor. See disneyworld.disney.go.com/guest-services/wheelchair-rentals for a list of approved rental agencies who can drop off and pick up equipment at your hotel. Don't let your pride keep you from having a good time. Sure, you could march 10 miles if you had to—but you don't have to!

Senior Lodging

If you can afford it, stay in Walt Disney World. If you're concerned about the quality of your accommodations or the availability of transportation, staying inside the Disney complex will ease your mind. The rooms are some of the nicest in the Orlando area and are always clean and well maintained. Plus, transportation is always available to any destination in Disney World at no additional cost. Disney hotels reserve rooms closer to restaurants and transportation for guests of any age who can't tolerate much walking. They also provide golf carts to pick up guests and deliver them to their rooms. Cart service can vary dramatically depending on the time of day and the number of guests requesting service. At check-in time (around 3 p.m.), for example, the wait for a ride can be as long as 40 minutes.

Disney hotels are spread out. It's easy to avoid most stairs, but it's often a long hike to your room from parking lots or bus stops. Seniors intending to spend more time at Epcot and Hollywood Studios than at the Magic Kingdom or Animal Kingdom should consider the Yacht & Beach Club Resorts, the Swan, the Dolphin, or BoardWalk Inn & Villas.

The Contemporary Resort and Bay Lake Tower are good choices for seniors who want to be on the monorail system. So are the Grand Floridian and Polynesian, though they cover many acres, necessitating a lot of walking. For a restful, rustic feeling, choose the Wilderness Lodge & Boulder Ridge Villas. If you want a kitchen and the comforts of home, book a resort with villa accommodations (see Part 2 for options). If you enjoy watching birds and animals, try Animal Kingdom Lodge & Villas. Try Saratoga Springs for golf.

RVers will find Disney's Fort Wilderness Resort & Campground pleasant. Several independent campgrounds are also within 30 minutes of Disney World. None offers the wilderness setting or amenities that Disney does, but they cost less.

Senior Dining

Eat breakfast at your hotel restaurant, or save money by having juice and rolls in your room. Follow with an early dinner and be out of the restaurants and ready for evening touring and fireworks long before the main crowd begins to think about dinner. We recommend fitting dining and rest times into the day. Plan lunch as your break in the day. Sit back, relax, and enjoy. Then return to your hotel for a nap or a swim.

▶ **UNOFFICIAL TIP** Make your Advance Reservations for dining before noon to avoid the lunch crowds.

Walt Disney World for Guests with Disabilities

Each theme park offers a free booklet describing disabled services and facilities at disneyworld.disney.go.com/guest-services/guests-with-disabilities. Or get it when you enter the parks, at resort front desks, and at wheelchair-rental locations inside the parks.

For specific requests, such as those for special accommodations at hotels or on the Disney transportation system, call ☎ 407-939-7807 (voice) or 407-939-7670 (TTY). When the recorded menu comes up, press 1. Limit your questions and requests to those regarding disabled services and accommodations (address other questions to ☎ 407-824-4321 or 407-827-5141 [TTY]). If you'll be staying at a Disney resort, let the reservation agent know of any special needs you have when you book your room.

Visitors with Special Needs

COMPLETELY OR PARTIALLY NONAMBULATORY GUESTS You may rent wheelchairs or electric convenience vehicles (ECVs) at the Disney World theme parks. These are available on a first-come, first-serve basis. If you will definitely need one, or will need one at your hotel or other nonpark venue, you're better off renting from an independent agency (see page 119 for details). With very few exceptions, most rides, shows, restaurants, and restrooms can accommodate nonambulatory guests. If you're in a theme park and need guidance about park touring in a wheelchair or ECV, stop by Guest Relations.

Handicapped parking areas are available for disabled visitors at all Disney World theme parks and resorts. A valid disability parking permit is required. The parking attendants can direct you to the appropriate lot.

An information booklet for disabled guests is available at wheelchair-rental locations in each park. Theme-park maps issued to each guest on admission are symbol-coded to show nonambulatory guests which attractions accommodate wheelchairs.

Even if an attraction doesn't accommodate wheelchairs, nonambulatory guests still may ride if they can transfer from their wheelchair to the ride's vehicle. Disney staff, however, aren't trained or permitted to assist in transfers. Guests must be able to board the ride unassisted or have a member of their party assist them. Either way, members of the nonambulatory guest's party will be permitted to go along on the ride.

Because waiting areas of most attractions won't accommodate wheelchairs, nonambulatory guests and their party should request boarding instructions from a Disney attendant as soon as they arrive at an attraction. Almost always, the entire group will be allowed to board without a lengthy wait.

VISITORS WITH DIETARY RESTRICTIONS Walt Disney World restaurants work very hard to accommodate guests' special dietary needs. When you make a dining reservation online or by phone, you'll be asked about food allergies and the like. The host or hostess and your server will also ask about this and send the chef out to discuss the menu; if you're not asked, just talk to your server when you're seated. For counter-service restaurants or kiosks, ask at Guest Relations or at the venue itself. For more information, e-mail special.diets@disneyworld.com or visit tinyurl.com/wdwspecialdiets.

SIGHT- AND/OR HEARING-IMPAIRED GUESTS Guest Relations at the theme parks provides complimentary assistive-technology devices to visually and hearing-impaired guests ($25–$100 refundable deposit, depending on the device). Sight-impaired guests can customize the given information through an interactive audio menu that is guided by a wireless GPS system in the device. Hearing-impaired guests can benefit from amplified audio and closed-captioning for attractions loaded into the same device.

Braille guide maps are available from Guest Relations at all theme parks ($25 refundable deposit). Closed captioning is provided on some rides, while many theater attractions provide reflective captioning. A sign-language interpreter performs at some live-theater presentations; for show information, call ☎ 407-824-4321 (voice) or 407-827-5141 (TTY).

NONAPPARENT DISABILITIES We receive many letters from readers whose traveling companion or child requires special assistance, but who, unlike a person in a wheelchair, is not visibly disabled. Autism, for example, makes it very difficult or impossible for someone with the disorder to wait in line for more than a few minutes or in queues surrounded by a crowd.

Visitors with nonapparent disabilities should obtain a Disability Access Service (DAS) card, a pass that accommodates guests who can't wait in regular standby lines. You can obtain a DAS card at the Guest Relations window of the first theme park you visit. The same card works in every subsequent park you visit. Allow 20–30 minutes to complete the sign-up process.

Complete details on how to acquire and use a DAS card can be found at tinyurl.com/DisneyDAScard; here are the basics. When you get to Guest Relations, you'll need to present identification and describe your or your family member's limitations. You don't need to disclose a disease or medical condition—what Disney's looking for is a description of how the condition affects you in the parks. Rather than an attempt to have you "prove" your condition, the goal here is to get you the right level of assistance. Be as detailed as possible in describing limitations. For instance, if your child is on the autism spectrum, has trouble waiting in long lines, and has sensory issues that make it difficult for him or her to hear loud noises, you need to let the cast member know each of these things. "He doesn't wait in lines" isn't enough to go on.

The DAS card requires a photograph. Pictures are taken with an iPad; the cast member will come to you if you can't make it up to the counter. If the DAS card is for a child, you may either use the child's photo or substitute your own if you'd rather not use the child's. Finally, you must sign the card and agree to be bound by its rules.

DAS cards can be used at any attraction or meet and greet with a FastPass+ line. Present the card to a cast member at the attraction you want to ride. If the ride's standby wait time is less than 10 minutes, you'll usually be escorted through the standby entrance or FastPass+ entrance. If the standby time is higher, the cast member will enter on the back of the DAS card the attraction name, time of day, wait time, and a return time for you to come back to ride. The return time will be the current wait time minus 10 minutes. So if you get to Splash Mountain at 12:20 p.m. and the standby time is 40 minutes, your return time will be 30 minutes later, at 12:50 p.m.

You may return at the specified time or at any time thereafter. When you return, you'll be admitted to the FastPass+ line. The cardholder need not be present to obtain a return time but must be present with his or her party for anyone to gain admission.

DAS cards are good for parties of up to six people. For parties of more than six, all members of the party must be present when the card is used. DAS cards are good (1) for the duration of your vacation, (2) for 60 days, or (3) until the back of the card is full, whichever comes first. If you fill your card, you must return to Guest Relations and get another.

Finally, note that you can use FastPass+ while you're using the DAS. In fact, cast members will suggest that you do so. It may take some extra planning on the front end, but using FastPass+ helps your DAS access.

GETTING THERE

Directions

Motorists can reach any Walt Disney World destination via World Drive off US 192; via Epcot Center Drive off I-4; via FL 536 and West Osceola Parkway from FL 417/ Central Florida GreeneWay; or from the Hartzog Road/Walt Disney World interchange off FL 429, also known as the Western Beltway (see map on pages iv–v).

WARNING! I-4 is an east–west highway but takes a north–south slant through the Orlando-Kissimmee area. This directional change complicates getting oriented in and around Disney World. Logic suggests that highways branching off I-4 should run north and south, but most run east and west here.

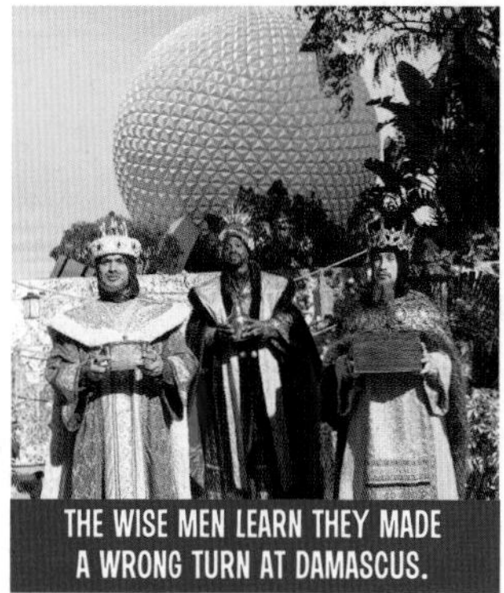

THE WISE MEN LEARN THEY MADE A WRONG TURN AT DAMASCUS.

FROM I-10 Take I-10 east across Florida to I-75 southbound at Exit 296A/Tampa; then take Florida's Turnpike (toll road) southbound at Exit 328 (on the left) toward Orlando. Take FL 429 (another toll road) to Exit 267A/Tampa southbound off the turnpike. Leave FL 429 at Exit 8, the Western Way interchange, in the direction of Walt Disney World, and follow the signs to your Disney destination. Also use these directions to reach hotels along US 192.

FROM I-75 SOUTHBOUND Take I-75 south onto Florida's Turnpike via Exit 328 (on the left) toward Orlando. Take FL 429 (toll) southbound off the turnpike. Leave FL 429 at Exit 8, the Western Way interchange, in the direction of Disney World, and follow the signs to your Disney destination. Also use these directions for hotels along US 192.

FROM I-95 SOUTHBOUND Take Exit 260B off I-95 onto I-4 West toward Orlando/ Tampa. In non-rush hours, continue on I-4 through downtown Orlando to WDW Exits 64, 65, 67, or 68, depending on your destination. During rush hour, exit I-4 south of Seminole Town Center at Exit 101B onto FL 417/Central Florida GreeneWay. Skirt Orlando to the southwest and continue on FL 417 to Exit 6/FL 536, marked Epcot/Disney Springs.

FROM THE ORLANDO INTERNATIONAL AIRPORT

There are two routes from the airport to Walt Disney World. Both take almost exactly the same amount of time to drive except during rush-hour traffic, when Route One via FL 417 is far less congested than Route Two via the Beachline Expressway. Also, Route One eliminates the need to drive on I-4, which is always horribly congested.

Route One: Drive southwest on FL 417/Central Florida GreeneWay, a toll road. Take Exit 6/International Drive toward FL 535. FL 536 will cross I-4 and become Epcot Center Drive. From here, follow the signs to your Walt Disney World destination. If you're going to a hotel on US 192 (Irlo Bronson Memorial Highway), follow the same route until you reach I-4. Take I-4 west toward Tampa. Take the first US 192 exit if your hotel is on West Irlo Bronson, the second exit if your hotel is on East Irlo Bronson. If your hotel is in Lake Buena Vista, take Exit 6 onto FL 536 as described previously, and then turn right on FL 535 to the Lake Buena Vista area.

Route Two: Take FL 528/Beachline Expressway, a toll road, west for about 19 miles to the intersection with I-4. Go west on I-4 to Exit 67/FL 536, marked Epcot/Disney Springs, and follow the signs to your Walt Disney World destination. This is also the route to take if your hotel is on International Drive or Universal Boulevard, near Universal Studios, near SeaWorld, or near the Orange County Convention Center. For these destinations, take I-4 east toward Orlando.

FROM MIAMI, FORT LAUDERDALE, AND SOUTHEASTERN FLORIDA
Head north on Florida's Turnpike to Exit 249/Osceola Parkway West, and follow the signs.

FROM TAMPA AND SOUTHWESTERN FLORIDA
Take I-75 northbound to I-4. Go east on I-4, take Exit 64 onto US 192 westbound, and follow the signs.

Walt Disney World Exits off I-4

Going east to west (in the direction of Orlando to Tampa), five I-4 exits serve Walt Disney World.

Exit 68 (FL 535/Lake Buena Vista) primarily serves the Disney Springs Resort Area and Disney Springs, including the Disney Springs Marketplace and West Side. It also serves non-Disney hotels with a Lake Buena Vista address. This exit puts you on roads with lots of traffic signals. Avoid it unless you're headed to one of the preceding destinations.

Exit 67 (Epcot/Disney Springs) delivers you to a four-lane expressway into the heart of Disney World. It's the fastest and most convenient way for westbound travelers to access almost all Disney destinations except Animal Kingdom and ESPN Wide World of Sports Complex.

Exit 65 (Osceola Parkway) is the best exit for westbound travelers to access Animal Kingdom, Animal Kingdom Lodge, Pop Century Resort, Art of Animation Resort, All-Star Resorts, and ESPN Wide World of Sports Complex.

Exit 64 (US 192/Magic Kingdom) is the best route for eastbound travelers to all Disney World destinations.

Exit 62 (Disney World/Celebration) is the first Disney exit you'll encounter if you're headed eastbound. This four-lane, controlled-access highway connects to the so-called Maingate of Walt Disney World. Accessing Walt Disney World via the next exit, Exit 64, also routes you through the main entrance.

Transportation to Walt Disney World from the Airport

If you arrive in Orlando by plane, there are six basic options for getting to Walt Disney World:

1. TAXI Taxis carry four to eight passengers, depending on the type of vehicle. Rates vary according to the distance traveled, not the number of passengers. If your hotel is on Disney World property, expect to pay $60–$72, not including tip. For the US 192 Maingate area, your fare will be about $60. If you go to International Drive or downtown Orlando, expect to pay about $38–$50. For a price estimate based on your exact destination, use taxifarefinder.com/main.php?city=Orlando

2. SHUTTLE SERVICE Mears Transportation Group (☎ 855-463-2776; mearstransportation.com) operates from Orlando International Airport. Although this is the shuttle service that will provide your transportation if airport transfers are included in your vacation package, you do not have to be on a package to avail yourself of their services. In practice, the shuttles collect passengers until they fill a van (or sometimes a bus). Once the vehicle is full or close to full, it's dispatched. Mears charges per-person rates (children under age 3 ride free). Both one-way and round-trip services are available. Round-trips to the World run about $36 for adults and $27 for children.

3. TOWN-CAR SERVICE Similar to taxi service, a town-car service will transport you directly from Orlando International Airport to your hotel. Instead of hailing a car outside the airport, however, the town-car driver will usually be waiting for you in the baggage claim area of your airline. Town-car companies we've had a good experience with include Tiffany Towncar Service (☎ 888-838-2161 or 407-370-2196; tiffanytowncars.com) and Quicksilver Tours & Transportation (☎ 888-GO-TO-WDW or 407-299-1434; quicksilver-tours.com). Round-trips to the World run about $125–$140, plus tip.

4. RENTAL CARS Rental cars are readily available for both short- and long-term rentals. Most rental companies allow you to drop a rental car at certain hotels or at one of their subsidiary locations in the Walt Disney World general area if you do not want the car for your entire stay. Likewise, you can pick up a car at any time during your stay at the same hotels and locations without trekking back to the airport. A list of discounts for rental cars can be found at mousesavers.com. With a little effort, you can often get a great deal.

Readers planning to stay in the World frequently ask if they will need a car. If your plans don't include restaurants, attractions, or other destinations outside of Disney World, the answer is a very qualified no. However, consider the following:

Plan to Rent a Car:

1. If your hotel is outside Walt Disney World;
2. If your hotel is in Walt Disney World and you want to dine someplace other than the theme parks and your own hotel;
3. If you plan to return to your hotel for naps or swimming during the day;
4. If you plan to visit other area theme parks or water parks (including Disney's).

▶ **UNOFFICIAL TIP** **Sign up for your car-rental company's frequent-renter program before your trip. Most programs are free and let you skip long waits in line to receive your car.**

5. UBER CARS Uber is a company that connects riders with drivers via a smartphone app. Download the Uber app and input your basic information, including a credit card number. Open the app to show your current location, then input your desired

destination. You'll see information about how long your wait will be for a car and an estimated fee. Fees vary based on demand. Uber can also be useful if you're traveling within the World but don't want to use Disney's transportation system—if, for example, you're traveling from hotel to hotel for a late-night dinner reservation.

6. DISNEY'S MAGICAL EXPRESS Disney's Magical Express is a free bus service that runs between the Orlando International Airport and most Walt Disney World hotels. All guests staying at a Disney-owned and -operated resort are eligible to use the service, even if the stay was booked independent of the Disney Travel Company. (Guests staying at the Swan, Dolphin, and Shades of Green are ineligible for Disney's Magical Express, as these hotels are independently owned.) Register your flight information with your resort reservation by calling ☎ 866-599-0951 or using mydisneyexperience.com. In addition to transportation, Magical Express provides free luggage-delivery service between your airline and Disney hotel, except for flights arriving after 10 p.m., when you'll need to pick up your suitcases from baggage claim.

You should receive special Magical Express luggage tags about 20–40 days prior to your departure date. Put a tag on any piece of luggage you plan to check with the airline. When you arrive at the airport, check the bags as you normally would. If you're traveling within the United States, you'll arrive in Orlando and follow the Magical Express signs to your bus; your luggage should be waiting in your hotel room when you check in. International travelers must retrieve their bags to go through customs. After passing through customs, you'll also head for a bus. Your bags are returned to baggage claim and Disney takes over from there. All tagged luggage is sent to an airport warehouse, where it's sorted by destination and then loaded onto a truck for delivery. At the resort, the luggage is matched to your reservation. If your room is ready, then the luggage is delivered there; otherwise it's held by the bellhops until you can check in.

The night before your flight home, you will receive a note from Disney with your return information. Buses typically pick up 3 hours before domestic US flights and 4 hours before international flights. You can check your baggage and receive your domestic flight boarding pass at the front desk of your Disney resort. Resort check-in counters are open 5 a.m.–1 p.m., and you must check in no later than 3 hours before your flight. Participating airlines are Alaska, American, Delta, JetBlue, Southwest, and United.

HOW TO TRAVEL AROUND THE WORLD

Transportation Trade-Offs for Guests Lodging Outside Walt Disney World

Disney day guests (those not staying inside Disney World) can use the monorail, bus, and boat systems. If, for example, you go to Disney's Hollywood Studios in the morning, and then decide to go to Epcot for lunch, you can take a bus directly there. The most important advice we can give day guests is to park in the lot of the theme park (or other Disney destination) where they plan to finish their day. This is critical if you stay at a park until closing time.

All You Need to Know About Driving to the Theme Parks

1. POSITIONING OF THE PARKING LOTS The Animal Kingdom, Disney's Hollywood Studios, and Epcot parking lots are adjacent to each park's entrance. The Magic Kingdom parking lot is adjacent to the Transportation and Ticket Center (TTC). From the TTC you can take a ferry, monorail, or bus to the Magic Kingdom entrance.

2. PAYING TO PARK Disney resort guests and Annual Pass holders park free. All others pay. If you pay to park, keep your receipt. If you move your car during the day to another theme park, you will not have to pay again if you show your receipt. Parking rates are steep, currently $20 per day per car or motorcycle.

3. FINDING YOUR CAR WHEN IT'S TIME TO DEPART The theme-park parking lots are huge. Jot down, text, or take a photo of the section and row where you park. If you are driving a rental car, jot down, text, or take a photo of the license number.

4. GETTING FROM YOUR CAR TO THE PARK ENTRANCE Each parking lot provides trams to transport you to the park entrance or, in the case of the Magic Kingdom, to the TTC. If you arrive early in the morning, it may be faster to walk to the entrance (or to the TTC) than to take the tram.

5. HOW MUCH TIME TO ALLOT FOR PARKING AND GETTING TO THE PARK ENTRANCE For Epcot and Animal Kingdom, it takes 10–15 minutes to pay, park, and walk or ride to the park entrance. At Disney's Hollywood Studios, allow 8–12 minutes; at the Magic Kingdom, it's 10–15 minutes to get to the TTC and another 20–30 to reach the park entrance via the monorail or the ferry. Allot another 10–20 minutes if you didn't buy your park admission in advance.

6. COMMUTING FROM PARK TO PARK You can commute to the other theme parks via a Disney bus, to and from the Magic Kingdom and Epcot by monorail, or to and from Epcot and Disney's Hollywood Studios by boat or on foot. You can also, of course, commute via your own car. Using Disney transportation or your own car, allow 45–60 minutes entrance-to-entrance one-way.

7. LEAVING THE PARK AT THE END OF THE DAY If you stay at a park until closing, expect the parking lot trams, monorails, and ferries to be mobbed. If the wait for the parking-lot tram is unacceptable, you can either walk to your car or walk to the first tram stop on the route and wait there until a tram arrives. When some people get off, you can get on and continue to your appropriate stop.

8. DINNER AND A QUICK EXIT One way to beat closing crowds at the Magic Kingdom is to arrange an Advance Reservation for dinner at one of the restaurants at the Contemporary Resort. When you leave the Magic Kingdom to go to dinner, move your car from the TTC lot to the Contemporary Resort. After dinner, either walk (8–10 minutes) or take the monorail back to the Magic Kingdom. When the park closes and everyone else is fighting their way onto the monorail or ferry, you can stroll leisurely back to the Contemporary, pick up your car, and be on your way. You can pull the same trick at Epcot by arranging an Advance Reservation at one of the Epcot resorts. After *IllumiNations* when the park closes, simply exit the park by the International Gateway and walk back to the resort where your car is parked.

9. SCORING A GREAT PARKING PLACE Anytime you arrive at a park after noon, there will be some empty spots up front vacated by early-arriving guests who have already departed.

Taking a Shuttle Bus from Your Out-of-the-World Hotel

Many independent hotels and motels near Walt Disney World provide trams and buses. They're fairly carefree, depositing you near theme-park entrances and saving you parking fees. The rub is that they might not get you there as early as you desire or be available when you're ready to leave. Also, some shuttles go directly to Disney World, while others stop at additional area lodgings. Each service is a bit different; check the particulars before you make reservations.

If you're depending on shuttles, you'll want to leave the park at least 45 minutes before closing. If you stay until closing and lack the energy to hassle with the shuttle, take Uber, Lyft, or a cab. Cab stands are near the Bus Information buildings at the Animal Kingdom, Epcot, Disney's Hollywood Studios, and the TTC. If no cabs are on hand, staff at Bus Information will call one for you. If you're leaving the Magic Kingdom at closing, it's easier to take the monorail to a hotel and hail a cab from there.

The Disney Transportation System

The Disney Transportation System is a hub-and-spoke system. Hubs include the TTC, Disney Springs, and all four major theme parks (from 2 hours before official opening time to 1 hour after closing). Although there are some exceptions, there is direct service from Disney resorts to the major theme parks and to Disney Springs, and from park to park. If you want to go from resort to resort or most anywhere else, you will have to transfer at one of the hubs.

If a hotel offers boat or monorail service, its bus service will be limited, meaning you'll have to transfer at a hub for many Disney World destinations. If you're staying at a Magic Kingdom resort served by the monorail (Polynesian, Contemporary–Bay Lake Tower, or Grand Floridian), you'll be able to commute efficiently to the Magic Kingdom via monorail. If you want to visit Epcot, you must take the monorail to the TTC and transfer to the Epcot monorail. (Guests at the Polynesian can eliminate the transfer by walking 5–10 minutes to the TTC and catching the direct monorail to Epcot.)

Walt Disney World Bus Service

Disney buses have an illuminated panel above the windshield that flashes the bus's destination. Also, theme parks have designated waiting areas for each Disney destination. To catch the bus to the Caribbean Beach Resort from Disney's Hollywood Studios, for example, go to the bus stop and wait in the area marked "To the Caribbean Beach Resort." At the resorts, go to any bus stop and wait for the bus displaying your destination on the illuminated panel. Directions to Disney destinations are available when you check in or at your hotel's Guest Relations desk. Guest Relations also can answer questions about the transportation system.

Buses begin service to the theme parks at about 7:30 a.m. on days when the parks' official opening time is at 9 a.m. Generally, buses run every 20 minutes. Buses to all four parks deliver you to the park entrance.

To be on hand for the real opening time (when official opening is at 9 a.m.), catch direct buses to Epcot, the Animal Kingdom, and Disney's Hollywood Studios between 7:30 and 8 a.m. Catch direct buses to the Magic Kingdom between 8 and 8:15 a.m. If you must transfer to reach your park, leave 15–20 minutes earlier. On days when official opening is at 7 or 8 a.m., move up your departure time accordingly.

For your return bus trip in the evening, leave the park 40 minutes to an hour before closing to avoid the rush. If you're caught in the mass exodus, you may be inconvenienced, but you won't be stranded. Buses, boats, and monorails continue to operate for 1 hour after the parks close.

Walt Disney World Monorail Service

Picture the monorail system as three loops. Loop A is an express route that runs counterclockwise, connecting the Magic Kingdom with the Transportation and Ticket Center (TTC). Loop B runs clockwise alongside Loop A, making all stops, with service to (in this order) the TTC, Polynesian Village, the Grand Floridian Resort & Villas, Magic Kingdom, Contemporary Resort and Bay Lake Tower, and back to the TTC. The long Loop C dips southeast, connecting the TTC with Epcot. The hub for all three loops is the TTC (where you usually park to visit the Magic Kingdom). The monorail system serving Magic Kingdom resorts normally starts operation an hour and a half before official opening. If you're staying at a Magic Kingdom resort and you wish to be among the first in the Magic Kingdom at official opening (usually 9 a.m.), board the monorail at the times indicated below.

From the Contemporary Resort–Bay Lake Tower	7:45–8:00 a.m.
From the Polynesian Village	7:50–8:05 a.m.
From the Grand Floridian Resort & Villas	8:00–8:10 a.m.

If you're a day guest, you'll be allowed on the monorail at the TTC between 8:15 and 8:30 a.m. on a day when official opening is 9 a.m. If you want to board earlier, walk from the TTC to the Polynesian Village and board there. The monorail loop connecting Epcot and the TTC begins operating at 7:30 a.m. on days when Epcot's official opening is 9 a.m. To be at Epcot when the park opens, catch the Epcot monorail at the TTC by 8:05 a.m.

▶ UNOFFICIAL TIP Monorails usually operate for 1 hour after the parks close. If a train is too crowded or you need transportation after the monorails have stopped running, catch a bus or boat.

Walt Disney World Boat Service

Boat service connects Disney's Hollywood Studios with Epcot, stopping at the Swan and Dolphin Resorts, Boardwalk Inn and Villas, Yacht Club Resort, and Beach Club Resort and Villas en route. There is a resort launch service to the Magic Kingdom from the Polynesian, Contemporary and Bay Lake, Grand Floridian, and Wilderness Lodge Resorts as well as from the Fort Wilderness Campground. For day guests, ferries serve as an alternative to the monorail from the TTC (Magic Kingdom parking lot) to the Magic Kingdom.

PROBLEMS AND HOW TO SOLVE THEM

CAR TROUBLE Security will help if you lock the keys in your parked car or find the battery dead. For more serious problems, the closest repair facility is the Car Care Center near the Magic Kingdom lot (☎ 407-824-0976).

The nearest off-World repair center is Maingate Citgo (on US 192 west of I-4; ☎ 407-396-2721). Disney security can help you find it. Farther away but highly recommended by one of our Orlando-area researchers is Riker's Automotive & Tire (5700 Central Florida Pkwy., near SeaWorld; ☎ 407-238-9800; rikersauto.com). Says our source: "They do great work and are the only car place that has never tried to get extra money out of me 'cause I know nothing about cars."

GASOLINE Three Speedway gas stations are on Disney property. One station is adjacent to the Car Care Center on the exit road from the TTC (Magic Kingdom) parking lot. It's also convenient to the Shades of Green, Grand Floridian, and Polynesian Resorts. Most centrally located is the station at the corner of Buena Vista Drive and Epcot Resorts Boulevard, near the BoardWalk Inn. A third station, also on Buena Vista Drive, is across from Disney Springs.

LOST AND FOUND If you lose (or find) something in the Magic Kingdom, go to City Hall. At Epcot, Lost and Found is behind Spaceship Earth. At Disney's Hollywood Studios, it's at Hollywood Boulevard Guest Relations, and at Animal Kingdom, it's at Guest Relations at the main entrance. If you discover your loss after you have left the park(s), call ☎ 407-824-4245 (for all parks). Ask to be transferred to the specific park's Lost and Found if you're still at the park(s) and discover something is missing.

LOST MAGICBANDS If you lose your MagicBand or Key to the World Card, your first step should be to disable the card via the My Disney Experience app or website (under the "MagicBands and Cards" tab). This will prevent others from using your FP+ selections or attempting to charge items to your account. Replacement bands or cards can be made at Guest Relations at any of the theme parks or at the concierge desk of any Disney resort hotel.

LOST CARS Don't forget where you parked—write down your section and row, send yourself a text, or snap a picture with your phone or camera.

RAIN Weather bad? Go to the parks anyway. The crowds are lighter on rainy days, and most of the attractions and waiting areas are under cover. Showers, especially during the warmer months, usually don't last very long. Ponchos cost about $10; umbrellas cost about $15. All ponchos sold at Disney World are made of clear plastic, so picking out somebody in your party on a rainy day can be tricky. Walmart sells an inexpensive green poncho that will make your family emerald beacons in a plastic-covered sea of humanity.

▶ **UNOFFICIAL TIP** Raingear is one of the few bargains at the parks. It isn't always displayed in shops; you have to ask for it.

Medical Matters

RELIEF FOR A HEADACHE Aspirin and other sundries are sold at the Emporium on Main Street in the Magic Kingdom (they're kept behind the counter; you must ask), at retail shops in Epcot's Future World and World Showcase, in Disney's Hollywood Studios, at the Animal Kingdom, and at each resort's gift shop.

ILLNESSES REQUIRING MEDICAL ATTENTION A Centra Care walk-in clinic is at 12500 South Apopka–Vineland Road (☎ 407-934-CARE). It's open 8 a.m.–midnight weekdays and 8 a.m.–8 p.m. weekends. Centra Care also operates a 24-hour physician house-call service and runs a free shuttle (☎ 407-938-0650). Buena Vista Urgent Care (8216 World Center Dr., Ste. D; ☎ 407-465-1110) comes highly recommended by Unofficial Guide readers.

The Medical Concierge (☎ 855-932-5252; themedicalconcierge.com) has board-certified physicians available 24/7 for house calls to your hotel room. They offer in-room X-rays and IV therapy service, as well as same-day dental and specialist appointments. They also rent medical equipment. Insurance receipts, insurance billing, and foreign-language interpretation are provided. Walk-in clinics are also available.

DOCS (Doctors on Call Service; ☎ 407-399-DOCS; doctorsoncallservice.com) offers 24-hour house-call service. All DOCS physicians are certified by the American Board of Medical Specialties.

Physician Room Service (☎ 407-238-2000; physicianroomservice.com) provides board-certified doctor house calls to Walt Disney World–area guest rooms for adults and children.

Several area Walgreens have in-house clinics that can diagnose and prescribe medication for basic illnesses, such as ear infections or strep throat. The Walgreens website has a tool that estimates how long the wait will be at each location; visit walgreens.com/pharmacy/healthcare-clinic/locations_wait_times.jsp.

PRESCRIPTION MEDICINE Two nearby pharmacies are Walgreens Lake Buena Vista (☎ 407-238-0600) and CVS Lake Buena Vista (☎ 407-239-1442). Turner Drugs (☎ 407-828-8125) charges $7.50–$15 to deliver a filled prescription to your hotel's front desk. The service is available to Disney and non-Disney hotels in Turner Drugs' area. The delivery fee will be charged to your hotel account.

DENTAL EMERGENCIES Call Celebration Dental Group (☎ 407-351-9704).

SERVICES

MESSAGES Messages left at City Hall in the Magic Kingdom, Guest Relations at Epcot, Hollywood Boulevard Guest Relations at Disney's Hollywood Studios, or Guest Relations at the Animal Kingdom can be retrieved at any of the four park facilities.

LOCKERS AND PACKAGE PICK-UP Guest lockers are available at each of the theme parks and water parks. At the Magic Kingdom, lockers are on the far right side of the entrance gate; Animal Kingdom lockers are on the left, just past Guest Services; Hollywood Studios lockers are on the right, near Oscar's and the wheelchair rental desk. There are two locker locations at Epcot: to the right of Spaceship Earth and at the International Gateway (back) entrance. Lockers cost $8–$10 per day and include a $5 refundable deposit. Epcot and Hollywood Studios also have large single-use coin-operated lockers located outside the park gates. These lockers cost only $1, but you'll have to go in and out of the park security checkpoints to use them.

Package Pick-Up is available at each major theme park. Ask the salesperson to send your purchases to Package Pick-Up. When you leave the park, they'll be waiting for you. Epcot has two exits, thus two Package Pick-Ups; specify the main entrance or International Gateway. If you're staying at a Disney resort, you can also have packages delivered to your resort's gift shop for pickup the following day.

CAMERA SUPPLIES Gift shops in the parks sell disposable cameras, camera cases, SD memory cards, and some batteries. The Camera Center near Spaceship Earth in Epcot carries a small selection of digital cameras.

GROCERY STORES Avoid the Gooding's Supermarket in the Crossroads Shopping Center, across FL 535 from the Disney World entrance. While its location makes it undeniably convenient, its selection is poor and you'll find the prices higher and more frightening than the Tower of Terror. For down-to-earth prices, try the Publix just north of the intersection of Reams Road and FL 535; Winn-Dixie on Apopka–Vineland Road, about a mile north of Crossroads Shopping Center; Winn-Dixie Marketplace, at US 192 on the west side of I-4; or the Super Target at 3200 Rolling Oaks Blvd., near the Western Way entrance.

GROCERY MARKETS THAT DELIVER If you don't have a car or you don't want to go to the supermarket, GardenGrocer (gardengrocer.com, ☎ 866-855-4350) will shop for you and deliver your groceries. The best way to compile your order is on GardenGrocer's website before you leave home. It's simple, and the selection is huge. Delivery arrangements are per your instructions. For orders of $200 or more, there's a $2 delivery fee; for orders less than $200, the delivery charge is $14; a minimum order of $40 is required.

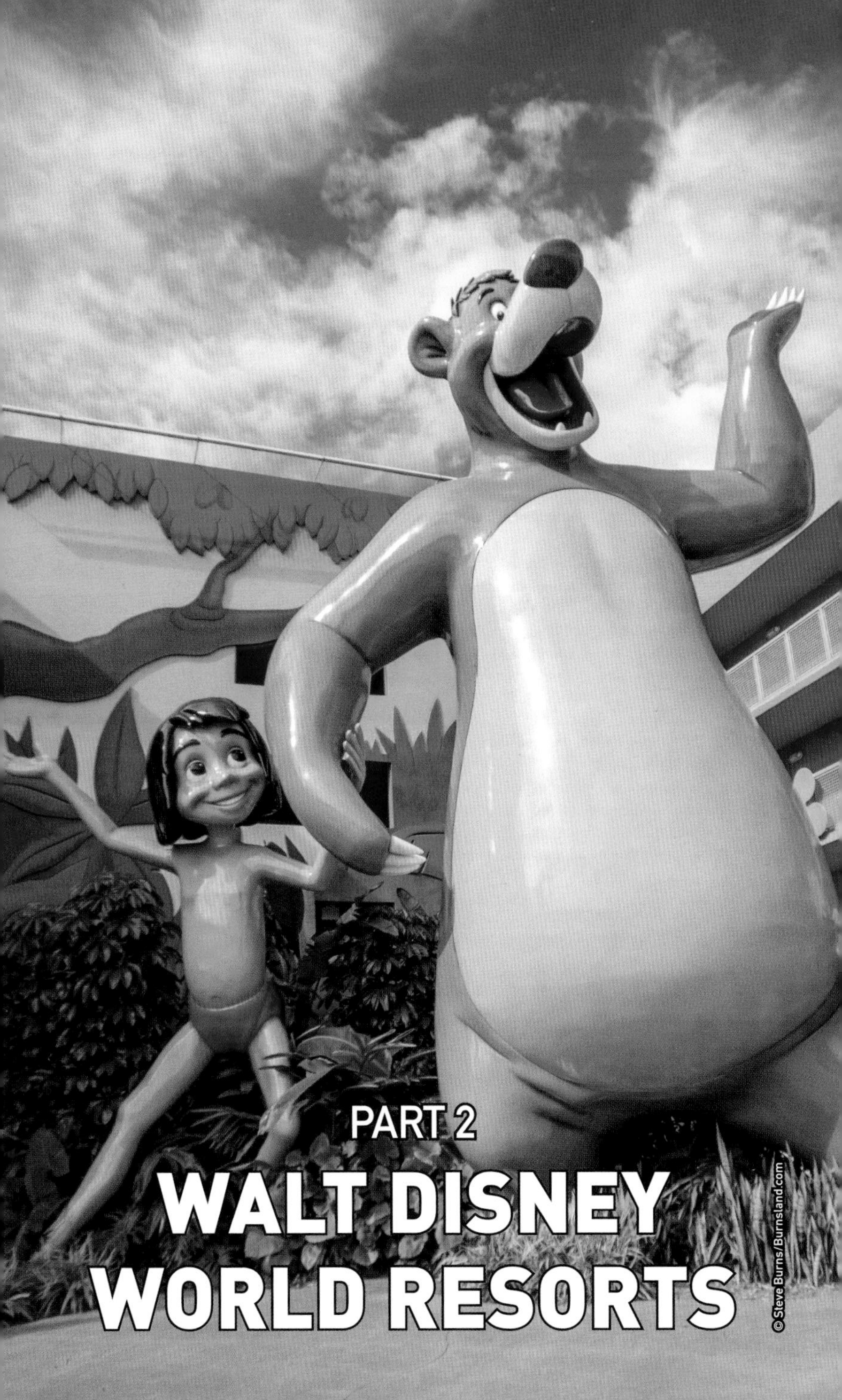

PART 2

WALT DISNEY WORLD RESORTS

CHOOSING A WALT DISNEY WORLD HOTEL

Staying at a Walt Disney World hotel means that you're surrounded by Disney's immersive detail and magic throughout your trip. If you've always wanted to stay at a national park lodge of the American West, for example, Disney has the Wilderness Lodge and Boulder Ridge Villas, complete with a five-story log-cabin lobby, a pool fed by a model mountain stream, and a miniature Old Faithful geyser that erupts on the hour, plus restaurants that serve everything from family-style camping fare to trendy Northwest cuisine. And that's just at one hotel! Disney World has more than 20 other such elaborately planned properties, each designed for a different theme and budget.

Regarding cost, the first thing to consider when choosing a Disney hotel is its resort classification. Disney's least-expensive hotels are its **value resorts,** including the All-Star, Pop Century, and Art of Animation properties. In general, these resorts offer the smallest rooms and fewest amenities. Disney's All-Star Music and Art of Animation resorts also have family suites, which are two standard rooms converted into a one-bedroom suite complete with kitchenette. All value resort buildings are essentially three- or four-story rectangles with open-air hallways and include a mall-style food court. Theming at the value resorts is provided by giant icons, such as 40-foot dogs from *101 Dalmatians.*

A step up in cost, architecture, and amenities are Disney's **moderate resorts,** including the Port Orleans properties and Caribbean Beach and Coronado Springs resorts. Theming at these resorts is much more developed than at the value resorts. Caribbean Beach, for example, has verdant green landscaping, tree-canopied walkways, and a laid-back island feel. Moderate resorts also feature larger rooms, more functional dressing areas, and storage space, as well as more dining options.

Disney's **deluxe resorts** are its top-of-the-line hotels, with the largest rooms, most amenities and recreational options, and best restaurant choices. Most deluxe resorts are located either within walking distance of one of the theme parks or offer direct monorail or boat service to one park's entrance. Besides transportation options, deluxe resorts also offer the most theming of any Disney properties, from the 19th-century Victorian gingerbread architectural ornamentation of the Grand Floridian to the African safari–themed Animal Kingdom Lodge, complete with wildlife roaming a savanna outside your window.

Besides these three main categories, Disney also offers **deluxe villa** resorts, including suites. These are studio, one-, two-, and three-bedroom accommodations, some with full kitchens. Many deluxe villa resorts, such as the Grand Floridian Villas, are attached to one of Disney's deluxe resorts. Regardless, deluxe villa rooms equal or surpass those found at the deluxe resorts.

Finally, there's Fort Wilderness Resort and Campground, offering both campsites (tent and RV) and fully equipped cabins, in an expansive wooded setting. Fort Wilderness offers everything from campfire sing-alongs to horseback riding.

Amenities and Recreation Disney resorts offer a staggering variety of amenities and recreational opportunities. All provide elaborate swimming pools, themed shops, restaurants or food courts, bars or lounges, and access to five Disney golf courses. The more you pay for your lodging, the more amenities and opportunities are at your disposal.

Making Reservations

DISNEY RESORTS	☎ **407-934-7639 or disneyworld.com**
DOLPHIN RESORT	☎ **407-934-4000 or swandolphin.com**
SWAN RESORT	☎ **407-934-3000 or swandolphin.com**
SHADES OF GREEN	☎ **407-824-3400 or shadesofgreen.org**

HOW TO FIND THE BEST ROOMS AT ANY DISNEY HOTEL

One of the first decisions you'll have when booking a hotel room at Walt Disney World is which view to select. If you're on the monorail loop, does a Magic Kingdom view really improve your chances of seeing the *Wishes* fireworks? Is the savanna view at the Animal Kingdom Lodge worth the money?

To help you decide, we spent over a year taking pictures of what you'll see from the window of every Disney World hotel room—more than 30,000 individual photos. Visit touringplans.com/hotel_maps to get started.

You can search for specific rooms using standard filters such as price, Disney's view category, bed type, and walking distance to the lobby and transportation. We'll show you all the rooms matching your criteria, and you can click on any room to see the view from that room. Here's the view from the Animal Kingdom Lodge's room 5412:

From here you can navigate left or right one room at a time, or up or down one floor. In addition to the room view, we can even set up an automatic fax so you can request rooms from Disney. While nothing is guaranteed, our faxes certainly help improve your chances of getting the room you want.

Don't Leave Your Room View Up to Chance

You're paying a premium to stay on-site. So consider the two views below, each of which is a room you could get at random if you let Disney make the decision for you.

Both of these All-Star Sports rooms are in Building 9, cost the same per night, face the same direction, and are the same walking distance to the lobby and transportation. The one below opens to a sweeping panorama of a pool and resort grounds. The other sees a hunk of gray metal.

COMPARING DISNEY WORLD RESORT ROOM SIZES

We had some colored duct tape lying around the office and decided to put it to use. The photo above shows the approximate size of standard Disney hotel rooms. The red tape represents a value resort at approximately 260 square feet; moderate resort rooms are represented by green tape and are 314 square feet; and deluxe resorts are in purple at around 402 square feet.

The shaded areas in the foreground represent the approximate size of the bathroom and dressing areas in each room type. The bed sheets shown are the same dimensions as a value resort's full-size beds (most moderate and all deluxe resorts have queen beds). The luggage includes one large- and one medium-size roller bag. The guy in the background is the size of a standard *Unofficial Guide* author.

We've omitted the standard nightstand, armoire, work table, and chairs found in Disney's hotel rooms. Keep that in mind, however, when you're looking at the area of a value resort while trying to determine whether your family can stay in one for a week. For our money, moderate resorts usually represent the best compromise between cost and convenience.

FORT WILDERNESS RESORT AND CAMPGROUND

If camping and cabin life are your thing, you've found a home at Fort Wilderness. With campsites that accommodate single-person tents up to bus-size RVs, and separate cabins that sleep six adults, Fort Wilderness is Disney's largest resort. It's also Disney's most diverse, with recreational options that include boating, biking, swimming, horseback riding, wagon rides, and walking trails, plus an outdoor movie theater and campfire sing-alongs at night.

Fort Wilderness's cabins are considered moderate rooms in Disney's resort categorization, but they have a full refrigerator, cooktop, and microwave, plus an outdoor charcoal grill. The living room features a sofabed that's comfortable enough for adults to use. The cabins also have one decent-sized bathroom and another separate bedroom that sleeps four. Restaurant options include the popular Trail's End buffet (occasionally featuring an ahead-of-its-time doughnut sampler) and the *Hoop-Dee-Doo Musical Revue* dinner show.

STRENGTHS

- Informality
- Children's play areas
- Best recreational options at WDW
- Special day and evening programs
- Campsite amenities
- Shower and toilet facilities
- *Hoop-Dee-Doo Musical Revue* show
- Convenient self-parking
- Off-site dining via boat at Magic Kingdom

WEAKNESSES

- Isolated location
- Complicated bus service
- Confusing campground layout
- Lack of privacy
- Very limited on-site dining options
- Crowding at beaches and pools
- Small baths in cabins
- Extreme distance to store and restaurant facilities from many campsites

ALL-STAR RESORTS

STRENGTHS

- Least expensive of the Disney resorts
- Rooms recently refurbished
- Family suites at All-Star Music are less expensive than those at Art of Animation
- Convenient parking
- Lots of pools
- In-room pizza delivery

WEAKNESSES

- Most likely Disney resorts to host large school groups
- Rooms are small
- No full-service dining; food courts often overwhelmed at mealtimes
- Bus stops often crowded
- Public spaces are showing wear

Disney's original version of a budget resort features three distinct themes executed in the same hyperbolic style. Spread over a vast expanse, the resorts comprise 30 three-story motel-style buildings. Although the three resorts are neighbors, each has its own lobby, food court, and registration area. The All-Star Sports Resort features huge sports icons: bright football helmets, tennis rackets, and baseball bats—all taller than the buildings they adorn. Similarly, the All-Star Music Resort features 40-foot guitars, maracas, and saxophones, while kids will get a kick out of seeing giant replicas of *Toy Story* characters and tongue-wagging Dalmatians at the All-Star Movies Resort. Lobbies of all are loud (in both decibels and brightness) and cartoonish, with checkerboard walls and photographs of famous athletes, musicians, or film stars. Each resort has two main pools; Music has a Piano Pool and a guitar-shaped Calypso Pool, and one of Movies' is star-shaped. Any All-Star Resort guest can freely use the pools or food courts at the other All-Stars.

All six pools feature plastic replicas of Disney characters, some shooting water pistols. Because of the decor, All-Star Sports is a popular resort for athletic teams participating at the ESPN Wide World of Sports complex. If you're looking for a quieter-than-average value resort, ask when booking about any group events that might be happening during your stay. Also, Sports is the first of the three All-Star Resorts visited on Disney's bus line, so guests here spend slightly less time in transit than at the other resorts.

Rooms at the All-Star Resorts are small, about 260 square feet, and feature two full beds or one king-size bed, a TV, desk and chairs, and a dresser. There's very little counter space, and the bathroom is small. Standard rooms are virtually identical at all three resorts. However, All-Star Music does have 182 suites (two formerly separate rooms connected by a doorway), which provide around 520 square feet of space for larger families. Pop Century and Art of Animation are better choices in Disney's value resort category. Choose All-Star if those aren't available, or if the $11–$22 per night cost difference is important.

Pools at all of the value resorts are large enough to handle big crowds.

A standard All-Star Music Resort room

... and bathroom.

All of the value resorts have themed, mall-style food courts.

ART OF ANIMATION RESORT

Opened in 2012, Art of Animation is a value resort located across Hourglass Lake from Pop Century. Similar to Pop, Art of Animation has multiple sections of rooms centered around pools and courtyards. Unlike the other value resorts, Art of Animation is mostly suites, which are double-sized rooms with kitchenettes. The suite areas also have interior hallways like Disney's deluxe resorts, as opposed to the exterior doors featured at other value resorts and in The Little Mermaid section of Art of Animation. All told, there are 864 standard rooms and 1,120 suites.

Theming uses characters from four Disney films: *Cars, Finding Nemo, The Lion King,* and *The Little Mermaid.* All but the *Mermaid*-themed rooms are suites. As at Pop Century, large, colorful icons stand in the middle of each group of buildings; here, though, they represent film characters rather than pop-culture touchstones. An interesting departure from the other value resorts is that Disney has decorated the building exteriors with giant murals stretching the length of each structure. Each of the Cars buildings, for example, display a four-story panoramic vista of the American desert, with the movie's iconic characters in the middle, while the Lion King buildings capture a single verdant jungle scene.

Three of the four sets of themed buildings have pools; the Lion King complex has a playground instead. Like the other value resorts, Art of Animation has a central building—here called Animation Hall—for check-in and bus transportation; it also holds the resort's food court, Landscape of Flavors; a gift shop; and a video-game arcade. We think the food court is the best of any value resort.

STRENGTHS

- Exceptional theming, particularly *Cars* and *Lion King* areas
- Best pool of the value resorts
- Landscape of Flavors food court is an *Unofficial Guide* favorite
- Family suites are innovatively designed
- Interior hallways in some buildings
- Walking trail around Hourglass Lake and connecting bridge to Pop Century
- Just one bus stop

WEAKNESSES

- Most expensive value resort
- Spotty in-room mobile reception
- The number of made-to-order meals at the food court can mean long waits in line
- The resort's family suites are rarely discounted
- Poor soundproofing

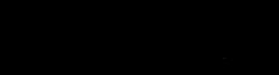

POP CENTURY RESORT

Pop Century's basic design is similar to that found in the Art of Animation and All-Star Resorts, with motel-style rectangular buildings decorated by large, colorful icons that represent various decades of late-20th-century American culture. Giant yo-yos, eight-track tapes, and Big Wheels will help you identify which building you're in. Swimming pools are shaped like bowling pins, computers, and flower petals.

Rooms at Pop Century are virtually identical to those at the All-Star value resorts. The big difference between Pop Century and the other value resorts is that Pop doesn't have family suites, which sleep six people. Pop Century rooms sleep four people in two full-size beds, plus one child under age 3 in a crib. All-Star Music and Art of Animation are value resorts with family suites.

Standard rooms at Pop Century are a little more expensive—and a little bit better—than those at the older All-Star Resorts. Pop Century's check-in desk, food court, laundry facilities, and bus stops are better at handling large crowds than the All-Star Resorts. Pop is less expensive than the newer—and better—Art of Animation value resort, for generally the same reasons.

STRENGTHS

- Theming is fun for anyone over age 35
- Our favorite pool bar of the value resorts
- One bus stop
- Walking trail around Hourglass Lake and connecting bridge to Art of Animation
- In-room pizza delivery
- Convenient parking

WEAKNESSES 

- The history of the theme may be lost on kids and teens, and the giant icons may be too in-your-face for adults
- Small rooms that are the same size as All-Stars' but slightly more expensive
- Bus stops at theme parks are a long distance from park entrances

Pop Century's pools are a hit with kids and adults.

CARIBBEAN BEACH RESORT

Opened in 1988, Caribbean Beach was Disney's first moderate resort. More than 20 years later, the building's bright colors, island-style theming, and lush landscaping are its strong points. Wandering the grounds, for example, you'll find tucked-away benches surrounded by tropical plants and faux cannon defenses to protect the resort from invaders. The scenery at night is among Disney World's most romantic. The check-in desk and food courts, however, are a long walk from many of the rooms, so you may want to have a car while staying here. Caribbean Beach also has a whopping seven bus stops, so expect 10–20 minutes of travel time just to get out of the resort.

Besides its standard tropical theme, Caribbean Beach's rooms are decorated in the style of two popular Disney films: *Finding Nemo* and *Pirates of the Caribbean*. Nemo rooms feature Nemo and Dory bedspreads and wall borders, while Pirates rooms have ship-shaped beds, carpet that looks like a wood deck, skull-draped curtains for the dressing area, and a profile of the *Flying Dutchman* etched into the shower wall. The heavily themed pirate rooms are more expensive but are consistently fully booked, despite their relatively remote location.

STRENGTHS

- Colorful Caribbean theme
- Rooms with *Pirates of the Caribbean* and *Finding Nemo* themes
- Lakefront setting
- Large food court
- Murphy beds in select rooms increase capacity to 5 people

WEAKNESSES

- Check-in is far from rest of resort
- Sit-down dining is mediocre at best
- Multiple bus stops
- Some "villages" are a good distance from restaurants and shops

© Disney

CORONADO SPRINGS RESORT

Coronado Springs Resort, near Animal Kingdom, is Disney's only midpriced convention property. Inspired by northern Mexico and the American Southwest, the resort is divided into three separately themed areas. The two- and three-story ranchos call to mind southwest cattle ranches, while the two- and three-story cabanas are modeled after Mexican beach resorts. The multistoried casitas embody elements of Spanish architecture found in Mexico's great cities. All buildings surround a 15-acre lake, and there are three small pools, as well as one large swimming complex with a reproduction of a Mayan steppe pyramid with a waterfall cascading down its side.

Rooms are decorated with sunset colors and feature hand-painted Mexican wall hangings. Lighting is above average for Disney's moderate resorts.

Coronado Springs offers one full-service restaurant as well as Disney World's most interesting food court, Pepper Market. It's also the only Disney moderate resort to offer concierge rooms ("Club Level" in Disneyspeak). Located in Cabana building 9B, rooms feature slightly nicer amenities as well as access to a lounge area stocked with drinks and snacks throughout the day.

STRENGTHS

- Most sophisticated room decor of the moderate resorts
- Setting is beautiful at night
- Themed swimming area with waterslides
- Large feature pool
- On-site business center
- Best public Wi-Fi at any Disney resort

WEAKNESSES

- Conventioneers may be off-putting to vacationing families
- Some rooms are a long distance from check-in, lobby, and restaurants
- Multiple bus stops

PORT ORLEANS FRENCH QUARTER

Easily the most romantic and intimate of Disney's moderate resorts, Port Orleans French Quarter is a perennial favorite of *Unofficial Guide* readers. Designed like a sanitized version of New Orleans, French Quarter is about half the size of the other moderate resorts. Features include colorful buildings, snug walkways, and a waterfront that practically begs you to walk alongside it at sunset—drink in one hand, sweetie in the other, and the kids off somewhere nearby not getting into too much trouble.

Rooms at French Quarter are about the same size as those at other moderate resorts. If you're worried about the counter space available with two separate sinks, a shelf runs along the back of both. The food court is relatively small and works best for breakfast and snacks. (The Port Orleans Riverside food court is a short walk away and offers slightly more variety.) The pool complex is great for small children, and guests of French Quarter can use the pool at the neighboring Riverside as well. The lovely path that connects the two resorts is worth a walk even if you're not pool hopping.

STRENGTHS

- Most compact of the WDW moderate resorts
- One bus stop
- Live entertainment in Scat Cat's Club
- Beignets in food court!
- Attractively themed lobby
- Good place to walk or run for fitness
- Short walk to Port Orleans Riverside's restaurants and bars

WEAKNESSES

- Shares bus service with Port Orleans Riverside during slower times of year
- No full-service dining

PORT ORLEANS RIVERSIDE

STRENGTHS

- Interesting narrative to theming
- Disney princess–themed rooms in Magnolia Bend
- Live entertainment in River Roost Lounge
- The only moderate resort (for now) that can sleep five (at Alligator Bayou)
- Very nice feature pool
- Close driving distance to Magic Kingdom
- Good place to walk or run for fitness
- Recreational options (bikes, boats)

WEAKNESSES

- Multiple bus stops; shares service with Port Orleans French Quarter during slower times of year
- Mediocre full-service restaurant

Readers consistently rank Port Orleans Riverside as one of Disney's best resorts in any category, and it's not hard to see why. Themed after Mississippi River communities in postwar Louisiana, the property includes buildings styled as three-story mansions with towering columns and red brick paths, as well as more rustic two-story bayou-style buildings. Guests enjoy incredibly detailed landscaping throughout the resort.

Regardless of whether you're in a mansion or a bayou shack, most rooms at Riverside look the same on the inside and are comparable to the other Disney moderate resorts. Exceptions are the 812 rooms refurbished into Royal Guest Rooms, with decor themed to Disney princesses and headboards animated with fiber-optic lights. Regardless of the room, the food court at Riverside is large enough to handle crowds well, and the swimming pools get top marks from readers.

ANIMAL KINGDOM LODGE AND VILLAS

Disney's Animal Kingdom Lodge combines African tribal architecture with the exotic, rugged style of grand East African national park lodges. Your entrance into the lodge's main-building (Jambo House), five-story lobby, featuring a thatched roof and native art and artifacts, will definitely make an impression. So too will the lodge's restaurants—Boma's buffet and Jiko's fine dining—which readers consistently rank among the best in Walt Disney World.

The Animal Kingdom Lodge's swimming complex is among the best in Walt Disney World, too, with a zero-entry pool for small children and enough space for everyone. The lodge's rooms feature hand-carved furnishings and colorful soft goods. Most rooms have balconies, and those that face the savanna offer the opportunity to see wildlife grazing throughout the day. At night, the lodge offers campfire storytelling and night-vision goggles to better see the nocturnal animals.

Kidani Village, sister resort to Animal Kingdom Lodge, has similar design, theming, and artwork, albeit on a smaller scale. Kidani rooms are decorated in lighter tones but feature hand-carved furniture and balconies similar to those in Jambo House.

Kidani has one restaurant located downstairs from the lobby. Sanaa (sah-NAH) is not as upscale as Jiko, the resort's African restaurant, but the kitchen offers diners a chance to sample and share a variety of Indian-African creations. The naan bread sampler is delicious.

STRENGTHS

- Beautiful lobbies
- Excellent on-site dining options
- Nice pools
- On-site cultural and nature programs
- Best theming of any Disney hotel

WEAKNESSES

- Jambo House rooms are among the smallest of the deluxe resorts
- Erratic bus service
- Savanna views vary in quality depending on location
- Only quick-service dining at Kidani Village is the pool bar

The lobby of the Animal Kingdom Lodge—Jambo House

BOARDWALK INN AND VILLAS RESORT

Disney's BoardWalk Inn is a detailed replica of an early-20th-century Atlantic coast boardwalk, complete with shopping, restaurants, and bakeries along a wide wooden walkway. Both the boardwalk and the resort's entrance are lighted like a landing strip at night, but you'll find the lobby more subdued, with a dignified decor grounded in weathered pastel blues, greens, and pinks. The BoardWalk's pool has an amusement-park theme that includes a great waterslide for families. That waterslide ends in a giant clown head, whose gaping mouth seems to spit children into the pool. Those who are coulrophobic may want to avert their eyes.

Rooms at the BoardWalk Inn are well appointed and decorated in yellow-and-white striped wallpaper and green curtains. Rooms typically have two queen beds, a daybed, desk and chair, and ceiling fans. Most rooms also have balconies, and the views are better than at most other resorts; however, not as many rooms overlook the BoardWalk as you might think. The bath and dressing areas have plenty of room for families, although the lighting here and in the room is a bit dark. The BoardWalk Villas, connected to the inn, are decorated in warmer colors and feature one- and two-bedroom villas in addition to the one-room studios.

STRENGTHS

- Walking distance to Epcot's International Gateway and Disney's Hollywood Studios
- Unique garden suites
- Vast selection of dining options for adults
- Fitness center is larger than Yacht & Beach Club's

WEAKNESSES

- Long, confusing hallways
- Some may find room theming overly fussy
- Limited quick-service dining options suitable for children
- Bus service to Magic Kingdom, Animal Kingdom, water parks, and Downtown Disney is shared with other Epcot resorts
- BoardWalk Villas have fewer baths per bedroom than newer DVC/DDV properties

FROZEN PRINCESS FREEZEY FREEZE RESORT

STRENGTHS

- Astonishingly good air-conditioning
- Bath parkas in each guest igloo
- Wild game specialties at restaurant
- No elevators

WEAKNESSES

- Tanning at pool limited to face
- Elks in rut in public areas
- Slippery pedestrian paths
- Possible frostbite

If you dig everything *Frozen,* you'll go wild for the Frozen Princess Freezey Freeze Resort. Each guest igloo features flat-screen television, comfy expedition-quality sleeping bags, and your own private reindeer. Baths are modern and fully equipped. Amenities include an electric hair defroster and Sunny Bun™ toilet seat warmers. When you're close to keeling over in the scorching Florida weather, chill out at the combination ice rink/swimming pool, where the lifeguards are fully trained in treating hypothermia. Hungry? Just take a resort sled to the Hare on Fire Grill, specializing in hare, caribou, elk, and weasel preparations served with frozen vegetables.

CONTEMPORARY RESORT AND BAY LAKE TOWER

It's no coincidence that for the opening of the Magic Kingdom in 1971, Disney designed its monorail to run right through the middle of the Contemporary Resort. The Contemporary was Disney's statement that a new era of design was underway at its Florida property, extending Disney's theming and entertainment architecture beyond the parks and into its entire urban landscape.

While the sleek angles and concrete-and-glass exterior might not be for everyone, rooms at the Contemporary are the nicest on Disney property. Wood accents and splashes of color are dotted throughout. Most tower rooms have views of either the Magic Kingdom or Bay Lake.

Bay Lake Tower is a 16-story, 295-unit resort that features studio, one-, two-, and three-bedroom villas, some with spectacular views of the Magic Kingdom. Laid out in a semicircle, Bay Lake Tower is connected to the Contemporary Resort by an elevated, covered walkway and shares monorail service with the Contemporary. Bay Lake Tower has a fabulous pool and pool bar but shares dining and recreational activities with the Contemporary.

The Contemporary's South Garden Wing rooms aren't located in the main building, but they're $50–$100 less per night, almost as glamorous, and also within walking distance of the Magic Kingdom.

STRENGTHS

- Iconic architecture; the only hotel that the monorail goes *through*
- Large, very attractive guest rooms with nice views of Bay Lake
- Easy walk to the Magic Kingdom
- Convenient parking
- Best lounge at WDW (Top of the World)
- Recreational options on Bay Lake
- Boat service to Fort Wilderness Resort

WEAKNESSES

- Magic Kingdom view rooms mostly look out at parking lots and are overpriced
- Very small studios in Bay Lake Tower
- Bus transportation to DHS, Animal Kingdom, water parks, and Disney Springs is shared with the other monorail resorts
- No on-site child care

The Contemporary features some of the nicest rooms on Disney property.

Bay Lake Tower pool

GRAND FLORIDIAN RESORT & VILLAS

Disney's flagship hotel is inspired by Florida's grand Victorian seaside resorts from the turn of the last century. The Grand Floridian integrates verandas, intricate latticework, dormers, and turrets beneath a red-shingle roof to capture the most memorable elements of 19th-century ocean-resort architecture. A five-story domed lobby encircled by enameled balustrades and overhung by crystal chandeliers establishes the resort's understated opulence.

Rooms at the Grand Floridian are luxurious yet warm and inviting, with wood trim and fabrics in beachy tones. The typical room has an armoire, two queen beds, a daybed, a reading chair, a table with side chairs, and marble-topped sinks. All rooms have been recently refurbished, and many include a balcony.

The Grand's pools are among the largest in Walt Disney World. The beachfront pool contains a waterslide perfect for little ones, plus a waterfall, while the courtyard pool offers more quiet for adults. In addition to swimming, the Grand offers a white-sand beach, fitness center, jogging trail, and watercraft options for Seven Seas Lagoon.

The Grand Floridian also has some of Disney's best dining options, including the seafood-centric Narcoossee's, upscale Cítricos, and flagship dining experience at Victoria & Albert's. Dining at V&A's is a 3-hour marathon of gustatory delight, complemented by the best service staff in Walt Disney World.

The Grand Floridian's 200 studio, one-, two-, and three-bedroom villas sit in a single T-shaped structure, separate and to the south of the main building. Inside, they're much nicer than the rooms at the main resort. Most have vaulted living room ceilings and faux-wood balconies or porches. Those balconies stretch the entire length of the room, giving everyone enough space for a good view. All except the studios have full kitchens with stainless steel appliances (the studios gets a kitchenette). The Villas share transportation, pools, and restaurants with the Grand Floridian. Service at the Villas is excellent, with a dedicated concierge desk inside the Villas' lobby.

STRENGTHS

- Low guest-to-staff ratio
- Excellent dining options for adults
- Large rooms with daybeds
- On-site spa
- *Alice in Wonderland*–themed splash area
- Boat and monorail transportation to the Magic Kingdom
- Diverse recreational options
- Close to Palm, Magnolia, and Oak Trail golf courses

WEAKNESSES

- Most expensive of the Disney resorts
- Self-parking is across the street
- Bus transportation to DHS, Animal Kingdom, water parks, and Disney Springs is shared by the other monorail resorts

The Grand Floridian Villas evoke calm with subdued decor.

The Grand Floridian's pools are among the best in Walt Disney World.

CAPTAIN NEMO'S ATOMIC SUB RESORT

If you think submarines cramp your style, wait until you see Captain Nemo's Atomic Sub Resort. Guest rooms are spacious, with floor-to-ceiling acrylic windows so you can watch your fish swim by on its way to the sushi bar. Enjoy the seafood delicacies of the Sequined Squid restaurant, and if you want to find your groove, let it all hang out at the Twerking Tuna Juke Joint. Topside there's shuffleboard and platform diving. There's no waterslide, but they'll load you up in a torpedo tube for the ride of your life (hold your nose!). Finally, relax in the Spa de Mer, where infant piranhas will gleefully nibble away all the dead skin on your feet.

STRENGTHS

- Super-fresh seafood in restaurants
- Excellent air-conditioning throughout
- Low radiation levels from reactor

WEAKNESSES

- Dinghy transportation to theme parks
- Occasional giant squid attacks
- Sub doesn't go anywhere

OLD KEY WEST RESORT

STRENGTHS

- Largest villas of the DVC/DDV resorts
- Often available at discounted rates or as DVC rental
- Mature landscaping
- Close to Lake Buena Vista golf course
- Homey, well-themed lounge (The Gurgling Suitcase)
- Grocery selection in gift shop
- Boat service to Disney Springs
- Convenient parking

WEAKNESSES

- Multiple bus stops
- No elevators in many buildings
- Fewer baths per bedroom than newer DVC/DDV properties
- Mediocre on-site dining

Old Key West is a large aggregation of two- to three-story buildings modeled after Caribbean residences and guesthouses of the Florida Keys. Set around a golf course and along Bonnet Creek, buildings are arranged in small, neighborhood-style clusters.

As the original Disney Deluxe Villa (that is, time-share) property, Old Key West has some of the roomiest accommodations in Walt Disney World. The one- and two-bedroom villas include a laundry room and a full kitchen, as well as a master bathroom big enough to hold a small party. All villas are tastefully decorated with wicker and upholstered furniture in light-colored schemes. Finally, each villa has a private balcony that overlooks either a private courtyard, garden, or water view.

Amenities at Old Key West include a full-service restaurant, modest fitness center, marina, and sundries shop. Each cluster of buildings has a quiet pool, and a larger pool is at the community hall with a waterslide in the shape of a giant sandcastle. Transportation from Old Key West is sometimes a challenge, so we recommend having access to a car.

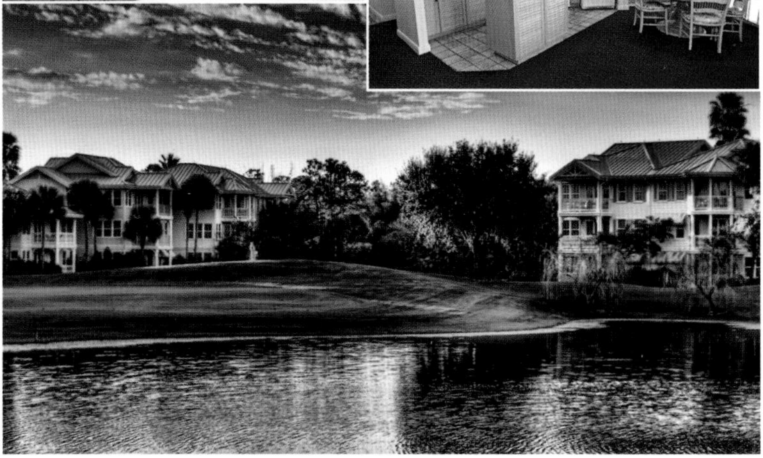

POLYNESIAN VILLAGE RESORT

Disney's Polynesian Village Resort would be the place we'd retire to if we ever hit the lottery. With its tropical landscaping, well-appointed rooms, and good on-site restaurants, it's one of the few Walt Disney World resorts where you could skip the parks entirely and be perfectly content just exploring the grounds. Everything about the Poly (as it's known to its fans) is designed to relax, from the exotic plants that greet you at the entrance to the white-sand beach complete with hammocks and lounge chairs.

Rooms at the Poly are among the nicest in Walt Disney World, and bathrooms have lots of counter space and larger-than-average showers.

The volcano-topped main pool offers a zero-entry end for smaller kids to splash and play (a separate "quiet pool" is in the middle of the resort). At night, the Poly's pool and beach offer excellent views of the Magic Kingdom's fireworks display.

STRENGTHS

- Most family-friendly dining on the monorail loop
- Fun South Seas theme
- On-site child care
- Boat and monorail transportation to the Magic Kingdom
- Walking distance to Epcot monorail
- Among the best club levels of the deluxe resorts
- Close to Palm, Magnolia, and Oak Trail golf courses

WEAKNESSES

- No spa or exercise facilities (guests must use those at the Grand Floridian)
- Bus transportation to DHS, Animal Kingdom, water parks, and Disney Springs is shared with the other monorail resorts

After a lengthy refurbishment, the Polynesian Village upgraded the lobby and both pools and added a fantastic new themed bar: Trader Sam's Grog Grotto. The rooms in the Moorea, Pago Pago, and Tokelau buildings have also been converted to Disney Vacation Club Villas, but the most noticeable, and priciest, addition is the 20 Bora Bora Bungalows that extend into Seven Seas Lagoon. The bungalows are 1,600-square-foot, two-bedroom, standalone structures surrounded by water, and they offer magnificent views at staggering prices—up to $3,400 per night!

© Disney

SARATOGA SPRINGS RESORT & SPA AND TREEHOUSE VILLAS

Saratoga Springs Resort & Spa is themed, Disney says, after an upstate New York Victorian lakeside retreat from the 1880s. And if the average New York Victorian lakeside retreat of the 1880s had about 18 gargantuan four-story pastel-color buildings situated around a massive lake, plus a pool complex, state-of-the-art fitness center and spa, on-site dining, and a golf course, then Disney's got themselves one heck of a history book! Or, it could be a sign that they need to stop paying the marketing guys by the adjective.

That said, Saratoga Springs's layout and architecture combine to hide the fact that the resort is fairly large. Most guest buildings are situated close to the water, and their size is the perfect scale to complement the lake. Taller buildings would have made it look like a pond, while smaller buildings would have made the resort seem too spread out. Walking trails around the grounds guide you both around the buildings and the water, with excellent views from almost any angle.

Rooms at Saratoga Springs are upscale and a little more masculine than in other Disney resorts. Chairs, sofas, and tables are quite substantial, perhaps a little too large for the rooms they inhabit. The overall effect, however, is sophisticated and restful. A total of 840 studio, one-, two-, and three-bedroom villas are available. Dining and bus transportation aren't the resort's strong points, so we suggest having access to a car.

STRENGTHS

- Often available at discounted rates or as a DVC/DDV rental
- Attractive main pool; multiple well-themed quiet pools with snack bars
- Closest resort to Disney Springs and Typhoon Lagoon
- Convenient parking
- Only WDW-owned resort with dedicated golf (Lake Buena Vista Golf Course)
- On-site spa and fitness center
- Grocery options in gift shop

WEAKNESSES

- On-site dining is limited for a resort of this size
- Theme is dull compared with those of other Disney resorts
- Bus service can take some time to get out of the huge resort
- Fewer baths per bedroom than newer DVC/DDV properties

Treehouse Villas is a complex of 60 villas situated between Old Key West and the Grandstand section of Saratoga Springs proper. True to their name, the villas stand on stilts 10 feet off the ground and are surrounded by densely wooded landscape. Each villa is an eight-sided structure with three bedrooms and two bathrooms in approximately 1,074 square feet—about the same size or slightly smaller than two-bedroom villas elsewhere. The treehouses have an open floor plan, however, that makes up for the smaller size.

The interior of each villa is decorated with natural materials, such as stone floors, granite countertops, and stained-wood furniture. Bathrooms are tiled and have excellent space and storage. One bedroom has bunk beds for small children, while the master bedroom and second bedroom have queen beds. A sleeper sofa and chairs in the living room means the treehouses can sleep nine if needed. Smaller families will love the extra space (ours did), as well as the layout and amenities.

SHADES OF GREEN

Shades of Green is a resort within Walt Disney World, but is owned and operated by the U.S. Armed Forces. Available only to US military personnel (including members of the National Guard and reserves, retired military, and employees of the U.S. Public Health Service and the Department of Defense), Shades of Green is the equivalent of Disney's deluxe resorts, at generally lower prices.

While Shades of Green doesn't have a major theme, the buildings and lobby interior have the rustic look and exposed wood beams of a mountain resort. Several pools are available within the resort, and Shades of Green is surrounded by Disney golf courses open to all guests.

Rooms at Shades of Green are large and well appointed, with light-oak furniture, soft hues, and the occasional bright accent. There's not a kernel of theming to be found here—no Aztec wallpaper or jaunty sailboat curtains—but for many folks that's a welcome relief. Most rooms have a private balcony.

STRENGTHS

- Large guest rooms
- Discount tickets for military personnel with ID
- Quiet setting
- Views of golf course from guest rooms
- Convenient self-parking
- Swimming complex, fitness center
- On-site car rental (Alamo)

WEAKNESSES

- No interesting theme
- Limited on-site dining
- Limited bus service
- Daily parking fee ($5)
- No Magical Express service from airport
- No free parking at theme parks

THE SWAN AND THE DOLPHIN

STRENGTHS

- Best-priced location on Crescent Lake
- Both hotels participate in Starwood Preferred Guest program
- Good on-site and nearby dining
- Only hotels within walking distance to mini-golf (Fantasia Gardens)
- Large variety of upscale restaurants; 24-hour food available at Picabu
- On-site car rental through National
- Very nice pool complex
- Impressive public spaces
- Walking distance to both Epcot International Gateway and DHS

WEAKNESSES

- Conventioneers may be off-putting to vacationing families
- Daily resort and parking fees
- No Disney's Magical Express or Disney Dining Plan
- Bus service to Magic Kingdom, Animal Kingdom, water parks, and Disney Springs is shared with other Epcot resorts
- Self-parking is quite distant from the hotels' entrances
- Tiny bathrooms (Swan)
- Spotty front-desk service and housekeeping (Swan)

It takes a special kind of architect to say, "and at the top of the hotels, we're going to have giant fish from outer space. Wait . . . giant swans! OK, a couple of each." Beyond the odd icons, however, are some of the nicest rooms available in Walt Disney World.

Though the hotels are on Disney property, next to the Yacht Club and BoardWalk Resorts, they're owned by Sheraton (Dolphin) and Westin (Swan). Perhaps because they're owned by hotel companies, rooms here tend to have better beds and soft goods and less theming than most comparable Disney resorts. Like Disney's deluxe resorts, the Swan and Dolphin are huge properties, with multiple restaurants and pools, and enough recreational options to keep you busy all day.

Rooms here are tastefully decorated in mostly neutral tones with accents of color. Most rooms feature excellent desk space and lighting, especially useful for business travelers. Bathrooms and dressing areas are on the smaller side but functional.

Swan and Dolphin guests are eligible for Extra Magic Hours and Magic Bands but not Magical Express. These hotels will nickel-and-dime you to death. Whatever rate you're quoted, figure on another $45 per day in miscellaneous costs.

WILDERNESS LODGE & BOULDER RIDGE VILLAS

With one of the more breathtaking lobbies at Walt Disney World, the Wilderness Lodge is styled after the lodges of the Adirondacks and national parks of the Western US. The eight-story atrium, with its 90-foot stone fireplace, interior waterfalls, and towering totem poles, is simply an introduction to the beautiful Wilderness Lodge grounds, which feature a free-form pool, views of Bay Lake, and an on-the-hour geyser.

The Disney Vacation Club Villas area of the Wilderness Lodge is getting a new name and undergoing major renovations in 2016–2017. Some rooms in the main lodge are being converted to villa-style rooms. Additional structures are being built in the villas area—one likely a table-service restaurant. Also expect to see the addition of over-the-water guest rooms, similar to the bungalows at the Polynesian Village.

STRENGTHS

- National-park-lodge theme is a favorite of kids and adults alike
- Along with Animal Kingdom Lodge, it's the least expensive Disney deluxe resort
- Excellent lounge for adults
- Great views from guest rooms
- Rooms with bunk beds available
- On-site child care
- Close to recreational options at Fort Wilderness

WEAKNESSES

- Transportation to Magic Kingdom is by bus or boat only
- No character dining
- Whispering Canyon Cafe noise can spill out into lobby and rooms near it
- Villa guests must access most services through main hotel
- Bus transportation to Magic Kingdom sometimes shared with Fort Wilderness
- Smallest rooms of Disney's deluxe resorts

YACHT AND BEACH CLUB RESORTS AND BEACH CLUB VILLAS

The two best features of the Yacht and Beach Club resorts are their location right next to Epcot (especially World Showcase's restaurants) and Stormalong Bay, easily the best swimming pool complex of any Walt Disney World resort. Both Yacht and Beach Club properties feature similar nautical theming, and except for the color scheme, you'd be hard-pressed to say which was which.

Rooms at both resorts have two queen beds or one king bed, a nice desk area for working, and lots of storage space. Some rooms have balconies, though a relatively small percentage look across the lake toward the BoardWalk. Dressing areas feature plenty of space for getting prepped in the mornings, and the bath features good lighting.

The Beach Club Villas offer studio, one-bedroom, and two-bedroom accommodations. Situated on the Epcot side of the resort, the villas' lack of a lake view is made up for by its surroundings, which are quiet enough to make you forget that you're next to a theme park.

STRENGTHS

- Best pool complex of any WDW resort
- Walking distance to Epcot's International Gateway
- Very underrated and relatively affordable full-service restaurant (Captain's Grille)
- Close to many BoardWalk and Epcot dining options
- Well-themed public spaces
- Bright and attractive guest rooms
- Boat transportation to DHS

WEAKNESSES

- Lack of good quick-service dining options
- Views and balcony size are hit-or-miss
- Bus service to Magic Kingdom, Animal Kingdom, water parks, and Disney Springs is shared with other Epcot resorts
- No three-bedroom Grand Villas at the Beach Club Villas
- Beach Club Villas have fewer baths per bedroom than newer DVC/DDV properties

Yacht Club

The Yacht and Beach Clubs share Stormalong Bay, Disney's best resort swimming complex.

Beach Club

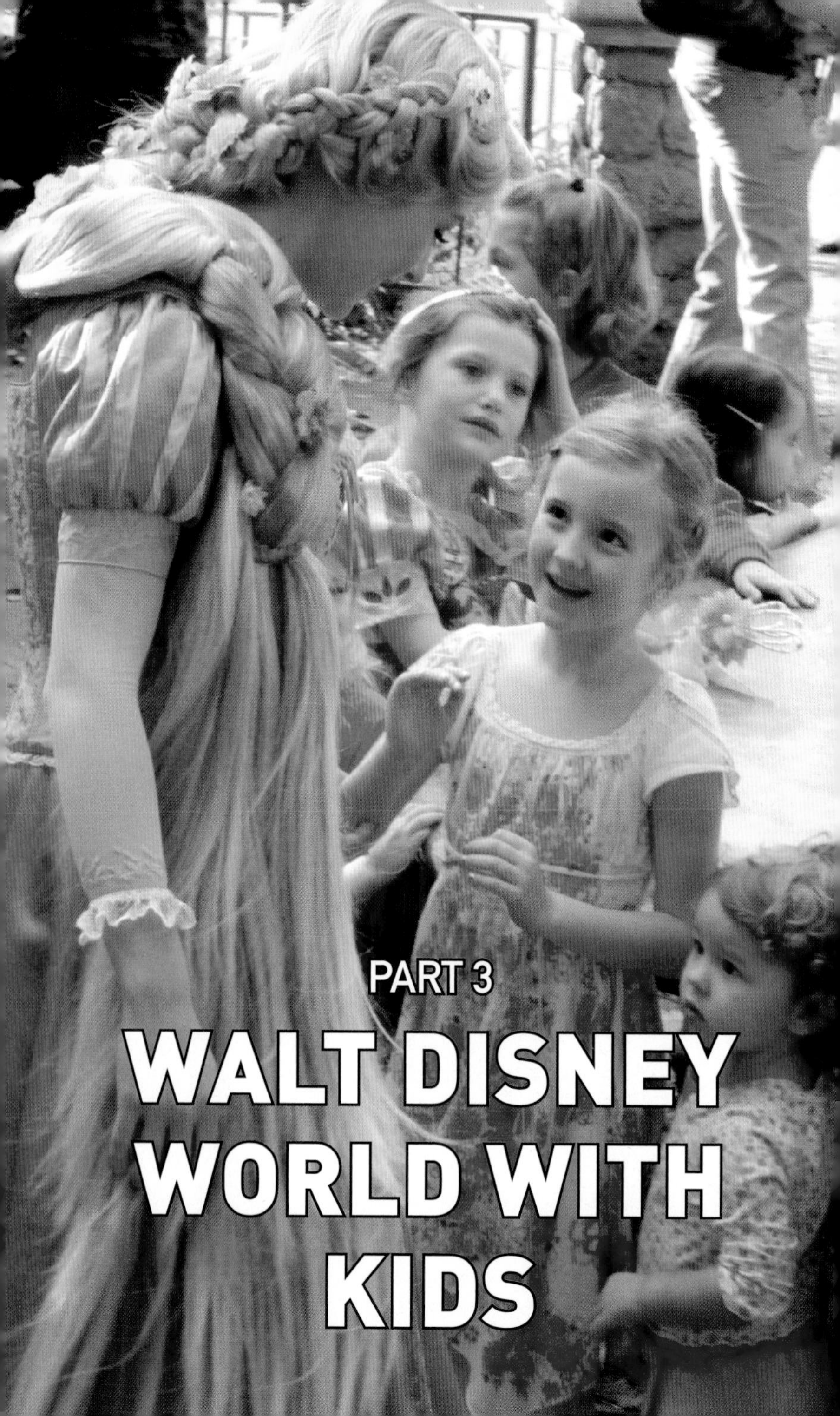

PART 3

WALT DISNEY WORLD WITH KIDS

ABOUT FAMILY VACATIONS

It has been suggested that the phrase *family vacation* is a bit of an oxymoron because you can never take a vacation from the responsibilities of parenting if your children are traveling with you. Though you leave work and normal routine far behind, your children require as much attention, if not more, when traveling as they do at home.

Parenting on the road is an art. It requires imagination and organization. Think about it: You have to do all the usual stuff (feed, dress, bathe, supervise, teach, comfort, discipline, put to bed, and so on) in an atmosphere where your children are hyper-stimulated, without the familiarity of place and the resources you take for granted while at home. Although it's not impossible—and can even be fun—parenting on the road is not something you want to learn on the fly, particularly at Walt Disney World.

The point we want to drive home is that preparation, or the lack thereof, can make or break your Walt Disney World vacation. Believe us, you don't want to leave the success of your expensive Disney vacation to chance. But don't confuse chance with good luck. Chance is what happens when you fail to prepare; good luck is when preparation meets opportunity. Also keep in mind that the risk of being overwhelmed increases with the size of your group, especially if you're traveling with extended family or friends. The larger the group, the greater the need for preparation.

Broadly speaking, you need to prepare yourself and your children mentally, emotionally, physically, organizationally, and logistically. You also need a basic understanding of the theme parks and a well-considered plan for how to go about seeing them.

Mental and Emotional Preparation

Mental preparation begins with realistic expectations about your Disney vacation and consideration of what each adult and child in your party most wants and needs from his or her Walt Disney World experience. Getting in touch with this aspect of planning requires a lot of introspection and good, open family communication.

1. Division of Labor Talk about what you and your partner need and what you expect to happen on the vacation. This discussion alone can preempt some unpleasant surprises mid-trip. If you are a two-parent (or two-adult) family, do you have a clear understanding of how the parenting workload is to be distributed?

2. Togetherness Another dimension to consider is how much togetherness seems appropriate to you. For some parents, a vacation represents a rare opportunity to really connect with their children, to talk, exchange ideas, and get reacquainted. For others, a vacation affords the time to get a little distance, to enjoy a round of golf while the kids are enjoying the theme park. The point here is to think about your and your children's preferences and needs concerning your time together.

3. Lighten Up Prepare yourself mentally to be a little less compulsive on vacation about correcting small behavioral deviations and pounding home the lessons of life. So what if Matt eats hamburgers for breakfast, lunch, and dinner every day? You can make him eat peas and broccoli when you get home. Roll with the little stuff.

4. Something for Everyone If you travel with an infant, toddler, or any child who requires a lot of special attention, make sure that you have some energy and time remaining for the rest of your brood. In the course of your planning, invite each child to name something special to do or see at Disney World with Mom or Dad alone.

5. Whose Idea Was This, Anyway? The discord that many vacationing families experience arises from the kids being on a completely different wavelength from Mom and Dad. Parents and grandparents are often worse than children when it comes to conjuring fantasy scenarios of what a Walt Disney World vacation will be like. It can be many things, but there's a lot more to it than just riding Dumbo and seeing Mickey.

6. Know Thyself and Nothing to Excess This good advice was made available to ancient Greeks courtesy of the oracle of Apollo at Delphi, who gave us permission to pass it along to you. First, concerning the "know thyself" part, we want you to do some serious thinking about what you want in a vacation. We also want you to entertain the notion that having fun and deriving pleasure from your vacation may be very different indeed from exhausting yourself trying to do and see as much as possible. Plan on seeing the theme parks in bite-size chunks with plenty of sleeping, swimming, napping, and relaxing in between.

7. Routines that Travel If you observe certain routines at home—for example, reading a book before bed or having a bath first thing in the morning—try to incorporate these familiar activities into your vacation schedule. They will provide your children with a sense of security and normalcy. Maintaining a normal routine is especially important with toddlers.

Physical Preparation

You'll find that some physical conditioning, coupled with a realistic sense of the toll that Disney World takes on your body, will preclude falling apart in the middle of your vacation. As one of our readers put it, "If you pay attention to eat, heat, feet, and sleep, you'll be OK."

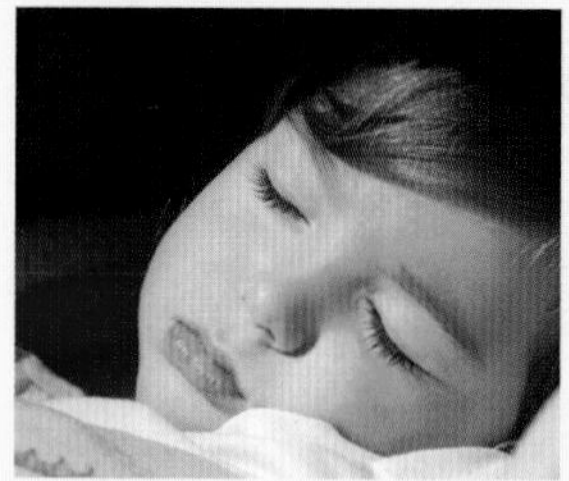

Build Naps and Rest into Your Itinerary The theme parks are huge; don't try to see everything in one day. Tour early in the morning and return to your hotel around 11:30 a.m. for lunch, a swim, and a nap. Even during off-season, when crowds are smaller and temperatures more pleasant, the size of the major theme parks will exhaust most children under age 8 by lunchtime. Return to the park in late afternoon or early evening and continue touring. When it comes to naps, this mom does not mince words:

One last thing for parents of small kids—take the book's advice. Get out of the park, and take the nap, take the nap, TAKE THE NAP! Never in my life have I seen so many parents screaming at, ridiculing, or slapping their kids. (What a vacation!) Disney [parks are] overwhelming for kids and adults.

A mom from Rochester, New York, was equally adamant:

[You] absolutely must rest during the day. Kids went from 8 a.m. to 9 p.m. in the park. Kids did great that day, but we were all completely worthless the next day. Definitely must pace yourself. Don't ever try to do two full days of park sightseeing in a row.

▶ **UNOFFICIAL TIP** Naps and relief from the frenetic pace of the theme parks, even during the off-season, are indispensable. If you plan to return to your hotel at midday and would like your room made up, let housekeeping know.

Build Endurance Though most children are active, their normal play usually doesn't condition them for the exertion required to tour a Disney theme park. We recommend starting a program of family walks four to six weeks before your trip to get in shape. Aim for being able to walk at least 6 miles without falling apart. A Pennsylvania mom tells how she got her first grader in shape:

Our 6-year-old began walking with us a bit every day one month before leaving—when we arrived, her little legs could carry her, and she had a lot of stamina.

A father of two had this to say:

My wife walked with my son to school every day when it was nice. His stamina was outstanding.

Other Recommendations for Making the Dream Come True

When planning a Disney World vacation with young children, consider the following:

AGE There really is something for everyone at Disney World, and any age will enjoy it. That said, the "ideal" age depends on your children and the expected frequency of visits. If you plan on making semiregular trips to the World, say every two or three years, there is no such thing as too young. If you plan on a once-in-a-generation trip, however, you probably want to wait until the kids are tall enough to ride everything and old enough to appreciate it. That tends to happen in the 7- to 10-year-old range.

TIME OF YEAR TO VISIT Avoid the hot, crowded summer months, especially if you have preschoolers. Go in October, November (except Thanksgiving), early December, January, February, or May. If you have children of varied ages and they're good students, take the older ones out of school and visit during the cooler, less-congested off-season. Arrange special assignments relating to the educational aspects of Disney World. If your children can't afford to miss school, take your vacation as soon as the school year ends in late May or early June. Alternatively, try late August before school starts.

WHERE TO STAY The time and hassle involved in commuting to and from the theme parks will be lessened if you stay in a hotel close to the theme parks. We should point out that this doesn't necessarily mean you have to lodge at a hotel in Walt Disney World. Because Walt Disney World is so geographically dispersed, many off-property hotels are actually closer to the theme parks than some Disney resorts. Regardless of whether you stay in or out of the World, it's imperative that you take young children out of the parks each day for a few hours of rest. Neglecting to relax is the best way we know to get the whole family in a snit and ruin the day (or the vacation).

If you have young children, you must plan ahead. Make sure your hotel is within 20 minutes of the theme parks. You can revive somewhat by retreating to a Disney hotel for lunch or by finding a quiet restaurant in the theme parks, but there's no substitute for returning to the familiarity and comfort of your own hotel. Regardless of what you have heard, children too large to sleep in a stroller won't relax unless you take them back to your hotel. If it takes renting a car to make returning to your hotel practicable, rent the car.

If you are traveling with children age 12 and younger and want to stay in the World, we recommend the Polynesian, Grand Floridian or its Villas, the Contemporary, Bay Lake Tower, or Wilderness Lodge & Boulder Ridge Villas Resorts (in that order), if they fit your budget. All are connected to the Magic Kingdom and Epcot (with transfer) by monorail. For less expensive rooms, try Port Orleans Resort. Bargain rooms are available at the All-Star, Art of Animation, and Pop Century Resorts. Fully equipped log cabins at Fort Wilderness Campground are also good economy lodging.

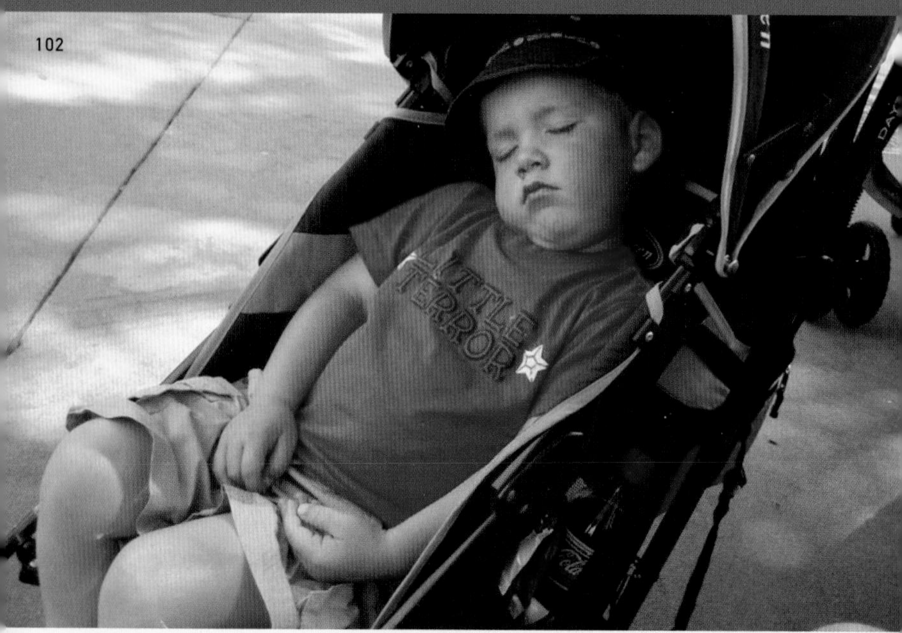

NOTHING MORE THAN FEELINGS When you or your children get tired and irritable, call a time-out and regroup. Trust your instincts. What would feel best? Another ride, an ice cream break, or going back to the room for a nap? The way to protect your considerable investment in your Disney vacation is to stay happy and have a good time. You don't have to meet a quota for experiencing attractions. Do what you want.

SETTING LIMITS AND MAKING PLANS Avoid arguments and disappointment by establishing guidelines for each day, and get everybody committed. Include the following:

1. Wake-up time and breakfast plans
2. When to depart for the park
3. What to take with you
4. A policy for splitting the group or for staying together
5. What to do if the group gets separated or someone is lost
6. How long you intend to tour in the morning and what you want to see, including plans in the event an attraction is closed or too crowded
7. A policy on what you can afford for snacks
8. A time for returning to the hotel to rest
9. When you will return to the park and how late you will stay
10. Dinner plans
11. A policy for buying souvenirs, including who pays: Mom and Dad or the kids
12. Bedtimes

WHAT KIDS WANT According to research by Yesawich, Pepperdine, Brown, and Russell, the chart on the facing page shows what kids want and don't want when taking a vacation. Kids have a lot in common about what they want, less so concerning what they don't want. The "don't want" entries in the chart are the four most common responses.

WHAT DO KIDS WANT?

To go swimming/have pool time	80%
To eat in restaurants	78%
To stay at a hotel or resort	76%
To visit a theme park	76%
To stay up late	73%

WHAT DO KIDS NOT WANT?

To get up early	52%
To ride in a car	36%
To play golf	34%
To go to a museum	31%

BE FLEXIBLE Any day at Walt Disney World includes some surprises; be prepared to adjust your plan. Listen to your intuition.

LEAST COMMON DENOMINATORS Somebody is going to run out of steam first, and when he or she does, the whole family will be affected. Sometimes a snack break will revive the flagging member. Sometimes, however, it's better to just return to your hotel. Pushing the tired or discontented beyond their capacity will spoil the day for them—and you. Accept that energy levels vary and be prepared to respond to members of your group who poop out.

AVOID MELTDOWNS

(At least the unpleasant kind)

Deal with fatigue and behavioral problems early before they get out of hand. Both children and adults have meltdowns every day at Walt Disney World, and once you or junior launch a stem-winder, it's tough to regain your vacation equilibrium. Don't push too hard or pressure kids to ride attractions that frighten them. If you sense that your group is getting testy, stop for a break or head back to the hotel for a swim and a nap. Choose your battles wisely. Avoid arguments and confrontations over insignificant issues.

▶ **UNOFFICIAL TIP** Just because they're on vacation doesn't mean that you should let the kids monopolize your trip—maintain some of your everyday rules, and you'll all have a better time together.

Good meltdowns

Sometimes a good meltdown will prevent a bad one.

Other Stuff to Think About

OVERHEATING, SUNBURN, AND DEHYDRATION These are the most common problems of younger children at Disney World. Carry and use sunscreen. Be sure to put sunscreen on children in strollers, and make sure that arms and legs are shaded by the stroller's canopy. To avoid overheating, rest regularly in the shade or in an air-conditioned restaurant or show. Hydration is exceptionally important, so carry a refillable water bottle and take plenty of drink breaks. A plastic squeeze bottle is sold in many shops for $4, and bottled water is sold everywhere.

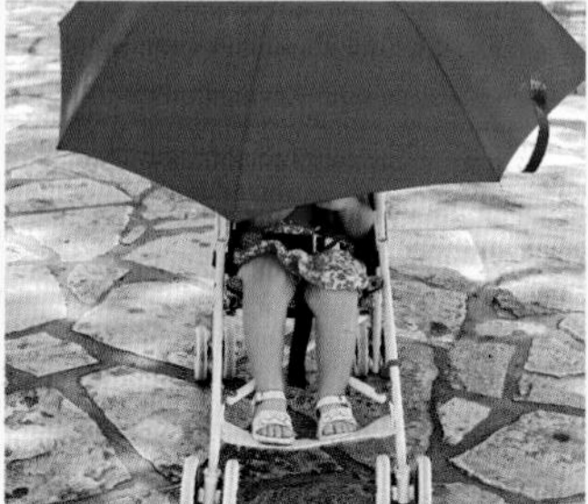

▶ UNOFFICIAL TIP Teaching your kids to tell you clearly what they want or need will help make the trip more enjoyable for everyone.

▶ UNOFFICIAL TIP We recommend using a stroller for children age 6 and younger and carrying plastic bottles of water.

BLISTERS AND SORE FEET Guests of all ages should wear comfortable, well-broken-in shoes and a pair of socks designed specifically for hiking (we've had great success with SmartWool socks). If you or your children are susceptible to blisters, bring precut moleskin bandages. When you feel a hot spot, stop, air out your foot, and place a moleskin bandage over the area before a blister forms. Young children may not tell you about a developing blister until it's too late, so inspect the feet of preschoolers two or more times a day. Johnson & Johnson makes bandages especially for blisters. These can be used after a blister has formed or as a substitute for moleskin when you feel a hot spot.

FIRST AID Each major theme park has a first-aid center. In the Magic Kingdom, it's at the end of Main Street to your left, between Casey's Corner and The Crystal Palace. At Epcot, it's on the World Showcase side of Odyssey Center. At Disney's Hollywood Studios, it's in the Guest Relations building inside the main entrance. At Animal Kingdom, it's in Discovery Island, on your left just before you cross the bridge to Africa. If you or your children have a medical problem, go to a first-aid center. The staff in these facilities are friendlier than the personnel in most doctor's offices and are accustomed to treating everything from paper cuts to allergic reactions.

CHILDREN ON MEDICATION Some parents of hyperactive children on medication discontinue or decrease the child's dosage at the end of the school year. If you have such a child, be aware that Disney World might overstimulate him or her. Consult your physician before altering your child's medication regimen.

SUNGLASSES If you want your younger children to wear sunglasses, put a strap or string on the frames, so the glasses will stay on during rides and can hang from the child's neck while indoors.

THINGS YOU FORGOT OR THINGS YOU RAN OUT OF Rain gear, diapers, diaper pins, formula, camera media, painkillers, topical sunburn treatments, and other sundries are sold at all major theme parks, all Disney resorts, Typhoon Lagoon, Blizzard Beach, and Disney Springs. Rain gear is a bargain, but most other items are high. Ask for goods you don't see displayed.

INFANTS AND TODDLERS AT THE THEME PARKS The major parks have centralized facilities for infant and toddler care. Everything necessary for changing diapers, preparing formulas, and warming bottles and food is available. Supplies are for sale, and there are rockers and special chairs for nursing mothers. At the Magic Kingdom, the Baby Care Center is next to The Crystal Palace at the end of Main Street. At Epcot, Baby Care is near the Odyssey Center, to the right of Test Track in Future World. At Disney's Hollywood Studios, Baby Care is in the Guest Relations building to the left of the entrance. At Animal Kingdom, Baby Care is behind the MyMagic+ service center. Dads are welcome at the centers and can use most services. In addition, many men's restrooms in the major parks have changing tables.

Infants and toddlers are allowed to experience any attraction that doesn't have minimum-height or age restrictions. If you think you might try nursing during a theater attraction, be advised that most shows run about 17–20 minutes. Exceptions are *The Hall of Presidents* at the Magic Kingdom and *The American Adventure* at Epcot, which run 23 and 29 minutes, respectively.

UNIFORMS We recommend springing for vacation uniforms. Buy for each child several sets of jeans (or shorts) and T-shirts, all matching, and all the same. For a one-week trip, for example, get each child three pairs of khaki shorts, three light-yellow T-shirts, and three pairs of SmartWool or CoolMax hiking socks. What's the point? First, you don't have to play fashion designer, coordinating a week's worth of stylish combos. Each morning the kids put on their uniform. It's simple, it saves time, and there are no decisions to make or arguments about what to wear. Second, uniforms make your children easier to spot and keep together in the theme parks. Third, the uniforms give your family, as well as the vacation itself, some added identity.

LABELS A great idea, especially for younger children, is to attach labels with your family name, hometown, the name of your hotel, the dates of your stay, and your cell phone number inside their shirts, on their shoelaces, or tattooed to their skin (seriously, they're temporary and available online).

DISNEY, KIDS, AND SCARY STUFF

Monsters and special effects at Disney's Hollywood Studios are more real and sinister than those in the other parks. If your child has difficulty coping with the ghouls in The Haunted Mansion, think twice about exposing him to machine-gun battles and the creature from *Alien* at the Hollywood Studios. Preschoolers should start with Dumbo and work up to the Jungle Cruise in late morning, after being revved up and before getting hungry, thirsty, or tired. Pirates of the Caribbean contains a naval battle (and lots of pirates), so may be out for preschoolers. You get the idea.

THE FRIGHT FACTOR

While each youngster is different, following are seven attraction elements that alone or combined could push a child's buttons and indicate that a certain attraction isn't age appropriate for that child:

1. NAME OF ATTRACTION Young children will naturally be more apprehensive about something called The Haunted Mansion or Tower of Terror than *Enchanted Tales with Belle.*

2. VISUAL IMPACT OF ATTRACTION FROM OUTSIDE Splash Mountain, the Tower of Terror, and Big Thunder Mountain Railroad look scary enough to give adults second thoughts, and they terrify many young children.

3. VISUAL IMPACT OF THE INDOOR-QUEUING AREA Pirates of the Caribbean's caves and dungeons and The Haunted Mansion's "stretch rooms" can frighten children.

4. INTENSITY OF ATTRACTION Some attractions are overwhelming, inundating the senses with sights, sounds, movement, and even smell. Animal Kingdom's *It's Tough to be a Bug!*, for example, combines loud sounds, lights, smoke, and animatronic insects with 3-D cinematography to create a total sensory experience. For some preschoolers, this is two or three senses too many.

5. VISUAL IMPACT OF THE ATTRACTION Sights in various attractions range from icky bugs to lurking buzzards, from grazing dinosaurs to waltzing ghosts. What one child calmly absorbs may scare the bejeepers out of another child the same age.

6. DARK Many Walt Disney World attractions operate indoors in the dark. For some children, this darkness triggers fear. A child who gets frightened on one dark ride (The Haunted Mansion, for example) may be unwilling to try other indoor rides.

7. THE TACTILE EXPERIENCE OF THE RIDE Some rides are wild enough to cause motion sickness, wrench backs, and discombobulate guests of any age.

As a footnote to the preceding, be aware that gaining the courage and confidence in regard to the attractions is not necessarily an upwardly linear process. A dad from Maryland explains:

As a 4-year-old, my daughter absolutely adored The Haunted Mansion. At 5 she was scared to death of it! At 6 she was fine again. Just because a child loves a ride at one age does not mean that he or she will love it on the next trip. The terror curve can go in either direction. (And then back again.)

SMALL-CHILD FRIGHT-POTENTIAL CHART

This is a quick reference to identify attractions to be wary of, and why. The chart represents a generalization, and all kids are different. It relates specifically to kids ages 3–7. On average, children at the younger end of the range are more likely to be frightened than children in their sixth or seventh year.

Magic Kingdom

Sorcerers of the Magic Kingdom Loud but not frightening.

MAIN STREET, U.S.A.

Town Square Theater Meet and Greets Not frightening in any respect.

Walt Disney World Railroad Not frightening in any respect.

ADVENTURELAND

Captain Jack Sparrow's Pirate Tutorial Not frightening in any respect.

Jungle Cruise Some macabre sights. A good test attraction for little ones.

Magic Carpets of Aladdin Much like Dumbo. A favorite of young children.

A Pirate's Adventure Some exhibits may frighten young children when playing at night.

Pirates of the Caribbean Slightly intimidating queuing area; intense boat ride with gruesome (though humorous) sights and a short, unexpected flume slide.

Swiss Family Treehouse May not be suitable for kids afraid of heights.

Walt Disney's Enchanted Tiki Room A thunderstorm, loud volume, and simulated explosions frighten some preschoolers.

FRONTIERLAND

Big Thunder Mountain Railroad Visually intimidating from outside, with moderately intense visual effects. Wild enough to frighten adults. Switching-off option (see p. 113).

Country Bear Jamboree Not frightening in any respect.

Frontierland Shootin' Arcade May be frightening to children who are scared of guns.

Splash Mountain Visually intimidating from outside, with moderately intense visual effects. Ride culminates in a steep 52-foot plunge. Switching-off option (see p. 113).

Tom Sawyer Island Some very young children are intimidated by dark tunnels that can be easily avoided.

LIBERTY SQUARE

The Hall of Presidents Not frightening, but boring for young ones.

The Haunted Mansion Name raises anxiety, as do sounds and sights of waiting area. Intense attraction with humorously presented macabre sights. Ride itself is gentle.

Liberty Belle Riverboat Not frightening in any respect.

FANTASYLAND

Ariel's Grotto Not frightening in any respect.

The Barnstormer (children's coaster) May frighten some preschoolers.

Casey Jr. Splash 'n' Soak Station Not frightening in any respect.

Dumbo the Flying Elephant A tame midway ride; great favorite of most young children.

Enchanted Tales with Belle Not frightening in any respect.

It's a Small World Not frightening in any respect.

Mad Tea Party Midway-type ride can induce motion sickness in all ages.

The Many Adventures of Winnie the Pooh Frightens a small percentage of preschoolers.

Meet Merida at Fairytale Garden Not frightening in any respect.

Mickey's PhilharMagic May frighten a small number of preschoolers.

Peter Pan's Flight Not frightening in any respect.

Pete's Silly Sideshow Not frightening in any respect.

Prince Charming Regal Carrousel Not frightening in any respect.

Princess Fairytale Hall Not frightening in any respect.

Seven Dwarfs Mine Train May frighten some preschoolers.

Under the Sea: Journey of the Little Mermaid Animatronic octopus character frightens some preschoolers.

TOMORROWLAND

Astro Orbiter Visually intimidating from the waiting area, but the ride is relatively tame.

Buzz Lightyear's Space Ranger Spin May frighten some preschoolers.

Monsters, Inc. Laugh Floor May frighten a small number of preschoolers.

Space Mountain Very intense roller coaster in the dark; the Magic Kingdom's wildest ride and a scary roller coaster by any standard. Switching-off option (see p. 113).

Stitch's Great Escape! Very intense. May frighten children age 9 and younger. Switching-off option (see p. 113).

Tomorrowland Speedway Noise of waiting area slightly intimidates preschoolers; otherwise, not frightening.

Tomorrowland Transit Authority PeopleMover Not frightening in any respect.

Walt Disney's Carousel of Progress Not frightening in any respect.

Epcot

FUTURE WORLD

Disney & Pixar Short Film Festival Not frightening in any respect.

Epcot Character Spot Not frightening in any respect.

Journey Into Imagination with Figment Loud noises and unexpected flashing lights startle younger children.

Innoventions Not frightening in any respect.

The Land: *Circle of Life* Not frightening in any respect.

The Land: Living with the Land Not frightening in any respect.

The Land: Soarin' May frighten children age 7 and younger or anyone with a fear of heights. Otherwise, a very mellow ride.

Mission: Space Extremely intense space-simulation ride known to frighten guests of all ages. Preshow may also frighten some children. Nonspinning version available. Switching-off option (see p. 113).

The Seas: Main Tanks and Exhibits Not frightening in any respect.

The Seas: The Seas with Nemo & Friends Very sweet but may frighten some toddlers.

The Seas: *Turtle Talk with Crush* Not frightening in any respect.

Spaceship Earth Dark, imposing presentation intimidates a few preschoolers.

Sum of All Thrills Intense roller-coaster simulator may frighten some children.

Test Track Intense thrill ride may frighten any age. Switching-off option (see p. 113).

Universe of Energy: *Ellen's Energy Adventure* Dinosaur segment frightens some preschoolers; visually intense, with some intimidating effects.

WORLD SHOWCASE

Agent P's World Showcase Adventure Not frightening in any respect.

Canada: *O Canada!* Not frightening in any respect, but audience must stand.

China: *Reflections of China* Not frightening in any respect.

France: *Impressions de France* Not frightening in any respect.

IllumiNations Not frightening in any respect.

Mexico: Gran Fiesta Tour Not frightening in any respect.

Norway: Frozen Ever After Dark. Ride ends with a plunge down a 20-foot flume, which may frighten a few preschoolers.

Norway: Royal Sommerhus Meet and Greet Not frightening in any respect.

United States: *The American Adventure* Not frightening in any respect.

World Showcase Pavilions Not frightening in any respect.

Animal Kingdom

The Oasis Not frightening in any respect.

DISCOVERY ISLAND

Meet Favorite Disney Pals at Adventurers Outpost Not frightening in any respect.

The Tree of Life/*It's Tough to Be a Bug!* Very intense and loud, with special effects that startle viewers of all ages and potentially terrify young children.

Wilderness Explorers Not frightening in any respect.

AFRICA

Conservation Station and Affection Section Not frightening in any respect.

Festival of the Lion King Not frightening in any respect, but a bit loud.

Gorilla Falls Exploration Trail Not frightening in any respect.

Kilimanjaro Safaris A "collapsing" bridge and proximity of real animals make a few young children anxious.

Wildlife Express Train Not frightening in any respect.

ASIA

Expedition Everest Can frighten guests of all ages. Switching-off option (see p. 113).

Flights of Wonder Swooping birds alarm a few small children.

Kali River Rapids Potentially frightening and certainly wet for all ages. Switching-off option (see p. 113).

Maharajah Jungle Trek Some children may balk at the bat exhibit.

Rivers of Light Loud with special effects but generally not frightening.

DINOLAND U.S.A.

The Boneyard Not frightening in any respect.

Dinosaur High-tech thrill ride rattles riders of all ages. Switching-off option (see p. 113).

Finding Nemo—The Musical Not frightening in any respect, but loud.

Primeval Whirl A beginner roller coaster. Most children age 7 and older take it in stride.

TriceraTop Spin Midway-type ride; will frighten only a small number of younger kids.

PANDORA: THE WORLD OF AVATAR

Avatar: Flight of Passage Not open at press time but should be similar to Epcot's Soarin'. May frighten children age 7 and younger or anyone with a fear of heights.

Na'vi River Journey Not open at press time. Expected to be dark, and may have small drops, but should be fairly tame.

Disney's Hollywood Studios

HOLLYWOOD AND SUNSET BOULEVARDS

Beauty and the Beast—Live on Stage Not frightening in any respect.

Fantasmic! Terrifies some preschoolers.

The Great Movie Ride Intense in parts, with very realistic special effects and some visually intimidating sights. Frightens many preschoolers.

Rock 'n' Roller Coaster The wildest coaster at Walt Disney World. May frighten guests of any age. Switching-off option (see p. 113).

The Twilight Zone Tower of Terror Visually intimidating to young children; contains intense and realistic special effects. The plummeting elevator at the ride's end frightens many adults as well as kids. Switching-off option (see p. 113).

ECHO LAKE

For the First Time in Forever: A Frozen Sing-Along Celebration Not frightening in any respect.

Indiana Jones Epic Stunt Spectacular! Intense show with powerful special effects, including explosions, but young children generally handle it well.

Jedi Training: Trials of the Temple Not frightening in any respect.

Star Tours—The Adventures Continue Extremely intense visually for all ages; too intense for children under age 8. Switching-off option (see p. 113).

MUPPET COURTYARD

Jim Henson's Muppet-Vision 3-D Intense and loud, but not frightening.

PIXAR PLACE

Toy Story Mania! Dark ride may frighten some preschoolers.

ANIMATION COURTYARD

Disney Junior—Live on Stage! Not frightening in any respect.

Star Wars Launch Bay Some children may be frightened by the villain costumes or by the villain character greetings.

Voyage of the Little Mermaid Some children are creeped out by Ursula.

Walt Disney: One Man's Dream Not frightening in any respect.

SWITCHING OFF (AKA THE BABY SWAP)

If you have a plucky child who doesn't meet the minimum-height requirement for her favorite attraction, bump her up a couple of feet with a big hairdo.

Several attractions have age and/or minimum-height requirements. Some couples with children too small or too young forgo these attractions, while others take turns riding. Missing some of Disney's best rides is an unnecessary sacrifice, and waiting in line twice for the same ride is a tremendous waste of time. Instead, take advantage of switching off, also known as the baby or rider swap.

To switch off, there must be at least two adults. Both adults and the child find a cast member at the FastPass+ entry and explain that you would like to switch off. The cast member will give you a rider exchange pass good for three people. One adult then waits in line (or uses a prescheduled FastPass+ reservation), while the other does something else with the child. After adult 1 is done riding, the second adult, along with two other people if they want, goes through the FastPass+ line using the rider exchange pass. If you have an older child who meets the height requirement, he or she gets to ride twice, once with each adult, under this method.

▶ **UNOFFICIAL TIP** You can incorporate FastPass+ with switching off to secure passes for multiple attractions at the same time.

THE DISNEY CHARACTERS

The large and friendly costumed versions of Mickey, Minnie, Donald, Goofy, and others—known as Disney characters—provide a link between Disney animated films and the theme parks. To people emotionally invested, the characters in Disney films are as real as next-door neighbors, never mind that they're drawings on plastic. In recent years, theme-park personifications of the characters also have become real to us. It's not a person in a mouse costume; it's Mickey himself. Similarly, meeting Goofy or Snow White is an encounter with a celebrity, a memory to be treasured.

While Disney animated-film characters number in the hundreds, only about 250 have been brought to life in costume. Of these, fewer than a fifth are "greeters" (characters who mix with patrons); the others perform in shows or parades. Originally confined to the Magic Kingdom, characters are now found in all major theme parks and at Disney deluxe resort character meals.

Character Watching

Watching characters has become a pastime. Families once were content to meet a character occasionally. They now pursue them relentlessly, armed with autograph books and cameras. Because some characters are only rarely seen, character watching has become character collecting. (To cash in on character collecting, Disney sells autograph books throughout the World.) Mickey, Minnie, and Goofy are a snap to bag; they seem to be everywhere. But some characters, like the Queen of Hearts and Friar Tuck, seldom come out, and quite a few appear only in parades or stage shows. Other characters appear only in a location consistent with their starring role. The Fairy Godmother is often near Cinderella Castle in Fantasyland, while the White Rabbit appears close to the *Alice in Wonderland*–themed Mad Tea Party.

Preparing Your Children To Meet The Characters

Almost all characters are quite large, and several, like Br'er Bear, are huge! Small children don't expect this, and preschoolers especially can be intimidated. Discuss the characters with your children before you go.

On first encounter, don't thrust your child at the character. Allow the little one to deal with this big thing from whatever distance feels safe. If two adults are present, one should stay near the youngster while the other approaches the character and demonstrates that it's safe and friendly. Some kids warm to the characters immediately; some never do. Most take a little time and several encounters. There are two kinds of characters: furs, or those whose costumes include face-covering headpieces (including animal characters and such humanlike characters as Captain Hook), and face characters, those for whom no mask or headpiece is necessary. These include Anna, Elsa, Tiana, Mary Poppins, Ariel, Jasmine, Aladdin, Cinderella, Belle, Snow White, Merida, Prince Charming, Peter Pan, and Jack Sparrow.

▶ UNOFFICIAL TIP Disney has been implementing technology to make some of the fur characters, most notably Mickey and Minnie, talk.

For now, it's still mostly only the face characters who speak. Because cast members couldn't possibly imitate the furs' distinctive cinema voices, Disney determined that it was more effective to keep such characters silent; although, as we mention in the tip above, technology may change this in the future. Lack of speech notwithstanding, headpiece characters are warm and responsive, and they communicate effectively with gestures. Tell children in advance that these characters may not talk. Some character costumes are cumbersome and give cast members very poor visibility. (Eyeholes

frequently are in the mouth of the costume or even on the neck or chest.) Children who approach the character from the back or side may not be noticed, even if the child touches the character. It's possible in this situation for the character to accidentally step on the child or knock him down. A child should approach a character from the front, but occasionally not even this works. Duck characters (Donald, Daisy, Uncle Scrooge), for example, have to peer around their bills. If a character appears to be ignoring your child, pick up your child and hold her in front of the character until the character responds. It's OK for your child to touch, pat, or hug the character. Understanding the unpredictability of children, the character will keep his feet still, particularly refraining from moving backward or sideways. Most characters will pose for pictures or sign autographs, but they will not hold your children or any other personal items. Costumes make it difficult for characters to wield a normal pen. If your child collects autographs, carry a pen the width of a Magic Marker.

The Big Hurt

Many children expect to meet Mickey as soon as they enter the park and are disappointed if they don't. If your children can't relax until they see Mickey, ask a cast member where to find him. If the cast member doesn't know, he or she can phone to find out.

▶**UNOFFICIAL TIP** Don't underestimate your child's excitement at meeting the Disney characters—but also be aware that very small children may find the large costumed characters a little frightening.

You can see Disney characters in live shows at all the theme parks and in parades at the Magic Kingdom and Disney's Hollywood Studios. Consult your daily entertainment schedule for times. If you want to meet the characters, get autographs, and take photos, consult the park map or the *Times Guide* provided as a daily supplement to the park map. If there is a particular character you're itching to meet, ask any cast member to call the character hotline for you. The hotline will tell you (via the cast member) if the character is out and about, and if so, where to find it.

▶**UNOFFICIAL TIP** To find out where any character is or will be appearing, call ☎ 407-824-2222.

WDW CHARACTER-GREETING VENUES

Magic Kingdom

MICKEY AND HIS POSSE

Chip 'n' Dale **Near Storybook Circus**

Daisy, Donald, Goofy, and Minnie **Pete's Silly Sideshow (FastPass+)**

Mickey **Town Square Theater (FastPass+)**

Pluto **Town Square**

DISNEY ROYALTY (PRINCESSES, PRINCES, SUITORS, AND SUCH)

Aladdin and Jasmine **Adventureland**

Anna and Elsa **Fantasyland during the Festival of Fantasy Parade and *Mickey's Royal Friendship Faire* stage show**

Ariel **Ariel's Grotto (FastPass+)**

Aurora, Cinderella, Rapunzel, and Tiana **Princess Fairytale Hall (FastPass+)**

Belle ***Enchanted Tales with Belle* (FastPass+)**

Gaston **Fountain outside Gaston's Tavern**

Merida **Fairytale Garden**

Snow White **Outside Town Square Theater**

The Tremaines **In Fantasyland near Cinderella's Castle**

MISCELLANEOUS

Alice and the Mad Hatter **Mad Tea Party**

Buzz Lightyear **Tomorrowland**

Jessie and Woody **Frontierland near Rivers of America**

Marie (*The Aristocats*) **Town Square**

Mary Poppins **Main Street, U.S.A next to Chappeau**

Peter and Wendy **Near Peter Pan's Flight in Fantasyland**

Tinker Bell **Town Square Theater (FastPass+)**

Winnie the Pooh and Tigger **Fantasyland near The Many Adventures of Winnie the Pooh**

Epcot

MICKEY AND HIS POSSE

Donald Mexico, at the Mexico Promenade

Goofy, Minnie, and Mickey Epcot Character Spot (FastPass+)

Pluto World Showcase Plaza

DISNEY ROYALTY (PRINCESSES, PRINCES, SUITORS, AND SUCH)

Aladdin and Jasmine Morocco

Anna, Elsa, and Frozen characters Norway

Belle France

Mulan China

Snow White Germany

MISCELLANEOUS

Alice, Mary Poppins, and Bert United Kingdom

Joy, Sadness, and Baymax Epcot Character Spot

Disney's Animal Kingdom

MICKEY AND HIS POSSE

Chip 'n' Dale Rafiki's Planet Watch at Conservation Station; The Oasis, just past the entrance turnstiles and to the right; and at park entrance

Donald DinoLand U.S.A., to the left of the Dinosaur exit on Cretaceous Trail

Goofy and Pluto DinoLand U.S.A., near Primeval Whirl

Mickey and Minnie Adventurers Outpost on Discovery Island (FastPass+)

DISNEY ROYALTY (PRINCESSES, PRINCES, SUITORS, AND SUCH)

Pocahontas Discovery Island trails that run behind the Tree of Life

MISCELLANEOUS

Flik (*A Bug's Life*) Discovery Island

King Louie and Baloo (*Jungle Book*) On the walkway between Asia and Africa

Dug and Russell (*Up!*) By *It's Tough to Be a Bug!*

Rafiki (*The Lion King*) Rafiki's Planet Watch at Conservation Station

Tarzan (*Jungle Book*) Discovery Island

Disney's Hollywood Studios

MICKEY AND HIS POSSE

Chip 'n' Dale Outside Red Carpet Dreams on Commissary Lane

Daisy, Donald At park entrance

Goofy Near Sci-Fi Dine-In Theater Restaurant

Minnie, Sorcerer Mickey Red Carpet Dreams on Commissary Lane

Pluto Animation Courtyard

MISCELLANEOUS

Buzz, Woody, Green Army Men Pixar Place

Olaf Celebrity Spotlight in Echo Lake

Sofia the First, Doc McStuffins, Jake (*Jake and the Never Land Pirates*) Animation Courtyard near *Disney Junior—Live on Stage!*

Star Wars: Chewbacca, Kylo Ren, Jawas Star Wars Launch Bay
Stormtroopers Animation Courtyard

*Characters are subject to change; check the *Times Guide* or kennythepirate.com for the latest information.

STROLLERS

The good news is that strollers are available for a daily rental fee at all four theme parks. If you rent a stroller at the Magic Kingdom and decide to go to Epcot, the Animal Kingdom, or Disney's Hollywood Studios, turn in your Magic Kingdom stroller and present your receipt at the next park. You'll be issued another stroller without additional charge. You can pay in advance for stroller rentals—this allows you to bypass the paying line and head straight for the pickup line. Disney resort guests can pay in advance at their resort's gift shop. Save receipts!

Single and double strollers are available. Obtain strollers at the Magic Kingdom entrance, to the left of Epcot's entrance plaza or at Epcot's International Gateway, and at Oscar's Classic Car Souvenirs just inside the entrance of Hollywood Studios. At Animal Kingdom, they are located to the right just inside the entrance. Rental is fast and efficient, and returning the stroller is a breeze. You can ditch your rental stroller anywhere in the park when you're ready to leave.

When you enter a show or board a ride, you must park your stroller, usually in an open, unprotected area. If it rains before you return, you'll need a cloth, towel, or diaper to dry it. Strollers are a must for infants and toddlers, but we have observed many sharp parents renting strollers for somewhat older children (up to 6 or so years old). The stroller prevents parents from having to carry children when they sag and provides a convenient place to carry water and snacks.

If you go to your hotel for a break and intend to return to the park, leave your rental stroller by an attraction near the park entrance, marking it with something personal like a bandanna. When you return, you'll know in an instant which stroller is yours.

Be aware that rental strollers are too large for all infants and many toddlers. It's permissible to bring your own stroller. Remember, however, that only collapsible strollers are allowed on monorails, parking-lot trams, and buses.

▶ **UNOFFICIAL TIP** Kingdom Strollers (kingdomstrollers.com), Orlando Stroller Rentals (orlandostroller rentals.com), and Magic Strollers (magicstrollers.com) offer folding strollers of higher quality than Disney's all-plastic models. All will drop off your stroller at your hotel and pick it up when you're done.

STROLLER WARS

Sometimes strollers disappear while you're enjoying an attraction. Cast members often rearrange strollers at the entrance to a ride or show in an effort to tidy up or clear a pedestrian path. If your stroller isn't exactly where it was left, you'll probably find it a few feet away. Sometimes, however, strollers are actually ripped off. Disney will replace one of its ripped-off strollers at no charge, but who wants the hassle? We recommend taking protective measures to ward off overly zealous cast members and stroller crooks. Sometimes just putting a personal item such as a bandanna on the stroller handle will suffice. Other times you might need to make a stronger statement.

CHARACTER DINING

Meeting characters has become so popular that Disney offers character breakfasts, brunches, lunches, and dinners where families can dine in the presence of Mickey, Minnie, Goofy, and other costumed versions of animated celebrities. These character meals provide a familiar, controlled setting in which young children can warm gradually to characters; several characters attend all meals. Adult prices apply to persons age 10 or older, children's prices to ages 3–9; little ones under age 3 eat free. For additional information on character dining, call ☎ 407-939-3463 (WDW-DINE).

Because character dining is very popular, we recommend arranging Advance Reservations as far in advance as possible, either online at disneyworld.disney.go.com/dining or by calling ☎ 407-939-3463 (WDW-DINE). The Disney dining reservations system makes Advance Reservations for character meals up to 180 days prior to the day you wish to dine. (The website opens at 6 a.m. Eastern each day; the phone lines open an hour later.) What's more, if you want to book a character meal, you must provide Disney with a credit card number. Your card will be charged $10 per person if you no-show or cancel your reservation less than 24 hours in advance; you may, however, reschedule with no penalty.

Breakfast at Cinderella's Royal Table is still the hottest Character Meal at Disney World, and spots are generally gone shortly after the opening of the 180-day reservation window. Reconfirm online or by phone all character-meal Advance Reservations three weeks or so before you leave home. Keep in mind that an Advance Reservation is not a reservation per se, only a commitment to seat you ahead of walk-in patrons at the scheduled date and time. A reserved table won't await you, but you will be seated ahead of patrons who failed to call ahead. Even with Advance Reservations, expect to wait at least 10–20 minutes to be seated. Due to its popularity, Cinderella's Royal Table requires full prepayment when the reservation is made. Don't worry, though: Even the fully paid reservation can be cancelled and refunded if you change your mind.

How to Choose a Character Meal

We receive a lot of mail asking for advice about character meals. Some meals are better than others, sometimes much better. Here's what we look for when we evaluate character meals:

1. THE CHARACTERS The various meals offer a diverse assortment of Disney characters. Selecting a meal that features your children's special favorites is a good first step. Check the Character-Meal Hit Parade chart that follows to see which characters are assigned to each meal.

2. ATTENTION FROM THE CHARACTERS In all character meals, the characters circulate among the guests hugging children, posing for pictures, and signing autographs. How much time a character spends with you and your children will depend primarily on the ratio of characters to guests. The more characters and fewer guests the better. Because many character meals never fill to capacity, the character-to-guest ratios found in our

Character-Meal Hit Parade chart have been adjusted to reflect an average attendance as opposed to a sell-out crowd. Even so, there's quite a range.

© Disney

3. THE SETTING Some character meals are staged in exotic settings, while for others, moving the venue to an elementary-school cafeteria would be an improvement. In our chart we rate the setting of each character meal with the familiar scale of zero to five stars. Two restaurants, Cinderella's Royal Table in the Magic Kingdom and The Garden Grill in the Land Pavilion at Epcot, deserve special mention. Cinderella's Royal Table is situated on the first and second floors of Cinderella Castle in Fantasyland, offering guests a look at the inside of the castle. The Garden Grill is a revolving restaurant that overlooks several scenes from the Living with the Land boat ride.

4. THE FOOD Although some food served at character meals is quite good, most is average—in other words, palatable but nothing to get excited about. In terms of variety, consistency, and quality, restaurants generally do a better job with breakfast than with lunch or dinner (if served). Some restaurants offer a buffet, while others opt for one-skillet, family-style service, in which all the hot items on the bill of fare are served from the same pot or skillet. To help you sort it out, we rate the food at each character meal in our chart using the tried-and-true five-star scale.

5. THE PROGRAM Some larger restaurants stage modest performances where the characters dance, head up a parade or conga line around the room, or lead songs. For some guests, these productions lend a celebratory air to the proceedings; for others, they turn what was already pandemonium into absolute chaos. In either event, the antics consume time that the characters could be spending with families at their table.

6. NOISE If you want to eat in peace, character meals are a bad choice. That having been said, some are much noisier than others. Once again, our chart gives you some idea of what to expect.

7. WHICH MEAL? Although character breakfasts seem to be the most popular, character lunches and dinners are usually more practical because they do not interfere with your early-morning touring. During hot weather especially, a character lunch at midday can be heavenly.

8. COST Breakfasts run \$25–\$58 for adults and \$15–\$36 for kids ages 3–9. For character lunches, expect to pay \$36–\$61 for adults and \$18–\$38 for kids. Dinners are \$36–\$73 for adults and \$17–\$43 for children. Kids age 2 years and younger eat free.

9. FRIENDS For some venues, Disney has stopped specifying the characters scheduled for a particular character meal. Instead, they tell you that it's a certain character "and friends." For example, "Pooh and friends," meaning Eeyore, Piglet, and Tigger, or some combination thereof, or "Mickey and friends" with some assortment chosen among Minnie, Goofy, Pluto, Donald, Daisy, Chip, and Dale. Most combos are pretty self-evident, but others, such as "Mary Poppins and friends," are unclear, but don't expect Dick Van Dyke.

10. THE BUM'S RUSH Most character meals are leisurely affairs, and you can usually stay as long as you want. An exception is Cinderella's Royal Table. Because Cindy's is in such high demand, the restaurant does everything short of pre-chewing your food to move you through.

CHARACTER-MEAL HIT PARADE

1. CINDERELLA'S ROYAL TABLE

LOCATION:	Magic Kingdom
MEALS SERVED:	Breakfast, Lunch, Dinner
CHARACTERS:	Cinderella, Ariel, Aurora, Snow White, Jasmine, Fairy Godmother
SETTING:	★★★★
TYPE OF SERVICE:	Fixed menu
FOOD VARIETY AND QUALITY:	★★★
NOISE LEVEL:	Quiet
CHARACTER-TO-GUEST RATIO:	1:26

2. AKERSHUS ROYAL BANQUET HALL

LOCATION:	Epcot
MEALS SERVED:	Breakfast, Lunch, Dinner
CHARACTERS:	4–6 characters chosen from Belle, Snow White, Aurora, Ariel, Mary Poppins, and Cinderella
SETTING:	★★★★
TYPE OF SERVICE:	Family-style (all you can eat); menu
FOOD VARIETY AND QUALITY:	★★★½
NOISE LEVEL:	Quiet
CHARACTER-TO-GUEST RATIO:	1:54

3. CHEF MICKEY'S

LOCATION:	Contemporary
MEALS SERVED:	Breakfast, Brunch, Dinner
CHARACTERS:	Minnie, Mickey, Donald, Pluto, Goofy (sometimes Chip 'n' Dale)
SETTING:	★★★
TYPE OF SERVICE:	Buffet
FOOD VARIETY AND QUALITY:	★★★ (breakfast/brunch); ★★★½ (dinner)
NOISE LEVEL:	Loud
CHARACTER-TO-GUEST RATIO:	1:56

4. THE CRYSTAL PALACE

LOCATION:	Magic Kingdom
MEALS SERVED:	Breakfast, Lunch, Dinner
CHARACTERS:	Pooh, Tigger, Eeyore, Piglet
SETTING:	★★★
TYPE OF SERVICE:	Buffet
FOOD VARIETY AND QUALITY:	★★½ (breakfast); ★★★ (lunch/dinner)
NOISE LEVEL:	Very loud
CHARACTER-TO-GUEST RATIO:	1:67 (breakfast); 1:89 (lunch/dinner)

5. 1900 PARK FARE

LOCATION:	Grand Floridian
MEALS SERVED:	Breakfast, Dinner
CHARACTERS:	Breakfast: Mary Poppins, Alice, Mad Hatter, Pooh; Dinner: Cinderella, Prince Charming, Lady Tremaine, stepsisters
SETTING:	★★★
TYPE OF SERVICE:	Buffet
FOOD VARIETY AND QUALITY:	★★★ (breakfast); ★★★½ (dinner)
NOISE LEVEL:	Moderate
CHARACTER-TO-GUEST RATIO:	1:54 (breakfast); 1:44 (dinner)

6. GARDEN GRILL RESTAURANT

LOCATION:	Epcot
MEALS SERVED:	Breakfast, Lunch, Dinner
CHARACTERS:	Mickey, Pluto, Chip 'n' Dale
SETTING:	★★★★½
TYPE OF SERVICE:	Family-style (all you can eat)
FOOD VARIETY AND QUALITY:	★★★½
NOISE LEVEL:	Very quiet
CHARACTER-TO-GUEST RATIO:	1:46

7. TUSKER HOUSE RESTAURANT	
LOCATION:	Animal Kingdom
MEALS SERVED:	Breakfast, Lunch, Dinner
CHARACTERS:	Mickey, Donald, Daisy, Goofy
SETTING:	★★★
TYPE OF SERVICE:	Buffet
FOOD VARIETY AND QUALITY:	★★★
NOISE LEVEL:	Very loud
CHARACTER-TO-GUEST RATIO:	1:112

8. CAPE MAY CAFE	
LOCATION:	Beach Club
MEALS SERVED:	Breakfast
CHARACTERS:	Goofy, Minnie, Donald
SETTING:	★★★
TYPE OF SERVICE:	Buffet (all you care to eat)
FOOD VARIETY AND QUALITY:	★★½
NOISE LEVEL:	Moderate
CHARACTER-TO-GUEST RATIO:	1:67

9. 'OHANA	
LOCATION:	Polynesian Village Resort
MEALS SERVED:	Breakfast
CHARACTERS:	Mickey, Pluto, Lilo, Stitch
SETTING:	★★
TYPE OF SERVICE:	Family-style (all you can eat)
FOOD VARIETY AND QUALITY:	★★½
NOISE LEVEL:	Moderate
CHARACTER-TO-GUEST RATIO:	1:57

10. HOLLYWOOD & VINE	
LOCATION:	Disney's Hollywood Studios
MEALS SERVED:	Breakfast, Lunch, Dinner
CHARACTERS:	Breakfast and lunch: Handy Manny, Sofia the First, Doc McStuffins, Jake (*Jake and the Never Land Pirates*); Dinner: Minnie's seasonal dining
SETTING:	★★½
TYPE OF SERVICE:	Buffet
FOOD VARIETY AND QUALITY:	★★★
NOISE LEVEL:	Moderate
CHARACTER-TO-GUEST RATIO:	1:71

11. GARDEN GROVE	
LOCATION:	Swan
MEALS SERVED:	Breakfast (Sat. & Sun. only), Dinner
CHARACTERS:	Goofy, Pluto, Chip 'n' Dale
SETTING:	★★★
TYPE OF SERVICE:	Buffet
FOOD VARIETY AND QUALITY:	★★★½
NOISE LEVEL:	Moderate
CHARACTER-TO-GUEST RATIO:	1:198, but often much better

BABYSITTING

CHILD-CARE CENTERS Child care isn't available inside the theme parks, but two Magic Kingdom resorts connected by monorail or boat (Polynesian Village and Wilderness Lodge & Boulder Ridge Villas), four Epcot resorts (the Yacht Club and Beach Club Resorts, the Swan, and the Dolphin), the Animal Kingdom Lodge & Villas, and the Hilton at Walt Disney World have child-care centers for potty-trained children age 3 and older. Services vary, but children generally can be left between 5 p.m. and midnight. Milk and cookies and blankets and pillows are provided at all centers, and dinner is provided at most. Play is supervised but not organized, and toys, videos, and games are plentiful. Guests at any Disney resort or campground may use the services.

The most elaborate of the child-care centers (variously called "clubs" or "camps") is **Lilo's Playhouse** at the Polynesian Village Resort. The rate for children ages 3–12 is $58.58 for the "duration of the evening." All the clubs accept reservations (some six months in advance!) with a credit card guarantee. Call the club directly (☎ 407-824-1639) or reserve through Disney central reservations at ☎ 407-WDW-DINE. Most clubs require a 24-hour cancellation notice and levy a hefty penalty of 2 hours' time or $30 per child for no-shows. A limited number of walk-ins are usually accepted on a first-come, first-serve basis. (*Note:* The Cub's Den at Wilderness Lodge & Boulder Ridge Villas will be closed through 2017 due to construction.)

IN-ROOM BABYSITTING Two companies provide in-room sitting in Walt Disney World and surrounding tourist areas: **Kid's Nite Out** (☎ 407-828-0920; kidsniteout.com) and **Fairy Godmothers** (☎ 407-277-3724). Kid's Nite Out also serves hotels in the greater Orlando area, including downtown. Both provide sitters older than age 18 who are insured, bonded, and trained in CPR. Some sitters have more advanced medical/first-aid training and/or education credentials. All sitters are screened, reference-checked, and police-checked. In addition to caring for your children in your guest room, the sitters will, if you direct (and pay), take your children to the theme parks or other venues of your choice. Many of the sitters arrive loaded with reading books, coloring books, and games. Both services offer bilingual sitters.

MONSTERS

POP SECRET
POPCORN

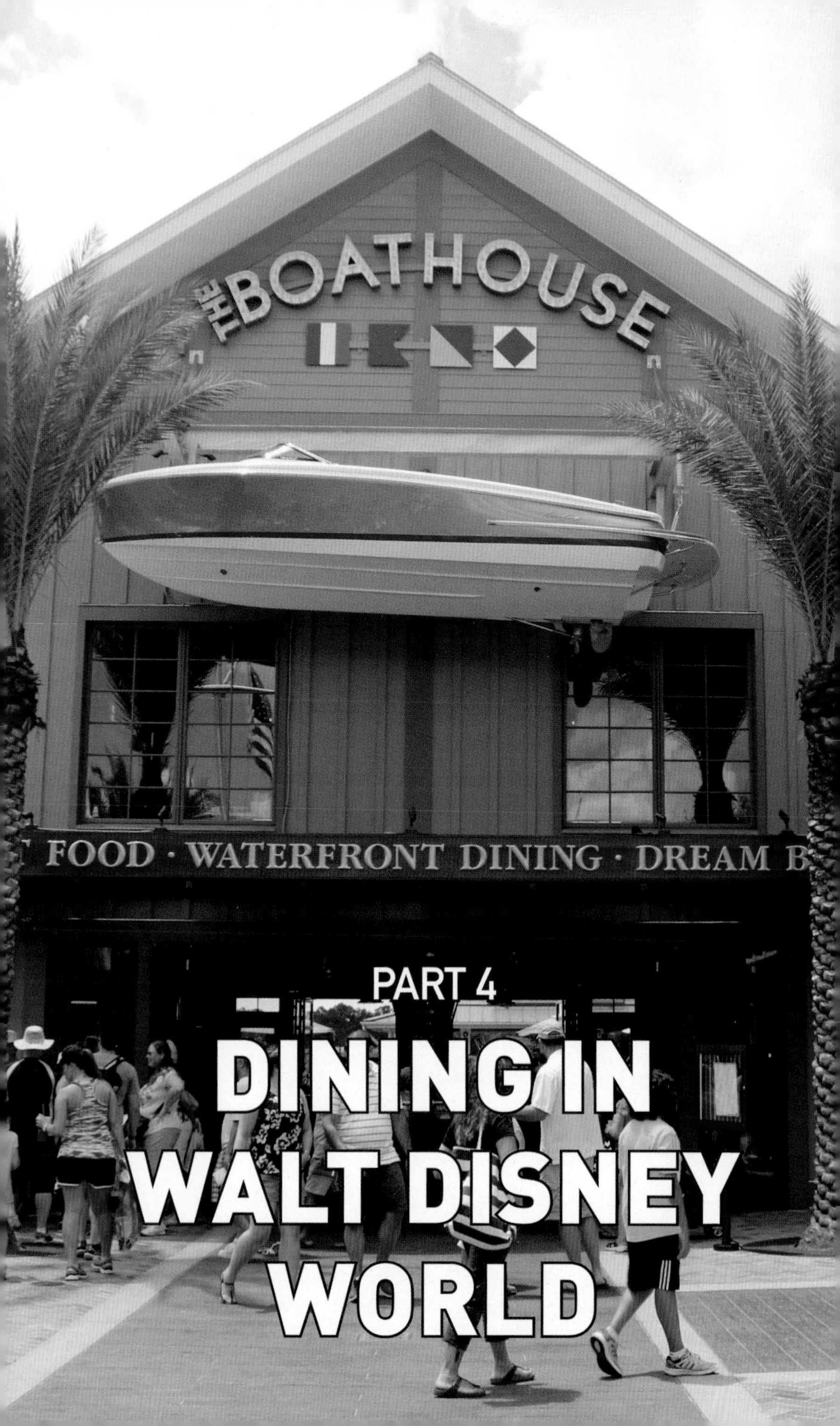

PART 4

DINING IN WALT DISNEY WORLD

DISNEY DINING 101

ADVANCE RESERVATIONS When you call Advance Reservations or book online, your name and essential information are taken as if you were making an honest to goodness reservation. The Disney representative or website fine print then says you have Advance Reservations for your restaurant of choice on the date and time you've requested and usually explains that this means you will be seated ahead of walk-ins—that is, those without Advance Reservations. Advance Reservations are recommended for all full-service restaurants except those in the Disney Springs Resort Area, which are operated independently of the Walt Disney Company. Advance Reservations are strongly recommended for character meals—many become fully booked months in advance—as well as for other buffets and for signature dining venues. The restaurants accept American Express, Diners Club, Japan Credit Bureau, MasterCard, and Visa, among others. For instructions on how to make an Advance Reservation, see page 31.

NO-SHOW FEES All Disney full-service restaurants now charge a no-show fee of $10–$25 per person. A couple of tips: Only one person needs to dine at the restaurant for Disney to consider your reservation fulfilled, even if your reservation is for more people. Also, while Disney says it requires 24 hours' notice, you can cancel up until midnight of the day before your meal. The upside to the no-show fee is that it's easier to book most restaurants closer to the date of your visit, as the fee discourages tentative plans.

DRESS Dress is informal at most theme park restaurants, but a business-casual dress code applies at Disney's Signature (read: upscale) restaurants, which means khakis, dress slacks, jeans, or dress shorts with a collared shirt for men and jeans, dresses, skirts, or dress shorts with a blouse or sweater for women. A full listing of the Signature restaurants is available on the Walt Disney World website.

▶ **UNOFFICIAL TIP** The only restaurant that requires jackets for men and dressy clothes for women is Victoria & Albert's at the Grand Floridian Resort.

SMOKING All Walt Disney World restaurants have a nonsmoking policy.

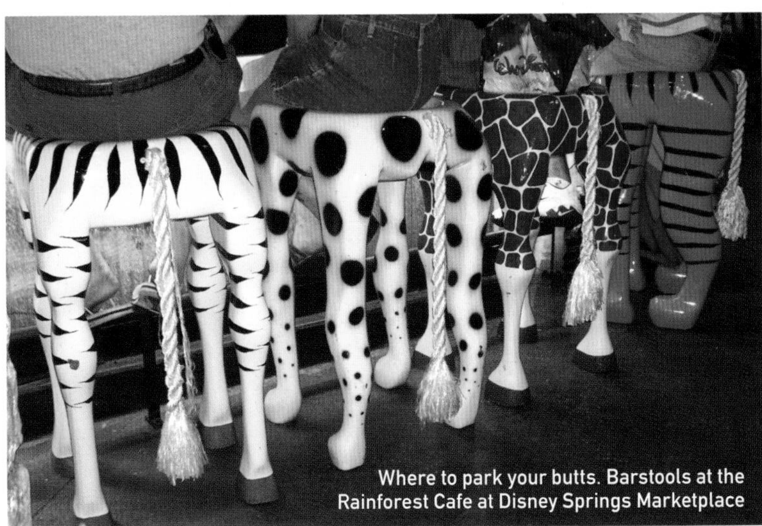

Where to park your butts. Barstools at the Rainforest Cafe at Disney Springs Marketplace

WALT DISNEY WORLD RESTAURANT CATEGORIES

In general, food and beverage offerings at Walt Disney World are defined by service, price, and convenience:

FULL-SERVICE RESTAURANTS Full-service restaurants are those where you are seated at a table, order from a menu, and a server brings your food. There are several full-service restaurants in each of the theme parks, at Disney Springs, and in most of the resorts. The All-Star resorts, Port Orleans French Quarter, Pop Century, and Art of Animation have other food options but no full-service restaurants.

Catch a flick at the Sci-Fi Dine-In Theater at Disney's Hollywood Studios.

Where the Jurassic set come to eat and be eaten: T-REX at Disney Springs Marketplace

BUFFETS AND FAMILY-STYLE RESTAURANTS At buffet restaurants, you are seated at a table and a server takes your beverage order, but you select your food yourself from a display line of options. At Walt Disney World, all the buffet restaurants are all-you-care-to-eat. Buffets may be a good option for young children who like to see what they're getting in advance. Several Disney World buffets offer character-greeting experiences; consider it killing two birds with one stone. A number of restaurants offer family-style service, some with character participation. Like buffets, these are prix fixe and all-you-care-to-eat; however, instead of selecting food from a displayed array, a server brings a platter with many dishes to your table and you fill your plate from the communal platter. Advance Reservations are recommended for all character meals. An automatic 18% gratuity is added for parties of six or more.

FOOD COURTS Featuring a collection of counter-service eateries under one roof, food courts can be found at all theme parks and at the moderate (Coronado Springs, Caribbean Beach, and Port Orleans) and value (All-Star, Art of Animation, Pop Century) resorts.

Be Our Guest restaurant in Fantasyland

COUNTER SERVICE Counter-service restaurants are those where a menu is posted on a wall, you order at a counter, and bring the food to your table yourself. Counter-service restaurants are in all the theme parks, water parks, resorts, and at Disney Springs. Reservations are not accepted at counter-service restaurants.

FAST CASUAL Somewhere between burgers and formal dining are the establishments in Disney's fast-casual category, including three in the theme parks: Be Our Guest in the Magic Kingdom, Sunshine Seasons in Epcot, and Starring Rolls Cafe in Disney's Hollywood Studios. Fast-casual restaurants feature menu choices that are a cut above what you'd normally see at a typical counter-service location. Entrées cost about $2–$3 more on average than traditional counter-service options, but the variety and quality make them worth the price.

VENDOR FOOD Vendors abound at the theme parks, Disney Springs, and Disney's BoardWalk and offer a variety of refreshments. Prices include tax, and many vendors accept credit cards, charges to your Disney resort room, and the Disney Dining Plan.

Coral Reef at The Seas in Epcot

MAGIC YOUR WAY DINING PLANS

Disney offers dining plans to accompany its Magic Your Way ticket system. They're available to all Disney-resort guests except those staying at the Swan, the Dolphin, the hotels of the Disney Springs Resort Area, and Shades of Green, none of which are Disney-owned or -operated. Guests must also purchase a Magic Your Way package from Disney (not an online reseller), have Annual Passes, or be members of the Disney Vacation Club (DVC) to participate in the plan. Except for DVC members, a three-night minimum stay is typically also required. Overall cost is determined by the number of nights you stay at a Disney resort.

Magic Your Way Plus Dining Plan The basic Disney Dining Plan (DDP) provides, for each member of your party, for each night of your stay, one counter-service meal, one full-service meal, and one snack at participating Disney dining locations. See disneyworld.disney.go.com/media/wdw_nextgen/CoreCatalog/WaltDisneyWorld/en_us/PDF/2016Dining.pdf for the complete list of participating restaurants. In addition to the meals and snacks, each person (age 3 and up) will receive one Rapid Fill mug. Mugs can be used for fountain beverages, coffee, tea, and cocoa at quick-service locations throughout the resorts during your current vacation. Cost for guests age 10 and up is about $64 per night and about $23 per night for guests ages 3–9. Children under age 3 may eat from a family member's plate at no additional charge.

The counter-service meal includes a main course, dessert, and nonalcoholic drink, or a complete combo meal (a main course and a side dish—think burger and fries), dessert, and nonalcoholic drink, including tax. Guests may now substitute a snack item for the dessert portion of their counter-service meal. The full-service sit-down meal includes a main course, dessert, a nonalcoholic drink, and tax. At some restaurants guests may substitute dessert for a side salad, cup of soup, or fruit plate. If you're dining at a buffet, the full-service meal includes the buffet, a nonalcoholic drink, and tax. The snack includes items normally sold from carts or small stands throughout the parks and resorts: ice cream, popcorn, soft drinks, fruit, chips, apple juice, and the like.

For instance, if you're staying for three nights, each member of your party will be credited with three counter-service meals, three full-service meals, and three snacks. All those meals will be put into a group meal account. Meals in your account can be used by anyone in your group, on any combination of days, so you're not required to eat every meal every day. Thus, you can skip a full-service meal one day and have two on another day.

Disney's top-of-the-line restaurants (dubbed Signature restaurants in the plan), along with Cinderella's Royal Table, all dinner shows, regular room service, and in-room pizza delivery, count as two full-service meals. If you dine at one of these locations, two full-service meals will be deducted from your account for each person dining.

In addition to the preceding, the dining plan comes with several other important rules:

- Everyone staying in the same resort room must participate in the plan.
- Children ages 3–9 must order from the kids' menu, if one is available. This rule is occasionally not enforced at Disney's counter-service restaurants, enabling older children to order from the regular (adult) menu.
- Alcoholic beverages and some bottled nonalcoholic beverages are not included in the plan.
- A full-service meal can be breakfast, lunch, or dinner. The greatest savings occur when you use your full-service meal allocations for dinner.
- The meal plan expires at midnight on the day you check out of the Disney resort. Unused meals are nonrefundable.
- The dining plan can usually be added to a discounted room-only reservation. You can't however, add Disney's Free Dining promotion.
- Gratuities are not included with any version of the plan. Be sure to budget 18%–20% for tips at all full-service, buffet, and family-style restaurants.

Quick Service Dining Plan This plan includes meals, snacks, and nonalcoholic drinks at most counter-service eateries in Walt Disney World. Guests may substitute a snack item for the dessert portion of their counter-service meal. The cost is about $44 per night for guests age 10 and up and about $19 per night for guests ages 3–9. The plan includes two counter-service meals and one snack per day, plus one Rapid Fill mug per person, per package (eligible for refills at resort counter-service locations during your current stay). The economics of the plan are difficult to justify unless you're drinking gallons of soda or coffee to offset Disney's inflated prices.

Magic Your Way Deluxe Dining Plan This dining option offers a choice of full- or counter-service meals for three meals a day at any participating restaurant. In addition to the three meals a day, the plan also includes two snacks per day and a Rapid Fill mug. The Deluxe Plan costs around $115 for adults and $36 for children for each night of your stay.

In addition to food, all plans include deal sweeteners such as a free round of miniature golf, discounts on spa treatments, and deals on recreation options.

Disney ceaselessly tinkers with the dining plans' rules, meal definitions, and participating restaurants. For example, it's possible (though not documented) to exchange a full-service-meal credit for a counter-service meal, although doing this even once can negate any savings you get from using a plan in the first place.

Things to Consider When Evaluating the Plus Dining Plan

If you prefer to always eat at counter-service restaurants, you'll be better off with the Quick Service plan. Other poor candidates for the Plus Plan include finicky eaters, light eaters, families who can't agree on restaurants, and those who can't get reservations at their first- or second-choice full-service restaurants.

If you opt for the plan, understand that skipping a single full-service meal during a visit of five or fewer days can mean the difference between saving and losing money. In our experience, having a scheduled sit-down meal for every day of a weeklong vacation can be mentally exhausting, especially for kids and teens. One option might be to schedule a meal at a Disney Signature restaurant, which requires two full-service credits, and have no scheduled sit-down meal on another night. Book your restaurants as soon as possible. Then decide whether the dining plan makes economic sense.

For an in-depth discussion of the various plans, including number crunching, visit touringplans.com/walt-disney-world/disney-dining-plan.

Pesky Technicalities and Administrative Problems

Readers report varying experiences with the Disney Dining Plan. Confused guests lead to longer lines at some counter-service locations. Some servers may not know what is included as a snack or what composes a meal, leading to frustration. The menu choices for kids age 9 and under are very limited but often include mac and cheese and chicken nuggets.

Readers also report difficulties in keeping their accounts straight. Check receipts after every purchase to make sure that your credits are deducted correctly.

A mom from Radford, Virginia, suggests eating a late lunch instead of dinner because the amount of food served is the same. She also recommends using the snacks as breakfast once you're in the parks.

▶UNOFFICIAL TIP If you're interested in trying a theme park full-service restaurant, be aware that the restaurants continue to serve after the park's official closing time. Incidentally, don't worry if you're depending on Disney transportation: Buses, boats, and monorails run 1–3 hours after the parks close.

GETTING A LEG UP AT WALT DISNEY WORLD

Fast food in the theme parks covers all the major food groups: cow, pig, turkey, and pizza. Vendors—offering such delights as fresh fruit, corn on the cob, popcorn, ice cream, churros, and giant smoked turkey legs (you can hardly taste the steroids)—abound at the parks. Of the vendor specialties, the smoked turkey legs are the most popular. At any time of day you can enjoy neo-Neanderthals lustily gnawing away on Butterball femurs. The legs are tasty, filling, and affordable. Did we mention messy? No? Well, these big boys are juicy to the max. When you bury your face in one, expect to come up dripping. Though prodigious numbers of legs are consumed daily, demand reaches its zenith on the Fourth of July. While normal Americans are eating pig, guzzling beer, and playing with gunpowder, Disney theme park guests are getting down with turkey legs. If you want to partake in this ritual, we recommend a bib and a pocketful of moist towelettes.

Orlando Convention & Visitors Bureau (opposite page)

WALT DISNEY WORLD FULL-SERVICE RESTAURANTS: RATED AND RANKED

OVERALL RATING The overall rating represents the entire dining experience: style, service, and ambience, in addition to taste, presentation, and quality of food. Five stars is the highest rating and indicates that the restaurant offers the best of everything. Four-star restaurants are above average, and three-star restaurants offer good, though not necessarily memorable, meals. Two-star restaurants serve mediocre fare, and one-star restaurants are below average. Our star ratings don't correspond to ratings awarded by AAA, Mobil, Zagat, or other restaurant reviewers.

COST The next rating tells how much a full-service entrée will cost. Appetizers, sides, soups/salads, desserts, drinks, and tips aren't included. We've rated the cost as inexpensive, moderate, or expensive.

Inexpensive	$12 or less per person
Moderate	$13–$23 per person

(Yeah, we know. Since when is $23 a head "moderate"? Welcome to Walt Disney World.)

Expensive	More than $23 per person

QUALITY RATING The food quality is rated on a scale of one to five stars, five being the best rating attainable. The quality rating is based expressly on the taste, freshness of ingredients, preparation, presentation, and creativity of food served. There is no consideration of price in this rating.

VALUE RATING If, on the other hand, you are looking for both quality and value, then you should check the value rating, expressed as stars.

★★★★★	Exceptional value, a real bargain
★★★★	Good value
★★★	Fair value, you get exactly what you pay for
★★	Somewhat overpriced
★	Significantly overpriced

READERS' RESTAURANT-SURVEY RESPONSES
For each Disney World restaurant profiled, we include the results of last year's reader-survey responses. Results are expressed as a percentage of responding readers who liked the restaurant well enough to eat there again (thumbs up 👍), as opposed to the percentage of responding readers who had a bad experience and wouldn't go back (thumbs down 👎).

CUISINE	LOCATION	OVERALL RATING
AFRICAN		
Jiko	Animal Kingdom Lodge	★★★★½
Boma	Animal Kingdom Lodge	★★★★
Sanaa	Animal Kingdom Lodge	★★★★
Jungle Navigation Co. Skipper Canteen	Magic Kingdom	★★★
Tusker House	Animal Kingdom	★★★
AMERICAN		
California Grill	Contemporary	★★★★★
Be Our Guest	Magic Kingdom	★★★★
The Hollywood Brown Derby	DHS	★★★★
Tiffins	Animal Kingdom	★★★★
Artist Point	Wilderness Lodge	★★★½
Cape May Cafe	Beach Club	★★★½
Captain's Grille	Yacht Club	★★★
Cinderella's Royal Table	Magic Kingdom	★★★
Crossroads at House of Blues	Disney Springs	★★★
The Crystal Palace	Magic Kingdom	★★★
50's Prime Time Cafe	DHS	★★★
Liberty Tree Tavern	Magic Kingdom	★★★
Olivia's Cafe	Old Key West	★★★
T-REX	Disney Springs	★★★
Tusker House	Animal Kingdom	★★★
The Wave	Contemporary	★★★
Whispering Canyon Cafe	Wilderness Lodge	★★★
Beaches & Cream	Beach Club	★★½
Boatwright's	Port Orleans	★★½
Chef Mickey's	Contemporary	★★½
ESPN Club	BoardWalk	★★½
Grand Floridian Cafe	Grand Floridian	★★½
Hollywood & Vine	DHS	★★½
Jock Lindsey's Hangar Bar	Disney Springs	★★½
1900 Park Fare	Grand Floridian	★★½
Planet Hollywood Observatory	Disney Springs	★★½
Rainforest Cafe	Disney Springs/Animal Kingdom	★★½
Splitsville	Disney Springs	★★½
Big River Grille & Brewing Works	BoardWalk	★★
The Diamond Horseshoe	Magic Kingdom	★★
The Fountain	Dolphin	★★
The Garden Grill	Epcot	★★
Garden Grove	Swan	★★
Plaza Restaurant	Magic Kingdom	★★
Las Ventanas	Coronado Springs	★★
Sci-Fi Dine-In Theater	DHS	★★
Trail's End	Fort Wilderness Resort	★★
Turf Club Bar & Grill	Saratoga Springs	★★
Wolfgang Puck Grand Cafe	Disney Springs	★★
The Edison *(opens 2017)*	Disney Springs	Too new
Homecoming	Disney Springs	Too new
BUFFET		
Boma	Animal Kingdom Lodge	★★★★
Cape May Cafe	Beach Club	★★★½
The Crystal Palace	Magic Kingdom	★★★
Tusker House	Animal Kingdom	★★★
The Wave	Contemporary	★★★
Chef Mickey's	Contemporary	★★½
Hollywood & Vine	DHS	★★½
1900 Park Fare	Grand Floridian	★★½
Akershus	Epcot	★★
Biergarten	Epcot	★★
Garden Grove	Swan	★★
Trail's End	Fort Wilderness Resort	★★

CUISINE	LOCATION	OVERALL RATING
CHINESE		
Nine Dragons	Epcot	★★
CUBAN		
Bongos Cuban Cafe	Disney Springs	★★
ENGLISH		
Rose & Crown	Epcot	★★★
FRENCH		
Be Our Guest	Magic Kingdom	★★★★
Monsieur Paul	Epcot	★★★★
Les Chefs de France	Epcot	★★★
GERMAN		
Biergarten	Epcot	★★
GLOBAL		
Paradiso 37	Disney Springs	★★½
GOURMET		
Victoria & Albert's	Grand Floridian	★★★★★
INDIAN		
Sanaa	Animal Kingdom Lodge	★★★★
IRISH		
Raglan Road	Disney Springs	★★★★
ITALIAN		
Tutto Italia	Epcot	★★★★
Via Napoli	Epcot	★★★★
Trattoria al Forno	BoardWalk	★★★½
Il Mulino	Swan	★★★
Mama Melrose's	DHS	★★½
Portobello	Disney Springs	★★½
Tony's Town Square Restaurant	Magic Kingdom	★★½
JAPANESE/SUSHI		
Kimonos	Swan	★★★★
Morimoto Asia	Disney Springs	★★★½
Teppan Edo	Epcot	★★★½
Tokyo Dining	Epcot	★★★
MEDITERRANEAN		
Cítricos	Grand Floridian	★★★½
Fresh Mediterranean Market	Dolphin	★★½
MEXICAN		
La Hacienda de San Angel	Epcot	★★★
San Angel Inn	Epcot	★★★
Maya Grill	Coronado Springs	★
Frontera Cocina	Disney Springs	Too new
MOROCCAN		
Spice Road Table	Epcot	★★★½
Restaurant Marrakesh	Epcot	★★
NORWEGIAN		
Akershus	Epcot	★★
PAN-ASIAN /POLYNESIAN		
Tiffins	Animal Kingdom	★★★★
Morimoto Asia	Disney Springs	★★★½
'Ohana	Polynesian Village	★★★
Kona Cafe	Polynesian Village	★★★
Trader Sam's Grog Grotto	Polynesian Village	★★★
Yak & Yeti	Animal Kingdom	★★

CUISINE	LOCATION	OVERALL RATING
SEAFOOD		
Narcoossee's	Grand Floridian	★★★★½
Flying Fish	BoardWalk	★★★★
bluezoo	Dolphin	★★★
The Boathouse	Disney Springs	★★★
Coral Reef	Epcot	★★½
Paddlefish	Disney Springs	★★½
Shutters	Caribbean Beach	★★
STEAK		
Shula's Steak House	Dolphin	★★★★
STK Orlando	Disney Springs	★★★½
Le Cellier Steakhouse	Epcot	★★★½
Yachtsman Steakhouse	Yacht Club	★★★
Shutters	Caribbean Beach	★★

FULL-SERVICE RESTAURANT PROFILES

Akershus Royal Banquet Hall ★★

NORWEGIAN/BUFFET EXPENSIVE QUALITY ★★ VALUE ★★★★
READER-SURVEY RESPONSES 89% 👍 11% 👎 DISNEY DINING PLAN Yes

Norway, World Showcase, Epcot; 407-939-3463
Reservations Required; credit card required to reserve at breakfast and lunch. **Dining Plan credits** 1/person/meal. **When to go** Anytime. **Cost range** Breakfast $44 (child $27), lunch $45 (child $27), dinner $50 (child $30). **Service** ★★★★. **Hours** Daily, 8–11:10 a.m., 11:55 a.m.–3:30 p.m., and 4:55–8:35 p.m.
Home to Princess Storybook Dining for breakfast, lunch, and dinner—the characters are the focus rather than the food. Modeled on a 14th-century fortress, Akershus offers all-you-can-eat *koldtbord* (cold buffet), roasted chicken with potatoes, pan-seared salmon, traditional *kjott-kake* (ground-beef-and-pork dumplings), and cold Carlsberg beer on tap.

Artist Point ★★★½

AMERICAN EXPENSIVE QUALITY ★★★★ VALUE ★★★
READER-SURVEY RESPONSES 88% 👍 12% 👎 DISNEY DINING PLAN Yes

Wilderness Lodge and Villas; 407-939-3463
Reservations Required. **Dining Plan credits** 2/person/meal. **When to go** Anytime. **Cost range** $30–$59 (child $9–$16). **Service** ★★★★★. **Hours** Daily, 5:30–9:30 p.m.
Enjoy roasted cedar-plank salmon, kettle-steamed Penn Cove mussels, diver scallops, smoky portobello soup, or berry cobbler in the cavernous Pacific Northwest–decorated dining room with a view of wildflowers, the lake, a waterfall, and even an erupting geyser.

Beaches & Cream Soda Shop ★★½

AMERICAN INEXPENSIVE QUALITY ★★½ VALUE ★★½
READER-SURVEY RESPONSES 92% 👍 8% 👎 DISNEY DINING PLAN Yes

Beach Club Resort; 407-934-8000
Reservations Accepted. **Dining Plan credits** 1/person/meal. **When to go** Anytime. **Cost range** $8.50-$16. **Service** ★★★. **Hours** Daily, 11 a.m.–11 p.m.
Casual eats and retro soda-fountain decor. Guests in bathing suits and flip-flops queue up for the burgers, sandwiches (corned beef Reuben, seafood salad), piles of hot fries, and hand-scooped ice cream, including the gargantuan $29 Kitchen Sink dessert.

Be Our Guest ★★★★

FRENCH/AMERICAN EXPENSIVE QUALITY ★★★★ VALUE ★★★★
READER-SURVEY RESPONSES 91% 👍 9% 👎 DISNEY DINING PLAN Yes

Fantasyland, Magic Kingdom; 407-939-5277
Reservations Accepted. **Dining Plan credits** 1/person/meal. **When to go** Anytime. **Cost range** Breakfast $22 (child $14), Lunch $10.50–$16 (child $9.50–$11.50), dinner $19 (child $9–$11). **Service** ★★★★. **Hours** Daily, 8–10 a.m., 10:30 a.m.–2:30 p.m., and 4–9:30 p.m.
Feast in Beast's Castle in a themed room inspired by *Beauty and the Beast:* the Grand Ballroom, the

 mysterious West Wing (which is smaller, darker, and a little quieter), and the pretty Rose Gallery. The quick-service lunch is crowded and noisy. Dinner offers table service, a tad more serenity, and wine and beer. Enjoy the catch of the day, New York strip, and cupcakes.

Biergarten ★★

GERMAN/BUFFET EXPENSIVE QUALITY ★★ VALUE ★★★★
READER-SURVEY RESPONSES 87% 👍 13% 👎 DISNEY DINING PLAN Yes

Germany, World Showcase, Epcot; 407-939-3463
Reservations Accepted. **Dining Plan credits** 1/person/meal. **When to go** Lunch or dinner. **Cost range** $30–$59 (child $13–$18). **Service** ★★★★. **Hours** Daily, noon–3:10 p.m. and 4–9 p.m.
Graze at a hefty German buffet that includes schnitzel, a variety of wursts, spaetzle, roast chicken, and sauerbraten (dinner only). You'll be seated with other guests, but the lively 25-minute dinner show (one every hour) and noisy dining room are part of the fun.

Big River Grille & Brewing Works ★★

AMERICAN MODERATE QUALITY ★★ VALUE ★★
READER-SURVEY RESPONSES 65% 👍 35% 👎 DISNEY DINING PLAN Yes

BoardWalk; 407-560-0253
Reservations Accepted at opentable.com. **Dining Plan credits** 1/person/meal. **When to go** Anytime. **Cost range** $15–$30. **Service** ★★★. **Hours** Sunday–Thursday, 11 a.m.–11 p.m.; Friday–Saturday, 11 a.m.–midnight.
This is the place for handcrafted beers. A good choice for late-night diners, it serves beer-cheese soup, meat loaf, ribs, and other pub fare. Outside seating, weather permitting.

bluezoo ★★★

SEAFOOD EXPENSIVE QUALITY ★★★★ VALUE ★★
READER-SURVEY RESPONSES 71% 👍 29% 👎 DISNEY DINING PLAN No

Dolphin Resort; 407-934-1111
Reservations Recommended. **When to go** Dinner. **Cost range** $32–$65 (child $12–$19). **Service** ★★★★. **Hours** Daily, 5–11 p.m.
In a dreamy setting designed by noted architect Jeffrey Beers, the menu features 2-pound Maine lobster and tenderloin of beef filet, but you can make a meal of the simple bowl of clam chowder.

The Boathouse ★★★

SEAFOOD EXPENSIVE QUALITY ★★★ VALUE ★★½
READER-SURVEY RESPONSES 91% 👍 9% 👎 DISNEY DINING PLAN Yes

The Landing, Disney Springs; 407-939-2628
Reservations Accepted. **Dining Plan credits** 2/person/meal. **When to go** Lunch or dinner. **Cost range** $12–$60 (child $10). **Service** ★★★. **Hours** Daily, 11 a.m.–11 p.m.
The airy restaurant seats up to 600 (200 outdoors) in nautically themed dining rooms. The three bars include one built over the water and attached to more than 300 feet of boardwalk and docks. Enjoy seafood of every sort, filet mignon topped with jumbo lump crab, and baked Alaska.

Boatwright's Dining Hall ★★½

AMERICAN/CAJUN MODERATE QUALITY ★★★ VALUE ★★
READER-SURVEY RESPONSES 84% 👍 16% 👎 DISNEY DINING PLAN Yes

Port Orleans Resort Riverside; 407-939-7639
Reservations Accepted. **Dining Plan credits** 1/person/meal. **When to go** Early evening. **Cost range** Dinner $17–$35 (child $9). **Service** ★★★. **Hours** Daily, 5–10 p.m.
Diners sit in a large, noisy room beneath the giant skeleton of a riverboat. The basic fare with a Cajun flair is pretty homogenized. The only table-service restaurant in the Port Orleans Resort, it gets busy and there can be waits. Try the jambalaya with chicken and andouille sausage.

Boma ★★★★

AFRICAN/BUFFET EXPENSIVE QUALITY ★★★★ VALUE ★★★★½
READER-SURVEY RESPONSES 92% 👍 8% 👎 DISNEY DINING PLAN Yes

Animal Kingdom Lodge & Villas—Jambo House; 407-934-7639
Reservations Recommended for dinner. **Dining Plan credits** 1/person/meal. **When to go** Breakfast or dinner. **Cost range** Breakfast $25 (child $14), dinner $43 (child $24). **Service** ★★★★. **Hours** Daily, 7:30–11 a.m. and 4:30–9:30 p.m.
A number of food stations encourage diners to roam about and graze on the pecan-caramel bread pudding (breakfast); papaya, avocado, and grapefruit salad; lamb curry; beef bobotie; hummus and breads; and house-made soups.

Bongos Cuban Cafe ★★

CUBAN MODERATE QUALITY ★★ VALUE ★★
READER-SURVEY RESPONSES 70% 👍 30% 👎 DISNEY DINING PLAN Yes

West Side, Disney Springs; 407-828-0999
Reservations Recommended. **Dining Plan credits** 1/person/meal. **When to go** Anytime. **Cost range** $12–$45 (child $6–$8). **Service** ★★★★. **Hours** Sunday–Thursday, 11 a.m.–11 p.m.; Friday–Saturday, 11 a.m.–midnight.
Gloria Estefan and her husband-producer, Emilio, created this large, multilevel restaurant that marries salsa music with Cuban cuisine. Other Cuban restaurants in the area do a better job with this wonderful cuisine—come here to have an umbrella drink and listen to Latin music.

California Grill ★★★★★

AMERICAN EXPENSIVE
QUALITY ★★★★★ VALUE ★★★
READER-SURVEY RESPONSES 92% 👍 8% 👎
DISNEY DINING PLAN Yes

Contemporary Resort; 407-939-3463
Reservations Required. **Dining Plan credits** 2/person/meal. **When to go** During evening fireworks. **Cost range** Brunch $80 (child $48), dinner $37–$69 (child $9–$18). **Service** ★★★★★. **Hours** Daily, 5–10 p.m. (Sunday brunch: 10 a.m.–1 p.m.)
The award-winning California Grill, on the 15th floor, offers one of the best spots for watching the Magic Kingdom fireworks. Try the sushi, pork two ways (grilled tenderloin and lacquered pork belly), oak-fired filet of beef, and Sonoma goat-cheese ravioli. Outstanding wine list.

Cape May Cafe ★★★½

AMERICAN/BUFFET MODERATE QUALITY ★★★½ VALUE ★★★★
READER-SURVEY RESPONSES 94% 👍 6% 👎 DISNEY DINING PLAN Yes

Beach Club Resort; 407-934-3358
Reservations Recommended. **Dining Plan credits** 1/person/meal. **When to go** Anytime. **Cost range** Breakfast $36 (child $21), dinner $48 (child $27). **Service** ★★★★★. **Hours** Daily, 7:30–11 a.m. and 5–9 p.m.
The buffet features peel-and-eat and fried shrimp, tasty (albeit chewy) clams, mussels, calamari, salmon, chicken, corn on the cob, lots of salads, and a good dessert bar. The kids' bar includes chicken nuggets and mac and cheese. Character breakfast with Goofy, Minnie, and Chip 'n' Dale. It's a convenient place to dine before *IllumiNations*.

Captain's Grille ★★★

AMERICAN MODERATE QUALITY ★★★½ VALUE ★★★
READER-SURVEY RESPONSES 84% 👍 16% 👎 DISNEY DINING PLAN Yes

Yacht Club Resort; 407-939-3463
Reservations Accepted. **Dining Plan credits** 1/person/meal. **When to go** Breakfast or lunch. **Cost range** Breakfast buffet $24 (child $13), lunch $13–$23 (child $9), dinner $16–$33 (child $9–11). **Service** ★★★★★. **Hours** Daily, 7:30–11:25 a.m., 11:30 a.m.–2 p.m., and 5–9 p.m.
This large dining room has a casual feel. Breakfast selections include a butter-poached lobster omelet and lemon-ricotta hot cakes. Lunch is coffee-shop fare, including New England lobster rolls and fish-and-chips. At dinner try New York strip, short ribs, or crab legs.

Le Cellier Steakhouse ★★★½

STEAK EXPENSIVE QUALITY ★★★½ VALUE ★★★
READER-SURVEY RESPONSES 90% 👍 10% 👎 DISNEY DINING PLAN Yes

Canada, World Showcase, Epcot; 407-939-3463
Reservations Required. **Dining Plan credits** 2/person/meal. **When to go** Before 6 p.m. **Cost range** $30–$60 (child $9–$17). **Service** ★★★★. **Hours** Daily, 12:30 p.m.–3:55 p.m. and 4–9 p.m.
With a wine cellar setting, Le Cellier specializes in Canadian Cheddar cheese soup and steaks. Le Cellier is Epcot's most popular restaurant. Make Advance Reservations as far ahead as possible.

Chef Mickey's ★★½

AMERICAN/BUFFET EXPENSIVE QUALITY ★★★ VALUE ★★★
READER-SURVEY RESPONSES 87% 👍 13% 👎 DISNEY DINING PLAN Yes

Contemporary Resort; 407-939-3463

Reservations Required. **Dining Plan credits** 1/person/meal. **When to go** Early evening. **Cost range** Breakfast and brunch $41 (child $25), dinner $50 (child $30). **Service** ★★★★. **Hours** Daily, 7–11:30 a.m., 11:35 a.m.–2:30 p.m. (brunch), and 5–9:30 p.m.
An open dining room with the monorail overhead, it's a popular Disney character restaurant with Mickey Mouse and pals on hand. It's noisy, busy, and fun for families. Breakfast: Carved ham, pancakes, pastries. Brunch: Mickey waffles, barbecue ribs. Dinner: Carved meats, sundae bar.

Les Chefs de France ★★★

FRENCH EXPENSIVE QUALITY ★★★ VALUE ★★★
READER-SURVEY RESPONSES 82% 👍 18% 👎
DISNEY DINING PLAN Yes

France, World Showcase, Epcot; 407-827-8709
Reservations Recommended. **Dining Plan credits** 1/person/meal. **When to go** Anytime. **Cost range** Lunch $15–$30, dinner $19–$36 (child $8–$10). **Service** ★★★★★. **Hours** Daily, noon–3 p.m. and 5–9 p.m.
This bustling bistro features dishes inspired by great French chefs: Paul Bocuse, the late Gaston Lenôtre, and Roger Vergé. At lunch, try the prix fixe bowl of onion soup topped with Gruyère and a croque monsieur (toasted ham-and-cheese sandwich); at dinner, enjoy duck breast with cherries, grilled tenderloin of beef, short ribs in Cabernet, and crème brûlée.

Cinderella's Royal Table ★★★

AMERICAN EXPENSIVE QUALITY ★★★ VALUE ★★
READER-SURVEY RESPONSES 92% 👍 8% 👎 DISNEY DINING PLAN Yes

Cinderella Castle, Fantasyland, Magic Kingdom; 407-939-3463
Reservations Required; credit card required to reserve; must prepay in full. **Dining Plan credits** 2/person/meal. **When to go** Early. **Cost range** Character breakfast $61 (child $36), character lunch $63 (child $39), character dinner $76 (child $45). **Service** ★★★★. **Hours** Daily, 8:05–10:40 a.m., 11:45–2:40 p.m., and 3:50–9:40 p.m.
A medieval banquet hall on the second floor of Cinderella Castle. All meals are fixed-price character affairs, with the menus changing periodically. Breakfast: caramel apple–stuffed French toast, goat cheese quiche, beef tenderloin, and cheese frittata. Lunch: fish of the day, braised short ribs with mashed potatoes, chicken with goat cheese polenta. Dinner: slow-roasted pork loin and flourless chocolate cake. Assorted princesses attend all three pricey meals.

Cítricos ★★★½

MEDITERRANEAN EXPENSIVE QUALITY ★★★★½ VALUE ★★★
READER-SURVEY RESPONSES 97% 👍 3% 👎 DISNEY DINING PLAN Yes

Grand Floridian Resort & Spa; 407-939-3463
Reservations Required; credit card required to reserve Chef's Domain. **Dining Plan credits** 2/person/meal. **When to go** Dinner. **Cost range** $33–$60 (child $9–$17). **Service** ★★★★★. **Hours** Daily, 5:30–10 p.m.
One of the best-kept dining secrets at Disney World. Try the sautéed shrimp with lemon, feta, tomatoes, and white wine; oak-grilled beef tenderloin; or pan-fried veal chop. For a treat, reserve the Chef's Domain, a private room for up to 12 guests where the chef creates a special menu.

Coral Reef ★★½

SEAFOOD EXPENSIVE QUALITY ★★ VALUE ★★
READER-SURVEY RESPONSES 91% 👍 9% 👎 DISNEY DINING PLAN Yes

The Seas with Nemo & Friends, Future World, Epcot; 407-939-3463
Reservations Required. **Dining Plan credits** 1/person/meal. **When to go** Lunch. **Cost range** Lunch $16–$33, dinner $20–$33 (child $11). **Service** ★★★★. **Hours** Daily, 11:30 a.m.–3:30 p.m. and 4–9 p.m.
Coral Reef offers one of the best theme-park views anywhere: below the water level of the huge saltwater tank in the Seas Pavilion. Sharks, rays, and even humans swim by. Enjoy creamy lobster soup, seared rainbow trout, grilled New York strip steak, and Chocolate Wave dessert.

Crossroads at House of Blues ★★★

REGIONAL AMERICAN MODERATE QUALITY ★★★½ VALUE ★★★
READER-SURVEY RESPONSES 82% 👍 18% 👎 DISNEY DINING PLAN Yes

West Side, Disney Springs; 407-934-2583

Reservations Recommended. **Dining Plan credits** 1/person/meal. **When to go** Lunch or early dinner; gospel brunch. **Cost range** $13–$30 (child $7–$10); brunch $40 (child $22). **Service** ★★★★. **Hours** Sunday–Thursday, 11:30 a.m.–11 p.m. (Sunday brunch: 10:30 a.m.–1 p.m.); Friday–Saturday, 11:30 a.m.– 1 a.m.

You'd think that it was a ramshackle hut in the bayou if the place weren't bigger than all of Louisiana. If you're planning on taking in one of the acts next door, you're better off seeing the show first so you can get a good seat, and then eating afterward. Menu items include flatbreads, burgers, jambalaya, shrimp and grits, lobster mac and cheese, and Bourbon bread pudding.

The Crystal Palace ★★★

AMERICAN/BUFFET MODERATE QUALITY ★★★½ VALUE ★★★
READER-SURVEY RESPONSES 91% 👍 9% 👎 DISNEY DINING PLAN Yes

Main Street, U.S.A., Magic Kingdom; 407-939-3463

Reservations Required. **Dining Plan credits** 1/person/meal. **When to go** Anytime. **Cost range** Breakfast $30 (child $18), lunch $38 (child $23), dinner $60 (child $36). **Service** ★★★. **Hours** Daily, 8–10:45 a.m. and 11:30 a.m.–9 p.m.

A turn-of-the-20th-century glass pavilion offers the best dining value in the Magic Kingdom. Menu items change often but may include waffles and pancakes layered with fresh fruit, shrimp and grits, pan-seared salmon, and an ice-cream sundae bar. Winnie the Pooh and friends dance about and pose with the kids. Kids get their own buffet with mac and cheese and chicken fingers.

The Diamond Horseshoe *(seasonal)* ★★

AMERICAN EXPENSIVE QUALITY ★★ VALUE ★★★
READER-SURVEY RESPONSES 70% 👍 30% 👎 DISNEY DINING PLAN Yes

Liberty Square, Magic Kingdom; 407-939-3463

Reservations Accepted. **Dining Plan credits** 1/person/meal. **When to go** Anytime. **Cost range** Lunch and dinner $33 (child $19). **Service** ★★★. **Hours** Daily, 11:30 a.m.–2:55 p.m. and 3–8:30 p.m.

This seasonal venue offers all-you-can-eat salad, pulled pork, turkey, smoked sausage, braised beef, and brownies topped with marshmallows. Visit Pecos Bill or Tortuga Tavern instead.

The Edison *(opens 2017)*

Town Center, Disney Springs; 407-939-3463

A lavish "Industrial Gothic"–style restaurant, bar, and nightclub, The Edison will feature classic American food, craft cocktails, and live entertainment. Themed to evoke a 1920s electric company, the space will have separate themed areas such as a Telegraph Lounge, The Tesla Lounge, The Radio Room, and the Patent Office. With live music, cabaret performances, contortionists, palm readers, and DJs, The Edison is aimed toward adult visitors; it's definitely not child-friendly.

ESPN Club ★★½

AMERICAN/SANDWICHES MODERATE QUALITY ★★★ VALUE ★★★
READER-SURVEY RESPONSES 74% 👍 26% 👎 DISNEY DINING PLAN Yes

BoardWalk; 407-939-1177

Reservations Not accepted. **Dining Plan credits** 1/person/meal. **When to go** Anytime. **Cost range** $13–$33 (child $9). **Service** ★★★. **Hours** Daily, 11:30 a.m.–1 a.m.

A sports bar to the *n*th degree, with basketball-court flooring, sports memorabilia, and, of course, lots of TVs. The bar area features sports-trivia video games. Family-friendly and affordable, with wings, burgers, sandwiches, and other pub fare. A good choice for late-night dining.

50's Prime Time Cafe ★★★

AMERICAN MODERATE QUALITY ★★★ VALUE ★★★
READER-SURVEY RESPONSES 85% 👍 15% 👎 DISNEY DINING PLAN Yes

Echo Lake, Disney's Hollywood Studios; 407-939-3463

Reservations Recommended. **Dining Plan credits** 1/person/meal. **When to go** Anytime. **Cost range** $15–$30 (child $9). **Service** ★★★★★. **Hours** Daily, 11 a.m.–3:15 p.m. and 3:30–8 p.m.

Like eating a meal in your own kitchen, 1950s style. Pot roast, meat loaf, chicken potpie, and other retro fare are served. The PB&J milk shake is worth every calorie. Diners really get a kick out of the classic comedies playing on black-and-white TVs, as well as the servers who nag you to "take your elbows off the table" or "finish every last bite."

Flying Fish ★★★★

SEAFOOD EXPENSIVE QUALITY ★★★★ VALUE ★★★
READER-SURVEY RESPONSES 94% 👍 6% 👎 DISNEY DINING PLAN Yes

BoardWalk; 407-939-3463
Reservations Required. **Dining Plan credits** 2/person/meal. **When to go** Anytime. **Cost range** $28–$47 (child $8–$15). **Service ★★★★★. Hours** Sunday–Thursday, 5:30–10 p.m.; Friday–Saturday, 5:30–10:30 p.m.

Following an extensive renovation, Flying Fish has unveiled sleek retro-Deco decor and a new bar called AbracadaBar. The most important addition, though, is chef Tim Majoras. The new menu still features seasonal seafood, along with the signature potato-wrapped red snapper.

The Fountain ★★

AMERICAN MODERATE QUALITY ★★ VALUE ★★
READER-SURVEY RESPONSES 88% 👍 12% 👎 DISNEY DINING PLAN No

Dolphin Hotel; 407-934-1609
Reservations Not accepted. **When to go** Lunch or dinner. **Cost range** $7.50–$16 (child $11). **Service ★★★★. Hours** Daily, 11 a.m.–11 p.m.

This soda shop offers build-your-own burgers and hot dogs (including black bean and turkey burgers), milk shakes (we love the PB&J), salads with seared salmon or chicken, and an ice-cream panini.

Fresh Mediterranean Market ★★½

MEDITERRANEAN/AMERICAN MODERATE QUALITY ★★½ VALUE ★★
READER-SURVEY RESPONSES 57% 👍 43% 👎 DISNEY DINING PLAN No

Dolphin Resort; 407-934-1609
Reservations Available but not necessary. **When to go** Breakfast or lunch. **Cost range** Breakfast (buffet or à la carte) $5–$26 (child $15), lunch $15–$18 (child $12). **Service ★★★★. Hours** Daily, 6:30–10:35 a.m.; Monday–Friday, 11:30 a.m.–2 p.m.; Saturday–Sunday, noon–2 p.m.

A pleasant, quiet spot for breakfast or lunch, with a breakfast buffet that's more healthful than many. At breakfast enjoy fresh fruit and vegetable juices and made-to-order omelets. Lunch options include burgers and salads. Ask for a veranda table if you want to have a quiet conversation away from the action in the open kitchen.

Frontera Cocina ★★★★

MEXICAN MODERATE QUALITY ★★★★ VALUE ★★★
READER-SURVEY RESPONSES Not enough to rate DISNEY DINING PLAN No

Town Center, Disney Springs; 407-939-3463
Reservations Recommended. **Dining Plan credits** 1/person/meal. **When to go** Anytime. **Cost range** $15–$35. **Service ★★★★. Hours** Daily, 11 a.m.–11 p.m.

Six-time James Beard honoree Rick Bayless recently opened this Mexican restaurant in Town Center, and we think it might be one of the best in Orlando. Try the cocina ancho-marinated half-chicken with queso añejo mashed potatoes, or the build-your-own carne asada tacos. Pair your meal with a Frontera margarita or agave flight. The pecan-pie-bar dessert is a Bayless family recipe.

The Garden Grill ★★

AMERICAN EXPENSIVE QUALITY ★★ VALUE ★★★
READER-SURVEY RESPONSES 92% 👍 8% 👎 DISNEY DINING PLAN Yes

The Land, Future World, Epcot; 407-560-6071
Reservations Required. **Dining Plan credits** 1/person/meal. **When to go** Anytime. **Cost range** $42 (child $23). **Service ★★★★. Hours** Daily, 8–10:30 a.m., 11:30 a.m.–3 p.m., and 4–8 p.m.

Tables revolve above scenes from Living with the Land, the pavilion's ride-through attraction. This is one of the quietest dining spots for getting photos with Mickey, Chip 'n' Dale, and various other Disney characters. Dishes include beef filet, turkey with stuffing and gravy, and fish of the day. Dessert is a seasonal cobbler with vanilla-bean whipped cream. The kids' menu includes mac and cheese, chicken drumsticks, sweet potato sticks, and broccoli.

Garden Grove ★★

AMERICAN/BUFFET MODERATE QUALITY ★★★ VALUE ★★
READER-SURVEY RESPONSES 71% 👍 29% 👎 DISNEY DINING PLAN No

Swan Hotel; 407-934-1609
Reservations Recommened. **When to go** Anytime. **Cost range** Breakfast $12–$23 (child $7–$14), lunch $14–$19 (child $9–$12), dinner $30–$37 (child $18); weekend Disney-character breakfast buffet $25 (child $16), Disney-character seafood buffet (Friday–Saturday nights) $36 (child $17). **Service** ★★★. **Hours** Daily, 6:30 a.m.–2 p.m. and 5–9:30 p.m.
Disney characters are the stars every night for dinner—and for breakfast on weekends—in this spacious dining room with a 25-foot faux oak tree in the center. For lunch, burgers, short-rib salad, and fish tacos. For dinner, unlimited salad and soup for starters, a protein (beef, salmon, chicken) or vegetarian entrée, and dessert buffet. The weekend seafood buffet features a raw bar, jumbo scallops, fried-seafood basket, paella, and salmon.

Grand Floridian Café ★★½

AMERICAN MODERATE QUALITY ★★★ VALUE ★★
READER-SURVEY RESPONSES 92% 👍 8% 👎 DISNEY DINING PLAN Yes

Grand Floridian Resort & Spa; 407-939-3463
Reservations Accepted. **Dining Plan credits** 1/person/meal. **When to go** Anytime. **Cost range** Breakfast $11–$19 (child $7), lunch $9–$18 (child $9), dinner $17.50–$33 (child $9). **Service** ★★★. **Hours** Daily, 7–11 a.m., 11:30 a.m.–2 p.m., and 5–9 p.m.
Light and airy decor with lots of sunlight, servers dressed in Victorian costumes, and pretty views of the pool and courtyard. The breakfast menu includes omelets, lobster hash, seasonal pancakes, and unique breakfast salads, including bacon and eggs on greens and quinoa. At lunch, the surf-and-turf burger (also at dinner) layers Angus beef and Maine lobster. Falafel fritters, deli sandwiches, penne pasta with shrimp or roasted chicken. For dinner, shrimp and sausage on mascarpone grits, strip steak, and miso-glazed salmon.

La Hacienda de San Angel ★★★

MEXICAN EXPENSIVE
QUALITY ★★★½ VALUE ★★½
READER-SURVEY RESPONSES 81% 👍 19% 👎 DISNEY DINING PLAN Yes

Mexico, World Showcase, Epcot; 407-939-3463
Reservations Required. **Dining Plan credits** 1/person/meal. **When to go** Dinner. **Cost range** $24–$59 (child $8.50–$9.50). **Service** ★★★★. **Hours** Daily, 4–8:35 p.m.
The simplest dishes on the menu are the best: excellent guacamole, *queso fundido;* pork confit carnitas; the taco sampler with pork, beef, battered fish, and chicken; short ribs with chimichurri; fried-shrimp tacos with chipotle-lime aioli. Margaritas are the real deal—or just go for a flight of fine sipping tequila. Back tables have choice views of World Showcase Lagoon and *IllumiNations.*

La Hacienda de San Angel

Hollywood & Vine ★★½

AMERICAN MODERATE QUALITY ★★★ VALUE ★★★
READER-SURVEY RESPONSES 83% 👍 17% 👎 DISNEY DINING PLAN Yes

Echo Lake, Disney's Hollywood Studios; 407-939-3463
Reservations Recommended. **Dining Plan credits** 1/person/meal. **When to go** Anytime. **Cost range** Breakfast buffet $32 (child $20), lunch buffet $41 (child $25), dinner buffet $50 (child $30). **Service** ★★★★. **Hours** Daily, 8–10:20 a.m., 11 a.m.–2:55 p.m., and 5–9 p.m.
Large Art Deco–style cafeteria, very noisy, with a menu that changes daily. Fare may include chilled salads, fish of the day, carved and grilled meats, vegetables and pasta, and fresh fruits and breads. Disney Channel characters visit at the breakfast and lunch all-you-can-eat buffets.

The Hollywood Brown Derby ★★★★

AMERICAN EXPENSIVE QUALITY ★★★★ VALUE ★★★
READER-SURVEY RESPONSES 90% 👍 10% 👎 DISNEY DINING PLAN Yes

Hollywood Boulevard, Disney's Hollywood Studios; 407-939-3463
Reservations Accepted. **Dining Plan credits** 2/person/meal. **When to go** Early evening. **Cost**

 range Lunch and dinner $16–$43 (child $6–$14). **Service** ★★★★★. **Hours** Daily, noon–3:25 p.m. and 3:30 p.m.–8 p.m.

A replica of the original Brown Derby restaurant (not the one shaped like a derby) in California, the elegant dining room has Cobb salad (named for Bob Cobb, the original restaurant's owner), original fettuccine Alfredo, and grapefruit cake. This is the Studios' top dining experience. *And* the dining room is quiet enough for conversation.

Homecoming: Florida Kitchen and Southern Shine by Art Smith

The Landing, Disney Springs; 407-939-3463

Florida born and raised, Art Smith is Oprah Winfrey's former private chef and is well known for his appearances on *Top Chef Masters* and *Iron Chef America.* With 200 seats, Homecoming focuses on traditional Southern cooking, highlighting Florida's produce and seafood bounty with dishes Smith is known for: pimento cheese, deviled eggs, Lowcountry shrimp and grits, and chicken and dumplings. Sweets from his bakery are shipped in daily. Cocktails feature artisanal moonshine.

Il Mulino New York Trattoria ★★★

ITALIAN EXPENSIVE QUALITY ★★★ VALUE ★★
READER-SURVEY RESPONSES 64% 👍 36% 👎 DISNEY DINING PLAN No

Swan Resort; 407-934-1199

Reservations Accepted. **When to go** Dinner. **Cost range** $16–$45 (child $12–$16). **Service** ★★. **Hours** Daily, 5–11 p.m.

Il Mulino takes an upscale-casual approach to Italian cuisine, with family-style platters for sharing in the noisy dining room. The cuisine focuses on Italy's Abruzzi region, with hearty pastas and big cuts of meat. Try the spaghetti carbonara or the veal saltimbocca.

Jiko—The Cooking Place ★★★★½

AFRICAN/FUSION EXPENSIVE QUALITY ★★★★½ VALUE ★★★½
READER-SURVEY RESPONSES 94% 👍 6% 👎 DISNEY DINING PLAN Yes

Animal Kingdom Lodge & Villas—Jambo House; 407-939-3463

Reservations Required. **Dining Plan credits** 2/person/meal. **When to go** Dinner. **Cost range** $30–$52 (child $9–$17). **Service** ★★★★★. **Hours** Daily, 5:30–10 p.m.

Young African exchange students greet guests as they enter Jiko's spacious dining room, inspired by the opening scenes of *The Lion King.* Jiko has won numerous accolades (including AAA's Four Diamond Award) for its interesting fare—such as Kalamata olive flatbread, oak-grilled filet mignon, and garam masala sea scallops—and stellar wine list, one of the largest collections of South African wines in any North American restaurant, with more than 1,800 bottles.

Jock Lindsey's Hangar Bar ★★½

AMERICAN MODERATE QUALITY ★★½ VALUE ★★½
READER-SURVEY RESPONSES 93% 👍 7% 👎 DISNEY DINING PLAN No

The Landing, Disney Springs; 407-939-3463

Reservations Not accepted. **When to go** Anytime. **Cost range** Appetizers $9–$16; cocktails $9.25–$21. **Service** ★★★★. **Hours** Sunday–Thursday, 11:30 a.m.–midnight; Friday–Saturday, 11:30 a.m.–1 a.m.

Lots of Indiana Jones movie references in the decor. Booth, bar, and table seating are available, all of it kid-friendly. Indoor and covered outdoor seating are available. Our favorites appetizers are Dr. Elsa's Shrimp BLT flatbread, with shrimp, bacon, roasted tomatoes, and basil pesto, and the Snack of Ra—salad and dips with bread and crisps.

Jungle Navigation Co. Ltd. Skipper Canteen ★★★

ASIAN/AFRICAN/LATIN
MODERATE QUALITY ★★★ VALUE ★★★
READER-SURVEY RESPONSES Too new to rate DISNEY DINING PLAN Yes

Adventureland, Magic Kingdom; 407-939-3463

Reservations Recommended. **Dining Plan credits** 1/person/meal (table-service credit for lunch and dinner). **When to go** Anytime. **Cost range** Lunch $7–$25 (child $10.50–$12.50), dinner $17–$34 (child $9.50–$12.50). **Service** ★★★★. **Hours** Daily, 11 a.m.–2:55 p.m. and 3 p.m.–9:30 p.m.

This place is chock-full of remnants from the late, lamented Adventurers Club. Food wanders from Chinese and Japanese rice bowls to curries, steak, and arepas, reflecting the wandering ways of the founding explorers. Lunch and dinner menus are the same. Kids' menu includes grilled fish, steak, beef arepas, or soup and fruit salad. Remarkably good desserts.

Kimonos ★★★★

JAPANESE MODERATE QUALITY ★★★★½ VALUE ★★★
READER-SURVEY RESPONSES 80% 👍 20% 👎 DISNEY DINING PLAN No

Swan Resort; 407-934-1609
Reservations Accepted for parties of 6 or more. **When to go** Dinner. **Cost range** Sushi and rolls à la carte, $5.25–$18. **Service** ★★★★★. **Hours** Daily, 5:30 p.m.–11 p.m.; bar opens at 5 p.m.
Although sushi and sashimi are the focus, Kimonos also serves hot appetizers, including tempura-battered shrimp and vegetables, beef *satay,* chicken *katsu,* and miso soup. There are no full entrées here—just good sushi and appetizers. The skill of the sushi artists is as much a joy to watch as is eating the wonderfully fresh creations. Karaoke starts at 9 p.m.

Kona Cafe ★★★

POLYNESIAN/PAN-ASIAN MODERATE QUALITY ★★★ VALUE ★★★★
READER-SURVEY RESPONSES 88% 👍 12% 👎 DISNEY DINING PLAN Yes

Polynesian Village Resort; 407-939-3463
Reservations Accepted. **Dining Plan credits** 1/person/meal. **When to go** Anytime. **Cost range** Breakfast $9–$14.50 (child $7), lunch $13–$18 (child $9), dinner $19–$33 (child $9). **Service** ★★★★. **Hours** Daily, 7:30–11:45 a.m., noon–2:45 p.m., and 5–10 p.m.
If you want to escape the Magic Kingdom for a quiet lunch, hop on the monorail or take the resort launch to the Polynesian to Kona Cafe. Breakfast: Tonga toast (a decadent French toast layered with bananas). Lunch: Fish tacos, crab cakes, stir-fried Asian noodles. Dinner: Sushi, pan-seared duck breast, New York strip steak, and sustainable fish. This isn't a fancy dining room, but the food is on a higher plane than your average java joint.

Liberty Tree Tavern ★★★

AMERICAN MODERATE QUALITY ★★★ VALUE ★★★
READER-SURVEY RESPONSES 91% 👍 9% 👎 DISNEY DINING PLAN Yes

Liberty Square, Magic Kingdom; 407-939-3463
Reservations Accepted. **Dining Plan credits** 1/person/meal. **When to go** Lunch or dinner. **Cost range** Lunch $14–$23 (child $9.50–$11), dinner $33 (child $19). **Service** ★★★★★. **Hours** Daily, 11:30 a.m.–3 p.m. and 3:05–9 p.m.
For lunch, New England–style pot roast, roast turkey, and sandwiches. Family-style dining at dinner, with all-you-can-eat turkey, carved beef, and ham. Though nothing much changes at Liberty Tree (the servers still wear those Colonial-style getups), it's still among the best of the Magic Kingdom's full-service restaurants. Make Advance Reservations here for about an hour or so before parade time—after you eat, you can walk right out and watch the parade.

Mama Melrose's Ristorante Italiano ★★½

ITALIAN MODERATE QUALITY ★★★ VALUE ★★
READER-SURVEY RESPONSES 87% 👍 13% 👎 DISNEY DINING PLAN Yes

Muppet Courtyard, Disney's Hollywood Studios; 407-939-3463
Reservations Required. **Dining Plan credits** 1/person/meal. **When to go** Lunch or dinner. **Cost range** $15–$33 (child $9). **Service** ★★★. **Hours** Daily, 11:30 a.m.–4:15 p.m. and 4:45 p.m.–8 p.m.
This casual restaurant sports checkered tablecloths, red vinyl booths, and grapevines hanging from the rafters. Ambience is generally quiet unless it's peak season. Portions here are fairly large—it's possible to dine cheaply on just an appetizer or two. Try the pork saltimbocca, penne alla vodka, campanelle pasta with chicken or shrimp, charred strip steak, flatbread pizzas, oak-fired mussels, tiramisu, and cannoli.

Maya Grill ★

MEXICAN/AMERICAN EXPENSIVE QUALITY ★ VALUE ★
READER-SURVEY RESPONSES 77% 👍 23% 👎 DISNEY DINING PLAN Yes

Coronado Springs Resort; 407-939-3463
Reservations Accepted. **Dining Plan credits** 1/person/meal. **When to go** Dinner. **Cost range** $20–$58 (child $7–$9.50). **Service** ★★★. **Hours** Daily, 5–10 p.m.
The food is ordinary, as is the setting. You're better off eating somewhere else. If you go, the mainstream menu offers overpriced Tex-Mex and Nuevo Latino dinner fare—such as rib eye, fajita skillet, and slow-cooked pork with corn tortillas—to suit the resort's convention crowd.

Monsieur Paul ★★★★

FRENCH EXPENSIVE QUALITY ★★★★½ VALUE ★★★
READER-SURVEY RESPONSES 93% 👍 7% 👎 DISNEY DINING PLAN Yes

France, World Showcase, Epcot; 407-939-3463
Reservations Required. **Dining Plan credits** 2/person/meal. **When to go** Late dinner. **Cost range** $39–$44 (child $13–$16). **Service ★★★★. Hours** Daily, 5:30–8:35 p.m.
An ode to legendary French chef Paul Bocuse, this is the more upscale of France's two full-service restaurants. Enjoy authentic, creative French cuisine such as black-truffle soup, classic cassolette d'escargots, and roasted duck breast with oxtail-stuffed cabbage. There's also a fixed-price menu ($89/person), and the wine list is solid. For a quiet dinner and conversation, this is the spot. Request a table at the windows to view World Showcase Lagoon. Seats just 120.

Morimoto Asia ★★★½

JAPANESE/PAN-ASIAN EXPENSIVE QUALITY ★★★½ VALUE ★★★★
READER-SURVEY RESPONSES Too new to rate DISNEY DINING PLAN Yes

The Landing, Disney Springs; 407-939-6686
Reservations Accepted. **Dining Plan credits** 2/person/meal. **When to go** Anytime. **Cost range** Lunch $9–$36, dinner $12–$54 (child $12). **Service ★★★★. Hours** Monday–Thursday, 11:30 a.m.–4:15 p.m. and 5 p.m.–midnight; Friday–Saturday, 11:30 a.m.–4:15 p.m. and 5 p.m.–1 a.m. (dinner served until 10 p.m.)
An ultrahip version of a big-city club with anime cartoons and graphic photographs throughout, framing the open kitchen. Japanese Iron Chef Masaharu Morimoto's specialties include pork, shrimp, chicken, and veggie dim sum; Peking duck; kung pao chicken; Morimoto spare ribs; lo mein, pad Thai, and ramen noodles; sushi rolls and sashimi. The outdoor terrace upstairs has what might be the best view of the Disney Springs lagoon. The Forbidden Lounge offers a late-night menu.

Narcoossee's ★★★★½

SEAFOOD EXPENSIVE QUALITY ★★★½ VALUE ★★
READER-SURVEY RESPONSES 93% 👍 7% 👎 DISNEY DINING PLAN Yes

Grand Floridian Resort & Spa; 407-939-3463
Reservations Required. **Dining Plan credits** 2/person/meal. **When to go** Sunday brunch, early evening. **Cost range** Brunch $69 (child $41); dinner $33–$75 (child $7–$17). **Service ★★★★★. Hours** Daily, 5:30–10 p.m.; Sunday brunch, 10 a.m.–2 p.m.
Narcoossee's is a freestanding octagonal building at the edge of Seven Seas Lagoon with an upscale yet noisy dining room. It offers a great view of the Magic Kingdom and the boat dock nearby. Try the Maine lobster, scallops, or grilled filet mignon.

Nine Dragons Restaurant ★★

CHINESE MODERATE QUALITY ★★ VALUE ★★
READER-SURVEY RESPONSES 69% 👍 31% 👎 DISNEY DINING PLAN Yes

China, World Showcase, Epcot; 407-939-3463
Reservations Recommended. **Dining Plan credits** 1/person/meal. **When to go** Lunch or dinner. **Cost range** Lunch $15–$23, dinner $15–$27 (child $8–$11). **Service ★★★. Hours** Daily, noon–3:25 p.m. and 3:30–8:50 p.m.
Nine Dragons features a lighter, more contemporary cuisine, such as roasted Beijing duck salad, vegetarian stir-fry, and five-spiced fish. It's pricey for Chinese, but the food is well prepared.

1900 Park Fare ★★½

AMERICAN/BUFFET MODERATE QUALITY ★★★ VALUE ★★★
READER-SURVEY RESPONSES 92% 👍 8% 👎 DISNEY DINING PLAN Yes

Grand Floridian Resort & Spa; 407-939-3463
Reservations Recommended. **Dining Plan credits** 1/person/meal. **When to go** Breakfast or dinner. **Cost range** Breakfast $32 (child $20), dinner $45 (child $27). **Service ★★★★. Hours** Daily, 8–11:50 a.m. and 4–9 p.m.

This bright, cavernous room is periodically filled with music from an antique band organ. Buffet usually includes mojo roast pork loin, Mongolian beef stir-fry, Mississippi fried catfish, and Florida strawberry soup. Separate buffet for kids includes cheese ravioli, hot dogs, chicken tenders, and a taco bar. A good choice for character dining, but too bright and loud for adults without children.

'Ohana ★★★

POLYNESIAN MODERATE QUALITY ★★★½ VALUE ★★★
READER-SURVEY RESPONSES 94% 👍 6% 👎 DISNEY DINING PLAN Yes

Polynesian Village Resort; 407-939-3463
Reservations Recommended. **Dining Plan credits** 1/person/meal. **When to go** Breakfast or dinner. **Cost range** Character breakfast $31 (child $20), dinner $43 (child $24). **Service ★★★★. Hours** Daily, 7:30 a.m.–10 p.m.
At any given moment, there may be a Hula-Hoop contest or a coconut race, where kids push coconuts around the room with broomsticks. There is no menu. As soon as you're seated, your server will begin to deliver food. Bread and salad are followed by honey-glazed chicken wings, pork dumplings, and pineapple-coconut bread. The main course is steak, chicken, and grilled shrimp, accompanied by stir-fried vegetables and lo mein noodles. Strolling singers and characters at breakfast provide entertainment. Sit in the main dining room, where the fire pit is located.

Olivia's Cafe ★★★

AMERICAN MODERATE QUALITY ★★★ VALUE ★★
READER-SURVEY RESPONSES 86% 👍 14% 👎 DISNEY DINING PLAN Yes

Old Key West Resort; 407-939-3463
Reservations Accepted. **Dining Plan credits** 1/person/meal. **When to go** Lunch. **Cost range** Breakfast $10–$15 (child $7), lunch and dinner $14.50–$33 (child $9). **Service ★★★★. Hours** Daily, 7:30–10:30 a.m., 11:30 a.m.–4:55 p.m., and 5–10 p.m.
This is Disney's idea of Key West: lots of pastels, mosaic-tile floors, and tropical trees in the center of the room. Some outside seating looks out over the waterway. At breakfast, try crab-cake eggs Benedict or banana-bread French toast. At lunch and dinner, conch fritters and conch chowder; Plantation Key pork chop with smoked-Gouda fondue; slow-cooked prime rib.

Paddlefish ★★½

SEAFOOD EXPENSIVE QUALITY ★★★½ VALUE ★★
READER-SURVEY RESPONSES Too new to rate DISNEY DINING PLAN Yes

The Landing, Disney Springs; 407-939-3463
Reservations Accepted. **Dining Plan credits** 2/person/meal. **When to go** Early evening. **Cost range** Lunch $9–$24, dinner $28–$49 (child $8–$12). **Hours** Daily, 11:30 a.m.–3:30 p.m. and 4–11 p.m.
On a permanently anchored boat formerly occupied by Fulton's Crab House, Paddlefish features an updated interior with a modern yachting theme, as well as a rooftop lounge that overlooks Disney Springs. An outdoor waterfront bar offers a build-your-own fish boil and private dining areas. The menu still features fresh seafood and steaks, as well as classic cocktails.

Paradiso 37 ★★½

GLOBAL INEXPENSIVE QUALITY ★★★ VALUE ★★★
READER-SURVEY RESPONSES 71% 👍 29% 👎 DISNEY DINING PLAN Yes

Disney Springs; 407-934-3700
Reservations Accepted. **Dining Plan credits** 1/person/meal. **When to go** Lunch or dinner. **Cost range** $10–$35 (child $8). **Service ★★★. Hours** Daily, 11:30 a.m.–11 p.m.
Prime location on the waterfront at Disney Springs. Ambience is festive and casual, with an open kitchen. Food is inspired by street foods of Central, South, and North America, from ceviche to enchiladas and barbecue ribs. The *37* in the name refers to the number of varieties of tequila, and the joint boasts "the coldest beer in the world," served at a crisp 29°F–32°F.

Planet Hollywood Observatory ★★½

AMERICAN MODERATE QUALITY ★★ VALUE ★★
READER-SURVEY RESPONSES 67% 👍 33% 👎 DISNEY DINING PLAN Yes

West Side, Disney Springs; 407-827-7827
Reservations Recommended. **Dining Plan credits** 1/person/meal. **When to go** Late lunch. **Cost range** $11–$31 (child $8). **Service ★★. Hours** Daily, 11 a.m.–1 a.m.
In 2016 the trademark globe structure was reimagined as a four-story observatory, in keeping with Disney Springs' turn-of-the-20th-century design aesthetic. An outdoor terrace and bar, called Stargazers, hosts live entertainment, while a DJ spins in the main dining room. You may see Kobe sliders, watermelon-and-feta salad, shrimp fajitas, ribs, L.A. Lasagna, and bananas Foster cheesecake.

Plaza Restaurant ★★

AMERICAN MODERATE QUALITY ★★ VALUE ★★
READER-SURVEY RESPONSES 90% 👍 10% 👎 DISNEY DINING PLAN Yes

Main Street, U.S.A., Magic Kingdom; 407-939-3463
Reservations Only accepted 11 a.m.–noon. **Dining Plan credits** 1/person/meal. **When to go** Anytime. **Cost range** $12–$19 (child $9). **Service** ★★★★. **Hours** 11 a.m.–9:30 p.m.
Tucked away on a side street at the end of Main Street, U.S.A., as you head to Tomorrowland, the Plaza evokes small-town diners across America. You pay top dollar for a tuna-salad sandwich or a burger, but on a hot Florida day, it's an air-conditioned respite. House specialties include the vegetarian sandwich, chicken-strawberry salad, and ice cream desserts such as the Plaza banana split or sundae.

Portobello ★★½

ITALIAN EXPENSIVE QUALITY ★★★ VALUE ★★
READER-SURVEY RESPONSES 74% 👍 26% 👎 DISNEY DINING PLAN Yes

Disney Springs; 407-934-8888
Reservations Recommended. **Dining Plan credits** 1/person/meal. **When to go** Anytime. **Cost range** Lunch $11–$15, dinner $11–$29 (child $5–$13). **Service** ★★★. **Hours** Daily, 11:30 a.m.–3:50 p.m. and, 4–11 p.m.
On the waterfront at Disney Springs, Portobello has a faux Tuscan interior designed to look like a "country Italian trattoria." Enjoy such dishes as wood-burning-oven pizzas, house-made lasagna, and grilled flat-iron steak.

Raglan Road Irish Pub & Restaurant ★★★★

IRISH MODERATE QUALITY ★★★½ VALUE ★★★
READER-SURVEY RESPONSES 90% 👍 10% 👎 DISNEY DINING PLAN Yes

Disney Springs; 407-938-0300
Reservations Recommended. **Dining Plan credits** 1/person/meal. **When to go** Monday–Saturday after 8 p.m. **Cost range** Sunday brunch $12–$25, lunch $15–$27, dinner $15–$29 (child $8–$11). **Service** ★★★½. **Hours** Daily, 11 a.m.–11 p.m., with pub food available until closing (1 a.m.-ish); Sunday brunch: 10 a.m.–3 p.m.

Courtesy of Raglan Road

Many elements of this pub, including the bar, were handcrafted from hardwoods in Ireland. Enjoy oven-roasted loin of ham with cabbage and mashed potatoes, beer-battered fish-and-chips, or beef stew infused with Guinness. The must-have appetizer is the Dalkey Duo: batter-fried cocktail sausages with a mustard dipping sauce. The real draw here is the knockout Celtic music. A talented band plays daily. Celtic dancers fill the stage and dance on tables.

Rainforest Cafe ★★½

AMERICAN MODERATE QUALITY ★★ VALUE ★★
READER-SURVEY RESPONSES 84% 👍 16% 👎 DISNEY DINING PLAN Yes

Disney Springs Marketplace, 407-827-8500; Animal Kingdom, 407-938-9100
Reservations Recommended. **Dining Plan credits** 1/person/meal. **When to go** After lunch crunch, in late afternoon, and before dinner hour. **Cost range** $13–$33 (child $9). **Service** ★★★. **Hours** *Disney Springs Marketplace:* Daily, 11 a.m.–10:35 p.m. *Animal Kingdom:* Daily, 8:30 a.m.–8:50 p.m. (closing time varies seasonally).
The Disney Springs version of the national chain sits beneath a giant volcano that can be seen (and heard) erupting all over the Marketplace. Inside is a huge dining room designed to look like a jungle, complete with animatronic elephants, bats, and monkeys. There is occasional thunder and even some rainfall. The Animal Kingdom version, featuring a huge waterfall, is easier on the eyes externally. Long waits are not worth the fare: coconut shrimp, burgers, slow-roasted pork ribs. If you're willing to pay to avoid the long wait, stop by the day before and purchase a Landry's Select Club membership for $25. By presenting your card on the day you want to dine, you'll be seated much faster (and get 10% off retail and other benefits). The shopping experience and the kid appeal must be the attractions because food preparations are spotty, and waits can be horrendous.

Restaurant Marrakesh ★★

MOROCCAN MODERATE QUALITY ★★½ VALUE ★★
READER-SURVEY RESPONSES 86% 👍 14% 👎 DISNEY DINING PLAN Yes

Morocco, World Showcase, Epcot; 407-939-3463
Reservations Accepted. **Dining Plan credits** 1/person/meal. **When to go** Lunch or dinner. **Cost range** Lunch $16–$23, dinner $22–$46 (child $8). **Service** ★★★★. **Hours** Daily, 11:30 a.m.–3:15 p.m. and 3:30–9 p.m.
Marrakesh re-creates a Moroccan palace and serves *bastilla* (a minced-chicken pie sprinkled with cinnamon sugar) and beef *brewat* (a pastry filled with beef, deep-fried, and sprinkled with cinnamon sugar), followed by lemon chicken or roast lamb. Split an order of couscous. If you're hungry, curious, or both, try the Berber Feast, with tastes of several courses. The creations are authentic but not too spicy. A Moroccan band and belly dancing provide entertainment. It's usually easy to get a table. Diners at Marrakesh sit at tables instead of on the floor and eat with utensils rather than with their hands. Picky kids can choose from chicken tenders, pasta, and burgers.

Rose & Crown Dining Room ★★★

ENGLISH MODERATE QUALITY ★★★½ VALUE ★★
READER-SURVEY RESPONSES 93% 👍 7% 👎 DISNEY DINING PLAN Yes

United Kingdom, World Showcase, Epcot; 407-939-3463
Reservations Accepted. **Dining Plan credits** 1/person/meal. **When to go** Lunch or dinner. **Cost range** Lunch $15–$29, dinner $16–$33 (child $9). **Service** ★★★★★. **Hours** Daily, noon–3:20 p.m. and 4–8 p.m.
The Rose & Crown is both a pub and a dining establishment. The traditional English pub has a large, cozy bar. The adjoining dining room is rustic and simple. Enjoy fish-and-chips, bangers and mash (sausage and mashed potatoes), and shepherd's pie washed down with Bass ale. This is a prime spot for viewing *IllumiNations,* so try to get a table on the patio for late evening.

Sanaa ★★★★

INDIAN/AFRICAN EXPENSIVE QUALITY ★★★★ VALUE ★★★★
READER-SURVEY RESPONSES 93% 👍 7% 👎 DISNEY DINING PLAN Yes

Animal Kingdom Villas–Kidani Village; 407-939-3463
Reservations Accepted. **Dining Plan credits** 1/person/meal. **When to go** Lunch or dinner. **Cost range** Lunch $15–$26, dinner $19–$35 (child $11–$12). **Service** ★★★★. **Hours** Daily, 11:30 a.m.–4 p.m. and 5–9:30 p.m.
One floor down from the Kidani Village lobby, Sanaa's dining room is inspired by Africa's outdoor markets with windows that look out on the resort's savanna—giraffes, water buffalo, and other animals wander within yards of you as you dine. A variety of Indian-African creations—such as Indian-style breads (naan, onion *kulcha,* and paneer paratha) with red-chile sambal, coriander chutney, and cucumber raita and tandoori chicken—is offered.

San Angel Inn ★★★

MEXICAN EXPENSIVE QUALITY ★★★ VALUE ★★
READER-SURVEY RESPONSES 79% 👍 21% 👎 DISNEY DINING PLAN Yes

Mexico, World Showcase, Epcot; 407-939-3463
Reservations Accepted. **Dining Plan credits** 1/person/meal. **When to go** Lunch or dinner. **Cost range** Lunch $19–$30, dinner $25–$30 (child $9). **Service** ★★★. **Hours** Daily, 11:30 a.m.–4 p.m. and 4:30 p.m.–park closing.
A romantically crafted open-air cantina, the restaurant overlooks both the Gran Fiesta Tour attraction and the bustling plaza of a small Mexican village. Mole poblano, chicken with a sauce made from several kinds of peppers and unsweetened Mexican chocolate; carne asada; and interesting regional fish preparations. The menu goes beyond typical Mexican selections, offering special and regional dishes that are difficult to find in the United States. Mariachi or marimba bands play in the courtyard.

Sci-Fi Dine-In Theater Restaurant ★★

AMERICAN MODERATE QUALITY ★★½ VALUE ★★
READER-SURVEY RESPONSES 86% 👍 14% 👎 DISNEY DINING PLAN Yes

Commissary Lane, Disney's Hollywood Studios; 407-939-3463
Reservations Recommended. **Dining Plan credits** 1/person/meal. **When to go** Anytime. **Cost range** $14–$32 (child $9). **Service** ★★★★★. **Hours** Sunday and Wednesday, 10:30 a.m.–8 p.m.; Monday–Tuesday and Thursday–Saturday, 11 a.m.–3:50 p.m. and 4–8 p.m.

Everyone gets a kick out of this unusual dining room—a facsimile of a drive-in from the 1950s, with faux classic cars instead of tables. Hop in, order, and watch cartoons and clips of vintage horror and sci-fi movies, such as *Attack of the 50 Ft. Woman, Robot Monster,* and *The Blob.* Servers take your order from the driver's seat. Fare consists of everything from burgers and shakes to pasta, ribs, and steak. We recommend making late-afternoon or late-evening Advance Reservations and ordering only dessert—the Sci-Fi is an attraction, not a good dining opportunity. If you don't have Advance Reservations, try walking in around 11 a.m. or 3 p.m.

Shula's Steak House ★★★★

STEAK EXPENSIVE QUALITY ★★★★ VALUE ★★
READER-SURVEY RESPONSES 90% 👍 10% 👎 DISNEY DINING PLAN No

Dolphin Resort; 407-934-1362
Reservations Required. **When to go** Dinner. **Cost range** $28–$130 (for the Australian lobster tail). Sides not included in entrée cost. **Service** ★★★★. **Hours** Daily, 5–11 p.m.
In a word, meat—really expensive but very high-quality meat. Only certified Angus beef is served: filet mignon, porterhouse (including a 48-ounce cut), and prime rib. This is part of a chain owned by former Miami Dolphins football coach Don Shula. The menu is printed on the side of a football and placed on a kickoff tee in the center of the table. Clubby and masculine is the atmosphere.

Shutters at Old Port Royale ★★

STEAK/SEAFOOD MODERATE QUALITY ★★½ VALUE ★★
READER-SURVEY RESPONSES 88% 👍 12% 👎 DISNEY DINING PLAN Yes

Caribbean Beach Resort; 407-939-3463
Reservations Accepted. **Dining Plan credits** 1/person/meal. **When to go** Dinner. **Cost range** $18–$35 (child $9–$11). **Service** ★★★. **Hours** Daily, 5–10 p.m.
The sparsely decorated dining room has kind of a neglected feel, but the chef is having fun in the kitchen whipping up Caribbean-inspired dishes. Pan-seared crab cakes, jerk-rubbed mahimahi, chicken wings with habanero sauce, and sustainable fish are house specialties.

Spice Road Table ★★★½

MOROCCAN MODERATE QUALITY ★★★★ VALUE ★★★
READER-SURVEY RESPONSES 88% 👍 12% 👎 DISNEY DINING PLAN Yes

Morocco, World Showcase, Epcot; 407-939-3463
Reservations Recommended. **When to go** Anytime, but primo spot for nightly fireworks. **Cost range** $22–$30 (child $6–$8). **Service** ★★★★★. **Hours** Daily, 11:30 a.m.–9 p.m.
A gorgeous, well-stocked bar is the centerpiece. The best seats, 120 in all, are on the covered terrace, but inside seats also have great views of World Showcase Lagoon—indoors or out, this is the place at Epcot to watch *IllumiNations.* The Mediterranean-style tapas menu includes hummus and olives, mussels tagine, fried calamari, lamb sliders, and rice-stuffed grape leaves. Entrées to try are coriander-crusted rack of lamb and yellowfin tuna with eggplant, zucchini, capers, and basil oil. Pair them with organic sangria, a Mediterranean beer, or a signature cocktail.

Spice Road Table

Splitsville ★★½

AMERICAN MODERATE QUALITY ★★½ VALUE ★★
READER-SURVEY RESPONSES 100% 👍 0% 👎 DISNEY DINING PLAN Yes

West Side, Disney Springs; 407-938-7467
Reservations Accepted. **Dining Plan credits** 1/person/meal. **When to go** Anytime. **Cost range** $11–$25 (child $9). **Service** ★★½. **Hours** Monday–Friday, 10:30 a.m.–11:55 p.m.; Saturday–Sunday, 10 a.m.–11:55 p.m.

Splitsville is part of a multistate chain of "luxury lanes"—hybrid bowling alleys/restaurants. The decor is vaguely midcentury modern. The menu is more spread out than a 7/10 split: Burgers, sushi, pizza, seafood, barbecue, Mexican, and Italian are represented. We've tried almost everything on the menu, and while all of it was OK, the only thing we'd order again is the sushi.

STK Orlando ★★★½

STEAK EXPENSIVE QUALITY ★★★★ VALUE ★★½
READER-SURVEY RESPONSES Too new to rate DISNEY DINING PLAN No

The Landing, Disney Springs; 407-917-7440
Reservations Required. **When to go** Anytime. **Cost range** $18–$98. **Service** ★★★★. **Hours** Sunday–Thursday, 11:30 a.m.–4 p.m. and 5–11 p.m.; Friday–Saturday, 11:30 a.m.–4 p.m. and 5 p.m.–midnight.

A lower level houses a bar and seating area with a Las Vegas/Miami–ultralounge feel, complete with DJ and lots of noise. The quieter, less-glitzy upstairs has both indoor and outdoor seating, the latter with fantastic views of Disney Springs. The steaks aren't cheap, but they're excellent, particularly the fork-tender porterhouse. Sides include mac and cheese, creamed spinach, and Parmesan-truffle fries.

Teppan Edo ★★★½

JAPANESE EXPENSIVE QUALITY ★★★★ VALUE ★★★
READER-SURVEY RESPONSES 93% 👍 7% 👎 DISNEY DINING PLAN Yes

Japan, World Showcase, Epcot; 407-939-3463
Reservations Recommended. **Dining Plan credits** 1/person/meal. **When to go** Lunch or dinner. **Cost range** $18–$35 (child $14). **Service** ★★★★★. **Hours** Daily, noon–3:45 p.m. and 4–8:55 p.m.

Upscale Japanese dining rooms, serving chicken, shrimp, beef, scallops, and Asian vegetables stir-fried on a teppanyaki grill by a knife-juggling chef. The menu includes sushi and appetizers such as edamame and tempura. Diners at the teppanyaki tables (large tables with a grill in the middle) are seated with other parties.

Tiffins ★★★★

PAN-ASIAN/AMERICAN EXPENSIVE QUALITY ★★★★ VALUE ★★★
READER-SURVEY RESPONSES Too new to rate DISNEY DINING PLAN Yes

Discovery Island, Disney's Animal Kingdom; 407-939-3463
Reservations Recommended. **Dining Plan credits** 2/person/meal. **When to go** Lunch and dinner. **Cost range** $29–$53. **Service** ★★★★. **Hours** Daily, 11 a.m.–park closing.

Tiffins is tucked behind Pizzafari, on a walking path to Pandora. Inside, Tiffins is divided into three relatively small, quiet dining rooms, plus the Nomad Lounge bar. A wraparound porch offers outdoor seating. Decor includes artifacts from Asia and Africa and carved-wood sculptures. Appetizers: marinated grilled octopus and black-eyed pea fritters. Entrées: whole fried sustainable fish, spiced lamb chops, Wagyu strip loin, or duck. Dessert: lime cheesecake or passion fruit tapioca. So far, we think Tiffins is one of the best restaurants in Disney World.

Tokyo Dining ★★★

JAPANESE MODERATE QUALITY ★★★★ VALUE ★★★
READER-SURVEY RESPONSES 90% 👍 10% 👎 DISNEY DINING PLAN Yes

Japan, World Showcase, Epcot; 407-939-3463
Reservations Accepted. **Dining Plan credits** 1/person/meal. **When to go** Lunch. **Cost range** $9–$30 (child $10.50–$11.50). **Service** ★★★★. **Hours** Daily, noon–3:45 p.m. and 4–8:55 p.m.

Modern Asian decor with a beautifully lighted sushi bar. Grilled meats and seafood; tempura chicken, shrimp, and vegetables; sushi and sashimi; and sake appear on the menu. It's a relatively quiet space in the Japan Pavilion. You can't beat a window seat here at fireworks time.

Tony's Town Square Restaurant ★★½

ITALIAN MODERATE QUALITY ★★★ VALUE ★★
READER-SURVEY RESPONSES 79% 👍 21% 👎 DISNEY DINING PLAN Yes

Main Street, U.S.A., Magic Kingdom; 407-939-3463

 Reservations Recommended. **Dining Plan credits** 1/person/meal. **When to go** Late lunch or early dinner. **Cost range** Lunch $15–$33, dinner $17–$30 (child $9). **Service** ★★★★. **Hours** Daily, 11:30 a.m.–2:55 p.m. and 3–9:30 p.m.

Tony's is a bit worn on the edges, with memorabilia from the Disney classic *Lady and the Tramp* on the walls. The best seats are on the glass-windowed porch. For lunch, flatbreads, paninis, and spaghetti; for dinner, chicken Parmigiana and New York strip. Tony's does a decent job with pasta (multigrain and gluten-free options available).

Trader Sam's Grog Grotto ★★★

PAN-ASIAN MODERATE QUALITY ★★★ VALUE ★★★
READER-SURVEY RESPONSES Too new to rate DISNEY DINING PLAN no

Polynesian Village Resort; 407-939-3463

Reservations Not accepted. **When to go** Dinner. **Cost range** Lunch $8.50–$15 (small plates only). **Service** ★★★. **Hours** Daily, 4 p.m.–midnight.

Off the Polynesian Village's main lobby and featuring views of the marina and Seven Seas Lagoon, this tiki bar has its own lore built in: it was started by Trader Sam, Adventureland's famous "head" salesman, who welcomes you to his enchanted South Seas hideaway to explore a menu of "magical tropical drinks and food." Cocktails are the big draw, with names like Castaway Crush and Tahitian Torch. Small plates include chicken lettuce cups with hoisin-ginger sauce, Hawaiian poke with Sriracha aioli, kalua pork tacos, pan-fried dumplings, and the Headhunter Sushi Roll. Trader Sam's is already a hit with Disneyphiles, so get there early—there are just 50 seats inside and 80 on the patio.

Trail's End Restaurant ★★

AMERICAN/BUFFET MODERATE QUALITY ★★ VALUE ★★
READER-SURVEY RESPONSES 95% 👍 5% 👎 DISNEY DINING PLAN Yes

Fort Wilderness Resort; 407-939-3463

Reservations Recommended. **Dining Plan credits** 1/person/meal. **When to go** Breakfast or dinner. **Cost range** Breakfast $19 (child $11), lunch $13–$18 (child $9), dinner $28 (child $16). **Service** ★★★. **Hours** Daily, 7:30–2 p.m. and 4:30–9:30 p.m.

Trail's End is what a pioneer buffet would have looked like had America's settlers built one out of a log cabin. Breakfast and dinner are served buffet-style; lunch transitions to an à la carte menu. Breakfast features eggs, sausage, bacon, waffles, biscuits, fruit, and pastries. Lunch includes shrimp and grits, flatbreads, and chicken and waffles, as well as s'mores and warm sticky-bun sundaes. The dinner lineup includes fried chicken, ribs, pasta, fish, and pizza. Trail's End makes a great midday break from the Magic Kingdom; take the boat from the park.

Trattoria al Forno ★★★½

ITALIAN MODERATE QUALITY ★★★½ VALUE ★★
READER-SURVEY RESPONSES 82% 👍 18% 👎 DISNEY DINING PLAN Yes

Disney's BoardWalk; 407-939-3463

Reservations Accepted. **Dining Plan credits** 1/person/meal. **When to go** Breakfast or dinner. **Cost range** Breakfast $7–$14 (child $7), dinner $17–$37 (child $10–$12). **Service** ★★★. **Hours** Daily, 7:30–11 a.m. and 5–10 p.m.

Our favorite spot here is the formal dining room right in front of the kitchen, where it's a little less noisy (and carpeted), or one of the booths at the back. For breakfast: poached egg over polenta with fennel sausage, red sauce, and Parmesan; waffle with espresso-mascarpone cream; cured Italian meats with hard-boiled egg, tomatoes, and cheeses. For dinner: thin-sliced cured meats; pizzas; linguine with clams; tagliatelle alla carbonara; T-bone steak; tiramisu and bomboloni (fried doughnuts). The wine list is carefully curated, with labels from all of Italy's major regions and more than 30 available by the glass or quartino. Breakfast is one of the best on Disney property.

T-REX ★★★

AMERICAN MODERATE QUALITY ★★ VALUE ★★
READER-SURVEY RESPONSES 79% 👍 21% 👎 DISNEY DINING PLAN Yes

The Marketplace, Disney Springs; 407-828-8739

Reservations Recommended. **Dining Plan credits** 1/person/meal. **When to go** Lunch or dinner. **Cost range** $16–$34 (child $9). **Service** ★★★. **Hours** Sunday–Thursday, 11 a.m.–11 p.m.; Friday–Saturday, 11 a.m.–midnight.

A cavernous dining room with life-size robotic dinosaurs, giant fish tanks, bubbling geysers, waterfalls, fossils in the bathrooms, and crystals in the walls. Volume: loud and louder, with meteor showers and growling dinos. Bronto Burger, New York strip, and Chocolate Extinction fudge cake are some of the offerings. Expect a wait unless there's an empty seat at the bar.

Tusker House

Turf Club Bar & Grill ★★

AMERICAN MODERATE QUALITY ★★★ VALUE ★★
READER-SURVEY RESPONSES 92% 👍 8% 👎 DISNEY DINING PLAN Yes

Saratoga Springs Resort; 407-939-3463

Reservations Accepted. **Dining Plan credits** 1/person/meal. **When to go** Dinner. **Cost range** $18–$35 (child $9). **Service** ★★★. **Hours** Daily, 5–10 p.m.

When the weather's nice, ask for an outdoor table; you can spot golfers on the adjacent Lake Buena Vista Golf Course while eating prime rib, pasta, or grilled chicken Caesar salad. (It has the best Caesar salad in Disney World.) Turf Club is worth the trip on a sunny day for a drink and appetizers on the shady terrace. It's rarely crowded.

Tusker House Restaurant ★★★

AMERICAN/AFRICAN/BUFFET MODERATE QUALITY ★★★ VALUE ★★★
READER-SURVEY RESPONSES 92% 👍 8% 👎 DISNEY DINING PLAN Yes

Africa, Animal Kingdom; 407-939-3463

Reservations Required for character meals. **Dining Plan credits** 1/person/meal. **When to go** Anytime. **Cost range** Breakfast $30 (child $18), lunch $38 (child $23), dinner $42 (child $25). **Service** ★★★. **Hours** Daily, 8–10:45 a.m., 11:30 a.m.–2:45 p.m., and 4 p.m.–park closing.

In Harambe Village. Character meals feature Donald, Daisy, Mickey, and Goofy. The setting is a bit austere, but the food (roasted meats, rotisserie chicken, seafood stew) is surprisingly good, with spices and taste combinations you won't find at other spots. The usual bacon, eggs, fruit, and pastries are served for breakfast.

Tutto Italia ★★★★

ITALIAN EXPENSIVE QUALITY ★★★★ VALUE ★★★
READER-SURVEY RESPONSES 89% 👍 11% 👎 DISNEY DINING PLAN Yes

Italy, World Showcase, Epcot; 407-939-3463

Reservations Recommended. **Dining Plan credits** 1/person/meal. **When to go** Midafternoon. **Cost range** Lunch $17–$34, dinner $23–$34 (child $10). **Service** ★★★★. **Hours** Daily, 11:30 a.m.–3:30 p.m. and 4:30–9 p.m.

The Roman decor features huge murals of an Italian piazza along the wall behind the upholstered banquettes. If the weather is pleasant, request a table on the piazza, away from the noisy dining room. House-made lasagna, grilled butcher's steak with rosemary potatoes, and cannoli are delicious. It's a little pricey, but the cuisine is authentic, and the servings are ample.

Las Ventanas ★★

AMERICAN MODERATE QUALITY ★★½ VALUE ★★
READER-SURVEY RESPONSES 78% 👍 22% 👎 DISNEY DINING PLAN Yes

Coronado Springs Resort; 407-939-3463
Reservations Recommended. **Dining Plan credits** 1/person/meal. **When to go** Anytime. **Cost range** Breakfast $7–$20 (child $9), lunch $15–$17 (child $10), dinner $15–$28 (child $10). **Service** ★★★★. **Hours** Daily, 7–10:30 a.m., 11 a.m.–2 p.m., and 4–10 p.m.
Las Ventanas is more refined and subdued than the nearby Pepper Market, with high ceilings, dark slate floors, and rust-colored walls. Try the huevos rancheros at breakfast, the ominous-sounding Huevos Divorciados, prime rib, and seared pork loin.

Via Napoli ★★★★

ITALIAN MODERATE QUALITY ★★★½ VALUE ★★★
READER-SURVEY RESPONSES 89% 👍 11% 👎 DISNEY DINING PLAN Yes

Italy, World Showcase, Epcot; 407-939-3463
Reservations Recommended. **Dining Plan credits** 1/person/meal. **When to go** Lunch or dinner. **Cost range** $18–$30, pizzas $17 (individual)–$41 (serves 3–5). **Service** ★★★★. **Hours** Daily, 11:30 a.m.–4:25 p.m. and 4:30–9 p.m.
The best pizza in Walt Disney World. Because the pies are cooked at inferno-like temperatures, they don't stay in the oven for long and vegetable toppings stay crunchy. The Capriciossa (eggplant, artichokes, prosciutto, and mushrooms) and four-cheese pies are our favorites. The main dining room is cavernous and loud, but it feels like a bustling Italian market. Shaded outdoor seating is available, and, occasionally, pizza by the slice is sold outside.

Victoria & Albert's ★★★★★

GOURMET EXPENSIVE QUALITY ★★★★★ VALUE ★★★★
READER-SURVEY RESPONSES 96% 👍 4% 👎 DISNEY DINING PLAN No

Grand Floridian Resort & Spa; 407-939-3463
Reservations Mandatory; must confirm by noon the day of your seating; credit card required to reserve. **When to go** Anytime. **Cost range** Fixed price, 7-course $185 (pairing $250), 10-course $235 (pairing $340), Queen Victoria's Room $235 (pairing $340), Chef's Table $250 (pairing $355). **Service** ★★★★★. **Hours** Variable seating starts nightly at 5:45 p.m.; plus 1 seating at 5:30 p.m. for Chef's Table. No children under age 10 except at Chef's Table.
With Frette linens, Riedel crystal, Christofle silver, and only 18 tables in the main dining room and Queen Victoria's Room, plus a private space with seating for eight, this is the top dining experience at Disney World. A winner of AAA's Five Diamond Award (the only restaurant in Central Florida so honored), Victoria & Albert's is civilized, lavish, and expensive. The menu changes

Via Napoli is The Unofficial Guide favorite for pizza in Walt Disney World.

daily, but Chef Scott Hunnel's favorites include Australian Kobe-style beef, Florida seafood, and Alaskan salmon. Pastry chef Erich Herbitschek's desserts are divine. A harpist or violinist entertains from the foyer. The best show is the Chef's Table, where chef Hunnel crafts a personal menu.

The Wave . . . of American Flavors ★★★

NEW AMERICAN/BUFFET MODERATE QUALITY ★★ VALUE ★★
READER-SURVEY RESPONSES 94% 👍 6% 👎 DISNEY DINING PLAN Yes

Contemporary Resort; 407-939-3463
Reservations Accepted. **Dining Plan credits** 1/person/meal. **When to go** Anytime. **Cost range** Breakfast $6.50–$12.50 à la carte, $24 buffet (child $13), lunch $12–$20, dinner $17.50–$34 (child $9). **Service** ★★★. **Hours** Daily, 7:30–11:45 a.m., noon–2 p.m., and 5–9:30 p.m.
The Wave has one of the coolest lounges at Disney World, adjoining a dining room with the feel of an upscale coffee shop, with organic beers and coffees, hip cocktails, and New World wines. For breakfast: a generous buffet, megaberry smoothie, and make-your-own muesli. For lunch: lump crab–Florida rock shrimp cakes, build-your-own burger. For dinner: grilled Colorado lamb chops, sustainable fish, vegetarian curry stew. The kitchen continues to create healthful dining options and source local products.

Whispering Canyon Cafe ★★★

AMERICAN MODERATE QUALITY ★★★½ VALUE ★★★★
READER-SURVEY RESPONSES 83% 👍 17% 👎 DISNEY DINING PLAN Yes

Wilderness Lodge & Villas; 407-939-3463
Reservations Accepted. **Dining Plan credits** 1/person/meal. **When to go** Anytime. **Cost range** Breakfast $10.50–$16.50 (child $7–$9), lunch $13.50–$22.50, dinner $19–$30 (child $9). **Service** ★★★★. **Hours** Daily, 7:30–11:15 a.m., 11:45 a.m.–2:30 p.m., and 5–10 p.m.
Enjoy all-you-can-eat skillets with corn bread, ribs, pulled pork, smoked brisket, roast chicken, mashed potatoes, baked beans, seasonal vegetables, and corn on the cob. There is also an à la carte option for those who don't care to share. Waitstaff engage children in impromptu parades and other rowdy demonstrations.

Wolfgang Puck Grand Café ★★

CREATIVE CALIFORNIAN EXPENSIVE QUALITY ★½ VALUE ★½
READER-SURVEY RESPONSES 75% 👍 25% 👎 DISNEY DINING PLAN Yes

West Side, Disney Springs; 407-938-9653
Reservations Recommended. **Dining Plan credits** 1/person/meal. **When to go** Early evening. **Cost range** Cafe $13–$30 (child $7–$10), upstairs $25–$49 (child $8–$10). **Service** ★★★. **Hours** *Cafe:* Daily, 11:30 a.m.–11 p.m. *Upstairs:* Daily, 6–10 p.m.
This is actually two restaurants in one—four if you count the attached Wolfgang Puck Express and the sushi bar that flows into the restaurant's lounge area. Downstairs is the actual café. The upstairs is a more formal dining room, but in name only. Both spaces are inordinately loud, making conversation difficult. Puck's has wood-fired pizzas, including barbecue chicken and spicy shrimp. Sushi is also a good bet. Upstairs, the menu features fresh fish, chicken, and beef.

Yachtsman Steakhouse ★★★

STEAK EXPENSIVE QUALITY ★★★½ VALUE ★★
READER-SURVEY RESPONSES 89% 👍 11% 👎 DISNEY DINING PLAN Yes

Yacht Club Resort; 407-939-3463
Reservations Required. **Dining Plan credits** 2/person/meal. **When to go** Dinner. **Cost range** $31–$59 (child $9–$17). **Service** ★★★★. **Hours** Daily, 5:30–9:30 p.m.
Take in the view of the sandy lagoon at the resort. The menu features seafood, lamb, fowl, and vegetarian creations. The adjacent Crew's Cup Lounge, with dozens of beers and fine wine by the glass, is a fun place to start the evening. Start with lobster bisque or Caesar salad. All steaks are cut and trimmed on the premises.

Yak & Yeti Restaurant ★★

PAN-ASIAN EXPENSIVE QUALITY ★★½ VALUE ★★
READER-SURVEY RESPONSES 93% 👍 7% 👎 DISNEY DINING PLAN Yes

Asia, Animal Kingdom; 407-939-3463
Reservations Recommended. **Dining Plan credits** 1/person/meal. **When to go** Dinner. **Cost range** $18–$29 (child $9). **Service** ★★★★. **Hours** Daily, 11 a.m.–3:30 p.m. and 4 p.m.–park closing.
Dine in a rustic two-story Nepalese inn . . . with seating for hundreds. Windows on the second floor overlook the Asia section of the park. Lo mein and curry noodle bowls, crispy honey tempura chicken, Kalbi flat-iron steak and coconut shrimp, and chicken tikka masala are good choices.

PART 5

THE MAGIC KINGDOM

The Magic Kingdom

FP+ FastPass+ Available

UseFP+ FastPass+ Recommended

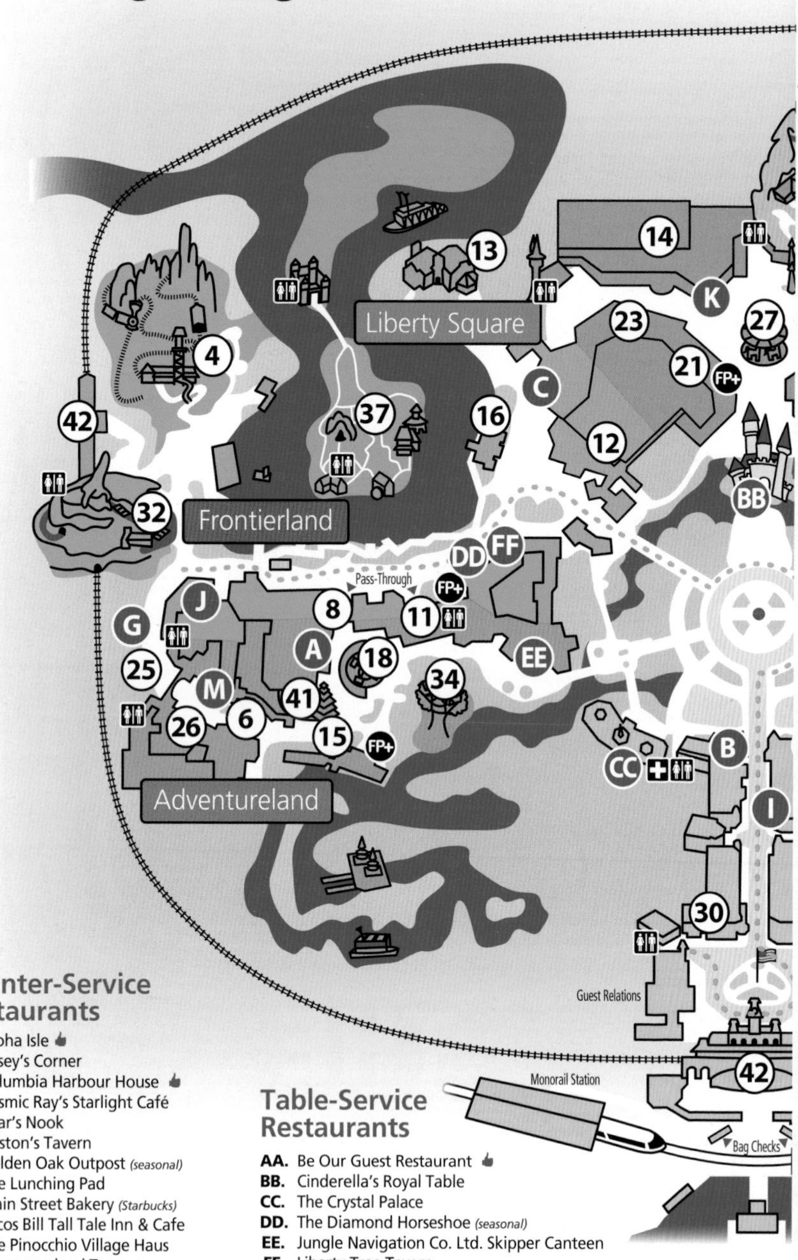

Counter-Service Restaurants

- **A.** Aloha Isle 👍
- **B.** Casey's Corner
- **C.** Columbia Harbour House 👍
- **D.** Cosmic Ray's Starlight Café
- **E.** Friar's Nook
- **F.** Gaston's Tavern
- **G.** Golden Oak Outpost *(seasonal)*
- **H.** The Lunching Pad
- **I.** Main Street Bakery *(Starbucks)*
- **J.** Pecos Bill Tall Tale Inn & Cafe
- **K.** The Pinocchio Village Haus
- **L.** Tomorrowland Terrace Restaurant *(seasonal)*
- **M.** Tortuga Tavern *(seasonal)*

Table-Service Restaurants

- **AA.** Be Our Guest Restaurant 👍
- **BB.** Cinderella's Royal Table
- **CC.** The Crystal Palace
- **DD.** The Diamond Horseshoe *(seasonal)*
- **EE.** Jungle Navigation Co. Ltd. Skipper Canteen
- **FF.** Liberty Tree Tavern
- **GG.** The Plaza Restaurant
- **HH.** Tony's Town Square Restaurant

First-Aid Station
Wishes! Dessert Party Viewing Spot
Parade Route
FastPass+ Kiosks
Restrooms
Recommended Dining
☑ Not to be Missed

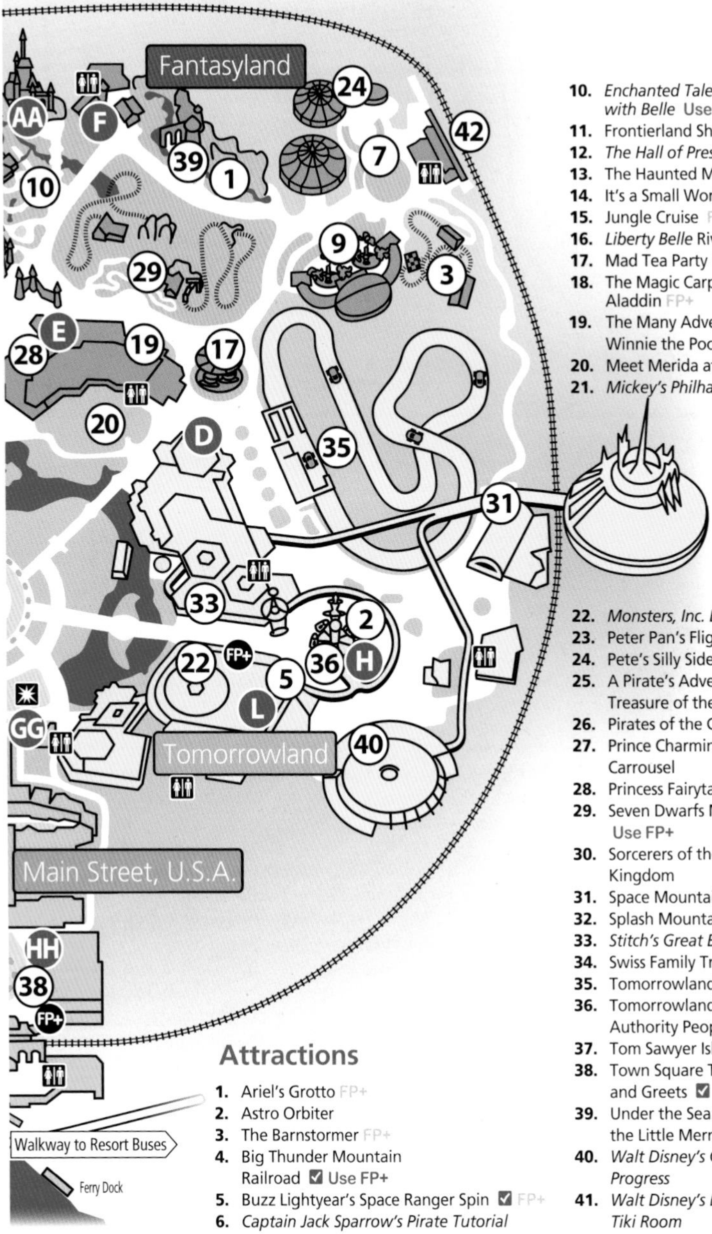

Fantasyland
Tomorrowland
Main Street, U.S.A.
Walkway to Resort Buses
Ferry Dock

Attractions

1. Ariel's Grotto FP+
2. Astro Orbiter
3. The Barnstormer FP+
4. Big Thunder Mountain Railroad ☑ Use FP+
5. Buzz Lightyear's Space Ranger Spin ☑ FP+
6. *Captain Jack Sparrow's Pirate Tutorial*
7. Casey Jr. Splash 'N' Soak Station
8. *Country Bear Jamboree*
9. Dumbo the Flying Elephant FP+
10. *Enchanted Tales with Belle* Use FP+
11. Frontierland Shootin' Arcade
12. *The Hall of Presidents*
13. The Haunted Mansion ☑ FP+
14. It's a Small World FP+
15. Jungle Cruise FP+
16. *Liberty Belle* Riverboat
17. Mad Tea Party FP+
18. The Magic Carpets of Aladdin FP+
19. The Many Adventures of Winnie the Pooh FP+
20. Meet Merida at Fairytale Garden
21. *Mickey's PhilharMagic* ☑ FP+
22. *Monsters, Inc. Laugh Floor* FP+
23. Peter Pan's Flight ☑ Use FP+
24. Pete's Silly Sideshow FP+
25. A Pirate's Adventure: Treasure of the Seven Seas ☑
26. Pirates of the Caribbean ☑ FP+
27. Prince Charming Regal Carrousel
28. Princess Fairytale Hall Use FP+
29. Seven Dwarfs Mine Train ☑ Use FP+
30. Sorcerers of the Magic Kingdom
31. Space Mountain ☑ Use FP+
32. Splash Mountain ☑ Use FP+
33. *Stitch's Great Escape!*
34. Swiss Family Treehouse
35. Tomorrowland Speedway FP+
36. Tomorrowland Transit Authority PeopleMover
37. Tom Sawyer Island
38. Town Square Theater Meet and Greets ☑ FP+
39. Under the Sea: Journey of the Little Mermaid FP+
40. *Walt Disney's Carousel of Progress*
41. *Walt Disney's Enchanted Tiki Room*
42. Walt Disney World Railroad *(multiple stations)*

Not to Be Missed at the Magic Kingdom

ADVENTURELAND	**A Pirate's Adventure** **Pirates of the Caribbean**
FANTASYLAND	***Mickey's PhilharMagic*** **Peter Pan's Flight** **Seven Dwarfs Mine Train**
FRONTIERLAND	**Big Thunder Mountain Railroad** **Splash Mountain**
LIBERTY SQUARE	**The Haunted Mansion**
MAIN STREET, U.S.A.	**Meet Mickey Mouse at Town Square Theater**
SPECIAL EVENTS	***Celebrate the Magic*** **Evening Parade** ***Wishes!***
TOMORROWLAND	**Buzz Lightyear's Space Ranger Spin** **Space Mountain**

Opened in 1971, the Magic Kingdom was the first built of Walt Disney World's four theme parks. Many of the attractions found here are originals from that park opening, and a few—including Cinderella Castle, Pirates of the Caribbean, and Splash Mountain—have helped define the basic elements of theme park attractions the world over. Indeed, the Magic Kingdom is undoubtedly what most people think of when Walt Disney World is mentioned.

Much of the Magic Kingdom was built by the same Disney staff who had built Disneyland more than a decade earlier. The remarkable achievement that Disney wrought in Orlando isn't that it could build a second, equally compelling theme park; it's that it could do so on a much larger scale while keeping many of the fine details that make visiting a Disney park such a completely immersive experience.

▶ **UNOFFICIAL TIP** If you don't already have a handout guide map and daily *Times Guide*, get them at the park entrance or at City Hall.

The Magic Kingdom is divided into six themed lands arranged around a circular hub. At the bottom of the hub is Main Street, replicating small-town American life, where all visitors enter and exit the park. Main Street leads to a central hub around which the other lands are distributed. Going clockwise from Main Street at the bottom, next is Adventureland, with its exotic jungle theme, and then Frontierland, Disney's take on the American West. Liberty Square follows, seamlessly integrating Frontierland's architecture with that of the early United States. At the top of the circular hub is Fantasyland, home of Cinderella Castle and the visual center of the park. Rounding out the lands is Tomorrowland, decorated in a retro (albeit incomplete) Jules Verne style. Tomorrowland is, along with Fantasyland, one of the most popular areas of the park.

MAIN STREET, U.S.A.

Begin and end your visit on Main Street, which may open 30 minutes before and close 30 minutes after the rest of the park. The Walt Disney World Railroad stops at Main Street. Get on to tour the park or ride to Frontierland or Fantasyland.

Main Street is a Disney-fied turn-of-the-19th-century small-town American street. Its buildings are real, not elaborate props. Along the street are shops, character-greeting venues, eating places, City Hall, and a fire station. What many visitors don't know, however, is that virtually all of the shops and restaurants are connected, and it's possible to walk almost from one end of Main Street to the other indoors. This is especially useful during parades and inclement weather. On most mornings, horse-drawn trolleys, fire engines, and horseless carriages transport visitors along Main Street to the central hub.

Main Street Services

Most park services are centered on Main Street, including:

Baby Center/Baby Care Needs: Next to The Crystal Palace, left around the central hub (toward Adventureland)
First Aid: Next to The Crystal Palace
Live Entertainment and Parade Information: City Hall at the railroad-station end of Main Street
Lost and Found: City Hall
Lost Persons: City Hall
Storage Lockers: On the right, just past the park entrance as you're heading into the park; lockers cleaned out each night
Wheelchair and Stroller Rental: Ground floor of the railroad station at the end of Main Street

SORCERERS OF THE MAGIC KINGDOM ★★★

APPEAL BY AGE			
	Preschool ★★★½	Grade School ★★★★½	Teens ★★★★
	Young Adults ★★★★	Over 30 ★★★★	Seniors ★★★

What it is Interactive video game. Scope and scale Minor attraction. When to go Before 11 a.m. or after 8 p.m. Comment Long lines to play. Authors' rating Great idea; ★★★. Duration About 2 minutes per step, 4 or 5 steps per game. Probable waiting time per step 10–15 minutes.

The Sorcerers of the Magic Kingdom combines aspects of role-playing games such as Dungeons and Dragons with Disney characters and theme park attractions. Your objective: to help the wizard Merlin keep evildoers from taking over the Magic Kingdom. Merlin sends you on adventures in different parts of the park to fight these villains. Each land hosts a different adventure within the game.

The game is played with a set of trading cards—similar to baseball cards—with a different Disney character on each card. Each character possesses special properties that help it fight certain villains. Pick up the cards (free), plus a map showing where in the park you can play the game, at the Fire Station on Main Street, U.S.A.

You'll need your MagicBand to pick up your first set of cards and start the game. One card, known as your key, is special because it links you to your game. You'll need to present your key card when you pick up a set of cards to start your next adventure.

When you pick up your first set of cards, you'll view an instructional video explaining how to use them and the object of the game. Then you'll be sent to another location to start your first adventure. Each location in the park is associated with a unique symbol: an eye, a feather, a dragonfly, or something along those lines. Look for these symbols on the map to find the best route to your starting point.

Each adventure consists of four or five stops in a particular land. At each stop, another story will play on a video screen, outlining what your villain is trying to do. Merlin will ask you to cast a spell to stop the villain—to do so, hold one or more of your cards up to the video display. Cameras in the display read your card, deploy the spell, and show you the results.

You'll probably encounter a line of 5–10 people ahead of you at each portal, especially if you play during the afternoon. One complete adventure should take about 30–60 minutes to play, depending on how crowded the park is. If the game sounds too confusing, A Pirate's Adventure in Adventureland (see page 171) is easier.

TOWN SQUARE THEATER MEET AND GREETS: MICKEY MOUSE AND TINKER BELL (FASTPASS+)

★★★★

APPEAL BY AGE Preschool ★★★★½ Grade School ★★★★½ Teens ★★★½ Young Adults ★★★½ Over 30 ★★★½ Seniors ★★★½

What it is Character-greeting venue. Scope and scale Minor attraction. When to go Before 10 a.m. or after 4 p.m., or use FastPass+. Comment Mickey and Tink have 2 separate queues, requiring 2 separate waits in line. Authors' rating It all started with this mouse; ★★★★. Duration 2 minutes per character. Probable waiting time 15–25 minutes.

Mickey Mouse and Tinker Bell greet guests throughout the day at Town Square Theater. Wait times usually drop following the afternoon parade. Note that Mickey at this location has a movable face and speaks. His facial movements are a bit unnatural, which can unsettle some small kids. If talking Mickey might be an issue for you, visit other Disney World locations where you can meet Mickey in his usual silent state.

Whoa. Nice costume, big guy.

GREAT DISNEY PERFORMANCES

Tinker Bell whistles "Flight of the Bumblebee."

TRANSPORTATION RIDES

In addition to the railroad, jitneys, omnibuses, old-timey fire engines, and horse-drawn streetcars bring guests from one end of Main Street to the other from park opening until midmorning on most days. As with the railroad, these are more fun than efficient transportation.

DISNEY DESIGN *with Sam Gennawey*

The experience of entering Main Street parallels that of entering a movie theater, almost certainly due to the filmmaking experience of Walt Disney and the first Imagineers who built Disneyland.

The moviegoing analogy begins at the front gate, where you present your ticket and enter the lobby. In this case, the lobby is the forecourt in front of the train station. Notice the red bricks beneath your feet, which represent a movie theater's red carpet. Also notice that the train station now blocks your view of everything behind it, in the way a movie curtain restricts your view of the screen.

You enter the Magic Kingdom through a tunnel under the railroad. Walking through the tunnel simulates the raising of the movie curtain and provides a transition from the lobby to the "theater." It's no accident that these tunnel passages are built wide, deep, and dark; they delay your view of an open and colorful Main Street, U.S.A. until the last moment.

With this initial glimpse of Main Street, it's clear that you're now truly in "Disney's World." Orientation in this new world is Main Street's Town Square, providing guide maps and advice to newcomers. By design, Guest Services are on the left side of most Disney theme parks.

The use of forced perspective is what makes the Main Street buildings seem taller than they really are and the castle seem farther away. If you turn around, the full-scale train station does the reverse, making the walk to the exit seem much closer for weary guests at the end of the day. The results are optical illusions that trick your mind and feet.

WALT DISNEY WORLD RAILROAD ★★★

APPEAL BY AGE			
Preschool ★★★★	Grade School ★★★★	Teens ★★★★
Young Adults ★★★½	Over 30 ★★★★	Seniors ★★★★

What it is Scenic railroad ride around perimeter of Magic Kingdom; transportation to Frontierland and Fantasyland. Scope and scale Minor attraction. When to go Anytime. Comment Main Street is usually the least congested station. Authors' rating Plenty to see; ★★★. Duration About 20 minutes for a complete circuit. Average wait in line per 100 people ahead of you 8 minutes; assumes 2 or more trains operating. Loading speed Moderate.

The Walt Disney World Railroad is a scenic trip around the perimeter of the Magic Kingdom aboard an actual steam-powered train. The primary boarding area is the two-story train station on Main Street, but alternate stops are in Frontierland and Fantasyland. The ride provides a glimpse of all lands except Adventureland, with most of the interesting stuff (such as an American Indian village, animatronic animals, and frontier structures) on the leg between Frontierland and Fantasyland. If you're in Frontierland and headed out of the park, it's a nice way to end your visit.

As a transportation method, the railroad is more effective in saving your feet than saving time. That is, it's probably faster to walk anywhere within the park, but the train is useful if you're just plain worn out. Parents, for example, who find themselves at the far end of Fantasyland when it's time to go home, should hop on the train at the Fantasyland station and ride to Main Street, where they can exit the park immediately after exiting the station. Note that Disney strollers aren't allowed on the train (although folding strollers are fine). Take your name card and receipt with you, and a new one will be issued at your destination. Finally, note that the railroad shuts down immediately before and during parades.

ADVENTURELAND

Adventureland in Walt Disney World's Magic Kingdom was essentially a cloned version of the same theme area and attractions at Disneyland. The Disneyland version was originally conceived as a zoological section of the park based on Disney's nature documentaries on Asia and Africa. However, when zoologists explained that the real animals would pretty much laze around or hide, the Imagineers launched a new cottage industry, cranking out mechanical animals and, later, Audio-Animatronic ones. Adventureland at Walt Disney World is larger than that of Disneyland and is divided into four subareas: the entrance with an African/jungle feel, an Arabian village, a Polynesian area centered on *Walt Disney's Enchanted Tiki Room*, and Caribbean Plaza, where the Pirates of the Caribbean attraction is situated.

It's also the home of the Dole Whip, a pineapple and soft-serve ice cream treat that is, by itself, proof that American civilization was still advancing in the last years of the 20th century.

DISNEY DESIGN *with Sam Gennawey*

The Imagineers make the transition from Main Street's small-town America to Adventureland's jungles of your imagination by using the vocabulary of Victorian architecture, the dominant style in America of the time period represented by Main Street as well as 19th-century British Colonial rule. The Crystal Palace, located at the end of Main Street, is the visual bridge to Adventureland and is modeled after historical Victorian buildings, including New York's Crystal Palace, San Francisco's Conservatory of Flowers, and England's Royal Botanic Gardens.

Adventureland's main pathway winds past the Victorian-era Swiss Family Treehouse and eventually opens onto an Arabian bazaar containing the Magic Carpets of Aladdin. This attraction adds a strong center to the area and helps to orient you. The Jungle Cruise is below you to the left, and Spanish Main beckons just ahead.

The plaza in front of Pirates of the Caribbean is a traditional element of towns created during the great age of Spanish exploration. The buildings on your left reflect the Spanish architectural style found throughout the Caribbean. On your right, the Imagineers reinterpret the same architectural vocabulary as Spanish-influenced buildings typical of the American Southwest circa 1850. This creates the equivalent of a filmmaker's cross-dissolve transition from the jungles of Adventureland to the deserts of the American frontier West without creating any visual contradictions to spoil your journey.

© Mona Collentine (inset)

CAPTAIN JACK SPARROW'S PIRATE TUTORIAL ★★★½

APPEAL BY AGE			
	Preschool ★★★★½	Grade School ★★★★½	Teens ★★★½
	Young Adults ★★★½	Over 30 ★★★½	Seniors ★★★

What it is **Outdoor stage show with guest participation.** Scope and scale **Diversion.** When to go **See *Times Guide* for show schedule.** Authors' rating **Sign us up; ★★★½.** Duration **About 20 minutes.**

Outside Pirates of the Caribbean, Cap'n Jack and a crew member teach would-be knaves and scoundrels the basics of a career in politics. Or maybe it's a career in piracy—it was a little hard to hear from the back row, and let's face it, the skills are the same. Some kids go on stage to train in the finer points of dueling. The show finishes with everyone taking a pirate's oath of questionable legal validity and singing a rousing round of "A Pirate's Life for Me." The shows attract decent crowds, but the first and last show seem to be the least popular.

JUNGLE CRUISE (FASTPASS+) ★★★½

! APPEAL BY AGE Preschool ★★★★ | Grade School ★★★★ | Teens ★★★½ | Young Adults ★★★★ | Over 30 ★★★★ | Seniors ★★★★

What it is **Outdoor safari-themed boat-ride adventure.** Scope and scale **Major attraction.** When to go **Before 10:30 a.m., during the last 2 hours before closing, or use FastPass+.** Comment **Fun to ride at night!** Authors' rating **A Disney classic; ★★★½.** Duration **8–9 minutes.** Average wait in line per 100 people ahead of you **3½ minutes; assumes 10 boats operating.** Loading speed **Moderate.**

Forget that the animals aren't real and the boat is tethered to a track. The genius of the Jungle Cruise is that every square inch of the ride is filled with humor. Corny jokes and puns abound, from the radio banter playing in the queue's background to the stand-up comedians who double as your boat skippers. Regarding the skippers, no two have the same script, and the best way to experience the attraction is to go along with your captain's gags, even if the jokes are older than they are. The nearby Skipper Canteen restaurant serves food with the same kind of humor.

Duck!

MAGIC CARPETS OF ALADDIN (FASTPASS+) ★★½

APPEAL BY AGE			
	Preschool ★★★★½	Grade School ★★★★	Teens ★★★½
	Young Adults ★★★½	Over 30 ★★★	Seniors ★★★½

What it is Elaborate midway ride. Scope and scale Minor attraction. When to go Before 11 a.m. or after 7 p.m. Authors' rating A visually appealing children's ride; ★★½. Duration 1½ minutes. Average wait in line per 100 people ahead of you 16 minutes. Loading speed Slow.

Magic Carpets is similar to Fantasyland's Dumbo, except you ride a carpet instead of an elephant. Its one different feature is that Magic Carpets features a water-spitting camel, which soaks unsuspecting riders and passersby. As with Dumbo, you have some control over the ride: those who sit up front control the carpet's height, while those in the back control tilt. Kids sitting up front naturally try to get everyone wet. It's their job.

SWISS FAMILY TREEHOUSE ★★★

APPEAL BY AGE			
	Preschool ★★★½	Grade School ★★★½	Teens ★★★
	Young Adults ★★★½	Over 30 ★★★½	Seniors ★★★

What it is Outdoor walk-through tree house. Scope and scale Minor attraction. When to go Anytime. Comment Requires climbing a lot of stairs. Authors' rating Incredible detail and execution; ★★★. Duration 10–15 minutes. Average wait in line per 100 people ahead of you 7 minutes.

The hallmark of Adventureland's attractions is their attention to setting and detail. It would have been impressive enough if Disney had merely created this 60-foot-tall tree house and added the parts of the Robinson abode you see. (The waterwheel is particularly clever.) For us, the best part of the attraction is how the tree's limbs work with the rest of Adventureland's landscape to ensure that what you see is consistent with the house's tropical setting. Because you're far off the ground, it's possible to get a glimpse of Tomorrowland or beyond, but for the most part the tree guides your eye either inward to the family's rooms, or outside to the plant life or water features that surround the attraction. That's impressive work considering that the attraction was designed before the advent of computers, so Disney's architects had to imagine what the views would be from the upper reaches of the tree before the first branch was built.

PIRATES OF THE CARIBBEAN (FASTPASS+) ★★★★

APPEAL BY AGE			
	Preschool ★★★½	Grade School ★★★★	Teens ★★★★½
	Young Adults ★★★★½	Over 30 ★★★★½	Seniors ★★★★½

What it is **Indoor pirate-themed boat ride.** Scope and scale **Headliner.** When to go **Before 11 a.m., after 7 p.m., or use FastPass+.** Comment **Frightens some kids.** Authors' rating **Disney Audio-Animatronics at their best; not to be missed; ★★★★.** Duration **About 7½ minutes.** Average wait in line per 100 people ahead of you **1½ minutes; assumes both waiting lines operating.** Loading speed **Fast.**

If there's one attraction that you'd live in for the rest of your life, it has to be Pirates of the Caribbean. As Disney theme park blogger Greg Maletic observed, Pirates is one of the most influential theme park attractions of all time, and its elaborate queuing, grand scope, and storytelling set the standard by which subsequent theme park rides are judged. Plus, it's one of the first attractions to have a catchy song: "Yo Ho (A Pirate's Life for Me)."

The Pirates ride itself is a virtual crash course in Disney attraction design. The line guides you through an old Caribbean fort, complete with cannon defenses and jail cells holding the skeletons of captured pirates. The line ends at a small wood pier, where you board a boat and set sail. We won't spoil the story for you, but first-time riders should notice how the first set of scenes, which take place in a series of caves, transition the mood from sleepy backwater dock to cursed pirate treasure hunt.

One other thing we love about Pirates: it's one of the Magic Kingdom's most efficient attractions and can handle more than 2,000 guests per hour. Unless the park is packed like a sardine can, wait times should be low.

A PIRATE'S ADVENTURE: TREASURE OF THE SEVEN SEAS ★★★½

APPEAL BY AGE Preschool ★★★½ | Grade School ★★★★½ | Teens ★★★★ | Young Adults ★★★½ | Over 30 ★★★½ | Seniors ★★★★

What it is **Interactive game.** Scope and scale **Diversion.** When to go **Anytime.** Authors' rating **Simple, fast, and fun—especially at night; not to be missed; ★★★½.** Duration **About 25 minutes to play the entire game.** Probable waiting time **5 minutes or less.**

A Pirate's Adventure features interactive areas with physical props and narrations that lead guests on a quest to find lost treasure in Adventureland.

Guests begin their journey at an old Cartography Shop near Golden Oak Outpost. Groups of up to six people are given a talisman (a small card with a radio-frequency identification chip inside) to help them on their journey. The talisman activates a video screen that assigns your group to one of five different missions. Your group is then given a map and sent off to find your first location. Once at the location, touch the talisman to the symbol at the station, and the animation begins. Each adventure has four or five stops, and each stop contains 30–45 seconds of activity. No strategy or action is required: Watch what unfolds on the screen, get your next destination, and head off.

A Pirate's Adventure serves as a good introduction to other interactive games, such as Sorcerers of the Magic Kingdom (see p. 162). The effects are better at night.

WALT DISNEY'S ENCHANTED TIKI ROOM ★★★

APPEAL BY AGE Preschool ★★★½ | Grade School ★★★½ | Teens ★★★ | Young Adults ★★★ | Over 30 ★★★½ | Seniors ★★★★

What it is **Audio-Animatronic Pacific-island show.** Scope and scale **Minor attraction.** When to go **Before 11 a.m. or after 3:30 p.m.** Comment **Frightens some preschoolers.** Authors' rating **Very, very unusual; ★★★½.** Duration **15½ minutes.** Preshow **Talking birds.** Probable waiting time **15 minutes.**

If we didn't love *Tiki Room* so much, we'd be tempted to call it strange. Let's just say that it's quaint. One of the original Magic Kingdom attractions, *Enchanted Tiki Room* is a musical show that stars four mechanical male birds, accompanied by a flock of feathered females. Guests are seated in a thatched-roof tiki hut and surrounded by tropical foliage. Tiki statues and carvings cover most of the remaining space, and the entire room's furnishings come alive for the finale.

Tiki Room's appeal, however, isn't from the music or the now decades-old effects. Rather, it seems to come from the fact that around 40 years ago, someone decided that the best way to show off the then-new Audio-Animatronic technology was by building an elaborate Polynesian-themed attraction and populating it with a hundred miniature mechanical birds. At that time, the only folks thinking in that direction were Disney. The show here is a shortened version of the original attraction, which premiered at Disneyland in 1963.

FRONTIERLAND

It may be argued that Frontierland is the Magic Kingdom's best land. Themed to mimic the architecture of the American West, Frontierland includes two of the Magic Kingdom's headliner rides (Splash Mountain and Big Thunder Mountain Railroad), one of the Magic Kingdom's best spots to relax and unwind (Tom Sawyer Island), and some of the best spots for viewing the afternoon and evening parades.

DISNEY DESIGN *with Sam Gennawey*

Frontierland is designed to be a journey through time and distance, celebrating America's great westward expansion following the Louisiana Purchase. Frontierland's story begins where Liberty Square ends and takes you on a journey from St. Louis in the early 1840s to a ghost town after the gold rush boom in the 1880s. Each building moves you farther west through the use of different architectural styles and materials. In addition, the physical building addresses themselves are clues to the year many of the building facades were erected.

The first building in Frontierland is, appropriately, Liberty Square's Diamond Horseshoe, a grand show palace common in St. Louis in 1830, when St. Louis was known as the gateway to the American West.

Moving westward, time passes into the 1850s. Here we find a north woods union hall featuring the *Country Bear Jamboree*. Farther down, the Town Hall came in 1867, and Pecos Bill's saloon is dated 1878. The Frontier Trading Post is owned by "Texas" John Slaughter, a real-life person from the 1870s, as well as the subject of a Disney TV series in the late 1950s. Turning the corner, we come to Splash Mountain, set in the antebellum South.

The last stop on our westward journey is the little mining town of Big Thunder. The mountain is influenced by the peaks of Monument Valley, and the designers used forced perspective to make them seem larger.

Because our journey goes from east to west, it is appropriate that the last thing you see in Frontierland is the Walt Disney World Railroad train station. The Rivers of America and the *Liberty Belle* Riverboat are a symbolic link between Liberty Square and Frontierland, highlighting the importance of rivers and canals to the start of the American expansion. The railroad station, in contrast, represents the completion of the transcontinental railroad and the end to the great expansion.

There is one more design element unique to Frontierland: the use of multiple pathways to provide variety to your experience. You can walk along the raised wooden plank sidewalk along the building frontier facades, in the street with the great masses migrating "West," or along the boardwalk at the edge of Rivers of America to get a taste of the rural life. Not only does this provide a set of options for the guests, but it also creates huge capacity to move people without looking like a giant sidewalk.

FRONTIERLAND SHOOTIN' ARCADE ★½

! APPEAL BY AGE			
	Preschool ★★★½	Grade School ★★★½	Teens ★★★★½
	Young Adults ★★★★	Over 30 ★★★½	Seniors ★★★★

What it is **Electronic shooting gallery.** Scope and scale **Diversion.** When to go **Whenever convenient.** Comment **Costs $1 per play.** Authors' rating **Very nifty shooting gallery; ★½.**

Perhaps it's because the arcade is one of the few interactive experiences in the park, but there's something satisfying about hitting a target and sending it spinning. In the Frontierland Shootin' Arcade, your rifles shoot beams of light at targets about 10–30 feet away. The rifles are a bit heavy for smaller children, and even adults will need to rest their arms after a few rounds. Still, it's a hoot. Would-be gunslingers get about 30 shots per $1 play.

BIG THUNDER MOUNTAIN RAILROAD

(FASTPASS+) ★★★★

! APPEAL BY AGE	Preschool ★★★½	Grade School ★★★★½	Teens ★★★★½
	Young Adults ★★★★½	Over 30 ★★★★½	Seniors ★★★★

What it is Western mining–themed roller coaster. Scope and scale Headliner. When to go Before 10 a.m., the hour before closing, or use FastPass+. Comments 40" minimum height requirement; children younger than age 7 must ride with an adult; switching-off option (see p. 113). Authors' rating Great effects; relatively tame ride; not to be missed; ★★★★. Duration About 3½ minutes. Average wait in line per 100 people ahead of you 2½ minutes; assumes 5 trains operating. Loading speed Moderate–fast.

Big Thunder Mountain Railroad is a roller coaster through a decaying Western mining town. The queue winds through the upper part of the mine and offers a good look at the mountains and canyons you'll be screaming through. The effects are even better at night, when colored lights cast shadows on the jagged rocks and landscape and create a completely different ride dynamic. It's also

possible to see the Magic Kingdom's nighttime fireworks from Big Thunder, if you time it correctly.

If you're in the standby queue, try the interactive props: Spin a metal wheel and push on a dynamite plunger to trigger an "explosion" (of water, steam, or noise) near a passing train; watch "home movies" of the workers in the mines; see (and smell!) what some proverbial canaries experience underground; and more. These toys are spaced far enough apart for little kids to have something to do the entire time in line.

Many Disney rides feature a transition scene, which sets the story and mood for the ride as you depart from the ride's loading area. Big Thunder's version takes you inside a mountain cave, complete with stalactites and mineral-colored pools. At the top of the cave is the basis for a clever ride effect: a fissure in the cave ceiling mists water on you from above, just before you're launched down the mountain. Then as you're riding and the wind whips by, the mist on your skin evaporates. Besides cooling you off, the evaporation makes you feel as if you're going faster than you really are.

As roller coasters go, Big Thunder is a step beyond Seven Dwarfs Mine Train, yet tamer than Space Mountain. It's certainly less intimidating than many headliner coasters found at regional amusement parks around the country. Most of the ride takes place outside, so children can see much of the track before deciding whether to ride. If your kids handled Mine Train well, give Big Thunder a try.

Another day, another runaway industrial vehicle

COUNTRY BEAR JAMBOREE ★★★½

APPEAL BY AGE Preschool ★★★½ Grade School ★★★½ Teens ★★★ Young Adults ★★★ Over 30 ★★★ Seniors ★★★★

What it is **Audio-Animatronic country-hoedown theater show.** Scope and scale **Major attraction.** When to go **Anytime.** Authors' rating **Old and worn but pure Disney; ★★★½.** Duration **11 minutes.** Probable waiting time **It's not terribly popular but has a comparatively small capacity. Waiting time between noon and 5:30 p.m. on a busy day will average 11–22 minutes.**

Country Bear Jamboree is a country-music themed variety show featuring animatronic singing bears. It's roughly the equivalent of Adventureland's *Enchanted Tiki Room*, with bears and country music instead of birds and Hawaiian songs. *Country Bear* has had its songs trimmed and sped up, as a concession to modern, short attention spans . . . Squirrel! However, many readers think the *Bear* show has passed from charming and quaint to stale. It's still a good attraction when you're trying to get out of the midday sun or when your feet need a break, and the waits are usually short.

TOM SAWYER ISLAND AND FORT LANGHORN ★★★

APPEAL BY AGE Preschool ★★★★ Grade School ★★★★½ Teens ★★★★ Young Adults ★★★½ Over 30 ★★★½ Seniors ★★★

What it is **Outdoor walk-through exhibit/playground.** Scope and scale **Minor attraction.** When to go **Midmorning–late afternoon.** Comment **Closes at dusk.** Authors' rating **The place for rowdy kids; ★★★.**

Tom Sawyer Island isn't one of the Magic Kingdom's more celebrated attractions, but it's one of the park's better conceived ones. Attention to detail is excellent, and the island is bigger than you might think. While the windmill is visible from almost all of Frontierland, the island hides a cave, climbing hills, barrel bridges, and children's play areas, as well as a replica pioneer fort (Fort Langhorn). It's a delight for adults and a godsend for children who have been in tow and closely supervised all day.

Fantasyland Jury

SPLASH MOUNTAIN (FASTPASS+) ★★★★★

APPEAL BY AGE

Preschool ★★★★†	Grade School ★★★★½	Teens ★★★★½
Young Adults ★★★★½	Over 30 ★★★★½	Seniors ★★★★½

† Many preschoolers are too short to ride, and others are intimidated when they see the attraction from the waiting line. Among preschoolers who actually ride, most give it high marks.

What it is **Indoor/outdoor water-flume adventure ride.** Scope and scale **Super-headliner.** When to go **As soon as the park opens, during afternoon or evening parades, just before closing, or use FastPass+.** Comments **40" minimum height requirement; children younger than age 7 must ride with an adult; switching-off option** **(see p. 113).** Authors' rating **A soggy delight, and not to be missed; ★★★★★.** Duration **About 10 minutes.** Average wait in line per 100 people ahead of you **3½ minutes; assumes ride is operating at full capacity.** Loading speed **Moderate.**

© Stefan Zwanzger/thethemeparkguy.com

The view from the top of Splash Mountain

One of the *Guide*'s authors (Len) thinks Splash Mountain is the best attraction in Walt Disney World. Writes Len: "The best Disney attractions combine five key traits: a grand scope or scale, attention to detail, a dynamic element that rewards repeated visits, the right amount of thrills for the family, and a ride long enough to justify the wait in line." Splash Mountain succeeds on every count. In terms of scope and scale, Splash is among Disney's largest and longest rides, covering more than half a mile and including swamps, caves, and briar patches. There's plenty of detail too—from the story of how Bre'r Rabbit leaves home to the grand showboat scene in his triumphant return. An especially nice touch is in an underground cave

Dad's "See no water, feel no water" theory fails its big test.

scene, where water jumps from geyser to geyser just in front of your ride vehicle. And there are plenty of hidden Mickeys to be found along the way.

Also, because your journey takes place in a waterborne log, each ride is slightly different, depending on the weight of passengers with you, speed of current, and a dozen other variables. The result is that you'll end up somewhere between slightly damp and completely soaked, with riders at the front of the log generally getting wetter.

Splash Mountain contains a couple of long drops, but don't let the view from outside the ride intimidate you or your kids—even the big drop is mild by any thrill ride standard, and many families report that Splash is their kindergartner's favorite attraction. Finally, Splash lasts anywhere from 10 to 12 minutes—an impressive amount of time for any thrill ride and an ample reward for most waits in line. It's hard to find a better theme park ride anywhere.

LIBERTY SQUARE

Liberty Square re-creates America at the time of the Revolutionary War. The architecture is Federal or Colonial and provides a seamless transition from the edge of Fantasyland to Frontierland. A real 130-year-old live oak, the Liberty Tree, lends dignity and grace to the setting.

DISNEY DESIGN *with Sam Gennawey*

Despite being one of the smallest lands in any Disney park, Liberty Square required an unusual level of detail because it reflects the qualities of places that really exist and are accessible to many of Disney World's visitors. The challenge for the design team was to create, in the Imagineers' words, an "enhanced reality" that is "better than real."

Just like Frontierland, the use of architectural details provides the clues for our trip through time and geography. For Liberty Square, our trip begins in New York along the banks of the Hudson River in the early 1700s, where The Haunted Mansion is based on the Gothic architecture used in the New York region when it was known as Dutch New Amsterdam. The nearby Columbia Harbour House would feel right at home in the port city of Boston in the mid-1700s. Traveling south, the buildings begin to take on the Georgian style popular in Williamsburg during the late 1700s. *The Hall of Presidents* is modeled after buildings in Philadelphia at the time of the Constitution's adoption in 1787. Liberty Square ends at the edge of the American frontier with The Diamond Horseshoe, which could have been in St. Louis during the 1830s. The westward expansion continues in Frontierland.

THE HALL OF PRESIDENTS ★★★½

! APPEAL BY AGE			
	Preschool ★★½	Grade School ★★★	Teens ★★★½
	Young Adults ★★★½	Over 30 ★★★★	Seniors ★★★★½

What it is Audio-Animatronic historical theater presentation. Scope and scale Major attraction. When to go Anytime. Authors' rating Impressive and moving; ★★★½. Duration Almost 23 minutes. Probable waiting time The lines for this attraction look intimidating, but they're usually swallowed up as the theater exchanges audiences. It would be exceptionally unusual not to be admitted to the next show.

© Disney

The Hall of Presidents combines a wide-screen theater presentation of the highlights and milestones in the United States' political history, with a short stage show, including life-size animatronic replicas of every US president. Morgan Freeman provides most of the narration, and additional speeches feature the words of George Washington, Abraham Lincoln, and Barack Obama.

The roll call of presidents, in which the name of every man ever to hold the office is read in the order in which he served, has long been an opportunity to boo or cheer the recent occupants of the White House. We encourage you to take this one step further by catcalling more of the earlier presidents. For example, it's time to jeer William Howard Taft's support of the Sixteenth Amendment (the income tax). We expect the new US president to be introduced in 2017, shutting down the attraction briefly while the new animatronic is added.

LIBERTY BELLE RIVERBOAT ★★½

! APPEAL BY AGE			
	Preschool ★★★½	Grade School ★★★½	Teens ★★★
	Young Adults ★★★½	Over 30 ★★★½	Seniors ★★★★

What it is Outdoor scenic boat ride. Scope and scale Major attraction. When to go Anytime. Authors' rating Slow, relaxing, and scenic; ★★½. Duration About 16 minutes. Average wait to board 10–14 minutes.

The *Liberty Belle* is a massive paddle wheel riverboat that takes passengers on a spin around Tom Sawyer Island and Fort Langhorn, passing settler cabins, old mining paraphernalia, a Plains Indian village, and some animatronic wildlife. It's not the fastest way around, and during summer it can be hot and humid. It's better at dusk, however, and the upper deck offers some especially good views of Liberty Square and Frontierland.

THE HAUNTED MANSION (FASTPASS+) ★★★★½

APPEAL BY AGE Preschool ★★★½ | Grade School ★★★★ | Teens ★★★★½ | Young Adults ★★★★½ | Over 30 ★★★★½ | Seniors ★★★★½

What it is **Haunted-house dark ride.** Scope and scale **Major attraction.** When to go **Before 11 a.m. or during the last 2 hours before closing.** Comment **Frightens some very young children.** Authors' rating **A masterpiece of detail and not to be missed; ★★★★½.** Duration **7-minute ride plus a 1½-minute preshow.** Average wait in line per 100 people ahead of you **2½ minutes; assumes both "stretch rooms" operating.** Loading speed **Fast.**

Although its roots are in the haunted houses of small amusement parks everywhere, Disney's version is done on a scale big enough to justify use of the word *mansion*. The Haunted Mansion is a masterpiece of detail, starting with the gravestones lining the lawn next to the exterior waiting area and extending into the wallpaper and paintings in preshow areas. Even the cast members get into the act as they gravely announce, "Your time has come," to enter the ride, and exhort you to move to the "dead center" of the foyer to begin the show.

The mansion is filled with room after room of visual effects, most of which are no more threatening than a whoopee cushion. Only the graveyard scene, which features a handful of skulls popping up from behind tombstones, might be considered

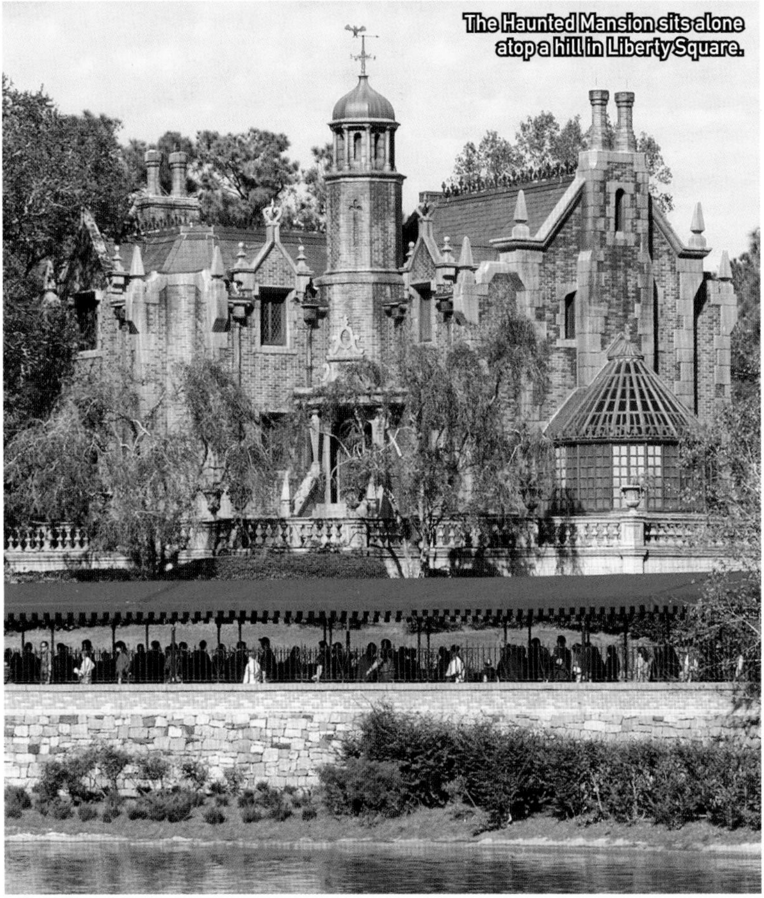

The Haunted Mansion sits alone atop a hill in Liberty Square.

© Stefan Zwanzger/thethemeparkguy.com

mildly scary. Other scenes include a room with stairs running every which way and a ballroom dancing scene that ranks among Disney's best (and oldest) effects. As with Disney's other classic attractions, The Haunted Mansion also features a catchy sound track ("Grim Grinning Ghosts") that will keep you humming on your way to the next attraction. Guests with registered MagicBands should pay close attention to the final "and a ghost will follow you home" scene; personalized messages often appear.

The standby waiting queue for Mansion has interactive elements that make noise and music when touched.

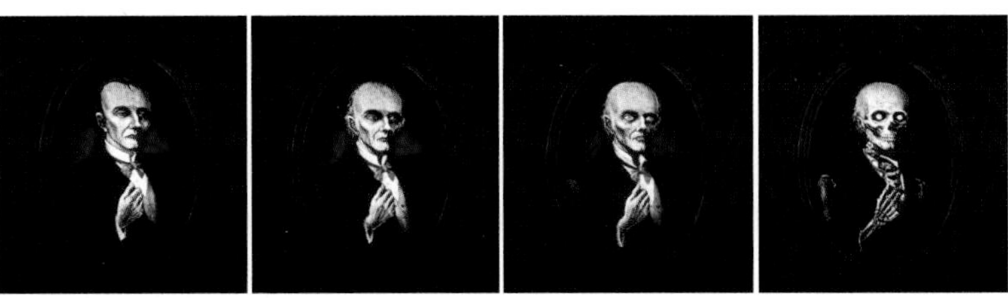

FANTASYLAND

Fantasyland is the center of the action in most Disney theme parks, both literally (in terms of crowds) and figuratively (in terms of theming and storytelling). Walt Disney World's version is modeled after an alpine village tucked behind the steepled towers of Cinderella Castle.

DISNEY DESIGN *with Sam Gennawey*

The largest land expansion in the Magic Kingdom's history was completed in 2014 with the opening of New Fantasyland. The construction added two large sections to the Fantasyland area of the park. First, directly behind Cinderella Castle is a snow-capped mountain and Beast's Castle, part of a *Beauty and the Beast*–themed area. Most of this section holds dining opportunities (Be Our Guest, see page 210, and Gaston's Tavern, see page 211), a gift shop, and the *Enchanted Tales with Belle* meet and greet. The second expanded area is at the far right corner of Fantasyland (much of which was previously occupied by the now-defunct Mickey's Toontown), themed as a small circus and called, not surprisingly, Storybook Circus. The circus theme is an homage to Disney's *Dumbo* film. Storybook Circus includes the Dumbo ride, a children's roller coaster called The Barnstormer, a themed water-play area, gift shops, and character meet and greets. The middle of Fantasyland territory holds the headliner attractions, including Under the Sea and Seven Dwarfs Mine Train. The placement of these two attractions allows good traffic flow either to the left (toward Beast's Castle) for dining, to the right for the circus area aimed at younger children, or back to the original area of Fantasyland with its classic rides, such as Peter Pan's Flight and The Many Adventures of Winnie the Pooh. The central part of Fantasyland also hosts the popular Princess Fairytale Hall meet and greet. Finally, when nature calls, don't miss the *Tangled*-themed restrooms located near It's a Small World.

ARIEL'S GROTTO (FASTPASS+) ★★★

APPEAL BY AGE Preschool ★★★★½ | Grade School ★★★★½ | Teens ★★★★ | Young Adults ★★★★ | Over 30 ★★★½ | Seniors ★★★★

What it is **Character-greeting venue.** Scope and scale **Minor attraction.** When to go **Before 10:30 a.m., during the last 2 hours before closing, or use FastPass+.** Authors' rating **★★★.** Duration **About 30–90 seconds.** Probable waiting time **45 minutes.**

This is Ariel's home base, next to the Under the Sea: Journey of the Little Mermaid ride. In the base of the seaside cliffs under Prince Eric's Castle, Ariel (in mermaid form) greets guests from a seashell throne. The queue isn't as detailed as other character-greeting venues in the park, and it can get hot. Try visiting after dinner if time permits. The Grotto may close an hour before the rest of the park.

THE BARNSTORMER (FASTPASS+) ★★

APPEAL BY AGE	Preschool ★★★★	Grade School ★★★★	Teens ★★★½
	Young Adults ★★★	Over 30 ★★★	Seniors ★★★½

What it is Small roller coaster. Scope and scale Minor attraction. When to go Before 11 a.m., during parades, or during the last 2 hours before closing; not a good use of FastPass+. Comment 35" minimum height requirement. Authors' rating Great for little ones but not worth the wait for adults; ★★. Duration About 53 seconds. Average wait in line per 100 people ahead of you 7 minutes. Loading speed Slow.

© Curtis Lannom

The Barnstormer is a very small roller coaster. The ride is zippy but super-short. In fact, of the 53 seconds the ride is in motion, 32 seconds are consumed in leaving the loading area, being ratcheted up the first hill, and braking into the off-loading area. Actual time spent careening around the track is 21 seconds. The Barnstormer is a fairly benign introduction to the roller coaster genre and a predictably positive way to help your children step up to more adventuresome rides. If your child does well on The Barnstormer, try the Seven Dwarfs Mine Train next.

CASEY JR. SPLASH 'N' SOAK STATION ★★★

APPEAL BY AGE	Preschool ★★★★½	Grade School ★★★★	Teens ★★★
	Young Adults ★★½	Over 30 ★★½	Seniors ★★★

What it is Opportunity to get wet. Scope and scale Diversion. When to go When it's hot. Authors' rating Great way to cool off; ★★★.

Casey Jr., the circus train from the film *Dumbo*, hosts an absolutely drenching experience in the Storybook Circus area next to the Fantasyland Train Station. In warm weather, captive circus beasts spray water on passersby in this elaborate water-play area. If your children need a break from waiting in lines, this is a great place to cool off, physically and emotionally. Bring a change of clothes and a big towel.

Disney security places a guest in time out.

DUMBO THE FLYING ELEPHANT (FASTPASS+) ★★★½

! APPEAL BY AGE			
	Preschool ★★★★½	Grade School ★★★★	Teens ★★★
	Young Adults ★★★½	Over 30 ★★★½	Seniors ★★★½

What it is **Disney-fied midway ride.** Scope and scale **Minor attraction.** When to go **Before 11 a.m. or after 6 p.m.; not a good use of FastPass+.** Authors' rating **Disney's signature ride for children; ★★★½.** Duration **1½ minutes.** Average wait in line per 100 people ahead of you **5 minutes.** Loading speed **Slow.**

A tame, happy children's ride based on the lovable flying elephant Dumbo. Parents and children sit inside small fiberglass "elephants" mounted on long metal arms, which spin around a central axis. Despite being little different from rides at state fairs and amusement parks, Dumbo is the favorite Magic Kingdom attraction of many younger children.

As part of the Fantasyland expansion, Dumbo moved to the upper-right corner of the land. The attraction's capacity doubled with the addition of a second ride—a clone of the first. These two changes, along with the addition of the newer Fantasyland attractions, have drastically reduced waits to ride. If you do find yourself with a wait, Dumbo also includes a covered queue featuring interactive elements (read: things your kids can play with to pass the time in line).

If Dumbo is essential to your child's happiness, ride within the first 2 hours the park is open. Or try Dumbo following the afternoon parade. Not only are crowds smaller, but the lighting and effects make the ride much prettier at night. With increased capacity and a remote location moderating its lines, Dumbo is rarely a good choice for FastPass+.

ENCHANTED TALES WITH BELLE

(FASTPASS+) ★★★★

! APPEAL BY AGE	Preschool ★★★★½	Grade School ★★★★½	Teens ★★★½
	Young Adults ★★★½	Over 30 ★★★★	Seniors ★★★★

What it is **Interactive character show.** Scope and scale **Minor attraction.** When to go **As soon as the park opens, during the last 2 hours before closing, or use FastPass+.** Authors' rating **The prettiest meet and greet in the park; ★★★★.** Duration **About 20 minutes.** Probable waiting time **25 minutes.**

This multiscene *Beauty and the Beast* experience takes guests into Maurice's workshop, through a magic mirror, and into Beast's library, where the audience shares a story with Belle. You enter the attraction through Maurice's cottage, where you see mementos tracing Belle's childhood. From there, you'll enter Maurice's workshop for a short tour. The workshop's magic mirror turns into a full-size doorway, through which guests enter into a wardrobe room. The attraction's premise is explained there: you're supposed to reenact the story of *Beauty and the Beast* for Belle on her birthday, and some guests are chosen to act in the play. There are generally enough parts for everyone who really wants one.

Once the parts are cast, everyone walks into the castle's library. Cast members explain how the play will take place and introduce Belle, who's (of course) thrilled to see everyone. The play is acted out within a few minutes, and all of the actors get a chance to take photos with Belle and receive a small bookmark as a memento.

Enchanted Tales with Belle is the prettiest and most elaborate meet and greet station in Walt Disney World. For those who perform in the play, it's also a chance to interact with Belle in a way that's different from other character encounters. Sure, it can be a 30-minute wait for a 3-minute play, but your kids will love it.

IT'S A SMALL WORLD (FASTPASS+) ★★★½

! APPEAL BY AGE			
	Preschool ★★★★½	Grade School ★★★★	Teens ★★★
	Young Adults ★★★	Over 30 ★★★½	Seniors ★★★★

What it is **World-brotherhood-themed indoor boat ride.** Scope and scale **Major attraction.** When to go **Before 11 a.m., during parades, or after 7 p.m.; FastPass+ is unnecessary.** Authors' rating **Exponentially cute; ★★★½.** Duration **Approximately 11 minutes.** Average wait in line per 100 people ahead of you **3½ minutes; assumes busy conditions with 30 or more boats operating.** Loading speed **Fast.**

One of Disney's oldest entertainment offerings, It's a Small World first unleashed its brainwashing song and lethally cute ethnic dolls on the real world at the 1964 New York World's Fair. Though it bludgeons you with its sappy redundancy, almost everyone enjoys the ride (at least the first time).

However, It's a Small World is one of the rides most frequently maligned by critics of Disney theme parks and American culture. Truth be told (and we're not exactly strangers to those aforementioned groups), the ride gets a bum rap mainly because it's an easy target. Yes, the Walt Disney World version plays second fiddle to the original Disneyland attraction, which is larger and features Mary Blair's iconic design. Yes, the imagery and message are trite, with your boat gliding past Hawaiian dancers predictably doing the hula, accompanied by the song's "wouldn't it be great if we all just got along" lyrics (of course, sung by small children).

All of that said, however, we're not sure that we could have come up with a better attraction given the scope, cost, and schedule constraints that Disney's Imagineers were surely under when the ride was built. While we like to think we would have gone with some sort of highbrow concept, our initial reaction to the first budget cut or schedule delay would have been to yell at the intern, "You know what Peru's all about? Llamas. Get me some llamas!"

Note: If you've registered your MagicBand, have your camera ready to grab a shot of a personalized good-bye just prior to the exit area.

© Disney

MAD TEA PARTY (FASTPASS+) ★★

! APPEAL BY AGE Preschool ★★★★½ Grade School ★★★★ Teens ★★★★
Young Adults ★★★½ Over 30 ★★★½ Seniors ★★★½

What it is **Midway-type spinning ride.** Scope and scale **Minor attraction.** When to go **Before 11 a.m. or after 5 p.m.; not a good use of FastPass+.** Comment **Turn the wheel in the center of the cup to make the teacups spin faster.** Authors' rating **Fun but not worth the wait; ★★.** Duration **1½ minutes.** Average wait in line per 100 people ahead of you **7½ minutes.** Loading speed **Slow.**

It looks so cute—oversize teacups! Inside every extra-large teacup, however, is a "metal wheel of death." OK, not death in the literal sense, but the *Guide*'s marketing reps note that "metal wheel of gastrointestinal discomfort" isn't as catchy. And our lawyers say the aesthetics justify the hyperbole.

The faster you spin the metal wheel, the faster your teacup spins about its central axis. And while your cup is spinning around its central axis, it's also spinning in a larger circle with two other cups. And all of the cups are spinning on one giant orbit around the middle of the ride. It's circles within circles within circles. Needless to say, the row of green hedges you see around the outside of the ride while you're waiting in line are there for you to vomit in afterward, without having to get janitors to clean it up. We write from experience. Sad, sad experience. Whatever you do, don't go on this ride with anyone to whom you've helped give birth.

© Steve Burns/Burnsland.com

THE MANY ADVENTURES OF WINNIE THE POOH (FASTPASS+) ★★★½

APPEAL BY AGE Preschool ★★★★½ | Grade School ★★★★ | Teens ★★★½ | Young Adults ★★★½ | Over 30 ★★★½ | Seniors ★★★★

What it is **Indoor track ride.** Scope and scale **Minor attraction.** When to go **Before 10 a.m., in the last hour before closing, or use FastPass+.** Authors' rating **Cute as the Pooh Bear himself; ★★★½.** Duration **About 4 minutes.** Average wait in line per 100 people ahead of you **4 minutes.** Loading speed **Moderate.**

Tigger tails are made for bouncing!

© MrChrisCornwell/Matt Shirky

Pooh is mostly sunny, upbeat, and charming without being saccharine. You ride a Hunny Pot through the pages of a huge picture book into the Hundred Acre Wood, where you encounter Pooh, Piglet, Eeyore, Owl, Rabbit, Tigger, Kanga, and Roo as they contend with a blustery day. Small children may be frightened by one short part of the ride, which contains dramatic lighting, Pooh talking in a worried tone, and an appearance by Heffalumps and Woozles. It all ends well, however, with the gang joining together for a big party. Pooh is a great way to assess how your youngest children react to dark rides.

MEET MERIDA AT FAIRYTALE GARDEN ★★★½

APPEAL BY AGE Preschool ★★★★★ | Grade School ★★★★½ | Teens ★★★½ | Young Adults ★★★½ | Over 30 ★★★½ | Seniors ★★★

What it is **Storytelling session and character meet and greet.** Scope and scale **Diversion.** When to go **See *Times Guide* for schedule.** Authors' rating **Lovely lass, lovely locale; ★★★½.** Duration **About 10 minutes.** Probable waiting time **1 hour or more.**

Merida, the flame-haired Scottish princess from *Brave,* greets guests in Fairytale Garden, on the Tomorrowland side of Cinderella Castle. In addition to meeting Merida, you can learn some kid-friendly archery or color pictures of scenes from the movie. It's a shady, relaxing respite from the bustle of the park.

Princess meet and greets tend to be quite popular, so expect long lines. If meeting Merida is a must-do for your family, get in line early in the morning.

MICKEY'S PHILHARMAGIC (FASTPASS+) ★★★★

APPEAL BY AGE Preschool ★★★★ Grade School ★★★★½ Teens ★★★★ Young Adults ★★★★½ Over 30 ★★★★½ Seniors ★★★★½

What it is 3-D movie. Scope and scale Major attraction. When to go Before 11 a.m. or during parades; FastPass+ is unnecessary. Authors' rating A zany masterpiece; not to be missed; ★★★★. Duration About 12 minutes. Probable waiting time 12–30 minutes.

The best of Disney World's 3-D movies, *Mickey's PhilharMagic* tells the tale of Donald Duck frantically trying to find Mickey Mouse's orchestra conductor's hat after losing it in a self-inflicted (what else?) tornado of time and space. Disney film buffs will recognize that the premise owes a lot to the 1935 Mickey Mouse short *The Band Concert*.

In *PhilharMagic*, Donald Duck whips through scenes from many of Disney's pre-Pixar animated films, including *The Little Mermaid*, *Beauty and the Beast*, and *The Lion King*, in a wide-angle 3-D presentation that is remarkably well done, both in terms of visual appeal and sound track. If you have small children and own these movies, you'll catch yourself singing along with the score, possibly at near operatic levels. Don't worry—everyone else is either singing along or watching the movie. In addition to sight and sound, there's something for your senses of smell and touch too.

PETER PAN'S FLIGHT (FASTPASS+) ★★★★

! APPEAL BY AGE			
	Preschool ★★★★½	Grade School ★★★★	Teens ★★★½
	Young Adults ★★★★	Over 30 ★★★★	Seniors ★★★★

What it is Indoor track ride. Scope and scale Minor attraction. When to go First or last 30 minutes the park is open, or use FastPass+. Authors' rating Nostalgic, mellow, and well done; ★★★★. Duration A little over 3 minutes. Average wait in line per 100 people ahead of you 5½ minutes. Loading speed Moderate–slow.

Peter Pan's Flight is the best of Fantasyland's midway-style attractions. It's superbly designed and absolutely delightful, with a happy theme uniting some favorite Disney characters, beautiful effects, and charming music. Peter Pan's Flight launches you into the London night sky onboard a miniature pirate ship suspended from a rail in the ceiling. Perhaps because you're up high, many of the effects had to be three-dimensional, rather than the painted flat panels you'll find in other Fantasyland attractions. Other neat tricks include simulated moving cars on the London streets (courtesy of a bicycle chain dotted with luminescent paint) and a neat fly-by of some imaginative mountain ranges. Unlike some dark rides, there's nothing here that will jump out at you or frighten young children. Peter Pan is one of the best FastPass+ choices in the Magic Kingdom. If you're unable to get a FP+, the standby queue is worth seeing (if the wait isn't too long). There's interactive art, and you can play games with Peter's shadow.

PETE'S SILLY SIDESHOW (FASTPASS+) ★★★½

APPEAL BY AGE Preschool ★★★★½ Grade School ★★★★½ Teens ★★★½ Young Adults ★★★★ Over 30 ★★★★ Seniors ★★★★½

What it is Character-greeting venue. Scope and scale Minor attraction. When to go Before 11 a.m. or during the last 2 hours before closing; not a good use of FastPass+. Authors' rating Well themed with unique character costumes; ★★★½. Duration 7 minutes per character. Probable waiting time 25 minutes.

© Daniel M. Brace

Pete's Silly Sideshow is a circus-themed character-greeting area in the Storybook Circus part of Fantasyland. The characters' costumes are distinct from the ones normally used around the parks. Characters include Goofy as The Great Goofini, Donald Duck as The Astounding Donaldo, Daisy Duck as Madame Daisy Fortuna, and Minnie Mouse as Minnie Magnifique. The queue is indoors and air-conditioned. There's one queue for Goofy and Donald and a second queue for Minnie and Daisy; you can meet two characters at once, but you have to line up twice to meet all four.

PRINCE CHARMING REGAL CARROUSEL ★★★

APPEAL BY AGE Preschool ★★★★½ Grade School ★★★★ Teens ★★★½ Young Adults ★★★½ Over 30 ★★★½ Seniors ★★★½

What it is Merry-go-round. Scope and scale Minor attraction. When to go Anytime. Comment Adults enjoy the beauty and nostalgia of this ride. Authors' rating A beautiful ride for children; ★★★. Duration About 2 minutes. Average wait in line per 100 people ahead of you 5 minutes. Loading speed Slow.

You'll have a long wait, but the beauty of the carousel (formerly known as Cinderella's Golden Carrousel) captures everyone. The carousel, built in 1917, was discovered in New Jersey, where it was once part of an amusement park. It is one of the most elaborate and beautiful merry-go-rounds you'll ever have the pleasure of seeing, especially when its lights are on. However, unless young children in your party insist on riding, appreciate this attraction from the sidelines. While lovely to look at, the carousel loads and unloads very slowly.

But consider this from a shy 9-year-old girl from Rockaway, New Jersey, who thinks our rating of the carousel should be higher:

> **I want to complain. I went on the Prince Charming Regal Carrousel four times, and I loved it! Raise those stars right now!**

PRINCESS FAIRYTALE HALL (FASTPASS+) ★★★

! APPEAL BY AGE	Preschool ★★★★	Grade School ★★★★	Teens ★★★
	Young Adults ★★½	Over 30 ★★★	Seniors ★★½

What it is **Character-greeting venue.** Scope and scale **Minor attraction.** When to go **Before 10:30 a.m., after 4 p.m., or use FastPass+.** Authors' rating **You want princesses? We got 'em! ★★★.** Duration **7–10 minutes.** Average wait in line per 100 people ahead of you **35 minutes.**

Princess Fairytale Hall is royalty central in the Magic Kingdom. Inside are two greeting venues, with each holding a small reception area for two royals. Thus, there are four royals meeting and greeting at any time, and you can see two of them at once. Signs outside the entrance tell you which line leads to which royal pair and how long the wait will be. Rapunzel leads one side and Cinderella the other. They each meet with a visiting princess, such as Aurora or Tiana. There's plenty of time for small talk, a photo, and a hug from each princess.

For the past few years, Anna and Elsa met here and were one of the hottest tickets in the World. With the Arendelle royalty now at the Norway Pavilion in Epcot (see page 243), Princess Fairytale Hall has much more reasonable waits. If you have a princess-obsessed child (or adult, no judgment), we still recommend FastPass+ reservations, however, as the line may still be substantial.

SEVEN DWARFS MINE TRAIN (FASTPASS+) ★★★★

APPEAL BY AGE Preschool ★★★★ Grade School ★★★★½ Teens ★★★★ Young Adults ★★★★ Over 30 ★★★★ Seniors ★★★★

What it is A musical roller-coaster journey into the diamond mine of the Seven Dwarfs. Scope and scale Super-headliner. When to go As soon as the park opens or use FastPass+. Comment 38" minimum height requirement. Authors' rating Great family coaster; not to be missed; ★★★★. Duration About 3 minutes. Average wait in line per 100 people ahead of you About 4½ minutes. Loading speed Fast.

In the pantheon of Disney coasters, Seven Dwarfs Mine Train fits somewhere between The Barnstormer and Big Thunder Mountain Railroad—that is, it's geared to older grade-school kids who've been on amusement park rides before. There are no loops, inversions, or rolls in the track, and no massive hills or steep drops; rather, the Mine Train's trick is that your ride vehicle's seats swing side to side as you go through turns, and Disney has designed a curvy track with steep turns. The swinging effect is more noticeable the farther back you're seated in the train. Also, the train seats are a bit snug for larger folks. An elaborate indoor section shows the dwarfs' underground operation.

© Curtis Lannom

The exterior design includes waterfalls, forests, and landscaping and is meant to join together all of the surrounding Fantasyland's various locations, including France and Germany.

If you have only a day to see the Magic Kingdom, make FastPass+ reservations in advance for around 9:30 a.m. at Big Thunder Mountain Railroad and around 3:30 p.m. at Space Mountain. On the day of your visit, ride Seven Dwarfs Mine Train as soon as the park opens, and then hotfoot it to Splash Mountain to ride immediately. Your FastPass+ reservation for Big Thunder Mountain will be valid by the time you're done, and you'll have experienced three of the park's four headliners in about an hour.

UNDER THE SEA: JOURNEY OF THE LITTLE MERMAID (FASTPASS+) ★★★½

APPEAL BY AGE			
	Preschool ★★★★½	Grade School ★★★★	Teens ★★★½
	Young Adults ★★★★	Over 30 ★★★★	Seniors ★★★★

What it is **Dark ride retelling the film's story.** Scope and scale **Major attraction.** When to go **Before 10:30 a.m. or during the last 2 hours before closing; not a good use of FastPass+.** Authors' rating **Colorful, but most effects are too simple for an attraction this big; ★★★½.** Duration **About 5½ minutes.** Average wait in line per 100 people ahead of you **3 minutes.** Loading speed **Fast.**

Under the Sea takes riders through almost a dozen scenes retelling the story of *The Little Mermaid,* this time with Audio-Animatronics, video effects, and a vibrant 3-D set the size of a small theater.

Guests board a clamshell-shaped ride vehicle running along a continuously moving track (similar to The Haunted Mansion's). Then the ride "descends" under water, past Ariel's grotto, and on to King Triton's undersea kingdom. The most detailed animatronic is of Ursula, the octopus, and she's a beauty.

Other scenes hit the film's highlights, including Ariel meeting Prince Eric, her deal with Ursula to become human, and, of course, the couple's happy ending. The attraction's exterior is attractive, with detailed rockwork, water, and story elements. Because the ride can handle so many people per hour, Under the Sea is rarely a good choice for FastPass+.

TOMORROWLAND

Tomorrowland's original vision was to showcase how man had developed technology and what that technology might hold for the future. The problem was that technology developed faster than Disney could keep up, so Tomorrowland eventually became a walk-through of what the future might look like from Watergate-era designers—the same people who brought you polyester pants and puffy disco shirts.

In the mid-1990s, however, Disney took that "what the future might look like" idea and pushed it back a few more decades, changing Tomorrowland's theme to what artists of the late 1800s and early 1900s had envisioned for their future. The new Tomorrowland features lots of Buck Rogers–like mechanical rockets, with plenty of brass fittings and other metallic bits. Several attractions feature characters from recent Disney films too, and they've more or less been worked into the new theming.

DISNEY DESIGN *with Sam Gennawey*

One of the signature hallmarks of Tomorrowland is all of the vehicles moving about. Moving vehicles dominate the land at all levels. On the ground plain, constantly queuing up are the cars of the Speedway. Up one level are the PeopleMover trains, which continue throughout the land and become a thread that ties many of the Tomorrowland structures together. Flying high overhead are the Astro Orbiter rockets. And when the *Carousel of Progress* is spinning, even the buildings add to the movement. There is no other spot in the Magic Kingdom with such diversity of vehicles on display.

This movement is due to the original Tomorrowland, which lived until 1994. In the relatively brief history of the Magic Kingdom, only Tomorrowland has received a significant makeover. (Fantasyland, while much larger, has essentially the same theme as before.) What you see today is the Imagineers' solution to a longtime vexing problem. How do you create the world of tomorrow when tomorrow happens so fast? What happens when the design and construction process takes so long that by the time the project is done, it isn't relevant anymore?

The first Tomorrowland, in Disneyland in 1955, was set in 1986, the return year for Haley's Comet. It was updated in 1967 to no specific date, but the place was the "world on the move." The Magic Kingdom's Tomorrowland 1.0 was the next generation of that concept. But 20 years later the "world on the move" was looking dated.

So the solution in 1994 was to rethink the entire question. Instead of projecting a place set into the future, why not just create a fantasy place influenced by visions of the future? The Imagineers decided to borrow elements from Disneyland Paris's Discoveryland and create "a future that never was." This created a place that is less about anticipating the future than creating a more timeless setting. To this end, the Imagineers borrowed heavily from predictions of Jules Verne, H. G. Wells, and Buck Rogers to create a Spaceport, a place where visitors from throughout the universe come and go. In some respects, Tomorrowland is the first postmodern land.

TOMORROWLAND

ASTRO ORBITER ★★

APPEAL BY AGE			
	Preschool ★★★★	Grade School ★★★★	Teens ★★★½
	Young Adults ★★★	Over 30 ★★★	Seniors ★★½

What it is Buck Rogers–style rockets revolving around a central axis. Scope and scale Minor attraction. When to go Before 11 a.m. or during the last hour before closing. Comment Not as innocuous as it appears. Authors' rating Not worth the wait; ★★. Duration 1½ minutes. Average wait in line per 100 people ahead of you 13½ minutes. Loading speed Slow.

Astro Orbiter is conceptually the same kind of spinning ride as Fantasyland's Dumbo or Adventureland's Magic Carpets, but with fanciful rocket ships instead of elephants or carpets. The other major difference is that while those attractions take off from ground level, Astro Orbiter's ride vehicles start on the third floor of the ride building and go up from there. As a result, you get some great views of Tomorrowland and the Contemporary Resort, but the experience frightens a fair number of children and adults. Besides the fright factor, Astro Orbiter is one of the slowest-loading rides in any Disney park, so expect long lines all day.

MONSTERS, INC. LAUGH FLOOR

(FASTPASS+) ★★★½

APPEAL BY AGE			
	Preschool ★★★★	Grade School ★★★★½	Teens ★★★★
	Young Adults ★★★★	Over 30 ★★★★	Seniors ★★★★

What it is Interactive animated comedy show. Scope and scale Major attraction. When to go Before 11 a.m. or after 4 p.m.; not a good use of FastPass+. Comment Audience members may be asked to participate in skits. Authors' rating Good concept; jokes are hit-and-miss; ★★★½. Duration About 15 minutes.

We learned in Disney–Pixar's *Monsters, Inc.* that children's screams could be converted into electricity, which was used to power a town inhabited by monsters. During the film, the monsters discovered that children's laughter was an even better source of energy. The concept behind this attraction is that the monsters have set up a comedy club to capture as many laughs as possible. Mike Wazowski, the one-eyed character from the film, serves as the emcee to the club's three comedy acts. Each consists of an animated monster (most not seen in the film) trying out various bad puns, knock-knock jokes, and Abbott and Costello–like routines. Using the same technology as Epcot's popular *Turtle Talk with Crush*, behind-the-scenes Disney employees voice the characters and often interact with audience members during the skits. Disney has shown a willingness to try new routines and jokes, so the show has remained relatively fresh to repeat visitors.

BUZZ LIGHTYEAR'S SPACE RANGER SPIN (FASTPASS+) ★★★★

! APPEAL BY AGE

Preschool ★★★★½	Grade School ★★★★½	Teens ★★★★
Young Adults ★★★★	Over 30 ★★★★	Seniors ★★★★

What it is **Whimsical space travel–themed indoor ride.** Scope and scale **Minor attraction.** When to go **First or last hour the park is open, or use FastPass+.** Authors' rating **Surreal shooting gallery; ★★★★.** Duration **About 4½ minutes.** Average wait in line per 100 people ahead of you **3 minutes.** Loading speed **Fast.**

Buzz Lightyear is a moving shooting gallery in which you board rocket ships equipped with two cartoon-style laser "cannons" and shoot at round orange targets in various configurations. Through a small joystick mounted in between the cannon, you can spin the entire ride vehicle around to get better aim at the targets. Of course, the ones hardest to hit are typically worth the most points. Fire off individual shots as opposed to keeping the trigger depressed.

The ride features characters from Disney-Pixar's *Toy Story* film, including Emperor Zurg, the little green aliens, and, of course, Buzz Lightyear. The marginal story line has you and Buzz trying to save the universe from the evil Emperor Zurg. The game play within Buzz Lightyear is great (even for small children), and it remains one of Tomorrowland's most popular attractions.

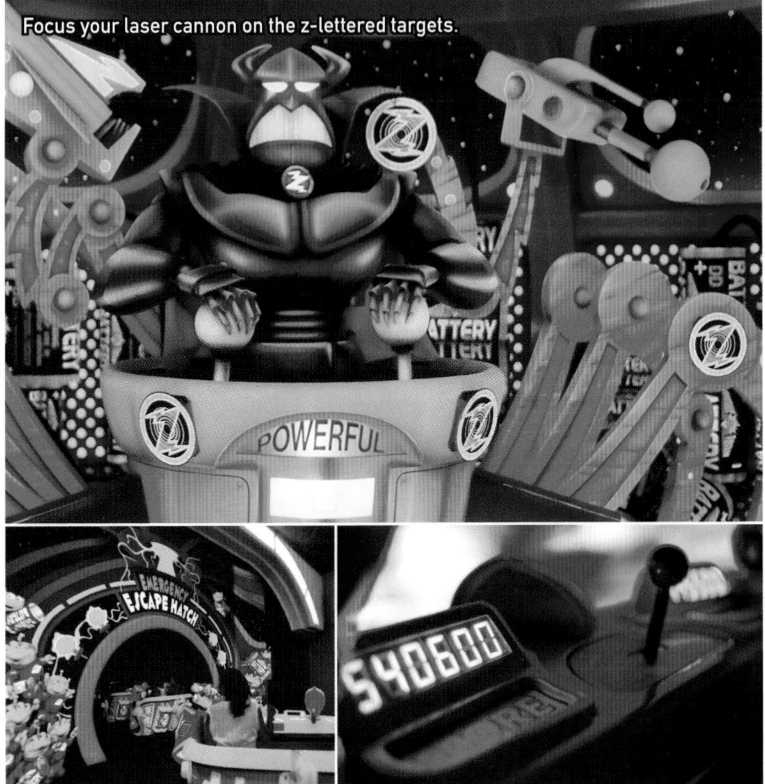

Focus your laser cannon on the z-lettered targets.

SPACE MOUNTAIN (FASTPASS+) ★★★★

! APPEAL BY AGE	Preschool ★★★†	Grade School ★★★★½	Teens ★★★★★
	Young Adults ★★★★½	Over 30 ★★★★½	Seniors ★★★½

† *Some preschoolers love Space Mountain; others are frightened by it.*

What it is **Roller coaster in the dark.** Scope and scale **Super-headliner.** When to go **When the park opens or use FastPass+.** Comments **Great fun and action; much wilder than Big Thunder Mountain Railroad. 44" minimum height requirement; children younger than age 7 must be accompanied by an adult; switching-off option (see p. 113).** Authors' rating **An unusual roller coaster with excellent special effects; not to be missed; ★★★★.** Duration **Almost 3 minutes.** Average wait in line per 100 people ahead of you **3 minutes; assumes 2 tracks, one dedicated to FastPass+ riders, dispatching at 21-second intervals.** Loading speed **Moderate–fast.**

Totally enclosed in a mammoth futuristic structure, Space Mountain has always been the Magic Kingdom's most popular attraction. It remains a rite of passage for Disney theme park fans, most of whom can still recite details from their first few rides. The theme is a space flight through dark recesses of the galaxy. Effects are superb, and the ride is the fastest and wildest in the Magic Kingdom. It's much zippier than Big Thunder Mountain Railroad, but much less than Rock 'n' Roller Coaster at Disney's Hollywood Studios or Expedition Everest at Animal Kingdom.

Conceptually, Space Mountain is an overgrown version of the small coasters found at local and regional amusement parks throughout the country for the past 50 years. Disney's is much bigger, of course, as well as indoors in the dark, and with much more elaborate special effects. Still, Space Mountain's thrills come from tight turns and unexpected drops, not from endless loops, corkscrews, or skin-flapping high speeds that other coaster designs turn to when they can't come up with a good story line. The top speed is only about 28 mph, a leisurely pace by 21st-century standards. Space Mountain has a queuing area with interactive games to help pass the time in line.

STITCH'S GREAT ESCAPE ★★

APPEAL BY AGE Preschool ★★½ | Grade School ★★½ | Teens ★★½ | Young Adults ★★½ | Over 30 ★★ | Seniors ★★½

What it is Theater-in-the-round sci-fi adventure show. Scope and scale Minor attraction. When to go Before 11 a.m., after 6 p.m., or during parades. Comments Frightens children of all ages. 40" minimum height requirement; switching-off option (see p. 113). Authors' rating It stinks; ★★. Duration About 12 minutes plus a 6-minute preshow. Probable waiting time 5–15 minutes.

Stitch's Great Escape is the worst attraction in Walt Disney World. Stitch, a prisoner of the galactic authorities, is being transferred to a processing facility en route to his final place of incarceration. He manages to escape by employing an efficient, though gross, trick that knocks out power to the facility.

Much of the show takes place in a darkened theater, which is filled with screams, shrieks, and sound effects. Worse, many effects come from shoulder harnesses lowered on to you. The harnesses also prevent you from reaching to comfort your children if they're scared. We're frankly surprised that the show has lasted as long as it has, and no one will be sorry to see it go.

TOMORROWLAND SPEEDWAY (FASTPASS+) ★★

APPEAL BY AGE Preschool ★★★★½ | Grade School ★★★★½ | Teens ★★★½ | Young Adults ★★★ | Over 30 ★★★ | Seniors ★★★

What it is Drive-'em-yourself miniature cars. Scope and scale Major attraction. When to go Before 10 a.m., during the last 2 hours before closing, or use FastPass+. Comment 54" minimum height requirement to drive unassisted; 32" minimum height requirement to ride with a parent. Authors' rating Boring for adults; great for preschoolers; ★★. Duration About 4¼ minutes. Average wait in line per 100 people ahead of you 4½ minutes; assumes 285-car turnover every 20 minutes. Loading speed Slow.

The Tomorrowland Speedway is an elaborate miniature raceway with gasoline-powered cars that travel up to 7 miles per hour. With its sleek cars and racing noises, the ride is quite alluring. Unfortunately, the cars poke along on a guide rail, leaving the driver little to do. Even with the guide rail, however, the steering wheel seems to be completely unconnected to the actual bits that steer the car. We're not the best drivers in the world, but we're always thrashed side to side on the Speedway like some sort of children's toy caught in the washing machine. And you spend so much energy pushing down the gas pedal in a futile attempt to go faster that your right leg is useless quivering jelly for an hour after you ride.

We're so doing this when we get home!

TOMORROWLAND TRANSIT AUTHORITY PEOPLEMOVER ★★★½

APPEAL BY AGE Preschool ★★★★ Grade School ★★★★ Teens ★★★★ Young Adults ★★★★ Over 30 ★★★★ Seniors ★★★★½

What it is Scenic tour of Tomorrowland. Scope and scale Minor attraction. When to go Anytime, but especially during hot, crowded times of day (11:30 a.m.–4:30 p.m.). Comment Good way to check out the line at Space Mountain and the Speedway. Authors' rating Scenic and relaxing; ★★★½. Duration 10 minutes. Average wait in line per 100 people ahead of you 1½ minutes; assumes 39 trains operating. Loading speed Fast.

A once-unique prototype of a linear-induction mass-transit system, the PeopleMover's trams take you on a spin past most of Tomorrowland, through Space Mountain, and past Buzz Lightyear's Space Ranger Spin on a covered, elevated track on Tomorrowland's second story.

Besides the view, the best things about the PeopleMover are that there's rarely a wait for it, you get to sit on comfortable padded seats, and there's enough combined breeze and air-conditioning to cool off. If you make pathetic faces to the cast members at the unloading area, they may let you ride again without getting off.

WALT DISNEY'S CAROUSEL OF PROGRESS ★★★

APPEAL BY AGE Preschool ★★★ Grade School ★★★ Teens ★★★½ Young Adults ★★★★ Over 30 ★★★★ Seniors ★★★★½

What it is Audio-Animatronic theater production. Scope and scale Major attraction. When to go Anytime. Authors' rating Nostalgic, warm, and happy; ★★★. Duration 21 minutes. Preshow Documentary on the attraction's long history. Probable waiting time Less than 10 minutes.

Carousel of Progress showcases how modern family life has evolved over the past century, using kitchen appliances as a backdrop for discussing social and familial changes in a four-act script. Originally conceived for the 1964–65 World's Fair, *Carousel* has gone through regular updates over the years; however, the underlying story is relatively unchanged, tracing how family life has improved for a father, mother, daughter, and son. Though the story spans roughly a hundred years, the characters age only slightly. *Carousel* is a great ride in the middle of the day. Because of its unique theater setup, waits are usually minimal at any time.

HOLIDAYS AT WALT DISNEY WORLD

© Disney

LIVE ENTERTAINMENT

Following is a sample of the best live entertainment offerings in the Magic Kingdom. Check the live-entertainment schedule in your guide map (free as you enter the park or at City Hall) or in the *Times Guide* available with the guide map.

Afternoon Parade Parade floats pay homage to Disney films, including *The Little Mermaid, Brave, Sleeping Beauty,* and the now inescapable *Frozen*. New in 2016, Festival of Fantasy (★★★★) is the most elaborate parade Walt Disney World has produced in ages. More than 100 cast members dance their way through the World, many on moving vehicles. The showpiece of the parade is the life-size steampunk Maleficent dragon, which periodically emits fiery breath.

Evening Parade This high-tech affair employs electroluminescent and fiber-optic technologies, light-spreading thermoplastics, and liquid-nitrogen smoke. For those who flunked chemistry and physics, the parade also offers music, Mickey Mouse, and twinkling lights. Evening-parade performances vary by season. The Main Street Electrical Parade (★★★★) is the current nightly cavalcade at the Magic Kingdom and is not to be missed.

▶ **UNOFFICIAL TIP** We like to sit along the shops in Frontierland rather than the waterside; the shops are usually in the shade, and in summer you can catch some of the cool air-conditioning wafting out of the stores. Note that parades occasionally incorporate seasonal themes. Also, FastPass+ is available for premium areas to view the afternoon and evening parades. You still need to show up early for a good spot, though.

***Celebrate the Magic* (★★★★½)** In this imaginative show, videos and special effects are set to music and projected nightly on Cinderella Castle. The effects are tremendous: in one vignette, the entire castle becomes a kaleidoscope of brightly colored Mickeys and Donalds; in another, flames appear throughout the castle's windows to emulate a scene from the Pirates of the Caribbean ride. Best of all, Disney regularly updates the show's content to keep it fresh. We rate this as not to be missed.

***Wishes* Fireworks (★★★★★)** *Wishes* features memorable vignettes and music from beloved Disney films, along with a stellar fireworks display, while Jiminy Cricket narrates a lump-in-your-throat story about making wishes come true.

Castle Forecourt Stage *Mickey's Royal Friendship Faire* debuted here in 2016. The cast includes Mickey, Minnie, Donald, and Goofy, with appearances by Anna, Elsa, Olaf, Rapunzel, Tiana, and others. Like its predecessors, the show is a bit of dialog stringing together several song-and-dance numbers involving the princesses. Check the daily *Times Guide* for showtimes.

Move It! Shake It! Dance and Play It! Street Party (★) This mini parade/party includes a handful of floats, Disney characters, and entertainers. The floats encircle the park's central hub and stop there, allowing guests to dance in the street with the performers. Guests are encouraged to post selfies to social media using the hashtag #MoveItShakeItPics in order to see their smiling faces shown on the floats' video screens. It's trying way too hard to be hip.

Disney Character Shows and Appearances A number of characters are usually on hand to greet guests when the park opens. Because they snarl pedestrian traffic and stop most children dead in their tracks, this is sort of a mixed blessing. Check the daily *Times Guide* for character-greeting locations and times.

Electrical Water Pageant Performed at nightfall (about 9 p.m. most of the year) on Seven Seas Lagoon and Bay Lake, this is one of our favorites among the Disney extras, but it's necessary to leave the Magic Kingdom to view it. The pageant is a stunning electric-light show aboard small barges and set to nifty electronic music. Leave the Magic Kingdom and take the monorail to the Polynesian Village Resort. Walk to the end of the pier to watch the show.

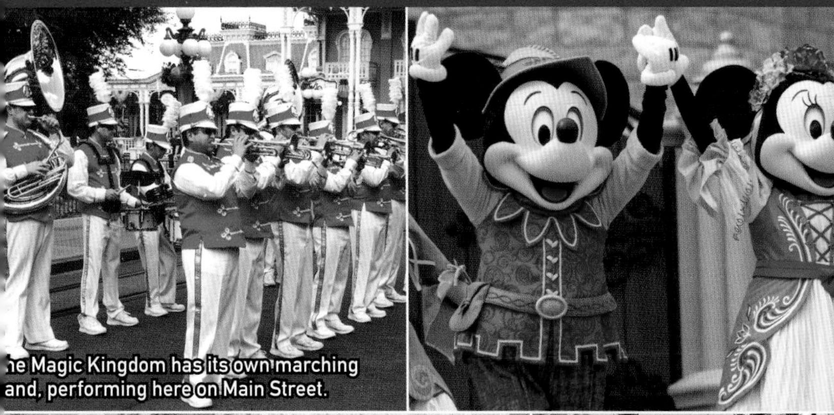

he Magic Kingdom has its own marching
and, performing here on Main Street.

FIREWORKS VIEWING LOCATIONS

In 2014 and 2015, the Magic Kingdom's central hub underwent extensive reconfiguration, which is now complete. The updates included more spacious walking paths, large lawn/garden areas, and an improved castle projection system. These all contribute to a more pleasant fireworks viewing experience, as well as a more pleasant exit from the park after the fireworks. If you're simply interested in a relatively uncrowded view of the evening fireworks, try viewing from Fantasyland. Our favorite spots include the bridge to the Be Our Guest restaurant; to the left of the entrance to Seven Dwarfs Mine Train; and between the Prince Charming Regal Carrousel and *Enchanted Tales with Belle.* Some of the minor pyrotechnics shot from Cinderella Castle will be behind you, but we think this gives the event a surround-sound feeling. The main fireworks will be much closer and brighter to you.

Not all Walt Disney World fireworks viewing locations are created equal. The best place within the Magic Kingdom to view fireworks is on Main Street, U.S.A.

Other locations in the park are tolerable if you're concerned with avoiding crowds, but Main Street, U.S.A. has the best view of the show.

To illustrate the best locations, we'll start at the end of Main Street closest to the castle and continue toward the exit of the park, showing the exact same fireworks burst (I call it "the fan") through photos, with an explanation of the location and the crowds you'll typically have if you want to view the fireworks from that location.

This first photo is the view of the fireworks if you stand about halfway between the *Partners* statue and Cinderella Castle. It's generally uncrowded, and for good reason: this close to the castle, you will miss about half of the show, as all but the highest bursts will be obscured by the castle. As a general rule, don't go beyond the *Partners* statue if you want a great fireworks view.

Our next vantage point is just to the right of the *Partners* statue. This location offers a pretty good view, especially if you like a more castle-centric look at the fireworks shows. However, this area (and the hub in general) is typically one of the most crowded locations because people will often stay here for the evening parade and fireworks.

This next location is the best, and my absolute favorite, location inside the Magic Kingdom: it is slightly north of Casey's Corner and the Main Street Ice Cream Parlor by about 20 feet. Scout out this spot during the day, and you'll notice that it's the high point of Main Street. In the photo at left, you'll see that I have a slightly higher vantage than the people in front of me. This is because of the incline, not because I'm tall. Often, this is an area where crowds are not allowed to congregate until around 15 minutes before the show (*Celebrate the Magic* does change this a bit), so you usually don't have to arrive early here.

If you continue heading down Main Street toward the train station, these bursts are often blocked by the buildings on Main Street.

Continuing down Main Street a tad farther, right in line with Casey's Corner and the Ice Cream Parlor, you'll notice that my view is no longer above the crowds, but the red and white burst that shoots off behind the fan is moving higher above the castle. This ends up being one of the more crowded areas, but again, cast members often keep traffic moving here, so you really don't need to worry too much about showing up early to get a spot here. Just be wary of tall people with small kids standing in front of you, and don't be surprised if that kid ends up on their shoulders, totally blocking your view!

The viewing locations get progressively worse as you move toward the train station, until you get right near the flagpole. For a unique view of the show, head to the second level of the train station. Viewing locations are very limited up there, and people camp out hours in advance of the Main Street Electrical Parade, as this spot also offers a great view of the parade. If you plan on taking photos of the fireworks, be warned, as the flagpole will be right in the center of your shots.

You may notice mentions of "inside" the Magic Kingdom littered throughout this text, as if to add an asterisk to certain viewing locations. This is because the best viewing locations aren't in the Magic Kingdom at all; they're at the Transportation and Ticket Center (TTC). Applying the principle of perspective distortion to the extreme, if you go all the way to the TTC, those bursts behind the castle will appear huge in relation to the castle.

Yes, the photo at left is the exact same burst as the first photo. Quite the stark contrast, right? Not only can you get an awesome view of the fireworks for free, but the music is played, and the crowds are incredibly light. We typically watch the special-events fireworks from here one night of our trip (sure beats paying $70 per person for a party ticket!) in addition to attending the party. The beach of the Polynesian Village Resort also offers a good view of the fireworks, but it's not nearly as good as the TTC.

COUNTER-SERVICE RESTAURANTS

The Magic Kingdom boasts lovingly crafted attractions, beautiful buildings, and timeless stories, but dining is not one of the park's strengths. More than likely, your dining choices for lunch will be made simply by finding the closest restaurant to where you are when you're hungry. It's not that counter-service food in the park is necessarily bad, but you probably won't find many places worth walking across the park for.

Our favorite restaurants are Liberty Square's **Columbia Harbour House** and Fantasyland's **Be Our Guest** for lunch.

Aloha Isle

QUALITY Excellent VALUE B+ PORTION Medium LOCATION Adventureland
READER RESPONSES 97% 👍 3% 👎 DINING PLAN No

Soft-serve ice cream, ice cream floats, fresh pineapple spears, juice. The pineapple Dole Whip soft-serve is a must-try. Be aware that Aloha Isle and Sunshine Seasons restaurants swapped places in 2015. Aloha Isle is now next to *Walt Disney's Enchanted Tiki Room*.

Be Our Guest

QUALITY Excellent VALUE B+ PORTION Medium LOCATION Fantasyland
READER RESPONSES 91% 👍 9% 👎 DINING PLAN Yes

Be Our Guest is the best counter-service restaurant in the Magic Kingdom, and one of the best in all of Walt Disney World. Breakfast is a prix-fixe meal that includes a beverage, a platter of pastries, and a hearty entrée. Entrées include an open-face bacon and egg sandwich, a croissant doughnut with a banana-caramel sauce and chocolate ganache topping, croque madame, veggie quiche, or a plate of assorted meats and cheeses. Kids choose from crepes, French toast, oatmeal, or cereal. The $24-per-person ($14-per-child) breakfast rate is steep, but you get a lot of food. For lunch, we like the braised pork or croque monsieur. The generous tuna Niçoise salad also hits the spot. The kids' menu has meat loaf, slow-cooked pork, whole-grain macaroni, grilled shrimp, carved-turkey sandwich, and grilled cheese with turkey noodle soup. Breakfast is only served 8–10 a.m., and waits for lunch can be an hour or more. Make a reservation if you don't want to wait. See page 137 for a review of Be Our Guest's sit-down dinner service.

Casey's Corner

QUALITY Good **VALUE** B **PORTION** Medium **LOCATION** Main Street, U.S.A.
READER RESPONSES 84% 👍 16% 👎 **DINING PLAN** Yes

Hot dogs, corn dog nuggets, fries, and brownies. The hot dogs are frequently lukewarm and the buns stale, so ask for an extra-hot dog and a toasted bun. Len recommends the barbecue slaw dog; our dining insider favors the chili-cheese dog. Die-hard fans should know that Casey's no longer offers hot melted cheese in its condiment area. If that was your reason for visiting, you can keep on walking.

Columbia Harbour House

QUALITY Good **VALUE** B **PORTION** Medium **LOCATION** Liberty Square
READER RESPONSES 94% 👍 6% 👎 **DINING PLAN** Yes

Healthful options such as grilled salmon with couscous and broccoli, the Lighthouse Sandwich with hummus and broccoli slaw, tuna on multigrain bread, or broccoli-peppercorn salad. Other choices: fried chicken and fish nuggets; lobster rolls; New England clam chowder; vegetarian chili; coleslaw; garden salad; chocolate cake, seasonal cobbler, strawberry yogurt; child's plate with macaroni and cheese, PB&J sandwich, garden salad with chicken, chicken nuggets and fish, or tuna sandwich with grapes; . No trans fats in the fried items, and the soups and sandwiches are a cut above most fast-food fare.

Cosmic Ray's Starlight Cafe

QUALITY Good **VALUE** B **PORTION** Large **LOCATION** Tomorrowland
READER RESPONSES 80% 👍 20% 👎 **DINING PLAN** Yes

Rotisserie chicken and ribs; burgers (and veggie burgers); hot dogs; Greek salad; chicken, turkey, and vegetable sandwiches; chicken nuggets; bacon-Cheddar dog; barbecue pork sandwich; Angus bacon chesseburger; chocolate or carrot cake for dessert. Kosher available on request. Each of the three "bays" has different offerings, so make sure you look at each menu before deciding—and note that some items show up on more than one menu. It can be difficult to manage a family with small children wanting items from different counters. The toppings bar is extensive; you can dress up your burger in style.

Friar's Nook

QUALITY Good **VALUE** B **PORTION** Medium–large **LOCATION** Fantasyland
READER RESPONSES 92% 👍 8% 👎 **DINING PLAN** Yes

Hot dogs, specialty macaroni and cheese (pot roast, barbecue chicken), veggies and chips with hummus, lemonade slush.

Gaston's Tavern

QUALITY Good **VALUE** C **PORTION** Medium **LOCATION** Fantasyland
READER RESPONSES 91% 👍 9% 👎 **DINING PLAN** Yes

Ham and cheese–stuffed pretzels, sliced fruit, mixed veggies with dip, hummus, croissants, and cinnamon rolls. The beverage of choice is LeFou's Brew, a frozen apple juice and toasted marshmallow concoction (it's Disney's answer to the popular Butterbeer at Universal Orlando); many adults find it too sweet, but kids seem to love it.

Golden Oak Outpost *(seasonal)*

QUALITY Good VALUE B+ PORTION Medium–large LOCATION Frontierland
READER RESPONSES 76% 👍 24% 👎 DINING PLAN Yes

The draw here is waffle fries topped with barbecue pork and coleslaw; waffle fries with brown gravy and white Cheddar; or BLT waffle fries with bacon, lettuce, tomato, and ranch dressing. You can also get chicken nuggets and chocolate chip cookies.

The Lunching Pad

QUALITY Good VALUE B– PORTION Medium LOCATION Tomorrowland
READER RESPONSES 74% 👍 26% 👎 DINING PLAN Yes

Ham and cheese–stuffed pretzel, frozen sodas, hot dogs. The frozen carbonated drinks—cola, cherry, blue raspberry—are a treat in summer's heat.

Pecos Bill Tall Tale Inn and Cafe

QUALITY Good VALUE C PORTION Medium–large LOCATION Frontierland
READER RESPONSES 84% 👍 16% 👎 DINING PLAN Yes

Steak or chicken fajita platter with rice and beans; spicy beef or chicken burrito; rice bowl with spicy beef, chicken, or veggies; salad with beef or chicken; chicken enchilada soup; churros, sopapillas, and yogurt for dessert.

The Pinocchio Village Haus

QUALITY Fair VALUE C PORTION Medium LOCATION Fantasyland
READER RESPONSES 77% 👍 23% 👎 DINING PLAN Yes

Flatbread pizzas, Italian flatbread sub; chicken nuggets; fries; Caesar salad with chicken or shrimp; chicken Parmesan sandwiches; Caesar salad with shrimp; kids' meal of pizza, chicken nuggets, mac and cheese, or PB&J.Village Haus is always filled with families taking a Fantasyland break. Consider Columbia Harbour House or Pecos Bill Tall Tale Inn and Cafe, both only a few minutes' walk away (and tastier too).

Tomorrowland Terrace Restaurant *(seasonal)*

QUALITY Fair VALUE C PORTION Medium–large LOCATION Tomorrowland
READER RESPONSES 83% 👍 17% 👎 DINING PLAN Yes

One-third-pound Angus bacon cheeseburger; chicken nuggets; chicken Caesar salad; lobster roll; chicken sandwich with bacon; citrus shrimp salad; chocolate cake, carrot cake, or yogurt for dessert. *The* place to grab an outdoor table and watch the castle lit by fireworks.

Tortuga Tavern *(seasonal)*

QUALITY Fair VALUE B PORTION Medium–large LOCATION Adventureland
READER RESPONSES 86% 👍 14% 👎 DINING PLAN Yes

Beef brisket, pulled pork, or grilled chicken sandwiches; roasted corn and vegetable salads. Sides include slaw and baked beans. Desserts are chocolate cake and gelato. Kids' meal is PB&J or mac & cheese. Even if the restaurant isn't open, you can often use the shaded seating area as a place to take a rest.

Magic Kingdom's Special Treats Menu

Mike Wazowski's Split Pea Soup

Keep an eye out for this hearty soup based on an award-winning Wazowski family recipe. Comes with bread and croutons for $6.50. Extra eyes are 75¢ each.

.... $6.50

Elsa's Chilled Free-Range Chicken

From the *Frozen Princess Cookbook* comes this refreshing rotisserie chicken, cooled to 32° and served on an ice ax. Each bite literally melts in your mouth.

.... $12.25

Bing Bong Sundae

Just the thing for a hot Florida day, the Bing Bong Sundae is two scoops of strawberry ice cream with hot fudge sauce and a Hershey Kiss on top. Kids will make it disappear faster than Bing Bong did in the movie. All Joy, no Sadness, guaranteed! $8.50

Pooh Pie

You'll be the happiest person in the 3-acre wood when you warm your innards with this piping hot honey and phyllo dessert.

.... $4.65

PART 6
EPCOT

It's probably safe to say that Epcot was what Walt Disney most wanted to build after the success of Disneyland. Designed to demonstrate new technology and innovation, Walt envisioned it as a sort of permanent world's fair for companies, universities, and governments to show off their latest creations.

On paper, that doesn't sound like the recipe for a fun vacation. Indeed, Epcot's educational theme and corporate imagery lack some of the obvious warmth and charm of the Magic Kingdom. And unlike the Magic Kingdom's attractions, many of which assume you're going to sit passively and watch whatever is in front of you, Epcot is a theme park about ideas, such as ecologies, energy sources, and the role communication systems play in human societies. Epcot's attractions work best when you consider the impact these ideas have—and will have—on the lives of everyday people.

Besides futuristic attractions, half of Epcot is devoted to World Showcase, a collection of elaborate pavilions representing the landmarks and cultures of various countries from around the world. Each country is staffed by young adults from that nation, so it's possible your children will hear French spoken in the France Pavilion or Mandarin in the China Pavilion. Every country has at least one restaurant too, making Epcot home to the most diverse set of dining options on property. Epcot has a wonderful nighttime fireworks display and music in *IllumiNations*. Given these, Epcot may be the best theme park ever built.

Not to Be Missed at Epcot

WORLD SHOWCASE	***The American Adventure***	**Frozen Ever After**
	IllumiNations	
FUTURE WORLD	**Living with the Land**	**Mission: Space**
	Soarin'	**Spaceship Earth**
	Sum of All Thrills	**Test Track**
	Turtle Talk with Crush	

▶UNOFFICIAL TIP Plan to arrive at the entrance gate 30–40 minutes before official opening time. Give yourself an extra 10 minutes or so to park and make your way to the entrance. First thing in the morning, walking may be quicker than taking the tram.

DISNEY DESIGN *with Sam Gennawey*

The popular story of Epcot's design is that Imagineers Marty Sklar and John Hench formed the park by pushing models together of two separate projects: Future World and a permanent world's fair called World Showcase. The resulting mash-up was one 260-acre park, more than twice as large as the Magic Kingdom.

The gateway for this new park would be a time machine, similar to the entrance at the Magic Kingdom. To illustrate my point, you might recall that at the Magic Kingdom, you pass below the railroad, through a small tunnel, and enter an idealistic American town circa 1900. The tunnel is like a time machine. At Epcot, Spaceship Earth serves this function.

Epcot

Attractions

1. Agent P's World Showcase Adventure *(multiple locations)*
2. *The American Adventure* ☑
3. *The Circle of Life*
4. Club Cool
5. Disney & Pixar Short Film Festival FP+
6. Epcot Character Spot FP+
7. Frozen Ever After FP+
8. Gran Fiesta Tour Starring the Three Caballeros
9. *IllumiNations: Reflections of Earth* ☑ FP+
10. *Impressions de France*
11. Innoventions East
12. Innoventions West
13. Journey Into Imagination with Figment FP+
14. Living with the Land ☑ FP+
15. Mission: Space ☑ Use FP+
16. *O Canada!*
17. *Reflections of China*
18. Royal Sommerhus *(Frozen meet and greet)*
19. The Seas Main Tank and Exhibits
20. The Seas with Nemo & Friends Use FP+
21. Soarin' ☑ Use FP+
22. Spaceship Earth ☑ Use FP+
23. Sum of All Thrills ☑
24. Test Track ☑ Use FP+
25. *Turtle Talk with Crush* ☑ FP+
26. Universe of Energy: *Ellen's Energy Adventure*

Recommended Dining ☑ Not to be Missed

FP+ FastPass+ Available · First-Aid Station · *IllumiNations* Top Viewing Spot

Use FP+ FastPass+ Recommended · FP+ FastPass+ Kiosks · Restrooms · "I Can't Believe It's Disney" Fountains

Table-Service Restaurants

AA. Akershus Royal Banquet Hall
BB. Biergarten Restaurant
CC. Le Cellier Steakhouse
DD. Chefs de France
EE. Coral Reef Restaurant
FF. Garden Grill Restaurant
GG. La Hacienda de San Angel
HH. Monsieur Paul
II. Nine Dragons Restaurant
JJ. Restaurant Marrakesh
KK. Rose & Crown Pub & Dining Room 👍
LL. San Angel Inn Restaurante
MM. Spice Road Table
NN. Teppan Edo 👍
OO. Tokyo Dining 👍
PP. Tutto Italia Ristorante 👍
QQ. Via Napoli Ristorante e Pizzeria

Counter-Service Restaurants

A. L'Artisan des Glaces 👍
B. La Cantina de San Angel
C. Crêpes des Chefs de France
D. Electric Umbrella
E. Fife & Drum Tavern
F. Fountain View *(Starbucks)*
G. Les Halles Boulangerie–Patisserie 👍
H. Katsura Grill 👍
I. Kringla Bakeri Og Kafe 👍
J. Liberty Inn
K. Lotus Blossum Café
L. Promenade Refreshments
M. Refreshment Cool Post
N. Refreshment Port
O. Sommerfest 👍
P. Sunshine Seasons 👍
Q. Tangierine Café 👍
R. Yorkshire County Fish Shop

FUTURE WORLD

Gleaming futuristic structures of immense proportions define the first themed area beyond the main entrance. Broad thoroughfares are punctuated with billowing fountains—all reflected in shiny, space-age facades. Everything, including landscaping, is sparkling clean and seems bigger than life. Front and center is Spaceship Earth, flanked by Innoventions East and West, while pavilions dedicated to mankind's past, present, and future technological accomplishments ring the perimeter of Future World.

Epcot Services

Baby Center/Baby Care Needs: On the World Showcase side of the Odyssey Center
Banking Services: ATMs outside the main entrance and on the Future World bridge, and in World Showcase at the United States Pavilion and at the International Gateway entrance
Dining Reservations: Make reservations on your phone, tablet, or computer via My Disney Experience; at Guest Relations, to the left of Spaceship Earth; or any restaurant podium.
First Aid: Next to the Baby Center on the World Showcase side of the Odyssey Center
Live Entertainment Information: Daily schedule listed in the *Times Guide* available at the entrance gates. Also on the My Disney Experience app and the Touring Plans Lines app.
Lost and Found: At the main entrance at the gift shop
Lost Persons: At Guest Relations and the Baby Center
Storage Lockers: Small lockers are on the right side of Spaceship Earth and at the International Gateway World Showcase entrance. Large coin-operated luggage lockers are located outside the park near the bus loading area. All lockers are emptied nightly.
Wheelchair and Stroller Rental: Inside the main entrance and to the left, toward the rear of the Entrance Plaza; a limited number may also be available at the International Gateway entrance.

Most Epcot services are concentrated in Future World's Entrance Plaza, near the main gate.

CLUB COOL

Attached to the fountain side of Innoventions West is a retail space–soda fountain called Club Cool. It doesn't look like much, but inside, this Coca-Cola–sponsored exhibit provides free unlimited samples of soft drinks from around the world. Some selections may taste like medicine to an American (Italy's offering, Beverly, could peel paint off walls), but others will please. Because it's centrally located in Future World, it makes a good meeting or break place, and you can slake your thirst while you wait for the rest of your party. Adventurous types may want to experiment with blending soda flavors, or even mixing the sodas into an adult beverage purchased at the World Showcase.

EPCOT CHARACTER SPOT (FASTPASS+) ★★★

APPEAL BY AGE			
	Preschool ★★★★½	Grade School ★★★★½	Teens ★★★★
	Young Adults ★★★★	Over 30 ★★★★	Seniors ★★★

What it is **Character-greeting venue.** Scope and scale **Diversion.** When to go **Before 11 a.m. or use FastPass+.** Authors' rating **Indoors and air-conditioned; ★★★.** Duration **About 8 minutes.** Probable waiting time **20–40 minutes.**

Epcot Character Spot offers the chance to meet Disney characters indoors, in air-conditioned comfort. Characters on hand typically include Mickey Mouse, Minnie Mouse, and Goofy. There are also two character-greeting areas directly across the covered pathway: one features Baymax from *Big Hero 6*, and the other has Joy and Sadness from *Inside Out*.

The Character Spot should be your first stop if you have small children. Please note that while the characters are all in the same location, they meet in separate areas with separate queues. The FastPass+ selection for Epcot Character Spot applies only to the original space where you can meet Mickey, Minnie, and Goofy. Make FastPass+ reservations for Soarin' for around 9:30 a.m. so you can proceed there directly after getting autographs. The venue typically stays open until 9 p.m., even when other Future World attractions close at 7 p.m., and usually later during evening Extra Magic Hours.

INNOVENTIONS ★★★½

APPEAL BY AGE Preschool ★★★½ | Grade School ★★★★ | Teens ★★★½ | Young Adults ★★★½ | Over 30 ★★★ | Seniors ★★★½

What it is Static and hands-on exhibits relating to products and technologies of the near future. Scope and scale Major diversion. When to go On your second day at Epcot or after you've seen all the major attractions. Comments Most exhibits demand time and participation to be rewarding. Authors' rating We're hoping for a spectacular refurbishment; ★★½.

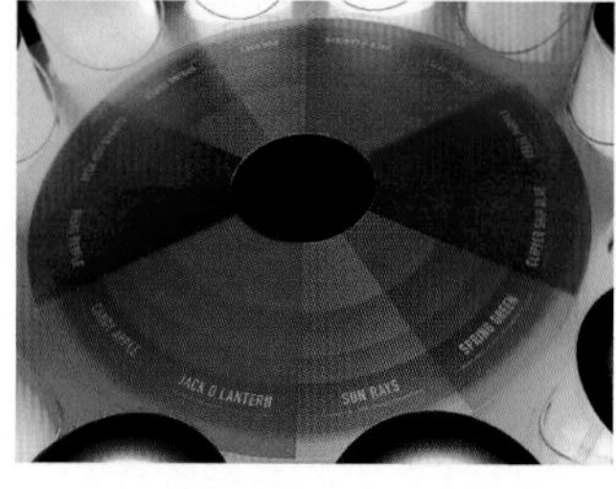

Innoventions—a collection of hands-on walk-through exhibits sponsored by corporations—consists of two huge, crescent-shaped, glass-walled structures separated by a central plaza. Electronics and entertainment technology exhibits play a prominent role, as do ecology and "how things work" displays. Because the future arrives faster and different than expected, large chunks of Innoventions are either closed or outdated. Some exhibits are definitely worth stopping for, however. Our favorite attraction is Sum of All Thrills (see below). An exhibit by Glidden Paint, Colortopia, has interactive kiosks where you can see how the rooms in your house look with different color schemes.

SUM OF ALL THRILLS ★★★★

APPEAL BY AGE Preschool ★★★½ | Grade School ★★★★½ | Teens ★★★★½ | Young Adults ★★★★½ | Over 30 ★★★★½ | Seniors ★★★★

What it is Hands-on exhibit and ride simulator. Scope and scale Minor attraction. When to go Before 10:30 a.m. or after 5 p.m. Comments 48" minimum height requirement; 54" minimum height requirement for track designs with inversions. Authors' rating Not to be missed; ★★★★. Duration 15 minutes. Average wait in line per 100 people ahead of you 40 minutes; assumes all simulators operating. Loading speed Slow.

Sum of All Thrills is a design-your-own-roller-coaster simulator in which you use a computer program to specify the drops and curves of a coaster track before boarding an industrial robotic arm to experience your creation. Three vehicle options are available: bobsled, roller coaster, and jet aircraft. You can program loops into both the coaster and jet courses, and the robot arm will swing you upside down. You can also select the kinds of turns, loops, and hills in your track design. Choices range from mild, broad curves to extreme multiple-loop inversions, making it unlikly you'll experience the same track twice. Be sure that the two people sharing this experience have a similar tolerance for thrills. What's mild to some might be terrifying to others. Go as early in the morning as possible.

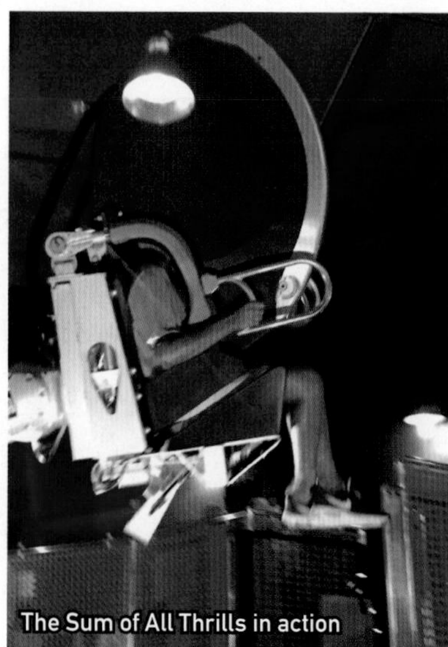
The Sum of All Thrills in action

SPACESHIP EARTH (FASTPASS+) ★★★★

APPEAL BY AGE Preschool ★★★★ Grade School ★★★★ Teens ★★★★ Young Adults ★★★★ Over 30 ★★★★ Seniors ★★★★½

What it is Educational dark ride through past, present, and future. Scope and scale Headliner. When to go Before 10 a.m., after 4 p.m., or use FastPass+. Comments If lines are long when you arrive, try again after 4 p.m. Authors' rating One of Epcot's best; not to be missed; ★★★★. Duration About 16 minutes. Average wait in line per 100 people ahead of you 3 minutes. Loading speed Fast.

This ride spirals through the 18-story interior of Epcot's premier landmark, taking visitors past Audio-Animatronic scenes depicting mankind's developments in communications. Key scenes in those developments are re-created in incredible detail, including everything from Phoenician merchants' invention of the alphabet, Greek theater, the movable-type printing press and its path to the Renaissance, and modern television, space communications, and computer networks. The ride is well done and an amazing use of the geosphere's interior.

Besides the story, Spaceship Earth has a few more features that make it one of Disney World's best rides. One is that its ride vehicles are loaded continuously. In addition, the ride's narration is available in a variety of languages. And the ride ends with an interactive, animated cartoon that lets you choose how your lifestyle might look in a Jetsons-like future.

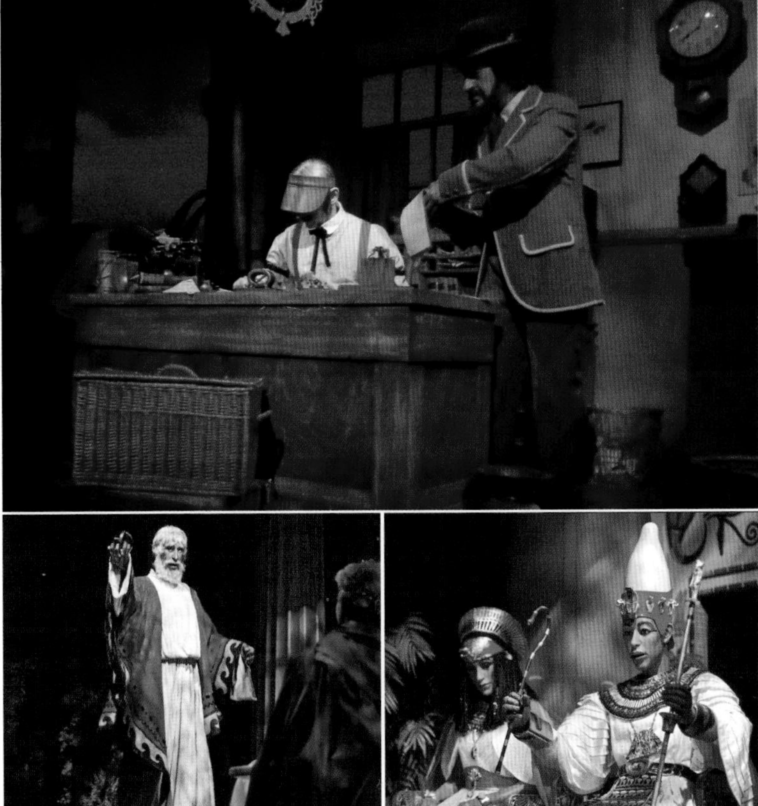

IMAGINATION! PAVILION

This glass pyramid-shaped pavilion is on the west side of Innoventions West and down the walk from The Land. Outside is an upside-down waterfall and one of our favorite Future World landmarks, the "jumping" water, a fountain that hops over the heads of unsuspecting passersby. Imagination! is home to two attractions and a post-show area with interactive computer art and music stations.

DISNEY & PIXAR SHORT FILM FESTIVAL

(FASTPASS+) ★★

What it is **Trailers for upcoming Disney-Pixar movies.** Scope and scale **Diversion.** When to go **If it's raining and you need shelter; not a good use of FastPass+.** Authors' rating **★★.** Duration **About 20 minutes.** Probable waiting time **13 minutes.**

This theater has shown just three films in its 35-year history, all of them 3-D: *Magic Journeys,* a look inside childhood imaginations, ran 1982–1986. *Captain EO,* an epic space opera and long-form music video starring singer Michael Jackson, ran 1986–1994 and again 2010–2015. *Honey, I Shrunk the Audience,* a spin-off of *Honey, I Shrunk the Kids*, ran for 17 years: 1994–2010. The air-conditioned space now houses Disney and Pixar animated 4-D short movies, 10–15 minutes long. The films are fun and enjoyable even for young viewers but in no way a headliner. Enjoy the attraction on your second day at Epcot, during inclement weather, or when it is hot and your feet need a break. These are the same movie previews you can see online for free, on Apple TV, or before actual movies in actual theaters.

JOURNEY INTO IMAGINATION WITH FIGMENT (FASTPASS+) ★★½

APPEAL BY AGE			
	Preschool ★★★★	Grade School ★★★½	Teens ★★★
	Young Adults ★★★	Over 30 ★★★	Seniors ★★★½

What it is **Dark fantasy-adventure ride.** Scope and scale **Major-attraction wannabe.** When to go **Anytime.** Authors' rating **★★½.** Duration **About 6 minutes.** Average wait in line per 100 people ahead of you **2 minutes.** Loading speed **Fast.**

This attraction takes you on a tour of the zany Imagination Institute. Sometimes you're a passive observer, and sometimes you're a test subject, as the ride provides a glimpse of the fictitious lab's inner workings. Stimulating all your senses and then some, you are hit with optical illusions, an experiment in which noise generates colors, a room that defies gravity, and other brainteasers. The ride features Figment, a purple winged dragon that is among the parks' most popular residents.

After the ride, you're led through an interactive exhibit area called ImageWorks, offering some hands-on imagery technology.

We told you God was watching!

THE LAND PAVILION

The Land is a huge themed area containing three attractions, a guided tour of a greenhouse, and several food court–style restaurants. When the pavilion was originally built, its emphasis was on farming, but it now focuses on the environment.

THE CIRCLE OF LIFE ★★★½

APPEAL BY AGE Preschool ★★★½ | Grade School ★★★½ | Teens ★★★½ | Young Adults ★★★½ | Over 30 ★★★ | Seniors ★★★½

What it is Film exploring humans' relationship with the environment. Scope and scale Minor attraction. When to go Anytime. Authors' rating Inspiring and enlightening; ★★★½. Duration About 20 minutes. Preshow Ecological slide show and trivia. Probable waiting time 10–15 minutes.

This playful yet educational film, starring Simba, Timon, and Pumbaa from Disney's animated feature *The Lion King*, spotlights the environmental interdependency of all creatures, demonstrating how easily the ecological balance can be upset. The message is sobering but one that enlightens.

LIVING WITH THE LAND (FASTPASS+) ★★★★

! APPEAL BY AGE Preschool ★★★½ | Grade School ★★★½ | Teens ★★★★ | Young Adults ★★★★ | Over 30 ★★★★ | Seniors ★★★★½

What it is Indoor boat ride chronicling the past, present, and future of farming and agriculture in the United States. Scope and scale Major attraction. When to go Before 11 a.m., after 1 p.m., or use FastPass+. Comments Go early in the morning and save other Land attractions (except for Soarin') for later in the day. The ride is on the pavilion's lower level. Authors' rating Informative without being dull; not to be missed; ★★★★. Duration About 14 minutes. Average wait in line per 100 people ahead of you 3 minutes; assumes 15 boats operating. Loading speed Moderate.

Living with the Land is a relaxing boat ride through the history of (mostly American) agriculture. As you float past swamps and inhospitable farm environments, you're shown how technology such as mechanization, fertilizers, and pest management help produce the food we eat.

The second half of the attraction showcases a futuristic greenhouse, where everything from fish and alligators to exotic and everyday plant crops are grown. Each room in the greenhouse displays innovative ways to grow these crops: In areas with little land space, for example, vertical walls grow lettuce. In areas with little natural rain, techniques are shown that limit the amount of water used by spraying the liquid directly on the plant's roots. And vegetables and gourds that typically sit on the soil are made rot-resistant by growing them in strong nets several feet off the ground.

It's inspiring and educational, with excellent effects and good narrative. Stars of the greenhouse include giant pumpkins and a tomato tree whose ancestors produced a world-record harvest of more than 30,000 tomatoes, with a total weight in excess of 850 pounds, in just 16 months. A walking tour of the greenhouse is also available for a small cost. If you're into this sort of thing, it's like a visit to the Willie Wonka chocolate factory (and you can sneak the occasional sample too).

Many Epcot guests who read about Living with the Land in guidebooks decide that it sounds too dry and educational for their tastes. We find smaller children to be much more engaged if they're asked to guess what kind of food comes from the plants being grown.

SOARIN' (FASTPASS+) ★★★★½

APPEAL BY AGE			
	Preschool ★★★★½	Grade School ★★★★★	Teens ★★★★½
	Young Adults ★★★★½	Over 30 ★★★★½	Seniors ★★★★★

What it is Flight simulator ride. Scope and scale Super-headliner. When to go First 30 minutes the park is open or use FastPass+. Comments Entrance on the lower level of the Land Pavilion. May induce motion sickness; 40" minimum height requirement; switching-off option (see p. 113). Authors' rating Exciting and mellow at the same time; not to be missed; ★★★★½. Duration 5½ minutes. Average wait in line per 100 people ahead of you 4 minutes; assumes 2 concourses operating. Loading speed Moderate.

Soarin' is a thrill ride for all ages, exhilarating as a hawk on the wing and as mellow as swinging in a hammock. If you are fortunate enough to have experienced flying dreams in your sleep, you'll have a sense of how Soarin' feels.

Once you enter the main theater, you are secured in a seat not unlike those on inverted roller coasters (where the coaster is suspended from above). When everyone is in place, the rows of seats swing into position, making you feel as if the floor has dropped away, and you are suspended with your legs dangling. Thus hung out to dry, you embark on a simulated hang glider tour with IMAX-quality images projected all around you, and with the flight simulator moving in sync with the movie.

A new ride film debuted at Soarin' in summer 2016, featuring film clips from flights around the world. Instead of being geographically constrained to California, the new film (created for the debut of Shanghai Disneyland) glides around the globe from the Matterhorn (the one in Switzerland, not Anaheim) and an arctic glacier to the Taj Mahal and the Great Wall of China. The visuals are stunningly sharp, thanks to laser IMAX projectors, and computer-animated animals are employed to create clever transitions, an improvement over the original's jarring location changes. Jerry Goldsmith's memorable musical theme returned with updated orchestrations, as did Patrick Warburton's flight attendant preshow, but there's a new trio of scents to inhale along the way; we're growing partial to Eau de Africa. The end result is a clear upgrade over what was already one of Walt Disney World's top-rated rides.

We're not sure what it's doing in Future World, but Soarin' is fun for everyone.

MEXICO
RING CARVERS

THE SEAS WITH NEMO AND FRIENDS PAVILION

This area comprises one of America's top marine aquariums, a ride that tunnels through the aquarium, an interactive animated film, and a number of first-class educational walk-through exhibits. Altogether it's a stunning package, one we rate as not to be missed. Characters from the animated feature *Finding Nemo* bring some whimsy and much-needed levity to what was educationally brilliant but somewhat staid. The 2016 release of the film *Finding Dory* has sparked interest in this pavilion.

TURTLE TALK WITH CRUSH (FASTPASS+) ★★★★

APPEAL BY AGE Preschool ★★★★½ | Grade School ★★★★½ | Teens ★★★★ | Young Adults ★★★★ | Over 30 ★★★★ | Seniors ★★★★½

What it is An interactive animated film. Scope and scale Minor attraction. When to go Before 11 a.m., after 3 p.m., or use FastPass+. Authors' rating A real spirit lifter; not to be missed; ★★★★. Duration 17 minutes. Probable waiting time 10–20 minutes.

Turtle Talk with Crush is an interactive theater show starring the 153-year-old surfer-dude turtle from the Disney-Pixar film *Finding Nemo*. Although it starts like a typical Disney theme park movie, *Turtle Talk* quickly turns into a surprise interactive encounter as the on-screen Crush begins to have actual conversations with guests in the audience. Real-time computer graphics are used to accurately move Crush's mouth when forming words, and he's voiced by a guy who went to the *Fast Times at Ridgemont High* school of diction. Disney added Dory (the blue tang, voiced by Ellen DeGeneres) and other characters from their film *Finding Dory* to this attraction in 2016.

All Crush needs is some tasty waves, kids.

THE SEAS MAIN TANK AND EXHIBITS ★★★½

! APPEAL BY AGE			
	Preschool ★★★★	Grade School ★★★★	Teens ★★★★
	Young Adults ★★★★	Over 30 ★★★★	Seniors ★★★★

What it is **A huge saltwater aquarium, plus exhibits on oceanography, ocean ecology, and sea life.** Scope and scale **Major attraction.** When to go **Before 11:30 a.m. or after 5 p.m.** Authors' rating **An excellent marine exhibit; ★★★½.**

The Seas is among Future World's most ambitious offerings. Scientists and divers conduct actual marine experiments in a 200-foot-diameter, 27-foot-deep main tank containing fish, mammals, and crustaceans in a simulation of an ocean ecosystem. Visitors can watch the activity through 8-inch-thick windows below the surface (including some in the Coral Reef restaurant). On entering The Seas, you're directed to the loading area for The Seas with Nemo & Friends, an attraction that conveys you via a plexiglass tunnel through the Seas' main tank.

The Seas' fish population is substantial, but the strength of this attraction lies in the dozen or so exhibits offered after the ride. Visitors can view fish-breeding experiments, watch short films about sea life, and more. A delightful exhibit showcases clownfish (Nemo), regal blue tang (Dory), and other species featured in *Finding Nemo* and *Finding Dory*. Other highlights include a haunting, hypnotic jellyfish tank; a sea horse aquarium; a stingray exhibit; and a manatee tank.

About two-thirds of the main aquarium is home to reef species, including sharks, rays, and a number of fish that you've seen in quiet repose on your dinner plate. The other third, separated by an inconspicuous divider, houses bottlenose dolphins and sea turtles.

THE SEAS WITH NEMO & FRIENDS

(FASTPASS+) ★★★

APPEAL BY AGE			
	Preschool ★★★★½	Grade School ★★★★	Teens ★★★½
	Young Adults ★★★½	Over 30 ★★★½	Seniors ★★★★

What it is **Ride through a tunnel in The Seas' main tank.** Scope and scale **Major attraction.** When to go **Before 10:30 a.m., after 3 p.m., or use FastPass+.** Authors' rating **★★★.** Duration **4 minutes.** Average wait in line per 100 people ahead of you **3½ minutes.** Loading speed **Fast.**

The Seas with Nemo & Friends is a high-tech ride featuring characters from the animated hit *Finding Nemo*. The ride likewise deposits you at the heart of The Seas, where the exhibits, *Turtle Talk with Crush*, and viewing platforms for the main aquarium are located.

Upon entering The Seas, you're given the option of experiencing the ride or proceeding directly to the exhibit area. If you choose the ride, you'll be ushered to its loading area, where you'll be made comfortable in a "clam mobile" for your journey through the aquarium. The attraction features technology that makes it seem as if the animated characters are swimming with live fish. Very cool.

Almost immediately you meet Mr. Ray and his class and learn that Nemo is missing. The remainder of the odyssey consists of finding Nemo with the help of Dory, Bruce, Marlin, Squirt, and Crush, all characters from the animated feature. Unlike the film, however, the ride ends with a musical finale.

Nemo's gone missing again? How unusual.

UNIVERSE OF ENERGY: *ELLEN'S ENERGY ADVENTURE* ★★★½

APPEAL BY AGE			
	Preschool ★★★	Grade School ★★★½	Teens ★★★
	Young Adults ★★★	Over 30 ★★★	Seniors ★★★★

What it is **Combination dark ride–theater presentation.** Scope and scale **Major attraction.** When to go **Anytime.** Comment **Don't be dismayed by long lines; 580 people enter the pavilion each time the theater changes audiences.** Authors' rating **Fun and informative but showing its age; ★★★½.** Duration **About 26½ minutes plus 8-minute preshow.** Probable waiting time **14 minutes.**

This pavilion focuses on energy sources, primarily the origin of fossil fuels. What would be an otherwise ponderous discussion is greatly enhanced by the addition of Ellen DeGeneres and Bill Nye, in both the preshow film and in narration throughout the presentation.

For the presentation, you're seated in what appears to be an ordinary theater. A short movie sets up the premise of the ride: Ellen falls asleep watching *Jeopardy*—her favorite game—and she dreams of competing on the show when all of the question categories involve energy. Bill Nye plays Ellen's neighbor in the film and appears in her dream to provide educational tips about the origins, types, and relative merits of energy in all its forms.

During all of this, you'll notice that the theater seats divide into six 97-passenger traveling cars that glide among the swamps and reptiles of a prehistoric forest. Special effects include the feel of warm, moist air from the swamp and the smell of sulfur from an erupting volcano.

If you enjoy Ellen's humor (and we do), parts of the ride are downright funny. For kids, Universe of Energy remains a toss-up. The dinosaurs frighten some preschoolers, and kids of all ages lose the thread during the educational segments. And no matter what, we recommend avoiding the ride right after lunch—the combination of arcane subject matter; smooth, dark ride; and air-conditioning is too great an opportunity to nap for many, many people. As we went to press, we heard rumors that a *Guardians of Galaxy* attraction would soon replace Universe of Energy.

TEST TRACK PAVILION

Sponsored by Chevrolet, this pavilion consists of the Test Track attraction and Inside Track, a collection of transportation-themed exhibits and multimedia presentations. The pavilion is the last on the left before the World Showcase. Many readers tell us that Test Track "is one big commercial" for Chevrolet. We agree that promotional hype is more heavy-handed here than in most other business-sponsored attractions. But Test Track is nonetheless one of the most creatively conceived attractions in Disney World.

© Stefan Zwanzger/thethemeparkguy.com

TEST TRACK (FASTPASS+) ★★★★

APPEAL BY AGE			
	Preschool ★★★★	Grade School ★★★★★	Teens ★★★★★
	Young Adults ★★★★½	Over 30 ★★★★½	Seniors ★★★★½

What it is **Automobile test-track simulator ride.** Scope and scale **Super-headliner.** When to go **The first 30 minutes the park is open, just before closing, or use FastPass+.** Comments **40" minimum height requirement.** Authors' rating **Not to be missed; ★★★★.** Duration **About 4 minutes.** Average wait in line per 100 people ahead of you **4½ minutes.** Loading speed **Moderate–fast.**

Test Track takes you through the process of designing a new vehicle and then "testing" your car in a high-speed drive through and around the pavilion. After hearing about auto design, you enter the Chevrolet Design Studio to create your own concept car. Using a large touch screen interface (like a giant iPad), groups of up to three guests drag their fingers to design their car's body, engine, wheels, trim, and color. For example, designing a large truck with a huge V-8 engine increases the car's capability and power but drastically reduces its efficiency.

Next, you board a six-seat ride vehicle, attached to a track on the ground, for an actual drive through Chevrolet's test track. The vehicle's tests include braking maneuvers, cornering, and acceleration, culminating in a spin around the outside of the pavilion at speeds of up to 65 miles per hour.

At various points during the ride, video screens show the virtual cars designed by the guests in your vehicle and a status update on how the vehicle's tests are progressing. Most guests figure out quickly that absolutely nothing in their car's design has any effect whatsoever on their ride experience: designing a fuel-sipping electric hybrid results in the exact same sensations as a monster truck with huge tires.

Test Track's postshow area continues the design process by allowing guests to create commercials for their concept cars. Farther into the pavilion are displays of actual Chevrolet cars, many of which you can sit in.

Test Track is a favorite attraction of teens. If nobody in your family wants to join you on the ride and you don't have FastPass+ reservations (they often run out by afternoon), join the single-rider line. It moves much faster.

MISSION: SPACE (FASTPASS+) ★★★★

APPEAL BY AGE			
	Preschool ★★★½	Grade School ★★★★	Teens ★★★★
	Young Adults ★★★★	Over 30 ★★★★	Seniors ★★★½

What it is Space-flight-simulation ride. Scope and scale Super-headliner. When to go First or last hour the park is open or use FastPass+. Comments Not recommended for pregnant women or people prone to motion sickness or claustrophobia; 44" minimum height requirement. Authors' rating Impressive; not to be missed; ★★★★. Duration About 5 minutes plus preshow. Average wait in line per 100 people ahead of you 4 minutes. Loading speed Moderate–fast.

Mission: Space was one of the hottest tickets at Walt Disney World until two guests died after riding it in 2005 and 2006. While neither death was linked directly to the attraction, the negative publicity caused many guests to skip it entirely. In response, Disney added a tamer, nonspinning version of Mission: Space in 2006.

Disney's lawyers probably clocked as much time as the ride engineers in designing the lite version. Even before you walk into the building, you're asked whether you want your ride with or without spin. Choose the spinning version, and you're on the orange team; the green team trains on the no-spin side. Either way, you're immediately handed the appropriate launch ticket containing the first of myriad warnings about the attraction. (In case you're wondering, the nonspinning version typically has much shorter wait times.)

Guests for both versions of the attraction enter the NASA Mission: Space Training Center, where they are introduced to the deep-space exploration program and then divided into groups for flight training.

After orientation, you are strapped into space capsules for a simulated flight, where, of course, the unexpected happens. Each capsule accommodates a crew consisting of a group commander, pilot, navigator, and engineer, with a guest functioning in each role. The crew's skill and finesse (or, more often, lack thereof) in handling their respective responsibilities have no effect on the outcome of the flight. The capsules are small, and both ride versions are amazingly realistic. The nonspinning version does not subject your body to g-forces, but it does bounce and toss you around in a manner roughly comparable to other Disney motion simulators.

Space Station replica

The queuing area and preshow are pretty dazzling. En route to the main event, guests pass space hardware, astronaut tributes and memorials, a cutaway of a huge space wheel showing crew working and living compartments, and a manned mission control where cast members actually operate the attraction. The postshow area features an electronic game called Mission: Space Race that almost three dozen guests, divided into two teams, can play at once. The winning team beats the other team's spaceship back from Mars to the home base. Individuals on each team are responsible for certain tasks essential to the mission and make their ship fly faster by hitting the correct keyboard buttons.

WORLD SHOWCASE

World Showcase, Epcot's second themed area, is an ongoing world's fair encircling a picturesque 40-acre lagoon. The cuisine, culture, history, and architecture of almost a dozen countries are permanently displayed in individual national pavilions spaced along a 1.2-mile promenade. Pavilions replicate familiar landmarks and present representative street scenes from the host countries. Critics might say that one cannot gain a full appreciation of any diverse nation by visiting a 2-acre theme park pavilion. We agree, but think they're missing the point. As with Future World, inspiration is a main goal of World Showcase—the inspiration to actually visit these countries. You'll be the judge as to whether it works. One way to tell is if you utter, "Paris looks like a lot of fun!" after leaving the France exhibit.

Besides the pavilions, World Showcase features some of the loveliest gardens in the United States. Located in Germany, France, England, Canada, and, to a lesser extent, China, they are sometimes tucked away and out of sight of pedestrian traffic on the World Showcase promenade. These are best appreciated during daylight hours. The World Showcase offers some of the most diverse and interesting shopping at Walt Disney World.

DISNEY DESIGN with Sam Gennawey

So how do you bring peace and harmony to the world? The formula at the World Showcase is to host countries in a suburban-like cul-de-sac around a lagoon and give each country the same amount of waterfront footage.

Instead of being a collection of exact replicas of famous buildings, the Imagineers use a cinematic trick called shrink and edit. This technique takes well-known iconic buildings, changes the scale and some of the details, and then arranges the structures to make the most compelling composition.

Architectural aficionados will have a field day strolling the 1.3-mile promenade around the lagoon. Going clockwise, you start with an Aztec-style pyramid with a Mexican village tucked inside. Next door, a Norwegian castle and village are out front with a stave church and sod roofs. A scale model of 1420 Hall of Prayer for Good Harvest dominates China, while Germany heavily leans on Bavarian influences. In Italy, the reproduction of Venice's Piazza of San Marco is reversed.

The American Adventure's Georgian manor uses forced perspective to hide its huge show building and to make the structure look smaller than it really is. The traditional torii gate along the waterfront and the 83-foot pagoda outside the entrance of a palace defines the Japan Pavilion. The king of Morocco brought over his own artists to create the amazing hand-made terra-cotta tile mosaics that line the rooms and corridors that connect the Ville Nouvelle section to the Medina section in Morocco.

France celebrates the period of La Belle Époque and includes a one-tenth scale model of the Eiffel Tower. A replica of the long-gone Pont des Arts (bridge) connects France to the United Kingdom. The UK Pavilion is a history lesson in British architecture and includes examples of Elizabethan, Tudor, Regency, Yorkshire, and Victorian buildings, plus a Shakespearian cottage. Finally, Canada presents nothing less than the Rockies and one of that country's most famous gardens.

EPCOT FOOD & WINE FESITVAL

For about 6–7 weeks each fall, the Epcot Food & Wine Festival becomes a prominent fixture in the World Showcase. Supplementing the already terrific dining options, 20–30 additional food-service booths are set up around the lagoon, representing countries, states, regions, or particular genres of food and drink (desserts, Champagne, craft beer, and more). The booths sell tasting-size portions for about $4–$7, depending on the offerings. It's a wonderful way to explore a new cuisine without making a substantial commitment. The festival also offers a concert series, cooking lessons with celebrity chefs, cookbook and wine bottle signings, full dinner and entertainment events, and more. To stay clear of the sometimes rowdy crowds, avoid weekend evenings. A more relaxed—and more beautiful but similar—event, the Epcot Flower & Garden Festival takes place for several weeks during the spring.

Kidcot Fun Stops

Designed to make Epcot more interesting for the 5- to 12-year-old crowd, Kidcot allows children to make small craft projects related to the host pavilion. While the setup usually consists of nothing more than a couple of tables, some chairs, and craft items, Kidcot Stops are an inexpensive way for your child to collect souvenirs from the park and to spend a few minutes in air-conditioning. Each pavilion offers a Kidcot Fun Stop.

Moving clockwise through the World Showcase promenade, here are the nations represented and their attractions.

MEXICO

Pre-Columbian pyramids dominate the architecture of this exhibit. One forms the pavilion's facade, and the other overlooks the restaurant and plaza alongside the boat ride, Gran Fiesta Tour, inside the pavilion. Romantic and exciting testimony to Mexico's charms, the pyramids contain a large number of authentic and valuable artifacts. Many people zip past these treasures without stopping to look.

The interior of the pavilion is designed as a nighttime village scene. It is beautiful and exquisitely detailed. The left half of the pavilion holds shops and Mexico's Kidcot stop. The center and right of the pavilion hold shopping and a fabulous little tequila bar, La Cava del Tequila (see page 260). At the rear of the pavilion is a restaurant, with some very romantic seats overlooking the water and boat ride.

San Angel Inn restaurant

© Linda O'Keefe

GRAN FIESTA TOUR STARRING THE THREE CABALLEROS ★★½

APPEAL BY AGE Preschool ★★★★ | Grade School ★★★½ | Teens ★★★ | Young Adults ★★★ | Over 30 ★★★½ | Seniors ★★★½

What it is **Indoor scenic boat ride.** Scope and scale **Minor attraction.** When to go **Before noon or after 5 p.m.** Authors' rating **Visually appealing, light, and relaxing; ★★½.** Duration **About 7 minutes (plus 1½-minute wait to disembark).** Average wait in line per 100 people ahead of you **4½ minutes; assumes 16 boats in operation.** Loading speed **Moderate.**

The Gran Fiesta Tour is a slow boat ride through an elaborate tour of Mexican landmarks. Gran Fiesta features animated versions of Donald Duck, José Carioca, and Panchito—an avian singing group called The Three Caballeros, from Disney's 1944 film of the same name—to enliven what some consider a Mexican-style It's a Small World.

The ride's premise is that the Caballeros are scheduled to perform at a fiesta later that day, but Donald has gone missing. Large video screens show Donald off enjoying Mexico's pyramids, monuments, and water sports while José and Panchito search other Mexican points of interest. Everyone is reunited in time for a rousing concert near the end of the ride. All of the scenes are done in eye-catching colors. At the risk of sounding like the Disney geeks we are, we must point out that Panchito is technically the only Mexican Caballero; José Carioca is from Brazil, and Donald is from Burbank. Either way, more of the ride's visuals seem to be situated on the left side of the boat. Have small children sit nearer to that side to keep their attention, and listen for Donald's humorous dialogue as you wait to disembark at the end of the ride.

NORWAY

The Norway Pavilion has recently emerged from a major reimagining, transitioning from a solely Scandinavian focus to a mixture of the real world blended with a heaping helping of the imaginary land of Arendelle, from the animated film *Frozen*. Surrounding a courtyard is an assortment of traditional Scandinavian buildings. Highlights include replicas of the 14th-century Akershus Castle in Oslo, now home to princess-hosted character meals, and a miniature version of a stave church built in 1212 in Gol, Norway (go inside—the doors open!). It's hard to say no to the mouthwatering pastries at Kringla Bakeri Og Kafe.

The popular Maelstrom boat ride through Norway was closed in late 2014 and repurposed as Frozen Ever After, now one of Epcot's major atrractions. Norway is also home to Anna and Elsa's incredibly popular Royal Sommerhus Meet and Greet. Due to the attractions' popularity, Norway opens at 9 a.m., earlier than the rest of World Showcase.

© Steve Burns/Burnsland.com

FROZEN EVER AFTER (FASTPASS+) ★★★★

! APPEAL BY AGE Preschool ★★★★½ Grade School ★★★★½ Teens ★★★★½
Young Adults ★★★★½ Over 30 ★★★★ Seniors ★★★★½

What it is **Indoor boat ride.** Scope and scale **Major attraction.** When to go **Before noon., after 7 p.m., or use FastPass+.** Comment **Expect long waits.** Authors' rating **Don't let this one go (unless the line is over 2 hours); ★★★★.** Duration **Almost 5 minutes.** Average wait in line per 100 people ahead of you **4 minutes; assumes 12–13 boats operating.** Loading speed **Fast.**

Frozen Ever After is a pleasant boat ride through *Frozen*'s Arendelle. The premise is that you've arrived just in time for Arendelle's Winter in Summer celebration, where Elsa will use her magical powers to make it snow during the hottest part of the year. Nearly every major and minor character from the film is represented, from Olaf the snowman to Sven the reindeer, along with much of the sound track's songs with brand-new lyrics.

If you've visited Epcot before, the flume ride's path is almost identical to the old boat ride, Maelstrom. The ride features detailed sets, augmented with digital projection mapping, and more than a dozen animatronics sporting video-screen faces (like Seven Dwarfs Mine Train).

ROYAL SOMMERHUS MEET AND GREET ★★★★

! APPEAL BY AGE Preschool ★★★★ Grade School ★★★★ Teens ★★★★
Young Adults ★★★★ Over 30 ★★★★ Seniors ★★★★

What it is **Meet and greet with the *Frozen* princesses.** Scope and scale **Minor attraction.** When to go **As soon as World Showcase opens, at lunch or dinner, or the last hour the park is open.** Authors' rating **★★★★.** Duration **About 3 minutes.** Probable waiting time **15–25 minutes.**

Royal Sommerhus is a new character greeting for Anna and Elsa. While *Frozen* wasn't explicitly set in Norway, the Royal Sommerhus meet and greet features traditional Norwegian architecture and crafts. This meet and greet is designed to have multiple rooms with Anna and Elsa operating simultaneously. This, coupled with Epcot's lower average attendance relative to the Magic Kingdom's, means that once the initial crowds die down after opening, waits should be shorter than when Anna and Elsa held court at Magic Kingdom's Princess Fairytale Hall. It does not offer FastPass+.

CHINA

A half-sized replica of the Temple of Heaven in Beijing identifies this pavilion. Gardens and reflecting ponds simulate those found in Suzhou, and an art gallery features a lotus-blossom gate and formal saddle roofline. Inside the temple is a short film about the history and people of China, shown on screens that form a complete 360-degree circle around the viewing area. Surprisingly well done (and with some really powerful air-conditioning), the only things the theater lacks are seats. Which is all for the best, since we'd probably end up asleep here after lunch. Exiting the film, you're deposited in one of the largest and prettiest gift shops on Disney property.

The pavilion also hosts regularly updated exhibits on Chinese history, culture, or trend-setting developments. The current exhibit displays scaled-down replicas of the terra-cotta "tomb warriors" buried with the Qin Dynasty emperor in the second century B.C. to guard him in the afterlife.

REFLECTIONS OF CHINA ★★★½

! APPEAL BY AGE			
Preschool ★★★	Grade School ★★★½	Teens ★★★★	
Young Adults ★★★★	Over 30 ★★★★	Seniors ★★★★½	

What it is Film about the Chinese people and culture. Scope and scale Major attraction. When to go Anytime. Comment Audience stands throughout performance. Authors' rating ★★★½. Duration About 14 minutes. Probable waiting time 10 minutes.

Pass through the Hall of Prayer for Good Harvest to view the Circle-Vision 360 film *Reflections of China*. Warm and appealing, it's a brilliant (albeit politically sanitized) introduction to the people and natural beauty of China.

GERMANY

A clock tower, adorned with boy and girl figures, rises above the *platz* (plaza) marking the Germany Pavilion. Dominated by a fountain depicting St. George's victory over the dragon, the platz is encircled by buildings in the style of traditional German architecture.

Germany has no film or attraction, and the main draw seems to be the popular (and tasty) Biergarten restaurant, where yodeling, folk dancing, and oompah-band music are part of the mealtime festivities. You know, just like the spread mom used to put out. Lederhosen are optional.

Another big draw in Germany is Karamell-Küche ("Caramel Kitchen"), offering small caramel-covered sweets, including apples, fudge, and cupcakes. We love coming here for a midday snack to tide us over before dinner.

Be sure to check out the large and elaborate model railroad located just beyond the restrooms as you walk from Germany toward Italy.

ITALY

The entrance to Italy is marked by a 105-foot-tall campanile (bell tower) said to mirror the tower in St. Mark's Square in Venice. Left of the campanile is a replica of the 14th-century Doge's Palace, also in the famous square. Having toured Veneto, we think the architectural detail in these buildings is incredible. Throw in a couple of gelato shops and shoe stores, and we'd call it done.

The pavilion extends to a waterfront on the lagoon, where gondolas are tied to striped moorings. This area offers some spectacular views of both Italy and other parts of World Showcase. Streets and courtyards in the Italy Pavilion are among the most realistic in the World Showcase. Like Germany, the Italy Pavilion has no film or attraction, and most of the space is dedicated to retail shops, a bar, and two sit-down restaurants. (One, Via Napoli, serves the best pizza in Walt Disney World—eat it on the go for complete authenticity.) The shops closest to the United States Pavilion often sell relatively inexpensive, individually wrapped candies and cookies, in case you're looking for a sugar boost to get you through to dinner. You'll have to make it to Morocco, however, to get coffee with them.

Where in the World?

Identify where each of these photos was taken.

A: The Temple of Heaven in Epcot's China B. Canada in Epcot's World Showcase
C. Expedition Everest in Animal Kingdom's Asia D. Polynesian Village Resort lobby

UNITED STATES

THE AMERICAN ADVENTURE ★★★★

APPEAL BY AGE			
Preschool ★★½	Grade School ★★★½	Teens ★★★½
Young Adults ★★★★	Over 30 ★★★★	Seniors ★★★★½

What it is Patriotic mixed-media and Audio-Animatronic theater presentation on US history. Scope and scale Headliner. When to go Anytime. Authors' rating Disney's best historic/patriotic attraction; not to be missed; ★★★★. Duration About 29 minutes. Preshow Voices of Liberty choral singing. Probable waiting time 25 minutes.

The United States Pavilion, generally referred to as *The American Adventure,* consists (not surprisingly) of a fast-food restaurant and a patriotic show.

The pavilion is an imposing brick structure reminiscent of colonial Philadelphia. The right wing of the building holds a small garden area often used for special events, and the left holds the restaurant. Inside the pavilion is a marble-floored gallery displaying artwork and crafts from American hands. Inside, under the rotunda, a singing group named The Voices of Liberty perform American classics (think "She'll Be Comin' Round the Mountain," not "Purple Rain") a capella prior to each show.

The American Adventure production is a composite of everything Disney does best. The 29-minute show is a stirring, but sanitized, rendition of American history narrated by an Audio-Animatronic Mark Twain (who carries a smoking cigar) and Ben Franklin (who climbs a set of stairs to visit Thomas Jefferson). Behind a stage (almost half the size of a football field) is a 28-by-55-foot rear-projection screen (the largest ever used) on which motion-picture images are interwoven with action on stage.

The sets are among the most ambitious ever constructed for a Disney attraction, considering they're all moved on and off stage. A detailed room in colonial Philadelphia, the World's Fair of 1876, and a Depression-era gas station are among the best.

THE AMERICAN ADVENTURE
The American Adventure
FORT MARION
NATIONAL MONUMENT
ST. AUGUSTINE, FLORIDA
A FREE GOVERNMENT SERVICE
GREAT SMOKY
NATIONAL
PARK
NATIONAL PARK
SERVICE

JAPAN

The five-story, blue-roofed pagoda, inspired by a 17th-century shrine in Nara, sets this pavilion apart. A hill garden behind it features waterfalls, rocks, flowers, lanterns, paths, and rustic bridges. On the right, as one faces the entrance, a building inspired by the ceremonial and coronation hall at Kyoto's Imperial Palace contains restaurants and a branch of Japan's Mitsukoshi department store. Through the center entrance and to the left is Bijutsu-kan Gallery, exhibiting colorful displays on Japanese pop culture. Recent subjects have included everything from comics to Japan's culture of "cute." Not to be missed are the Matsuriza Taiko drummers. The drums can often be heard throughout the World Showcase, but you need to be up close to see the graceful way they're played. Tasteful and elaborate, the pavilion creatively blends simplicity, architectural grandeur, and natural beauty.

At Kabuki Cafe try kakigōri, shaved ice that comes in such unique flavors as honeydew melon, strawberry, and tangerine. It's a little on the sweet side but lighter than ice cream.

MOROCCO

The bustling market, winding streets, lofty minarets, and stuccoed archways re-create the romance and intrigue of Marrakesh and Casablanca. Attention to detail makes Morocco one of the most exciting World Showcase pavilions. It also has a museum of Moorish art and the Restaurant Marrakesh, which serves some unusual and difficult-to-find North African specialties, as well as belly dancers at dinnertime. Another interesting item in Morocco is the waterwheel in World Showcase Lagoon that provides irrigation to the flower beds opposite the pavilion.

For quick bites, try the excellent Tangierine Cafe counter-service restaurant (with adjacent coffee and pastry bar); it's one of Epcot's highest rated restaurants. Across the walkway, Spice Road Table serves up tapas-style Mediterranean dishes and uncrowded views of *IllumiNations*.

RIGHT: Restaurant Marrakesh has some of the most exotic food in Epcot, but for some reason it took us a couple of visits to realize they had, you know, menus. Not sure why.

FRANCE

Naturally, a replica of the Eiffel Tower (a big one) is this pavilion's centerpiece. In the foreground, streets recall Belle Époque, France's "beautiful age" between 1870 and 1910. Detail and the evocation of a bygone era enrich the atmosphere of this pavilion. Streets are small—just like Paris. Less-explored areas of the pavilion include the perfume store and gardens, both featured prominently during Epcot's annual spring Flower & Garden Festival.

The pavilion includes a popular counter-service restaurant, Boulangerie Patisserie, which serves pastries, sandwiches, and coffees; and L'Artisan des Glaces, an ice cream and sorbet shop with toppings such as Grand Marnier and whipped cream–flavored vodka. Because Mommy loves you kids, but sometimes she needs something to take the edge off, OK? Now run along and get some croissants with your father.

IMPRESSIONS DE FRANCE ★★★½

APPEAL BY AGE	Preschool ★★★½	Grade School ★★★½	Teens ★★★½
	Young Adults ★★★★	Over 30 ★★★★	Seniors ★★★★½

What it is **Film essay on the French people and country.** Scope and scale **Major attraction.** When to go **Anytime.** Authors' rating **Exceedingly beautiful film; ★★★½.** Duration **About 18 minutes.** Probable waiting time **15 minutes (at suggested times).**

Impressions de France is an 18-minute movie projected over 200 degrees onto five screens. Unlike the films at China and Canada, the audience sits to view this well-made film, introducing France's people, cities, and natural wonders.

UNITED KINGDOM

A variety of period architecture attempts to capture Britain's city, town, and rural atmospheres. One street alone has a thatched-roof cottage, a four-story timber-and-plaster building, a pre-Georgian plaster building, a formal Palladian exterior of dressed stone, and a city square with a Hyde Park bandstand (whew!).

The pavilion is composed mostly of shops. The Rose & Crown Pub and Dining Room is the only World Showcase full-service restaurant with dining on the waterside of the promenade. The pub doesn't require reservations. For fast food try the Yorkshire County Fish Shop and sit by the water.

254 QUEEN'S CORGI CATASTROPHE

What it is **Chariot challenge of a lifetime.** Scope and scale **Major attraction.** When to go **After months of training, when you and your corgis are at peak performance.** Comment **Watch out for the queen and her corgis.** Authors' rating **Pure corgi cuteness; ★★★★.** Duration **About 20 minutes.**

Who says the World Showcase is boring? Strap on your safety harness, take a deep breath, and get set for a wild and crazy ride inspired by the chariot race featured in the movie *Ben Hur.* In this attraction, 14 teams of corgis pull royal carriages around a replica of London's Trafalgar Square. A full-size animatronic statue of Admiral Horatio Nelson waves a checkered flag at the start and finish of each race. To augment the excitement, loud speakers blare Eliza Doolittle's famous exhortation, "Move your bloomin' arse!" from the film *My Fair Lady.* If your corgis wimp out, not to worry. Before boarding, you can buy Red Bull Puppy Peppers, available in both dog biscuit and suppository form.

CANADA

Canada's cultural, natural, and architectural diversity is reflected in this large and impressive pavilion. Thirty-foot-tall totem poles embellish an American Indian village at the foot of a magnificent château-style hotel. Nearby is a rugged stone building said to be modeled after a famous landmark near Niagara Falls and reflecting Britain's influence on Canada. Behind the facades are rugged mountain rock formations, complete with a waterfall. These are hidden photo-op gems for your family.

Le Cellier, a steak house on the pavilion's lower level, is one of Disney World's most popular restaurants. It almost always requires reservations for dinner; you'd have to be lucky to get a walk-in spot, but it doesn't hurt to ask.

O CANADA! ★★★½

! APPEAL BY AGE			
	Preschool ★★★	Grade School ★★★	Teens ★★★★
	Young Adults ★★★★	Over 30 ★★★★	Seniors ★★★★

What it is **Film essay on the Canadian people and their country.** Scope and scale **Major attraction.** When to go **Anytime.** Comment **Audience stands during performance.** Authors' rating **Makes you want to catch the first plane to Canada; ★★★½.** Duration **About 15 minutes.** Probable waiting time **9 minutes.**

O Canada! showcases Canada's natural beauty and population diversity and demonstrates the immense pride Canadians have in their country. Visitors leave the theater through Victoria Gardens, which was inspired by the famed Butchart Gardens of British Columbia.

Speaking of Canada's immense pride, cast members often run a preshow quiz on Canadian trivia outside the theater before the show. Helpful tips for Americans: Canada's capital is Ottawa; its $1 coin is nicknamed the Loonie, after the bird engraved on it; and the $2 coin is the Toonie—not, unfortunately, the Doubloonie.

AGENT P'S WORLD SHOWCASE ADVENTURE ★★★★

APPEAL BY AGE			
Preschool ★★★½	Grade School ★★★★	Teens ★★★★½
Young Adults ★★★½	Over 30 ★★★½	Seniors ★★★½

What it is Interactive scavenger hunt in select World Showcase pavilions. Scope and scale Minor attraction. When to go Anytime. Authors' rating One of our favorite additions to the parks; ★★★★. Duration Allow 30 minutes per adventure.

In their eponymous Disney Channel show, Phineas and Ferb have a pet platypus named Perry. In the presence of humans, Perry doesn't do a whole lot. When the kids aren't looking, though, Perry takes on the role of Agent P—a fedora-wearing, James Bond–esque secret agent who battles the evil Dr. Doofenshmirtz to prevent world domination (or at least domination of the tristate area in which the show is based).

In Agent P's World Showcase Adventure, you're a secret agent helping Perry, and you receive a cell phone–like device before you're dispatched on a mission to your choice of seven World Showcase pavilions. Once you arrive at the pavilion, the device's video screen and audio provide various clues to help you solve a set of simple puzzles necessary for defeating Doofenshmirtz's plan. As you discover each clue, you'll find special effects such as talking statues and flaming lanterns, plus live "secret agents" stationed in the pavilions just for this attraction. For example, in a prior version of the game you were instructed to utter the phrase "Danger is my cup of tea" to someone working behind the counter at the United Kingdom's tea shop; he or she would respond by handing you a Twinings tea packet on which was printed a clue to solve a puzzle.

Agent P makes static World Showcase pavilions more interactive and kid-friendly. The adventures have simple clues, fast pacing, and neat rewards for solving the puzzles. Many kids will happily spend an entire afternoon in World Showcase playing this game and snacking on whatever's available in a nearby store.

Playing the game is free, and no deposit is required for the device. You'll need proof of park admission to sign up before you play, and you can choose both the time and location of your adventure. Register and pick up your devices at the Italy or Norway Pavilion, the International Gateway (near the UK Pavilion), or the east side of the main walkway from Future World to World Showcase.

Each group can have up to three devices for the same adventure. Because you're working with a device about the size of a cell phone, it's best to have one device for every two people in your group.

© Daniel M. Brace

LIVE ENTERTAINMENT

Live entertainment in Epcot is more diverse than in the Magic Kingdom. In World Showcase, it reflects the nations represented. Future World provides a perfect setting for new and experimental offerings. Information about live entertainment on the day you visit is contained in the Epcot guide map, often supplemented by a *Times Guide*.

Here are some performers and performances you'll encounter:

America Gardens Theatre This large amphitheater, near the United States Pavilion, faces World Showcase Lagoon. It hosts pop (and oldies pop) [Oldies pop? I grew up with this music. What are you saying? —Len] musical acts throughout much of the year, as well as Epcot's popular Candlelight Processional for the Christmas holidays.

Around the World Showcase Impromptu performances take place in and around the World Showcase pavilions. They include a strolling mariachi group in Mexico; a singing group (The Voices of Liberty) at *The American Adventure*; traditional songs, drums, and dances in Japan; street comedy and a Celtic folk music group in the United Kingdom; and flag throwers in Italy, among other offerings. Street entertainment occurs about every half hour.

Disney Characters

Characters appear at the Epcot Character Spot (see page 219), elsewhere throughout the park (see page 117), and in live shows at America Gardens Theatre and the Showcase Plaza between Mexico and Canada. Times are listed in the *Times Guide*. Finally, The Garden Grill restaurant in The Land and Akershus Royal Banquet Hall in Norway offer character meals.

In Future World A musical crew of drumming janitors works near the front entrance and at Innoventions Plaza (between the two Innoventions buildings and by the fountain) according to the daily entertainment schedule. They're occasionally complemented by an electric-keyboard band playing what today's wouldn't-know-good-music-if-it-bit-them-on-the-keister kids would call oldies.

Innoventions Fountain Show

Numerous times each day, the fountain situated between the two Innoventions buildings comes alive with pulsating, arching plumes of water synchronized to a musical score.

Future World Stage

The area next to the central Future World fountain provides a showcase for several forms of entertainment. At various times of the day and year, you may find gospel choirs, high school dance teams, a cappella groups, or percussion bands.

ILLUMINATIONS: REFLECTIONS OF EARTH (FASTPASS+) ★★★★½

IllumiNations is Epcot's great outdoor spectacle, integrating fireworks, laser lights, neon, and music in a stirring tribute to the nations of the world. It's the climax of every Epcot day. The show, loaded with symbolism, has a plot as well as a theme. We'll provide the CliffsNotes version here, because it all sort of runs together in the show itself.

The show kicks off with colliding stars that suggest the big bang, following which "chaos reigns in the universe." This display is soon replaced by twittering songbirds and various other manifestations signaling the nativity of the Earth. Next comes a brief history of time, from the dinosaurs to ancient Rome, all projected in images on a huge, floating globe. Man's art and inspiration then flash across the globe "in a collage of creativity." All this stimulates the globe to unfold "like a massive flower," bringing on the fireworks crescendo heralding the dawn of a new age. Although only the artistically sensitive will be able to differentiate all this from, say, the last 5 minutes of any Transformers movie, we thought you'd like to know what Disney says is happening. The sound track is excellent and can often be heard throughout the *Guide*'s offices while we're working on the book.

The best viewing location for *IllumiNations* is on the lakeside veranda of La Cantina de San Angel in Mexico. Come early (at least 90 minutes before the show) and relax with a drink or snack while you wait. For a really fantastic view, you can charter a pontoon boat for $346. To reserve call ☎ 407-WDW-PLAY 18 days in advance.

DRINKING AROUND THE WORLD (SHOWCASE)

A popular adult pastime at Epcot is to make a complete circuit of the World Showcase, sampling the exceptional alcoholic drinks native to each country represented. Perhaps knowing this, Disney has stand-alone bars in six pavilions.

La Cava del Tequila, Mexico Inside the pyramid, La Cava stocks more than 100 kinds of tequila and mezcal, almost a dozen kinds of margaritas, and a few light appetizers. A dedicated tequila expert is on hand most days to explain the different types of tequila and provide tasting notes. La Cava is the most popular bar in Epcot, and Len's favorite in Walt Disney World. On weekends or during special events such as the Food & Wine Festival or Cinco de Mayo, expect a wait to get a table.

A typical Friday night at La Cava includes *Unofficial Guide* staff and friends.

Tutto Gusto Wine Cellar, Italy Tutto Gusto serves wine, spirits, and light appetizers in a setting reminiscent of an underground wine cellar. Our favorite spot is a small room just inside the entrance, to the right, with a fireplace, a couple of comfy chairs, and tables big enough to hold your food and drinks. The menu's "small plates" section offers four choices that each serve two people: combinations of cured meats and salamis, cheeses, olives, veggies, and seafood. There's also a selection of so-so panini, and pasta that's both tasty and reasonably priced. The cannoli are the last words in desserts.

Sake Bar, Japan Sake Bar is not much more than a small circular table at the far end of the retail space on the first floor of the Japan Pavilion. It's common to see customers lined up two deep to sip and discuss their favorite rice wines. Ask how to say "Fall down, go boom" in Japanese while you're still able.

Weinkeller, Germany Serves wines by the glass (around $5) and in flights of three 2-ounce pours (about $10). If you like sweet white wines, this is the place to be. Selections usually include a couple of Rieslings, a Liebfraumilch, dessert wines, and ice wines. The bar has no seating and serves no food, but the wine pours are generous.

Spice Road Table, Morocco Menu includes beer, wine, cocktails, and tapas-style small plates, including mussels, lamb sausage, and spicy chicken rolls. Most of the food gets mixed reviews, and at $7–$12 for the appetizers (up to $30 for entrées), the prices are on the high side for what you get. The result is a theme park bar that's rarely busy at any time of day.

Rose & Crown Pub, United Kingdom World Showcase's original destination bar, Rose & Crown serves UK-based beers and wines, malt whisky, other spirits, and cocktails, plus a full menu of pub fare from Scotch eggs to bangers and mash. If you're looking for a light and fruity drink, try the Pimm's Cup.

COUNTER-SERVICE RESTAURANTS

For the most part, Epcot's restaurants have always served decent food, although World Showcase restaurants have occasionally been timid about delivering an honest representation of the host nation's cuisine. While these eateries have struggled with authenticity, they are bolder now, encouraged by America's expanding appreciation of ethnic dining. True, the less adventuresome can still find sanitized and homogenized meals, but the same kitchens will serve up the real thing for anyone with a spark of curiosity and daring.

L'Artisan des Glaces

QUALITY Excellent VALUE C PORTION Large LOCATION France
READER RESPONSES 97% 👍 3% 👎 DINING PLAN Yes

Flavors change but can include vanilla, chocolate, mint chocolate, pistachio, hazelnut, caramel with salt, cherry, and coffee ice creams. Sorbet flavors can include strawberry, mango, melon, lemon, pomegranate, and mixed berry. Over-21s can enjoy two scoops in a martini glass, topped with a shot of Grand Marnier, rum, or whipped cream–flavored vodka. The ice cream is freshly made on the spot. Our profiterole sample had chunks of chocolate-covered cookie pieces, and our white chocolate–coconut had fresh shaved coconut in it. And the chocolate macaroon ice-cream sandwich is worth every calorie.

La Cantina de San Angel

QUALITY Good VALUE B PORTION Medium–large LOCATION Mexico
READER RESPONSES 84% 👍 16% 👎 DINING PLAN Yes

Chicken, beef, or fried-fish tacos; cheese empanada; Mexican salad with cabbage, lettuce, black beans, and corn; grilled chicken with Mexican rice, corn, cascabel sauce, and pickled onions; guacamole and chips; churros and frozen fruit pops; margaritas. Lots of covered outdoor seats.

Crêpes des Chefs de France

QUALITY Excellent VALUE B+ PORTION Medium LOCATION France
READER RESPONSES 84% 👍 16% 👎 DINING PLAN No

Crêpes filled with chocolate, strawberry preserves, ice cream, or sugar; ice cream; specialty beer (Kronenbourg 1664); espresso. These crêpes rate high—even with French guests.

Electric Umbrella Restaurant

QUALITY Fair VALUE B– PORTION Medium LOCATION Innoventions East
READER RESPONSES 72% 👍 28% 👎 DINING PLAN Yes

Angus bacon cheeseburger, French dip burger, sausage and pepper sub, salad with roasted chicken, veggie and tofu sandwich, chicken nuggets, cheesecake, no-sugar-added brownie, chocolate cupcake. For the kids, veggie flatbread, chicken wrap, cheeseburger, or mac and cheese. World Showcase has more-interesting fast food.

Fife & Drum Tavern

QUALITY Fair VALUE C PORTION Large LOCATION United States
READER RESPONSES 86% 👍 14% 👎 DINING PLAN Yes

Turkey legs, popcorn, ice cream, frozen slushes, beer, and alcoholic lemonade and root beer. Home of the Doofenslurper—frozen lemonade topped with passion fruit sorbet foam. Seating is available in and around the Liberty Inn, behind the Fife & Drum.

Les Halles Boulangerie Patisserie

QUALITY Good VALUE A PORTION Small–medium LOCATION France
READER RESPONSES 96% 👍 4% 👎 DINING PLAN Yes

Tuna Niçoise salad; sandwiches (ham and cheese; Brie, cranberry, and apple); imported-cheese plate; quiches; soups; pastries. For an authentic Parisian experience, grab a baguette or baguette sandwich and eat it while walking around the France Pavilion. It opens at 9 a.m.—2 hours before World Showcase—so it's a great spot for a quiet breakfast (come in via International Gateway). Breads and pastries are made in the bakery above Chefs de France. Usually crowded starting at lunch and throughout the day.

Katsura Grill

QUALITY Good VALUE B PORTION Small–medium LOCATION Japan
READER RESPONSES 89% 👍 11% 👎 DINING PLAN Yes

Udon noodles with beef, curry, or tempura shrimp; chicken, beef, or salmon teriyaki; chicken curry; Japanese curry rice with beef; edamame; sushi; miso soup; green-tea ice cream and cheesecake; teriyaki chicken kids' plate; Kirin beer, sake, and plum wine. Pleasant gardens and outdoor seating offer a nice respite, but seating is limited.

Kringla Bakeri og Kafé

QUALITY Good–excellent VALUE B PORTION Small–medium LOCATION Norway
READER RESPONSES 95% 👍 5% 👎 DINING PLAN Yes

Sandwiches such as ham and apple or Norwegian club with lingonberry mayo; vegetable tortes; meatballs; lattes; imported beers. Pastries are a cult item, particularly the troll horn, often filled with cloudberries or lingonberries, and the school bread (see photo), a sweet cream-filled bread topped with coconut. One of our favorites is the fruit-topped rice cream (not a typo). Shaded outdoor seating.

Liberty Inn

QUALITY Fair VALUE C PORTION Medium LOCATION United States
READER RESPONSES 80% 👍 20% 👎 DINING PLAN Yes

Angus bacon cheeseburger, grilled chicken BLT, New York strip steak, Southwest chicken salad, fried shrimp, hot dog, veggie sandwich with guacamole and sweet potato tortilla chips on the side. Brownies, fruit, or warm peach cobbler for dessert. Kosher items also available.

Lotus Blossom Cafe

QUALITY Fair VALUE C PORTION Medium LOCATION China
READER RESPONSES 70% 👍 30% 👎 DINING PLAN Yes

Pork and vegetable egg rolls, pot stickers, Hong Kong–style vegetable curry (chicken optional), sesame chicken salad, shrimp fried rice with egg roll, orange chicken, beef-noodle soup bowl, caramel-ginger or lychee ice cream, plum wine, Tsingtao beer.

Promenade Refreshments

QUALITY Fair VALUE C PORTION Large LOCATION World Showcase Promenade
READER RESPONSES 79% 👍 21% 👎 DINING PLAN Yes

Chili dogs, hot dogs, kettle chips, beer. Seating is limited—be prepared to walk and chew.

Refreshment Cool Post

QUALITY Good VALUE B– PORTION Small LOCATION Between Germany and China
READER RESPONSES 85% 👍 15% 👎 DINING PLAN Yes

Hot dogs, soft-serve in a cone, slushes, coffee or tea, draft Safari Amber beer. Home of the Frozen Elephant—an adult slushy of frozen Coke and Amarula, a cream liqueur from South Africa. Look for special items during the Epcot Food & Wine and Flower & Garden Festivals.

Refreshment Port

QUALITY Good VALUE B– PORTION Medium LOCATION Near Canada
READER RESPONSES 93% 👍 7% 👎 DINING PLAN Yes

The croissant doughnut (the star here) shares this little spot with chicken nuggets and fries, flavored coffees, hot chocolate, and soft-serve ice cream.

Rose & Crown Pub

QUALITY Good VALUE C+ PORTION Medium LOCATION United Kingdom
READER RESPONSES 91% 👍 9% 👎 DINING PLAN No

Fish-and-chips; Scotch egg (hard-boiled, wrapped in sausage, and deep-fried); Indian-style chicken masala; bangers and chips; Guinness, Harp, and Bass beers, as well as other spirits. Most of the crowd is here to drink in an authentic British pub. See the full-service restaurant profile for the Rose & Crown Dining Room on page 149.

Sommerfest

QUALITY Good VALUE B– PORTION Medium LOCATION Germany
READER RESPONSES 86% 👍 14% 👎 DINING PLAN Yes

Bratwurst; frankfurter with sauerkraut; *nudelgratin* (baked macaroni with Cheddar and Swiss); cold potato salad; apple strudel; Black Forest cake; German wine and beer. Tucked in the entrance to the Biergarten restaurant, Sommerfest is hard to find from the street. Very limited seating. Skip the *nudelgratin*.

Sunshine Seasons

QUALITY Excellent VALUE A PORTION Medium LOCATION The Land
READER RESPONSES 95% 👍 5% 👎 DINING PLAN Yes

Comprises the following four areas: (1) wood-fired grills and rotisseries; (2) made-to-order sandwiches; (3) Asian shop, with noodle bowls and various stir-fry combos; (4) and soup-and-salad shop, with unusual creations such as seared tuna-noodle salad or the chicken, quinoa, and almond salad. Breakfast includes the usual suspects: pastries, bacon, eggs, and the like. The breakfast panini (eggs, bacon, roast pork, and cheese) is an Unofficial favorite.

Tangierine Cafe

QUALITY Good VALUE B PORTION Medium LOCATION Morocco
READER RESPONSES 93% 👍 7% 👎 DINING PLAN Yes

Chicken and lamb shawarma; hummus; tabbouleh; lentil salad; couscous salad; chicken, lamb, and falafel wraps; vegetarian hummus, tabbouleh, and lentils platter; child's burger or chicken tenders with carrot sticks and apple slices; Moroccan wine and beer; baklava. Good food with an authentic flavor. The best seating is at the outdoor tables.

Yorkshire County Fish Shop

QUALITY Good VALUE B+ PORTION Medium LOCATION United Kingdom
READER RESPONSES 94% 👍 6% 👎 DINING PLAN Yes

Fish-and-chips, Victorian sponge cake, Bass Ale draft, and Harp lager. A fast-food window attached to the Rose & Crown Pub (see profile above). Outdoor seating overlooks the lagoon.

PART 7
ANIMAL KINGDOM

With its lush flora, winding streams, meandering paths, and exotic setting, Animal Kingdom is a stunningly beautiful theme park. The landscaping conjures images of rain forests, velds, and formal gardens. Add to this loveliness a population of more than 1,000 animals, replicas of Africa's and Asia's most intriguing architecture, and a diverse array of original attractions, and you have the most distinctive of all Disney theme parks.

Although it was the fourth Disney theme park built in Orlando, the wildlife exhibits at Animal Kingdom did break some new ground. For starters, there's lots of space, thus allowing for the sweeping vistas that Discovery Channel viewers would expect in, say, an African veld setting. The enclosures, natural in appearance, have few or no apparent barriers between you and the animals. The operative word, of course, is *apparent*. That flimsy stand of bamboo separating you from a gorilla is actually a neatly disguised set of steel rods embedded in concrete. The Imagineers even take a crack at certain animals' stubborn unwillingness to be on display. A lion that would rather sleep out of sight under a bush, for example, is lured to center stage with nice, cool, climate-controlled artificial rocks. Your journey into these exhibits begins just past the park entrance at The Oasis.

▶**UNOFFICIAL TIP** Three attractions—Dinosaur, Expedition Everest, and Kilimanjaro Safaris—are among the best in the Disney repertoire.

Not to Be Missed at Animal Kingdom

AFRICA	**Kilimanjaro Safaris** ***Festival of the Lion King***
ASIA	**Expedition Everest**
DINOLAND U.S.A.	**Dinosaur** ***Finding Nemo—The Musical***
DISCOVERY ISLAND	***It's Tough to Be a Bug!*** **Wilderness Explorers**

Disney's Animal Kingdom

Attractions

1. Avatar: Flight of Passage *(opens 2017)* Use FP+
2. The Boneyard
3. Conservation Station and Affection Section
4. Dinosaur ☑ Use FP+
5. Expedition Everest ☑ Use FP+
6. *Festival of the Lion King* ☑ FP+
7. *Flights of Wonder*
8. Gorilla Falls Exploration Trail
9. Habitat Habit!
10. *It's Tough to Be a Bug!*/ The Tree of Life
11. Kali River Rapids Use FP+
12. Kilimanjaro Safaris ☑ Use FP+
13. Maharajah Jungle Trek
14. Meet Favorite Disney Pals at Adventurers Outpost Use FP+
15. Na'vi River Journey *(opens 2017)* Use FP+
16. Primeval Whirl FP+
17. *Rivers of Light (opens 2016)* FP+
18. Theater in the Wild/ *Finding Nemo–The Musical* FP+
19. TriceraTop Spin
20. Wilderness Explorers Sign-Up Station ☑
21. Wildlife Express Train

Table-Service Restaurants

AA. Rainforest Café
BB. Tiffins
CC. Tusker House Restaurant
DD. Yak & Yeti Restaurant

Counter-Service Restaurants

A. Creature Comforts *(Starbucks)*
B. Flame Tree Barbecue 👍
C. Harambe Market
D. Kusafiri Coffee Shop & Bakery
E. Pizzafari
F. Restaurantosaurus
G. Royal Anandapur Tea Company
H. Thirsty River Bar and Trek Snacks
I. Yak & Yeti Local Food Cafés

Animal Kingdom's breathtaking natural scenery begins at The Oasis. Unlike other Disney theme-park entrances, there's not a gift shop in sight.

THE OASIS

Your first look at The Oasis should tell you that the Animal Kingdom is a different kind of Disney theme park. Once past the turnstiles, there's no clear road to follow. Instead, you see two garden paths heading in seemingly opposite directions. Each path leads you to Discovery Island, but the path you choose and what you see on the way is up to you. This transition experience is unique among Disney's parks, and the lesson is that the Animal Kingdom is a park to linger in and appreciate. If it's critical for your family's happiness that they're the first riders on Expedition Everest, then by George, send the husband or teenagers off to the races while you maintain your serenity.

DISNEY DESIGN *with Sam Gennawey*

From the time you arrive, Disney Imagineers use contrast to signal that Animal Kingdom is going to be different than any other theme park. The parking lot is a barren, treeless, lifeless field. Not a very inviting first impression. Off in the distance, beyond the edge of the parking lot, is a lush forest—The Oasis.

Functionally, The Oasis serves the same purpose as Main Street, U.S.A., Hollywood Boulevard, or walking under Spaceship Earth: to create a shared experience that sets up the adventures that lie ahead. The pathways meander and cross under a land bridge acting like a curtain to set up the big reveal—your first view of the Tree of Life.

Here's something to watch for throughout the park: in the field of ecology, naturalists use the concept of transects—a series of zones that transition from one type of land to another—to describe the characteristics of an ecosystem and how it changes. When the transition is sudden or is severely disrupted, significant environmental impacts can be felt. Virtually every attraction in the Animal Kingdom and every land deals with a disruption in the natural transect to move the story along.

Animal Kingdom Services

Most of the park's service facilities are located inside the main entrance and on Discovery Island as follows:

Baby Center/Baby Care Needs: On Discovery Island, behind the MyMagic+ Service Center
Banking Services: ATMs located at the main entrance by the turnstiles and near Dinosaur in Dinoland U.S.A.
Camera Supplies: Just inside the main entrance at Garden Gate Gifts, in Africa at Mombasa Marketplace, and in other shops around the park
First Aid: On Discovery Island, next to the MyMagic+ Service Center
Guest Relations and Information: Inside the main entrance to the left
Live Entertainment and Parade Information: Included in the park guide map, available free at Guest Relations
Lost and Found: Inside the main entrance to the left
Lost Persons: Can be reported at Guest Relations and at the Baby Center on Discovery Island
Storage Lockers: Inside the main entrance to the left
Wheelchair and Stroller Rental: Inside the main entrance to the right

These children are going into the FBI's witness protection program.

DISCOVERY ISLAND

Discovery Island occupies the center of the Animal Kingdom and is the first land you reach after exiting The Oasis and crossing a bridge. Most of Discovery Island's shops are decorated in equatorial African architecture, with vibrant hues of teal, yellow, red, and blue. Surrounded by water, the island is connected to the other lands by bridges. A number of animal exhibits are found on Discovery Island, and at the middle of the island is the park's signature landmark, The Tree of Life.

© Daniel M. Brace

IT'S TOUGH TO BE A BUG / THE TREE OF LIFE (FASTPASS+) ★★★★

! APPEAL BY AGE			
	Preschool ★★★½	Grade School ★★★★	Teens ★★★★
	Young Adults ★★★★	Over 30 ★★★★	Seniors ★★★★½

What it is 3-D theater show. Scope and scale Major attraction. When to go Before noon or after 4 p.m. Comments The theater is inside the tree. Authors' rating Zany and frenetic; not to be missed; ★★★★. Duration About 7½ minutes. Probable waiting time 12–20 minutes.

The Tree of Life is quite a work of art. Although from afar it is certainly magnificent and imposing, it is not until you examine the tree at close range that you truly appreciate its rich detail. What appears to be ancient gnarled bark is, in fact, hundreds of carvings depicting all manner of wildlife, each integrated seamlessly into the trunks, roots, and limbs of the tree. A stunning symbol of the interdependence of all living things, The Tree of Life is the most visually compelling structure found in any Disney theme park.

In sharp contrast to the grandeur of the tree is the subject of the attraction within its trunk. Starring the cast of Disney/Pixar's *a bug's life, It's Tough to Be a Bug!* is a humorous 3-D presentation about the difficulties of being a small insect. Flik, the main character from *a bug's life,* is the host and shows the audience how many insects perform vital roles in the ecosystem. Along the way

the audience gets to see, hear, smell, and—ick alert!—feel various bugs during the film. (Parents should be aware of this when considering whether the attraction is too intense for small children.) We generally leave just thankful that there wasn't a taste requirement, but unlike the relatively serious tone of Animal Kingdom in general, *It's Tough to Be a Bug* stands virtually alone in providing some much needed levity and whimsy. *It's Tough to Be a Bug* is rarely crowded, even on the busiest days.

MEET FAVORITE DISNEY PALS AT ADVENTURERS OUTPOST (FASTPASS+) ★★★½

APPEAL BY AGE Preschool ★★★★ | Grade School ★★★★½ | Teens ★★★★ | Young Adults ★★★★ | Over 30 ★★★★ | Seniors ★★★★

What it is Character-greeting venue. Scope and scale Minor attraction. When to go First thing in the morning, after 5 p.m., or use FastPass+. Authors' rating Nicely themed (and air-conditioned); ★★★½. Duration About 2 minutes. Probable waiting time About 20 minutes.

An indoor, air-conditioned character-greeting location for Mickey and Minnie Mouse, Adventurers Outpost is decorated with memorabilia from the Mouses' world travels. The Outpost features two greeting rooms with two identical sets of characters, so lines move fairly quickly. Good use of FastPass+ if you have kids too small to ride Expedition Everest or Dinosaur.

Reto's wife begged him not to wear the cat's head hat to meet two mice.

WILDERNESS EXPLORERS ★★★★

APPEAL BY AGE Preschool ★★★★ | Grade School ★★★★½ | Teens ★★★½ | Young Adults ★★★★ | Over 30 ★★★★ | Seniors ★★★★★

What it is Park-wide scavenger hunt and puzzle-solving adventure game. Scope and scale Diversion. When to go Sign up first thing in the morning and complete activities throughout the day. Comments Collecting all 32 badges takes 3–5 hours, which can be done over several days. Authors' rating One of the best attractions in any Disney park; not to be missed; ★★★★.

Wilderness Explorers is a scavenger hunt based on Russell's Boy Scout–esque troop from the movie *Up!* Players earn "badges" (stickers given out by cast members) for completing predefined activities throughout the park. For example, to earn the Gorilla Badge, you walk the Gorilla Falls Exploration Trail to observe how the primates behave, and then mimic that behavior back to a cast member to show what you've seen. Cast members can tailor the activities based on the age of the child playing. Register for the game near the bridge from The Oasis to Discovery Island. You'll be given an instruction book and a map showing the park location for each badge to be earned. It's tons of fun for kids and adults.

Activities are spread throughout the park, including areas to which many guests never venture. You have to ride specific attractions to earn certain badges, so using FastPass+ for those will save time.

PANDORA: THE WORLD OF AVATAR (OPENS 2017)

James Cameron's *Avatar* is still the highest-grossing movie the world has ever seen, despite being given a run for its money (and passed in the United States) by *Star Wars: The Force Awakens*. Part of what made the film so popular were the incredible visuals of the planet of Pandora. In 2017 Disney brings those stunning surrounds to life in Pandora: The World of Avatar, replacing the former Camp Minnie-Mickey. A.C.E. (Alpha Centauri Expeditions) is your way into this "planet," providing travel between the rest of Animal Kingdom and Pandora.

An exact release date was unknown as we went to press. But one of the more visible constructs is sure to be one of the most awe-inspiring sights of Pandora: the floating mountains. Disney has somehow worked out how to get a few giant "rock" structures suspended above the ground, appearing to float. The other dramatic feature of Pandora is its bioluminescent plants, which fans of the movie are sure to remember. The plants of the Avatar planet glowed softly at night, and the plants of this Avatar land do too.

AVATAR FLIGHT OF PASSAGE

This attraction allows guests to simulate flight with banshees, small dragonlike creatures from Pandora. According to Disney Imagineers, it is similar in style to Epcot's Soarin', but turned up a few levels. This will no doubt become a popular attraction very quickly; luckily Disney seems to be building two, and maybe even three, theaters to house it.

NA'VI RIVER JOURNEY

The other, calmer, more family-friendly attraction found on Pandora is the Na'vi River Journey. The Na'vi, inhabitants of Pandora, are a spiritual species. This boat expedition floats guests through a glowing rain forest full of creatures and a Na'vi shaman. It is a calm attraction, but the scale isn't small. Think more Pirates of the Caribbean than Gran Fiesta Tour.

AFRICA

Africa is the largest of Animal Kingdom's lands, and guests enter through Harambe, Disney's idealized, sanitized version of a rural African village. There is a market (with modern cash registers), as well as counter-service restaurants and snack carts, and table-service dining is available. The seemingly weathered structures and charming, engaging live entertainment help give Animal Kingdom's Africa one of the best atmospheres in Disney World. Recent expansions have made Harambe much larger, which is good news—now you can spend even more time exploring this rich area.

Harambe serves as the gateway to the African veld habitat, Animal Kingdom's largest and most ambitious zoological exhibit. Access to the veld is via the Kilimanjaro Safaris attraction, located at the end of Harambe's main drag near the fat-trunked baobab tree. Harambe is also the departure point for the train to Rafiki's Planet Watch and Conservation Station, the park's veterinary headquarters. *Festival of the Lion King* is also staged in Africa.

DISNEY DESIGN *with Sam Gennawey*

Africa represents the most "urban" environment in the Animal Kingdom. Inspired by an island town called Lamu off the east coast of Kenya, the Swahili-style structures represent a village that has learned to benefit by conserving nearby natural resources and becoming a tourist destination. It has a main street, and the safari's entrance next to a baobab tree (a real tree) acts like Cinderella Castle in the Magic Kingdom and draws you forward. The roof over the entrance was weaved by 13 thatchers from Zululand in South Africa. The grass roof is expected to last 30–40 years. The Imagineers say it is "so imperfect that it's perfect."

The spark of imagination that solidified this version of Africa as the central theme was a visit to Lake Nakuru, a popular safari park in Kenya. As described by Imagineer Kevin Brown, the group was driving around the park looking for animals in jeeps. A call came over the radio that somebody had spotted a leopard in a tree. By the time Kevin's truck made it to the spot, there were more than 40 vehicles with people hanging out taking photos. This is when the lightbulb went off for Joe Rohde, executive designer and vice president of creative for Walt Disney Imagineering.

As Kevin describes it, "Africa is a theme park—just not a particularly well-run one. We knew the experience we could provide in the Animal Kingdom would be as good as or better than that." So they created the fictional town of Harambe. *Harambe* is Swahili for "let us all pull together." The village is layered in history, with the walls of the ancient fort and canyons behind the Dawa Bar and remnants of the time when the area was under British Colonial control.

The safari is the big draw, and the locals manage the savanna. They collectively fear poaching, which threatens the ecosystem and their livelihood. The historic buildings have been readapted to accommodate the tourist trade with a hotel, a bar, a restaurant, and other necessary facilities. The posters on the walls reinforce the commercial nature of the village.

CONSERVATION STATION AND AFFECTION SECTION ★★★½

APPEAL BY AGE Preschool ★★★½ Grade School ★★★★ Teens ★★★ Young Adults ★★★½ Over 30 ★★★½ Seniors ★★★★

What it is **Behind-the-scenes educational exhibit and petting zoo.** Scope and scale **Minor attraction.** When to go **Anytime.** Comments **Opens 30 minutes after the rest of the park; must take Wildlife Express Train to and from this location.** Authors' rating **Not bad; ★★★½.** Duration **About 20 minutes.**

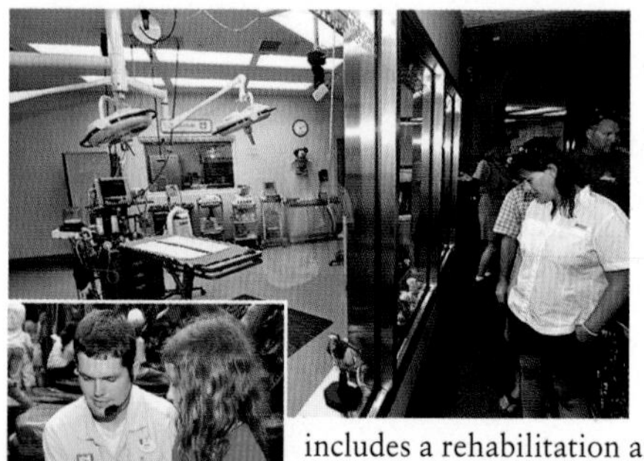

Conservation Station is Animal Kingdom's veterinary and conservation headquarters. Located on the perimeter of the African section of the park, in an area Disney calls Rafiki's Planet Watch, Conservation Station is, strictly speaking, a backstage, working facility. Here guests can meet wildlife experts, observe some of the station's ongoing projects, and learn about the behind-the-scenes operations of the park. The station includes a rehabilitation area for injured animals and a nursery for recently born (or hatched) critters. Vets and other experts are on hand to answer questions.

While there are several permanent exhibits, including Affection Section (an animal-petting area), what you see at Conservation Station will largely depend on what's going on when you arrive. If you trek there during the summer heat only to find nothing of interest, comfort yourself in knowing that Conservation Station has undoubtedly the best air-conditioning in the Animal Kingdom, and that must be worth something.

WILDLIFE EXPRESS TRAIN ★★

APPEAL BY AGE Preschool ★★★★ Grade School ★★★½ Teens ★★★½ Young Adults ★★★ Over 30 ★★★½ Seniors ★★★½

What it is **Scenic railroad ride to Rafiki's Planet Watch and Conservation Station.** Scope and scale **Minor attraction.** When to go **Anytime.** Comments **Opens 30 minutes after the rest of the park.** Authors' rating **Ho-hum; ★★.** Duration **About 5–7 minutes one way.** Average wait in line per 100 people ahead of you **9 minutes.** Loading speed **Moderate.**

This transportation ride snakes behind the African wildlife reserve as it makes its loop connecting Harambe to Rafiki's Planet Watch and Conservation Station. En route, you see the nighttime enclosures for the animals that populate Kilimanjaro Safaris. Similarly, returning to Harambe, you see the backstage areas of Asia. It's a pleasant, if visually unspectacular, experience.

FESTIVAL OF THE LION KING (FASTPASS+) ★★★★

! APPEAL BY AGE	Preschool ★★★★½	Grade School ★★★★½	Teens ★★★★½
	Young Adults ★★★★½	Over 30 ★★★★½	Seniors ★★★★★

What it is Theater-in-the-round stage show. Scope and scale Major attraction. When to go First show in the morning or one of the last two shows at night. Performance times are listed in the handout park map or *Times Guide*. Authors' rating Upbeat and spectacular, not to be missed; ★★★★. Duration 30 minutes. When to arrive 20–30 minutes before showtime.

This energetic production is part stage show, part parade, and part circus. Disney's official line is that it's inspired by Disney's *Lion King* film. We think it's more like a documentary into the everyday life of Elton John. We're not sure, but here are the details:

First, there's the music, for which Sir Elton won a 1994 Academy Award. By our count, every tune from *The Lion King* is belted out and reprised a couple of times. This is either what's running through Elton's head every day, or is a canny way to build up royalty payments for when he's retired.

Besides the music, there is a great deal of parading around by limber acrobats, a lot of dancing, and some incredible costuming. It's all spectacular, but as you're sitting through the show, ask yourself whether any of it would seem truly out of place in Elton's living room. Heck, the costumes probably came from Elton's spare closet!

Kidding aside, *Unofficial Guide* readers have been almost unanimous in their praise of *Festival of the Lion King*, and we consider it one of the best stage shows in all of Walt Disney World.

KILIMANJARO SAFARIS (FASTPASS+) ★★★★★

APPEAL BY AGE			
	Preschool ★★★★½	Grade School ★★★★½	Teens ★★★★½
	Young Adults ★★★★½	Over 30 ★★★★½	Seniors ★★★★★

What it is Ride through an African wildlife reservation. Scope and scale Super-headliner. When to go As soon as the park opens, in the 2 hours before closing, or use FastPass+. Authors' rating Truly exceptional; not to be missed; ★★★★★. Duration About 20 minutes. Average wait in line per 100 people ahead of you 4 minutes; assumes full-capacity operation with 18-second dispatch interval. Loading speed Fast.

The park's premier zoological attraction, Kilimanjaro Safaris offers an exceptionally realistic, albeit brief, imitation of an actual African photo safari. Thirty-two guests at a time board tall, open safari vehicles and are dispatched into a simulated African veld. Animals such as zebras, wildebeests, impalas, Thomson's gazelles, giraffes, and even rhinos roam apparently free, while predators such as lions, as well as potentially dangerous large animals such as hippos, are separated from both prey and guests by all-but-invisible, natural-appearing barriers. Though the animals have more than 100 acres of savanna, woodland, streams, and rocky hills to call home, careful placement of water holes, forage, and salt licks ensures that the critters are hanging out by the road when safari vehicles roll by, no matter the time of day. (Just to be sure about that, we had the researchers ride the safari for days on end during the summer. Those results showed that you'll see, on average, the same number of large and small critters at any time of day.)

Having traveled in Kenya and Tanzania, Bob will tell you that Disney has done an amazing job of replicating the sub-Saharan east African landscape. The main difference that an east African would notice is that Disney's version is greener and (generally speaking) less barren. Like on a real African safari, what animals you see (and how many) is pretty much a matter of luck. We've tried Disney's safari upward of 100 times and had a different experience on each trip. In 2016 Disney started offering evening runs of the safari. Guests have seen different animals active in the evenings, so if you're a daytime fan, you might want to try it later in the day. Be aware that there are some lighting effects at night that are somewhat less than realistic.

Mr. King of the Jungle loses his naptime spot.

ABOVE: OK, we're going to take the class photo now. Zebra and giraffe, you stand in the back by the big ol' truck. What do you mean you have to go to the bathroom? OK, but make it quick.

GORILLA FALLS EXPLORATION TRAIL ★★★★

APPEAL BY AGE Preschool ★★★★ | Grade School ★★★★ | Teens ★★★★ | Young Adults ★★★★½ | Over 30 ★★★★ | Seniors ★★★★½

What it is **Walk-through zoological exhibit.** Scope and scale **Major attraction.** When to go **Anytime.** Authors' rating **★★★★.** Duration **About 20–25 minutes.**

When you're done with Kilimanjaro Safaris, you have the choice of either returning to the village of Harambe in Africa or taking a stroll through the Gorilla Falls Exploration Trail. Winding between the domain of two troops of lowland gorillas, it's hard to see what, if anything, separates you from the primates. The trail also features a hippo pool with an underwater viewing area and a chance to view skulls of various creatures. A highlight of the trail is an exotic-bird aviary so craftily designed that you can barely tell you're in an enclosure.

ASIA

Crossing the bridge from Discovery Island, you enter Asia through the village of Anandapur. Situated near the bank of the Chakranadi River (translation: "the river that runs in circles") and surrounded by lush vegetation, Anandapur provides access to a gibbon exhibit and to Asia's two feature attractions, Kali River Rapids whitewater raft ride and Expedition Everest. Also in Asia is *Flights of Wonder,* an educational production about birds.

DISNEY DESIGN *with Sam Gennawey*

Asia is a remarkable land that sprawls from the *Flights of Wonder* theater all the way to Expedition Everest. Unlike Africa, which features a strong center in Harambe, the little village of Anandapur weaves in and out of the jungle along the floodplains and lower foothills of the Himalayas. Asia is not set in any one country but reflects the design and urban form of rural communities throughout Nepal, India, Thailand, and Indonesia.

Anandapur means "place of delight" in Sanskrit, and the underlying theme is the conflict between the population explosion and traditional respect for animals and wild places. On Discovery Island, nature and the built environment were in balance. In Africa, that balance was being restored, but there is a clear distinction between the urban and rural edge. In Asia, nature seems to have the upper hand, as many structures are being reclaimed, and the foliage is taking over.

The architecture varies from Nepalese, Javanese, and Thai influences. The hand-built feel is everywhere. But the real star of the show is the landscape architecture. One of the designers, Paul Comstock, said, "If you've been in the wild, surrounded by the foliage and flowers, you know you have to go over the top. We had to convince them that landscape was the show." As you move toward Serka Zong (Fortress of the Chasm), the little village at the base of Expedition Everest, you will see a greater use of red, the color of protection. Enhancing the authenticity of place is the use of prayer flags, which are common in Tibetan villages and meant to bring prosperity, long life, and happiness to those who put them on display. The flags also add kinetic energy to the landscape.

The paving materials along the pathways add to the story. Look down (carefully) and you will see—imprinted on the rough surface—footprints, bicycle and truck treads, leaves, and animal prints. As you move toward Everest, the bicycle tires fade away as that mode of travel becomes impractical. Here you will find more hoof marks. It's as if you just missed the residents.

EXPEDITION EVEREST (FASTPASS+) ★★★★½

APPEAL BY AGE			
	Preschool ★★★½	Grade School ★★★★½	Teens ★★★★★
	Young Adults ★★★★★	Over 30 ★★★★★	Seniors ★★★★

What it is **High-speed outdoor roller coaster through Nepalese mountain village.** Scope and scale **Super-headliner.** When to go **Before 9:30 a.m. or after 3 p.m., or use FastPass+.** Comments **44" minimum height requirement; switching-off option** **(see p. 113).** Authors' rating **Contains some of the park's most stunning visual elements; not to be missed; ★★★★½.** Duration **3½ minutes.** Average wait in line per 100 people ahead of you **4 minutes; assumes 2 tracks operating.** Loading speed **Moderate–fast.**

Expedition Everest reprises that Disney-storyboard staple, the runaway train, though this time the scenery includes bamboo forests, waterfalls, glacier fields, and vertiginous peaks. You're chugging up Mount Everest on an old pack-track in search of the legendary Abominable Snowman. But the track turns out to have collapsed (of course), and as the cars pick up speed—both forward and backward, and in the dark—riders find themselves perilously close to an elephant-size and pretty irascible yeti, protector of the Himalayas. The attraction also includes an especially intriguing type of queue, designed by uber-Imagineer Joe Rohde: while waiting to load onto the train, visitors walk through a meticulously re-created Himalayan village. Indeed, everyone should at least see it even if they don't wish to ride the coaster.

WARNING:
THIS RIDE WILL
MUSS YOUR DO

© Corey Dorsey

The outline of an Asian shrine mimics the shape of Mount Everest behind it.

ANANDAPUR

FLIGHTS OF WONDER ★★★★

APPEAL BY AGE Preschool ★★★★ Grade School ★★★★½ Teens ★★★★
Young Adults ★★★★½ Over 30 ★★★★½ Seniors ★★★★½

What it is Stadium show about birds. Scope and scale Major attraction. When to go Anytime. Performance times are listed in the handout park map or *Times Guide*. Authors' rating Unique; ★★★★. Duration 30 minutes. When to arrive 10–15 minutes before showtime.

Both interesting and fun, *Flights of Wonder* is well paced and showcases a surprising number of bird species. The show has a straightforward educational presentation, yet is still riveting. The focus of *Flights of Wonder* is on the natural talents and characteristics of the various species, so don't expect to see any parrots riding bicycles. The natural behaviors, however, far surpass any tricks learned from humans. Overall, the presentation is fascinating and exceeds most guests' expectations.

MAHARAJAH JUNGLE TREK ★★★★

APPEAL BY AGE Preschool ★★★★ Grade School ★★★★ Teens ★★★★
Young Adults ★★★★½ Over 30 ★★★★ Seniors ★★★★½

What it is Walk-through zoological exhibit. Scope and scale Headliner. When to go Anytime. Comments Opens 30 minutes after the rest of the park. Authors' rating A standard-setter for natural habitat design; ★★★★. Duration About 20–30 minutes.

The Maharajah Jungle Trek is a zoological nature walk similar to the Gorilla Falls Exploration Trail, but with an Asian setting and Asian animals. You start with Komodo dragons and then work up to Malayan tapirs. Next is a cave with fruit bats. Ruins of the maharaja's palace provide the setting for Bengal tigers. From the top of a parapet in the palace, you can view a herd of blackbuck antelope and Asian deer. The trek concludes with an aviary. Labyrinthine, overgrown, and elaborately detailed, the temple ruin would be a compelling attraction even without the animals.

Did someone say, "Here, kitty, kitty?"

KALI RIVER RAPIDS (FASTPASS+) ★★★½

! APPEAL BY AGE

Preschool ★★★★	Grade School ★★★★½	Teens ★★★★½
Young Adults ★★★★½	Over 30 ★★★★½	Seniors ★★★★½

What it is **Whitewater raft ride.** Scope and scale **Headliner.** When to go **First or last hour the park is open, or use FastPass+.** Comments **Guaranteed to get wet. Opens 30 minutes after the rest of the park. 38" minimum height requirement; switching-off option (****see p. 113****).** Authors' rating **Short but scenic; ★★★½.** Duration **About 4 minutes.** Average wait in line per 100 people ahead of you **5 minutes.** Loading speed **Moderate.**

Whitewater raft rides have been a hot-weather favorite of theme-park patrons for more than 20 years. The ride itself consists of an unguided trip down a man-made river in a circular rubber raft with a top-mounted platform seating 12 people. The raft essentially floats freely in the current and is washed downstream through rapids and waves. Because the river is fairly wide, with numerous currents, eddies, and obstacles, there is no telling exactly where the raft will drift. Thus, each trip is different and exciting. The only certainty, however, is that you will be utterly soaked. Lockers are available near the entrance to store your non-water-resistant belongings.

What distinguishes Kali River Rapids from other theme-park raft rides is Disney's trademark attention to visual detail. Where many raft rides essentially plunge down a concrete ditch, Kali River Rapids flows through a dense rain forest and past waterfalls, temple ruins, and bamboo thickets; emerging into a cleared area where greedy loggers have ravaged the forest; and finally drifting back under the tropical canopy as the river cycles back to Anandapur. Along the way, your raft runs a gauntlet of raging cataracts, logjams, and other dangers.

Disney has done a great job with the visuals on this attraction. The queuing area, which winds through an ancient Southeast Asian temple, is one of the most striking and visually interesting settings of any Disney attraction. And though the sights on the raft trip itself are also first-class, the attraction is marginal in two important respects. First, it's only about 3.5 minutes on the water, and second, well . . . it's a weenie ride. Sure, you get wet, but otherwise the drops and rapids are not all that exciting.

DINOLAND U.S.A.

The brightest and most playful of Animal Kingdom's lands, this is a cross between a paleontological dig and a quirky roadside attraction. Accessible via the bridge from Discovery Island, DinoLand U.S.A. is home to a children's play area, a nature trail, a 1,500-seat amphitheater, and Dinosaur, one of Animal Kingdom's two thrill rides. Also in DinoLand are a couple of natural-history exhibits, including Dino-Sue, an exact replica of the largest, most complete *Tyrannosaurus rex* discovered to date. Named after the fossil hunter Sue Hendrickson, the replica (like the original) is 40 feet long and 13 feet tall. It doesn't dance, sing, or whistle, but it will get your attention nonetheless.

DISNEY DESIGN *with Sam Gennawey*

The key to appreciating DinoLand is understanding its backstory. A backstory is a Disney specialty and becomes the organizing tool that creates continuity between design elements. A writer provides a story, and all of the design elements and attractions are created to support that story, just like set design for a movie.

In this case, the backstory starts with the famous Dino Institute, filled with mischievous students who have taken over a small roadside stop. Next door, the owners of the gas station, Chester and Hester, have decided to cash in and create a carnival in their parking lot. After all, it was their dog that found the bone that led to all of the excavation in the first place.

Each physical element is created to add to the story in subtle layers. The Dino Institute is a formal structure with a proper plaza and educational trail. Right in front of the institute is the students' contribution: the rambling and ever-expanding Restaurantosaurus made up of permanent and temporary additions, including an Airstream trailer. Puns and artifacts are everywhere. Well worth the time to check out.

Even the plant material supports the theme. The area is heavy on primitive plants that include monkey puzzle trees with nasty spines, one of the largest collections of cycads, and 20 different species of magnolias, which go back to the dinosaur era.

Dino-Sue

THE BONEYARD ★★★

! APPEAL BY AGE	Preschool ★★★★½	Grade School ★★★★½	Teens ★★★★
	Young Adults ★★★½	Over 30 ★★★	Seniors ★★★

What it is Elaborate playground. Scope and scale Diversion. When to go Anytime. Comments Opens 30 minutes after the rest of the park. Authors' rating Stimulating fun for children; ★★★.

This attraction is an elaborate playground, particularly appealing to kids age 10 and younger, but visually appealing to all ages. Arranged in the form of a rambling open-air dig site, the Boneyard offers plenty of opportunity for exploration and letting off steam. Playground equipment consists of the skeletons of *Triceratops, Tyrannosaurus rex, Brachiosaurus,* and the like, on which children can swing, slide, and climb. In addition, there are sandpits where little ones can scrounge around for bones and fossils.

DINOSAUR (FASTPASS+) ★★★★

! APPEAL BY AGE Preschool ★★★ Grade School ★★★★ Teens ★★★★½
Young Adults ★★★★ Over 30 ★★★★ Seniors ★★★★

What it is Motion-simulator dark ride. Scope and scale Headliner. When to go Before 10:30 a.m., after 4:30 p.m., or use FastPass+. Comments 40" minimum height requirement; switching-off option (see p. 113). Authors' rating Not to be missed;★★★★. Duration 3½ minutes. Average wait in line per 100 people ahead of you 3 minutes; assumes full-capacity operation with 18-second dispatch interval. Loading speed Fast.

Dinosaur is a combination track ride and motion simulator. In addition to moving along a cleverly hidden track, the ride vehicle also bucks and pitches (the simulator part) in sync with the visuals and special effects encountered. The plot has you traveling back in time on a mission of rescue and conservation. Your objective, believe it or not, is to haul back a living dinosaur before the species becomes extinct. Whoever is operating the clock, however, cuts it a little close, and you arrive on the prehistoric scene just as a giant asteroid is hurtling toward Earth. General mayhem ensues as you evade carnivorous predators, catch the dino, and make your escape before the asteroid hits.

Dinosaur serves up nonstop action from beginning to end with brilliant visual effects. Elaborate even by Disney standards, the attraction provides a tense, frenetic ride that's embellished by the entire Imagineering arsenal of high-tech gimmickry. Although the ride is jerky, it's not too rough for seniors. The menacing dinosaurs, however, along with the intensity of the experience, make Dinosaur a no go for younger children. To its credit, Disney is unafraid to keep Dinosaur a dark, fast ride.

FINDING NEMO—THE MUSICAL / THEATER IN THE WILD (FASTPASS+) ★★★★

! APPEAL BY AGE Preschool ★★★★½ Grade School ★★★★½ Teens ★★★★ Young Adults ★★★★½ Over 30 ★★★★½ Seniors ★★★★½

What it is **Enclosed venue for live stage shows.** Scope and scale **Major attraction.** When to go **Anytime. Performance times are listed in the handout park map or *Times Guide*.** Authors' rating **Not to be missed; ★★★★.** Duration **About 35 minutes.** When to arrive **30 minutes before showtime.**

Another chapter in the Pixar-ization of Disney theme parks, *Finding Nemo* is arguably the most elaborate live show in any Disney World theme park. Incorporating dancing, special effects (including trapezes), and sophisticated digital backdrops of the undersea world, it features onstage human performers retelling Nemo's story with colorful, larger-than-life puppets. To be fair, *puppets* doesn't adequately convey the impressiveness of these props, some of which are huge. An original musical score was written by Robert Lopez, composer of the Tony Award–winning *Avenue Q* and *The Book of Mormon* and, of course, the uberpopular movie *Frozen*. The musical is a must-see for most Animal Kingdom guests. A few scenes, such as one in which Nemo's mom is eaten, may be too intense for some very small children. Some of the midshow musical numbers slow the pace, so the main concern for parents is whether the kids can sit still for an entire show. With that in mind, we advise parents to catch an afternoon performance—around 3 p.m. would be great—after seeing the rest of Animal Kingdom. If the kids get restless, you can either leave the show and catch the afternoon parade, or end your day at the park.

PRIMEVAL WHIRL (FASTPASS+) ★★★

APPEAL BY AGE			
	Preschool ★★★½	Grade School ★★★★	Teens ★★★★
	Young Adults ★★★½	Over 30 ★★★½	Seniors ★★★

What it is **Small coaster.** Scope and scale **Minor attraction.** When to go **First two hours the park is open, the hour before park closing, or use FastPass+.** Comments **48" minimum height requirement; switching-off option** **(see p. 113).** Authors' rating **"Wild mouse" on steroids; ★★★.** Duration **Almost 2½ minutes.** Average wait in line per 100 people ahead of you **4½ minutes.** Loading speed **Slow.**

Primeval Whirl is a small coaster with short drops and curves, and it runs through the jaws of a dinosaur, among other things. This coaster is different in that the cars also spin. It's like being on one of the Magic Kingdom's teacups, mounted on a roller coaster track. Because guests cannot control the spinning, the cars spin and stop spinning according to how the ride is programmed. Sometimes the spin is braked to a jarring halt after half a revolution, and sometimes it's allowed to make one or two complete turns. The complete spins are fun, but the screeching-stop half spins are almost painful. If you subtract the time it takes to ratchet up the first hill, the actual ride time is about 90 seconds. Like Space Mountain, the ride is duplicated side by side, but with only one queue.

The spinning takes a toll on yet another visitor.

© Andrew Petersen

TRICERATOP SPIN ★★

APPEAL BY AGE			
	Preschool ★★★★½	Grade School ★★★★	Teens ★★★
	Young Adults ★★★	Over 30 ★★★	Seniors ★★★½

What it is **Hub-and-spoke midway ride.** Scope and scale **Minor attraction.** When to go **Before noon or after 3 p.m.** Authors' rating **Dumbo's prehistoric forebear; ★★.** Duration **1½ minutes.** Average wait in line per 100 people ahead of you **10 minutes.** Loading speed **Slow.**

Another Dumbo-like ride. Here you spin around a central hub until a dinosaur pops out of the top of the hub. You'd think with the collective imagination of the Walt Disney Company, they'd come up with something a little more creative.

LIVE ENTERTAINMENT

Animal Encounters Throughout the day, Disney staff conduct impromptu short lectures on specific animals at the park. Look for a cast member in safari garb holding a bird, reptile, or small mammal. ***Winged Encounters—The Kingdom Takes Flight*** showcases macaws and their handlers on Discovery Island. Guests can talk to the animal's trainers and see the birds fly around the middle of the park. It's a lot like *Flights of Wonder* (see page 285) on a much smaller scale, and the macaws are very pretty. Check the *Times Guide* for performances and the exact location.

Goodwill Ambassadors A number of Asian and African natives are on hand throughout the park. Both gracious and knowledgeable, they are delighted to discuss their country and its wildlife. Look for them in Harambe and along the Gorilla Falls Exploration Trail in Africa, and in Anandapur and along the Maharajah Jungle Trek in Asia. They can also be found near the main entrance, at The Oasis, and as part of Wilderness Explorers (see page 272).

Street Performers Street performers can be found most of the time at Harambe in Africa and Anandapur in Asia. Far and away the most intriguing street performer is the one you can't see—at least not at first. Totally bedecked in foliage and luxuriant vines is a stilt walker named DiVine, who blends so completely with Animal Kingdom's dense flora that you don't notice her until she moves. We've seen guests standing less than a foot away gasp in amazement as DiVine brushes them with a leafy tendril. Usually found on the path between Asia and Africa, DiVine is a must-see. If you don't encounter her, ask a cast member when and where she can be

found. Video of her is available on YouTube (go to youtube.com and search for "DiVine Disney's Animal Kingdom").

Rivers of Light Animal Kingdom never had a nighttime event along the lines of the Magic Kingdom's *Wishes* or Disney Hollywood Studios' *Fantasmic!* One reason is that fireworks would startle the animals; another was that, up to now, there simply weren't enough attractions to keep the park open much after dark. In preparation for the 2017 opening of Pandora: The Land of Avatar, Animal Kingdom has added *Rivers of Light*, nighttime safaris (see page 278), and more dining options. The show takes place on the lagoon formed by the Discovery River in between Discovery Island and Expedition Everest. Two amphitheaters hold a maximum of 5,000 guests.

Two shamans take to the river as part of a traditional Asian lantern celebration. The visual elements grow quickly from there as the celebration expands to include animals and the natural world. At one point the river is filled with 100 lantern floats, the largest of which also shoot water high into the air. Similar to *Fantasmic!*, colorful nature scenes are displayed on tall mist curtains, while other imagery is projected on to The Tree of Life. While all of this is happening, four floats emerge, each 15 feet tall and 30 feet long. Each float contains one or two massive owls, elephants, tigers, or turtles, their bodies seemingly assembled the way pieces of stained glass are made into a complete window. These animal bodies are lit from within by a rainbow of bright lights synchronized to music. Throw in the colorful reflections off the Discovery River, and it's a visual treat.

The show got off to a difficult start, and official opening was delayed by several months. For a limited-time engagement Disney used the setting of the amphitheaters to stage *Jungle Book: Alive,* a live show filled with music and special effects celebrating the Disney live-action film *The Jungle Book*.

The seating capacity of 5,000 guests, with some partly obstructed viewing areas, is likely to continue to be a problem, especially during the peak holiday times when guests also pay premium prices for park admission. In comparison, *Fantasmic!* at Disney's Hollywood Studios has a capacity of 6,900. So until Pandora: The World of Avatar opens, guests will still leave the Animal Kingdom early if they did not get a FastPass+ for the viewing of *Rivers of Light*.

Discovery Island Carnivale Various performers and musicians bring their energy, costumes, and music to a party inspired by celebrations from around the world. The event lasts several hours, so guests can flit in and out, seeing different experiences each time.

Harambe Wildlife Parti The Wildlife Parti brings the African village of Harambe to life with a street party and bustling marketplace. The Parti consists of a goodwill shaman on stilts, dancing, people playing instruments, women who call on the spirit of the African crane to entertain, soccer players interacting with the crowd and performing tricks, and acrobats.

Tree of Life *Awakening* One of the new nighttime offerings, *The Awakening* runs several times per night. It combines digital video projections with music and other special projection effects. Some effects make it appear that animals carved into the tree trunk have come alive, while others happen in the tree's leaves and branches. It's similar to the Magic Kingdom's popular *Celebrate the Magic* show.

COUNTER-SERVICE RESTAURANTS

Counter-service food is a cut above the average at the Animal Kingdom, and both ethnic and standard fare (hot dogs, burgers, and so on) are available. Our two favorites are **Flame Tree Barbecue** with outdoor waterfront dining and **Yak & Yeti Local Food Cafes** for casual Asian fare.

Flame Tree Barbecue

QUALITY Excellent VALUE B– PORTION Large LOCATION Discovery Island
READER RESPONSES 92% 8% DINING PLAN Yes

St. Louis–style ribs; smoked half chicken; pulled-pork sandwich; roasted-chicken salad; rib, chicken, and pulled-pork platter; watermelon salad; child's plate of baked chicken drumstick, chicken sandwich, hot dog, or PB&J sandwich; fries or onion rings; lime or chocolate mousse; Safari Amber beer, Bud Light, and wine.

Harambe Market

QUALITY Good VALUE B PORTION Large LOCATION Africa
READER RESPONSES 90% 10% DINING PLAN Yes

Spice-rubbed Karubi ribs, beef and pork or tikka masala chicken sausages, grilled-chicken skewers, all-beef gyro flatbread, or grilled-vegetable stack, each served with a side of green papaya–carrot slaw and a black-eyed pea, corn, and tomato salad. Beer and South African wines also available. Kids' menu includes child-size versions of the adult selections or a snack pack with yogurt, apple slices, carrot sticks, and crackers. Disney Imagineers modeled the marketplace setting after a typical real-life market in an African nation during the 1960s Colonial era.

Kusafiri Coffee Shop and Bakery

QUALITY Good VALUE B PORTION Medium LOCATION Africa
READER RESPONSES 92% 8% DINING PLAN Yes

Fruit turnovers, Danish and other pastries, muffins, croissants, cookies, brownies, cupcakes, cake, fruit cups, yogurt, coffee, cocoa, and juice. Breakfast wrap (egg, sausage, spinach, and goat cheese) served until 10:30 a.m. Get your morning sugar rush on the way to Kilimanjaro Safaris.

Pizzafari

QUALITY Fair VALUE B PORTION Medium LOCATION Discovery Island
READER RESPONSES 80% 👍 20% 👎 DINING PLAN Yes

Shrimp flatbread; cheese, pepperoni, sausage, or veggie personal pizza; meatball sub; Romaine salad with chicken or shrimp. Kids' choices: mac and cheese, pasta with turkey marinara, cheese pizza, or PB&J. Chocolate mousse or tiramisu for dessert. Beer and wine available. Kids love it. Hectic at peak mealtimes. The pizza is unimpressive but popular. Kosher menu available.

Restaurantosaurus

QUALITY Good VALUE B+ PORTION Medium–large LOCATION DinoLand U.S.A.
READER RESPONSES 77% 👍 23% 👎 DINING PLAN Yes

Angus bacon cheeseburger; chicken nuggets; black-bean burger; chili-cheese hot dog; roasted-chicken salad; grilled-chicken sandwich; kids' turkey wrap, corn dog nuggets, cheeseburger, or PB&J. Good burger-toppings bar.

Royal Anandapur Tea Company

QUALITY Good VALUE B PORTION Medium LOCATION Asia
READER RESPONSES 91% 👍 9% 👎 DINING PLAN No

Wide variety of hot and iced teas (fantastic frozen chai); lattes; coffee, espresso, and cappuccino; large pastries. Offers several loose-leaf teas from Asia and Africa, some organic.

Thirsty River Bar and Trek Snacks

QUALITY Good VALUE B PORTION Medium LOCATION Asia
READER RESPONSES Too new to rate DINING PLAN Yes

Smoked-turkey sandwich; roasted-pork *bánh mì* sandwich with cilantro and sriracha sauce; Thai papaya salad with shrimp, peanuts, and chiles; Asian noodle salad; hummus; fresh fruit and vegetables; ice cream novelties; chips and other snacks. Full bar serving cocktails and a few beers and wines. A new food stand to help the Asia area prep for *Rivers of Light* crowds. Try the Himalayan Ghost, a scary-smooth mix of vodka, guava juice, and lemonade.

Yak & Yeti Local Food Cafes

QUALITY Fair VALUE B PORTION Large LOCATION Asia
READER RESPONSES 90% 👍 10% 👎 DINING PLAN Yes

Crispy honey chicken with steamed rice (best choice), Korean stir-fry barbecue chicken, ginger chicken salad, Asian chicken sandwich, roasted-vegetable couscous wrap, teriyaki beef bowl, egg rolls, chicken fried rice. Kids' menu: chicken tenders, PB&J, or cheeseburger with fresh fruit.

Animal Kingdom Carnivore Treats

Goofy Burger

Observing the sausage factory code of silence, we can't tell you what's in it. But it's served on a bun, golden brown, and makes your lips jump up and down! Comes with fries and a medium-size drink.

....$8.95 ($10.95 with supersize ears)

Captain Hook Shish Ke-Bob

If you're a real carnivore, this one's for you. Tucker in for a whole pound of real cow meat grilled on a stainless steel prosthetic device over an open grill. Try it once and you'll be hooked! Gluten free.

..............................$11.37

Tinkerburger

Looking for a burger that will literally take you away? The Tinkerburger fits the bill. Served with Monterey Jack cheese, chipotle sauce, and a heaping measure of pixie dust, this is a burger you can't put (or keep) down.

.....$8.95 ($12.95 with butterfly net)

Mulan Shoe Pork

This colorful dish features barbecue pork ribs served in a decorative souvenir Chinese shoe. If you like pigs in a blanket, you'll be over the moon with this treat.

..............................$10.00

PART 8

DISNEY'S HOLLYWOOD STUDIOS

Disney's Hollywood Studios is a theme park dedicated to the process of making films, theater productions, TV shows, and music. The park also pays tribute to classic achievements in film and the other arts, especially those that have become part of popular American culture.

Formerly known as Disney-MGM Studios, the Disney Company built the park in response to the creation of Universal Studios Florida, a movie- and film-based theme park, in the late 1980s. When Disney-MGM opened, Disney promoted it as a working TV- and movie-production facility. And for a time it was common to see both animated films (such as Disney's animated *Lilo & Stitch*, *Mulan*, and *Brother Bear*) and TV shows in production as you walked through the park. Eventually, however, the costs of running duplicate facilities in both California and Florida became too great, and most Florida work stopped. While the buildings are still present, it's extremely rare to see actual television or film work being done nowadays.

The name Disney-MGM Studios also went by the wayside, with the more generic Disney's Hollywood Studios taking its place. Most park-goers now simply refer to it as DHS or the Studios. In the coming years Disney's Hollywood Studios will undergo major changes. Large portions of the park will be completely reimagined, with construction already visible. Toy Story Land, which will expand the Pixar Place area, will likely be the first section open within the next couple of years. The big deal, however, is a full Star Wars–themed land that will encompass much of the former Streets of America side of the park. To visit Star Wars Land you will need patience, though: it's going to be a few years.

Not to Be Missed at Disney's Hollywood Studios

Fantasmic!	***Muppet-Vision 3-D***
Rock 'n' Roller Coaster	**Star Tours—The Adventures Continue**
Toy Story Mania!	**Twilight Zone Tower of Terror**

Disney's Hollywood Studios

Attractions

1. *Beauty and the Beast–Live on Stage*/ Theater of the Stars FP+
2. *Disney Junior–Live on Stage!* FP+
3. *Fantasmic!* ☑ Use FP+
4. *For the First Time in Forever: A Frozen Sing-Along Celebration* FP+
5. The Great Movie Ride ☑ Use FP+
6. *Indiana Jones Epic Stunt Spectacular!* FP+

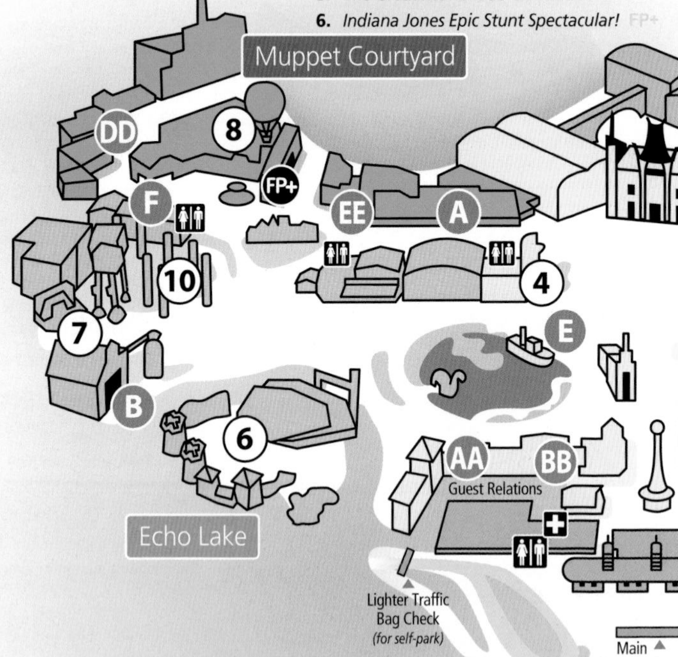

Counter-Service Restaurants

- **A.** ABC Commissary 👍
- **B.** Backlot Express 👍
- **C.** Catalina Eddie's
- **D.** Fairfax Fare
- **E.** Min and Bill's Dockside Diner
- **F.** Pizza Rizzo
- **G.** Rosie's All-American Cafe
- **H.** Starring Rolls Cafe
- **I.** Toluca Legs Turkey Co. 👍
- **J.** Trolley Car Cafe *(Starbucks)*

Table-Service Restaurants

- **AA.** 50's Prime Time Café
- **BB.** Hollywood & Vine
- **CC.** The Hollywood Brown Derby 👍
- **DD.** Mama Melrose's Ristorante Italiano
- **EE.** Sci-Fi Dine-In Theater Restaurant

7. *Jedi Training: Trials of the Temple*
8. *Jim Henson's Muppet-Vision 3-D* ☑ FP+
9. Rock 'n' Roller Coaster Starring Aerosmith ☑ Use FP+
10. Star Tours—The Adventures Continue ☑ Use FP+
11. Star Wars Launch Bay
12. Toy Story Mania! ☑ Use FP+
13. The Twilight Zone Tower of Terror ☑ Use FP+
14. *Voyage of the Little Mermaid* FP+
15. *Walt Disney: One Man's Dream*

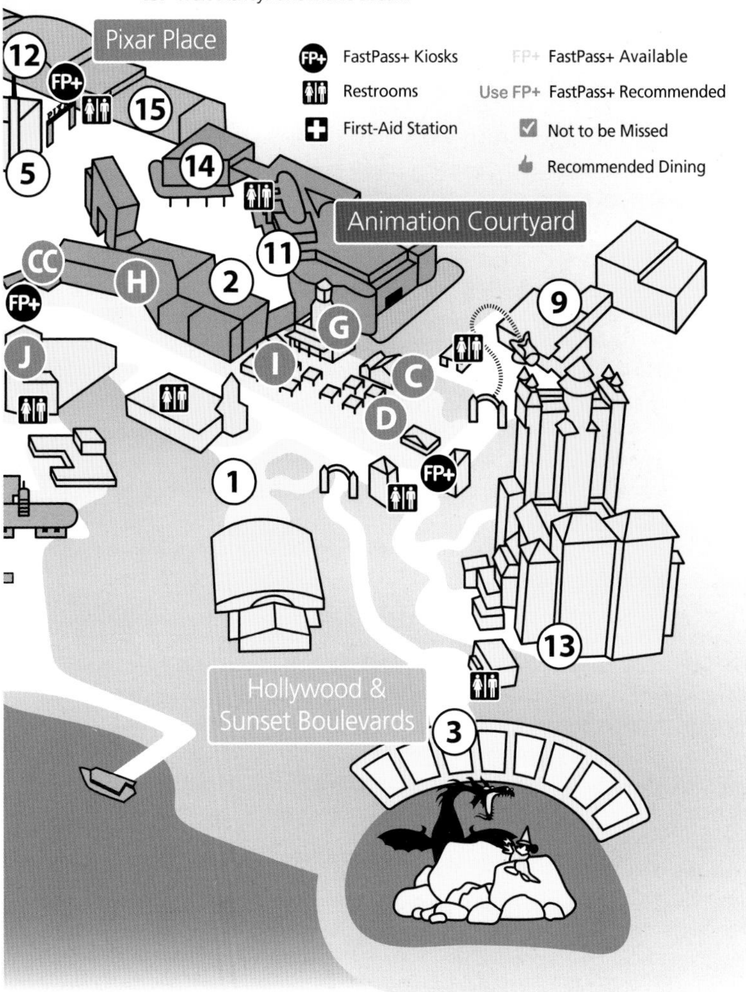

HOLLYWOOD AND SUNSET BOULEVARDS

Hollywood Boulevard is a palm-lined re-creation of Hollywood's main drag during Los Angeles's golden age. Architecture is Streamline Moderne, which is a version of Art Deco from the 1930s. Most service facilities are here, interspersed with eateries and shops. Merchandise includes Disney trademark items, as well as Hollywood and movie-related souvenirs. Hollywood characters and roving performers entertain on the boulevard, and daily parades and other happenings pass this way.

Sunset Boulevard, evoking the 1940s, is a major component of DHS. The first right off Hollywood Boulevard, Sunset Boulevard provides another venue for dining, shopping, and street entertainment.

DISNEY DESIGN *with Sam Gennawey*

In 1989 Michael Eisner proclaimed that Walt Disney World's third park would be dedicated to Hollywood, "not a place on a map, but a state of mind," and "a Hollywood that never was—and always will be."

While Disney's Hollywood Studios (then Disney-MGM Studios) is meant to be an imaginary Hollywood, it is one rooted in tangible real-world references. For example, many of the facades along Hollywood and Sunset Boulevards are replicas of classic Los Angeles–area structures; some of those buildings still stand in Los Angeles, while others have been torn down. The buildings include an electric substation (1907) from Culver City that is now a performance space, the Baine Building (1926), a J.J. Newberry (1928), a bank on Wilshire Boulevard (1929), the Chapman Market (1929), Max Factor Building (1931), Owl Drug Store (1933), and many others. A highlight is The Hollywood Brown Derby (1929), a treasure inside and out.

Disney's Imagineers were inspired by early filmmakers who used Los Angeles as the background for their movies. Here, the Imagineers applied a design trick called shrink and edit that takes a real building for inspiration and then changes the scale, color, or detail to support the story.

Your adventure starts at the park entrance as you pass through a reproduction of the Streamline Moderne Pan-Pacific Auditorium, Hollywood's primary convention center from 1935 to 1972. The entry plaza is at the intersection of Hollywood and Prospect Avenue. The central building is the Crossroads building (1936), a tribute to an early Los Angeles mini-mall. It is topped by a 5-foot Mickey Mouse, with one of Mickey's ears functioning as a lightning rod.

The Hollywoodland billboard refers to a subdivision that opened in 1923, the same year Walt Disney moved to Hollywood. Adjacent is a billboard for the 1945 Hollywood Canteen, a Hollywood oasis for soldiers fighting in World War II.

As the park ventures into a period of flux, the focus is transitioning from a representation of physical Hollywood to the imaginary by-products of Hollywood film releases. For example, instead of featuring the studio making Star Wars, the park will feature the intergalactic world represented within the Star Wars films. The change is subtle but significant.

Hollywood Boulevard Services

Most of the park's service facilities are on Hollywood Boulevard, including:

Baby Center/Baby Care Needs: At Guest Relations; baby food and other necessities available at Oscar's Classic Car Souvenirs
Banking Services: ATM outside the park to the right of the turnstiles and near Pizza Rizzo
Camera Supplies: At the Darkroom on the right side of Hollywood Boulevard as you enter the park, just past Oscar's Classic Car Souvenirs
First Aid: At Guest Relations
Live Entertainment and Parade Information: Available free at Guest Relations and elsewhere in park
Lost and Found: At Package Pick-Up, to the right of the entrance
Lost Persons: Report lost persons at Guest Relations
Storage Lockers: Rental lockers to the right of the main entrance, to the left of Oscar's Classic Car Souvenirs
Wheelchair and Stroller Rental: To the right of the entrance, at Oscar's Classic Car Souvenirs

FANTASMIC! (FASTPASS+) ★★★★½

APPEAL BY AGE			
Preschool ★★★★	Grade School ★★★★½	Teens ★★★★½
Young Adults ★★★★½	Over 30 ★★★★½	Seniors ★★★★½

What it is **Mixed-media nighttime spectacular.** Scope and scale **Super-headliner.** When to go **Check *Times Guide* for schedule; if two shows are offered, the second is less crowded.** Comments **Disney's very best nighttime event.** Authors' rating **Not to be missed; ★★★★½.** Duration **25 minutes.** Probable waiting time **50–90 minutes for a seat; 35–40 minutes for standing room.**

Fantasmic! is a mixed-media show presented off Sunset Boulevard behind the Tower of Terror. *Fantasmic!* is staged on an island opposite a 6,900-seat amphitheater. By far the largest theater facility ever created by Disney, the amphitheater can accommodate an additional 3,000 standing guests for an audience of nearly 10,000.

Fantasmic! is far and away the most innovative outdoor spectacle ever attempted at any theme park. Starring Mickey Mouse in his role as the sorcerer's apprentice from *Fantasia*, the production uses lasers, images projected on a shroud of mist, fireworks, lighting effects, and music in combinations so stunning that you can scarcely believe what you are seeing. The plot is simple: good versus evil. The story gets lost in all the special effects at times, but no matter; it's the spectacle, not the story line, that is so overpowering. While *beautiful*, *stunning*, and *powerful* are words that immediately come to mind, they fail to convey the uniqueness of this presentation.

Though we do not receive many reports of young children being terrified by *Fantasmic!*, we suggest that you spend a little time preparing your younger children for what they will see. You can mitigate the fright factor somewhat by sitting back a bit. Also, make sure to hang on to your children after *Fantasmic!* and to give them explicit instructions for regrouping in the event you are separated.

THE GREAT MOVIE RIDE (FASTPASS+) ★★★½

! APPEAL BY AGE			
	Preschool ★★★	Grade School ★★★½	Teens ★★★½
	Young Adults ★★★½	Over 30 ★★★½	Seniors ★★★★

What it is **Indoor movie-history ride.** Scope and scale **Headliner.** When to go **Before 11 a.m., during dinner, after 8 p.m., or use FastPass+.** Comments **Elaborate, with several surprises.** Authors' rating **Unique; ★★★½.** Duration **About 19 minutes.** Average wait in line per 100 people ahead of you **2 minutes; assumes all cars operating.** Loading speed **Fast.**

Entering through a re-creation of Hollywood's Chinese Theatre, guests board vehicles for a fast-paced tour through soundstage sets from classic films, including *Casablanca*, *Tarzan*, *The Wizard of Oz*, *Alien*, and *Raiders of the Lost Ark*. Each set is populated with Disney Audio-Animatronic characters, as well as an occasional human, all augmented by sound and lighting effects. One of Disney's larger and more ambitious dark rides, The Great Movie Ride encompasses 95,000 square feet and showcases some of the most famous scenes in filmmaking, in some of the largest sets ever constructed for a Disney ride.

We're fans of Great Movie Ride—it's elaborate and well engineered—but that doesn't mean it's perfect. For one thing, many of the film references—which may have been appropriate for audiences in the late 1980s—are hopelessly outdated for many guests under age 40, and certainly most under 30. We think we'd be hard-pressed to find someone in those demographics who's actually seen a James Cagney or Busby Berkeley film (or, for that matter, Disney's *Fantasia*). Perhaps it's time to update the attraction. Or to bring back musicals with swimming starlets. Either one is fine with Bob and Len.

Ever wonder how those huge theater cars in The Great Movie Ride operate? Or how the Imagineers created the sets and props for this affectionate tribute to the Golden Age of Hollywood? You'll find some of the answers in the *Walt Disney: One Man's Dream* exhibit (see page 323), where models and schematics reveal The Great Movie Ride's inner workings. So if you really wanna know how the gangster sequence works, youse should get your mugs over to *One Man's Dream*, see?

The Great Movie Ride draws decent crowds (and lines) from midmorning on. Actual wait times usually run about one-third shorter than the time posted.

ROCK 'N' ROLLER COASTER STARRING AEROSMITH (FASTPASS+) ★★★★

! APPEAL BY AGE Preschool ★★½ Grade School ★★★★½ Teens ★★★★★ Young Adults ★★★★★ Over 30 ★★★★½ Seniors ★★★★

What it is Rock music–themed roller coaster. Scope and scale Headliner. When to go First 30 minutes the park is open or use FastPass+. Comments 48" minimum height requirement; children younger than age 7 must ride with an adult; switching-off option (see p. 113). Single-rider line available. Authors' rating Disney's wildest American coaster; not to be missed; ★★★★. Duration Almost 1½ minutes. Average wait in line per 100 people ahead of you 2½ minutes; assumes all trains operating. Loading speed Moderate–fast.

Exponentially wilder than Space Mountain or Big Thunder Mountain in the Magic Kingdom, Rock 'n' Roller Coaster is an attraction for fans of high-tech thrill rides. Though the rock icons and synchronized music add measurably to the experience, the ride itself, as opposed to sights and sounds along the way, is the focus. Rock 'n' Roller Coaster offers loops, corkscrews, and drops that make Space Mountain seem like the Jungle Cruise. What really makes this metal coaster unusual, however, is that at first, it's in the dark (like Space Mountain, only with Southern California nighttime scenes instead of space), and second, you're launched up the first hill like a jet off a carrier deck. By the time you crest the hill, you'll have gone from 0 to 57 miles per hour in less than 3 seconds. When you enter the first loop, you'll be pulling five g's. By comparison, that's two more g's than astronauts experienced at liftoff on a space shuttle.

The ride lasts less than 2 minutes, but there might be enough entertainment in the queue and preshow to make up for any long waits in line. Classic concert posters line the halls of the queue, providing the opportunity to point out that you could once see Jimi Hendrix for what it costs to park at concerts these days. Roll your eyes and sigh deeply if your kids say, "Jimi who?" The preshow features Aerosmith in a short video setting up the premise to the ride. It's funny as much for the band's stilted delivery as it is for Steven Tyler's background antics when others are talking.

The ride's launch point. And honey, you're headin' down a one-way street.

THE TWILIGHT ZONE TOWER OF TERROR (FASTPASS+) ★★★★★

! APPEAL BY AGE			
	Preschool ★★★	Grade School ★★★★	Teens ★★★★½
	Young Adults ★★★★★	Over 30 ★★★★	Seniors ★★★★½

What it is **Sci-fi–themed indoor thrill ride.** Scope and scale **Super-headliner.** When to go **First or last 30 minutes the park is open, or use FastPass+.** Comments **40" minimum height requirement; switching-off option (see p. 113).** Authors' rating **Walt Disney World's best attraction; not to be missed; ★★★★★.** Duration **About 4 minutes plus preshow.** Average wait in line per 100 people ahead of you **4 minutes; assumes all elevators operating.** Loading speed **Moderate.**

The Tower of Terror is a different species of Disney thrill ride, though it borrows elements of The Haunted Mansion at the Magic Kingdom. The story is that you're touring a once-famous Hollywood hotel gone to ruin. As at Star Tours, the queuing area immerses guests in the adventure as they pass through the hotel's once-opulent public rooms. From the lobby, guests are escorted into the hotel's library, where Rod Serling, speaking from an old black-and-white television, greets the guests and introduces the plot.

The Tower of Terror is a whopper at 13-plus stories. Breaking tradition in terms of visually isolating themed areas, it lets you see the entire Studios from atop the tower . . . but you have to look quickly. The ride vehicle, one of the hotel's service elevators, takes guests to see the haunted hostelry. The tour begins innocuously, but at about the fifth floor, things get pretty weird. Guests are subjected to a full range of eerie effects as they cross into *The Twilight Zone.* The climax of the adventure occurs when the elevator reaches the top floor (the 13th, of course) and the cable snaps.

The Tower of Terror is an experience to savor. Though the final plunges (yep, make that plural) are calculated to thrill, the extraordinary visual and audio effects are the meat of the attraction. There's richness and subtlety here, enough to keep the ride fresh and stimulating after many repetitions. Disney tinkers with The Tower of Terror incessantly. Random ride and drop sequences make the attraction faster and keep you guessing about when, how far, and how many times the elevator will drop. In addition to random sequencing, visual and auditory effects add to the experience . . . if you can pay that much attention.

The next time you check in to a deserted hotel on the dark side of Hollywood, be sure you know just what kind of vacancy you're filling.

How great would it be if the Tower were an actual hotel? We'd take the stairs, of course.

THEATER OF THE STARS / *BEAUTY AND THE BEAST—LIVE ON STAGE* (FASTPASS+) ★★★★

APPEAL BY AGE			
Preschool ★★★★½	Grade School ★★★★	Teens ★★★★
Young Adults ★★★★	Over 30 ★★★★	Seniors ★★★★½

What it is Live Hollywood-style musical, usually featuring Disney characters; performed in an open-air theater. Scope and scale Major attraction. When to go Anytime; evenings are cooler. Comments Performances are listed in the daily *Times Guide*. Authors' rating Excellent; ★★★★. Duration 25 minutes. When to arrive 20–30 minutes before showtime.

Theater of the Stars combines Disney characters with singers and dancers in upbeat and humorous Hollywood musicals. *The Beauty and the Beast* show, in particular, is outstanding. The singing is a cut above most theme park shows in Disney or elsewhere. The story, necessarily abbreviated from the film, is clear and has no slow moments. The sets and costume design are colorful and dynamic, without being distracting. *Beauty and the Beast* ranks up there with *Festival of the Lion King* (at Animal Kingdom) and *Aladdin* (formerly at Disney California Adventure park).

The theater offers a clear field of vision from almost every seat, and a canopy protects the audience from the Florida sun (or rain). The theater still gets mighty hot in the summer, but you should make it through a performance without suffering a heatstroke.

ECHO LAKE

DISNEY DESIGN *with Sam Gennawey*

The real Echo Lake is a man-made lake near downtown Los Angeles and served as the background for many early silent film comedies. Just like the park's Hollywood Boulevard, the buildings that surround Echo Lake are from Los Angeles. Hollywood & Vine is modeled after a cafeteria (once the Hollywood Post Office) that was within walking distance of all the moviemaking action and burned down in 1990. The 50's Prime Time Cafe is influenced by residential buildings by Richard Neutra, Frank Lloyd Wright, and Pierre Koenig. The Streamline Moderne theater and adjacent buildings that house *For the First Time in Forever: A Frozen Sing-Along Celebration* are based on NBC Radio City (1938) and CBS Columbia Square (1938).

At that time, Los Angeles was filled with what is known interchangeably as programmatic architecture, California Crazy, or duck. A building of this type, as defined by architect Robert Venturi, is one whose "exterior is in the shape of the everyday object they relate to" and is "a building in which the architecture is subordinate to the overall symbolic form." The boat you see in the corner of Echo Lake is a tribute to a 1930 film called *Min and Bill* that won Marie Dressler an Academy Award. The dinosaur at the other end of Echo Lake is Gertie, an animated character who toured along with Winsor McCay on the vaudeville circuit in 1914. His hand-painted film was a huge influence on Walt Disney.

As you walk away from Echo Lake, you also move away from the architectural history of Los Angeles and into a studio back lot. Things become less real. *Indiana Jones Epic Stunt Spectacular!* is just a backdrop. The Star Tours facade is a reproduction of the Ewok Village movie set, with no pretension of being anything other than a stage. And the Backlot Express is a prop storage area.

FOR THE FIRST TIME IN FOREVER: A FROZEN SING-ALONG CELEBRATION

(FASTPASS+) ★★★

APPEAL BY AGE			
Preschool ★★★★½	Grade School ★★★★★	Teens ★★★★½	
Young Adults ★★★★	Over 30 ★★★	Seniors ★★★	

What it is Sing-along stage show retelling the story of *Frozen,* with appearances by Anna and Elsa. Scope and scale Minor attraction. When to go Check your *Times Guide* for showtimes. Authors' rating You'll learn all the words whether you want to or not; ★★★. Duration 25 minutes. When to arrive 15 minutes before showtime.

This attraction started out as a hastily assembled stage show during the summer of 2014, when Disney's Hollywood Studios began closing other attractions and needed something for guests to do, but it has grown into a legitimately enjoyable performance that retells the plot of *Frozen* in 25 minutes. That's enough time to sing every song in the movie and have a quick visit from Anna and Elsa—but nothing new. The hosts of the show are funny enough to keep guests giggling between musical numbers, and the finale with the Arendelle royalty will thrill young ones and even many slightly older ones. The format and production values make the show interesting even if you're on *Frozen* overload, and if you somehow don't already know all the words, lyrics are provided on a giant screen.

A mom from Richmond, Virginia, says that even with *Frozen* overload, the sing-along is a definite upper:

> **The sing-along was fantastic—along with *Fantasmic,* it was the highlight of the day. Even if you're a bit sick of *Frozen,* the atmosphere and the humor involved make it a lot of fun.**

Using FastPass+ on this attraction grants you access to a preferred seating section near the front of the stage. Guests experiencing the show via stand-by will be seated in whatever seats are left.

INDIANA JONES EPIC STUNT SPECTACULAR! (FASTPASS+) ★★★½

APPEAL BY AGE	Preschool ★★★½	Grade School ★★★★½	Teens ★★★★
	Young Adults ★★★★	Over 30 ★★★★	Seniors ★★★★

What it is **Movie-stunt demonstration and action show.** Scope and scale **Headliner.** When to go **First two shows or last show.** Comments **Performance times posted on a sign at the entrance to the theater.** Authors' rating **Done on a grand scale; ★★★½.** Duration **30 minutes.** Preshow **Selection of extras from audience.** When to arrive **20–30 minutes before showtime.**

This stage show features professional stuntmen and stuntwomen who demonstrate dangerous stunts with an insider's look at how it's done. Key scenes from the first Indiana Jones film, *Raiders of the Lost Ark*, are re-created on an enormous covered stage, and those scenes provide an opportunity to explain how moviemaking stunt work is done.

Indiana Jones's opening, which reenacts the big rolling ball intro of *Raiders*, is well done and certainly gets the audience's attention. In fact, sets throughout the entire show are elaborate and detailed. Besides the intro, other highlights include the German flying-wing airplane scene and the chase through Cairo's streets, with plenty of fire and explosions. Audience members (selected right before the show begins) get a chance to be extras in some of the scenes that don't involve things blowing up.

Indiana Jones's stunt work ranges from audience participation in fight scenes to large-scale explosions involving elaborate props.

JEDI TRAINING: TRIALS OF THE TEMPLE ★★★½

! APPEAL BY AGE			
	Preschool ★★★★½	Grade School ★★★★★	Teens ★★★★
	Young Adults ★★★★	Over 30 ★★★★½	Seniors ★★★★

What it is Outdoor stage show. Scope and scale Minor attraction. When to go First two shows. Comments To sign up your children to go on stage, visit the Indiana Jones Adventure Outpost shop early in the morning; spots are first come, first serve. Authors' rating A treat for young Star Wars lovers; ★★★½. Duration About 15 minutes. When to arrive 15 minutes before showtime.

Jedi Training: Trials of the Temple is staged several times daily to the left of the Star Tours building entrance, opposite Backlot Express. Young Skywalkers-in-training are selected from the audience to train in the ways of The Force and do battle against Darth Vader and the Seventh Sister Inquisitor from the *Star Wars Rebels* cartoon. A choreographed battle between Darth Maul and the Jedi Master's apprentice finishes off the show, which is not as intense as it sounds—it is for 4- to 12-year-olds, after all. Register your Obi-wannabes by the Indiana Jones Adventure Outpost shop (near 50's Prime Time Cafe) for their chance to get on stage and battle the Dark Side.

Do light sabers have an "on" button, or do you just use The Force?

STAR TOURS— THE ADVENTURES CONTINUE

(FASTPASS+) ★★★½

! APPEAL BY AGE	Preschool ★★★★	Grade School ★★★★½	Teens ★★★★½
	Young Adults ★★★★½	Over 30 ★★★★½	Seniors ★★★★

What it is Indoor space flight–simulation ride. Scope and scale Headliner. When to go Before 10 a.m., after 6 p.m., or use FastPass+. Comments Expectant mothers and anyone prone to motion sickness are advised against riding. Too intense for many children younger than age 8; 40" minimum height requirement; switching-off option (see p. 113). Authors' rating A classic adventure; ★★★½. Duration About 7 minutes. Average wait in line per 100 people ahead of you 5 minutes; assumes all simulators operating. Loading speed Moderate–fast.

Based on the Star Wars movie series, this was Disney's first modern simulator ride. Guests ride in a flight simulator modeled after those used for training pilots and astronauts. Hold on tight as you experience dips, turns, twists, and light speed only to exit hyperspace above Coruscant; on Naboo, Tatooine, or Endor; or inside the dreaded Death Star.

The ride film, based on the pod racing scene from Episode I: The Phantom Menace, is projected in high-definition 3-D and has more than 50 combinations of opening and ending scenes. You could ride Star Tours all day without seeing the same film segment twice.

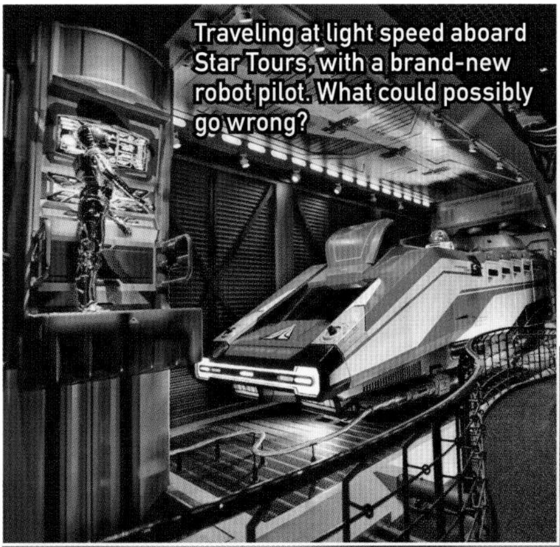

Traveling at light speed aboard Star Tours, with a brand-new robot pilot. What could possibly go wrong?

MOTION SICKNESS WARNING

STAR WARS LAND

The big news regarding Hollywood Studios is that it will become home to a galaxy that was previously far, far away. Star Wars has been a favorite among many for a long time, and the latest megahit, *The Force Awakens,* has emboldened Disney to finally build a full land dedicated to all things Star Wars. This 14-acre land will be near the current Star Tours attraction, but an exact location has not yet been announced. What we know is that it will be a new fictional planet with a trading port, allowing a mixture of characters and cultures from all of the various Star Wars offerings. There will be two attractions, one that puts guests into a major battle and one that puts guests at the controls of the iconic *Millennium Falcon.* As we go to print, construction has just begun, so our best guess right now for an opening date is 2019 or 2020.

MUPPET COURTYARD

Formerly part of the extinct Streets of America movie scene back lot, Muppet Courtyard is now a designated themed area home to *Muppet-Vision 3-D.* The street sets have been removed, and most of the area around it is a construction zone.

MUPPET-VISION 3-D

(FASTPASS+) ★★★★

APPEAL BY AGE Preschool ★★★★ | Grade School ★★★★ | Teens ★★★★ | Young Adults ★★★★ | Over 30 ★★★★ | Seniors ★★★★½

What it is **3-D movie starring the Muppets.** Scope and scale **Major attraction.** When to go **Anytime.** Authors' rating **Uproarious; not to be missed; ★★★★.** Duration **17 minutes.** Preshow **Muppets on television.** Probable waiting time **12 minutes.**

Muppet-Vision features the cast of Jim Henson's *Muppets* demonstrating an improvement to late-1980s 3-D animation. While that might sound boring, the actual plot represents perhaps 10% of the overall film. The rest is a series of classic Muppet gags and skits, featuring the entire cast of characters from Kermit and Miss Piggy, to Gonzo, the Swedish Chef, and the elder grouches, Statler and Waldorf. There are enough funny one-liners and jokes here that you'll be repeating them for the rest of the day. (One of our favorites: In answer to a question about how they got a place in the attraction, Statler and Waldorf answer, "We entered a contest. Yeah, we lost.")

It's a tribute to the show's writers that although the film hasn't been updated in almost two decades, some of the jokes can still get giggles from repeat visitors. If you're tired and hot, this zany presentation will make you feel brand-new. Arrive early and enjoy the hilarious preshow video and stage props.

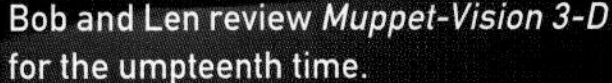

Bob and Len review *Muppet-Vision 3-D* for the umpteenth time.

ANIMATION COURTYARD

DISNEY DESIGN *with Sam Gennawey*

In 1989 the Studios were more than just a theme park. It was a real working studio with live production facilities as well as an animation studio. Films such as *Mulan, Lilo & Stitch, Brother Bear,* and *Home on the Range* were produced in Florida. You used to be able to take a tour, watch animators working at their desks, and view an informative film that made every adult male in the audience sob uncontrollably. The architecture for this area is based on the work of Kem Weber, who designed Walt Disney's Burbank Studio (1939).

DISNEY JUNIOR—LIVE ON STAGE! ★★★★

! APPEAL BY AGE			
	Preschool ★★★★★	Grade School ★★★★	Teens ★★½
	Young Adults ★★★	Over 30 ★★★	Seniors ★★★

What it is Live show for children. Scope and scale Minor attraction. When to go Per the daily entertainment schedule. Comments Audience sits on the floor. Authors' rating A must for families with preschoolers; ★★★★. Duration 25 minutes. When to arrive 20–30 minutes before showtime.

The show features characters from the Disney Channel's *Sofia the First, Doc McStuffins,* and *Jake and the Never Land Pirates,* plus other Disney Channel characters. *Disney Junior* uses elaborate puppets instead of live characters on stage. A simple plot serves as the platform for singing, dancing, some fantastic puppetry, and a great deal of audience participation. The characters rally throngs of tots and preschoolers to sing and dance along with them. All the jumping, squirming, and high-stepping is facilitated by having the audience sit on the floor so that kids can spontaneously erupt into motion when the mood strikes. Even for adults without children, it's a treat to watch the tykes rev up. If you have a younger child in your party, all the better: just stand back and let the video roll. *Disney Junior* is a highlight for preschoolers.

STAR WARS LAUNCH BAY ★★★

APPEAL BY AGE Preschool ★★★ | Grade School ★★★ | Teens ★★★ | Young Adults ★★★ | Over 30 ★★★ | Seniors ★★★

What it is Displays of a few Star Wars movie models and props, a movie trailer, and character greetings. Scope and scale Minor attraction. When to go Anytime. Authors' rating ★★★. Duration 9-minute film; 5 minutes for character greeting; 45 minutes to see and do everything. Probable waiting time 20 minutes for each character.

The first room of this walk-through exhibit displays replica props and models of the vehicles and weapons of the Rebel Alliance and Galactic Empire, as seen in Episodes IV–VI. The highlight of this area is a detailed scale reproduction of Boba Fett's *Slave I,* with a tiny figure of the infamous bounty hunter inside the cockpit. The hallway contains objects actually used in making the Star Wars films, such as Anakin's pod racer from *The Phantom Menace* and an Endor speeder bike from *Return of the Jedi.* There are a few interesting models here for the serious Star Wars fan, but they're spread out over such a large space that it makes the whole building seem emptier.

Two character-greeting opportunities are available: One leads to a Rebel base where Chewbacca, the world's favorite Wookie, awaits; the other leads to an Imperial bunker occupied by Kylo Ren, Dark Lord of the First Order. While you wait, overhead TVs display head-scratchingly tough Star Wars trivia. Chewbacca can move his mouth and growl in response to your questions, while Kylo has a full vocabulary of sinister phrases to taunt you with. Visit first thing in the morning for shorter character-greeting lines.

The 9-minute movie trailer summarizes the existing films and includes a short preview of Star Wars Land. Lines for the movie and character greetings run about 15–30 minutes each.

VOYAGE OF THE LITTLE MERMAID (FASTPASS+) ★★★½

APPEAL BY AGE			
	Preschool ★★★★½	Grade School ★★★★	Teens ★★★★
	Young Adults ★★★½	Over 30 ★★★½	Seniors ★★★★

What it is Musical stage show featuring characters from the Disney movie *The Little Mermaid.* Scope and scale Major attraction. When to go Before 9:45 a.m., just before closing, or use FastPass+. Authors' rating Romantic, lovable, and humorous in the best Disney tradition; ★★★½. Duration 17 minutes. Preshow Taped ramblings about the decor in the preshow holding area. Probable waiting time Less than 25 minutes.

Voyage of the Little Mermaid is a winner, appealing to every age. Cute without being silly or saccharine, and infinitely lovable, *Voyage of the Little Mermaid* is the most tender and romantic entertainment offered anywhere in Disney World. The story is simple and engaging, the special effects impressive, and the Disney characters memorable. When you enter the preshow lobby, stand near the doors to the theater. When they open, go inside, pick a row of seats, and let 6–10 people enter the row ahead of you. This will allow you to obtain a good seat and be near the exit.

Sandy feints with the left, then catches Daisy with a devastating right hook.

WALT DISNEY: ONE MAN'S DREAM ★★★

APPEAL BY AGE	Preschool ★★★	Grade School ★★★½	Teens ★★★½
	Young Adults ★★★★	Over 30 ★★★★½	Seniors ★★★★½

What it is **Tribute to Walt Disney.** Scope and scale **Minor attraction.** When to go **Anytime.** Authors' rating **Excellent; ★★★.** Duration **25 minutes.** Preshow **Disney memorabilia.** Probable waiting time **For film, 10 minutes.**

One Man's Dream is a tribute to Walt Disney. Launched in 2001 to celebrate the 100th anniversary of Disney's birth, the attraction consists of an exhibit area showcasing Disney memorabilia and recordings, followed by a film documenting Disney's life. The exhibits chronicle his life and business. On display are a replica of Walt's California office, various innovations in animation developed by Disney, and early models and working plans for Walt Disney World, as well as various Disney theme parks around the world. The film provides a personal glimpse of the man and offers insights regarding both Disney's successes and failures.

Give yourself some time here. Every minute spent among these extraordinary artifacts will enhance your visit, taking you back to a time when the creativity and vision that created Walt Disney World were personified by one struggling entrepreneur. *Walt Disney: One Man's Dream* will not be difficult to see.

Sometimes overlooked is the wonderful

PIXAR PLACE

DISNEY DESIGN *with Sam Gennawey*

Welcome to the world of Pixar. Headquartered in Emeryville, California, the architecture of its studio is legendary and designed in a very specific way to maximize the creativity and productivity of its employees. The major design criteria for the Studios park were to match those materials and bring a piece of California to Florida. The gateway you pass under is a scale model of the one at the studio, and all of the bricks used were hand-kilned from the same factory to match the look, texture, and color of the ones in California. Characters from Toy Story decorate the corridor and play with your perception of scale. If you want to see how the puzzle is put together, look for and check out Andy's instruction hanging on a wall.

TOY STORY MANIA! (FASTPASS+) ★★★★½

APPEAL BY AGE			
Preschool ★★★★½	Grade School ★★★★★	Teens ★★★★½
Young Adults ★★★★½	Over 30 ★★★★½	Seniors ★★★★½

What it is **3-D ride through indoor shooting gallery.** Scope and scale **Headliner.** When to go **As soon as the park opens or use FastPass+.** Authors' rating **Not to be missed; ★★★★½.** Duration **About 6½ minutes.** Average wait in line per 100 people ahead of you **4½ minutes.** Loading speed **Fast.**

Toy Story Mania! ushered in a whole new generation of Disney attractions: virtual dark rides. Since Disneyland opened in 1955, ride vehicles have moved past two- and three-dimensional sets often populated by Audio-Animatronic figures. These amazingly detailed sets and robotic figures defined the Disney Imagineering genius in attractions such as Pirates of the Caribbean, The Haunted Mansion, and Peter Pan's Flight.

For Toy Story Mania! the elaborate sets and endearing Audio-Animatronic characters are gone. Imagine long corridors, totally empty, covered with reflective material. There's almost nothing there . . . until you put on your 3-D glasses. Instantly, the corridor is full and brimming with color, action, and activity, thanks to projected computer-graphic images (CGI).

Conceptually, this is an interactive shooting gallery much like Buzz Lightyear's Space Ranger Spin, but in Toy Story Mania!, your ride vehicle passes through a totally virtual midway, with booths offering such games as ring tossing and ball throwing. You use a cannon on your ride vehicle to play as you move along from booth to booth. Unlike the laser guns in Buzz Lightyear, however, the pull-string cannons in Toy Story Mania! take advantage of CGI technology to toss rings, shoot balls, and even throw eggs and pies.

Each game booth is manned by a Toy Story character who is right beside you in 3-D glory, cheering you on. In addition to 3-D imagery, you experience various smells, vehicle motion, wind, and water spray. The ride begins with a training round to familiarize you with the nature of the games, and then continues through a number of "real" games in which you compete against your riding mate. The technology has the ability to self-adjust the level of difficulty, and there are plenty of easy targets for small children to reach. *Tip:* Let the pull string retract all the way back into the cannon before pulling it again.

Finally, and also of note, in the preshow queuing area, a 6-foot-tall Mr. Potato Head, a "living character" Audio-Animatronic figure, interacts with and talks to guests in real time (similar to Epcot's *Turtle Talk with Crush*).

3-D glasses? Check. Hands on cannon? Check. Disembodied hand creeping around the corner? Check.

TOY STORY LAND

An area aimed at younger guests that can also be enjoyed by adults, Toy Story Land will figuratively shrink guests by surrounding them with larger-than-life toys as they explore Andy's backyard. Tucked into an area behind the current site of Toy Story Mania!, Toy Story Land will feature the Slinky Dog Dash family coaster and Alien Swirling Saucers among other familiar sights from the Toy Story franchise. This land may open as soon as early 2018.

LIVE ENTERTAINMENT

The Studios' live-entertainment roster includes theater shows, musical acts, roaming bands of street performers, and *Fantasmic!* (see pages 304–305), a nighttime water, fireworks, and laser show that draws rave reviews. Of all of these, the theater shows, musical acts, and street performers are generally as good as or better than comparable acts at the other Disney parks.

Disney Characters Donald, Daisy, Goofy, and Pluto are usually in front of the Chinese Theatre, while Toy Story's Buzz and Woody are in Pixar Place near Toy Story Mania! Other Disney Junior stars are in Animation Courtyard too, near *Disney Junior—Live on Stage!* Check the *Times Guide* for times and locations of character appearances.

Street Entertainment The Studios has the best collection of roving street performers in all of Walt Disney World. Appearing primarily on Hollywood and Sunset Boulevards, the cast of characters includes Hollywood stars and wannabes, their agents, film directors, gossip columnists, various police officers, and Hollywood public-works crews. Performers are not shy about asking you to join in their skits—you may be asked to explain why you came to "Hollywood" or to recite a couple of lines in one of the directors' new films. If you're looking for a spot to rest and a bit of entertainment, grab a drink and seek out these performers.

Star Wars Entertainment In recent years Disney has warmed to the idea of regular fireworks at Hollywood Studios to supplement its very popular *Fantasmic!* show. In 2016 Disney unveiled Hollywood Studios' most ambitious fireworks ever. ***Star Wars: A Galactic Spectacular,*** set to popular music from the science-fiction

mega-franchise, shows on select nights. Along with hundreds of pyrotechnics, the show features projection effects and lasers. To view *Galactic Spectacular,* you won't want to be in a galaxy far, far away, but rather in a good spot along Hollywood Boulevard. Crowds will be thick, so we recommend securing a spot 30–60 minutes early. Make sure to check the schedule for your trip.

The live-action entertainment features various characters from the Star Wars films. During ***March of the First Order,*** Captain Phasma leads a procession of Stormtroopers through Animation Courtyard. They march in step around the stage as Phasma and two of the Stormtroopers make their way to the stage in front of a First Order banner. Phasma gives the troop orders and puts them through a pace routine. Finding the Stormtroopers acceptable, Phasma then joins the troops, gives them a once-over, and leads them back toward Star Wars Launch Bay.

The stage show, ***A Galaxy Far, Far Away,*** takes place at the stage in front of The Great Movie Ride. Clips from all seven Star Wars movies play on a screen in the middle of the stage, as characters such as C-3PO and R2-D2 come on stage. Other characters—including Chewbacca, Darth Maul, Darth Vader, Boba Fett, Stormtroopers, Captain Phasma, and Kylo Ren—join them. Last but not least, everyone's favorite ball droid, BB-8, rises from the stage to create a fantastic grouping of Star Wars characters as pyrotechnics boom from the stage.

COUNTER-SERVICE RESTAURANTS

Counter-service food at DHS consists mostly of burgers, hot dogs, pizza, and chicken strips, with the occasional salad tossed in. Slightly more variety can be found at the **ABC Commissary.**

ABC Commissary

QUALITY Fair **VALUE** B– **PORTION** Medium–large **LOCATION** Commissary Lane
READER RESPONSES 69% 31% **DINING PLAN** Yes

New York strip steak; Asian salad (chicken optional); chicken club sandwich; Angus bacon cheeseburger; shrimp platter; seafood platter; child's chicken nuggets, cheeseburger, or turkey sandwich; chocolate mousse; cupcakes; no-sugar-added strawberry parfait; wine and beer. Offers kosher food. One of the lowest-rated counter-service places in the parks.

Backlot Express

QUALITY Fair **VALUE** C **PORTION** Medium–large **LOCATION** Echo Lake
READER RESPONSES 83% 17% **DINING PLAN** Yes

One-third-pound Angus bacon cheeseburger, with or without barbecue brisket on top; chicken nuggets; chicken and waffles; chicken salad; Parmesan and garlic fries; chili-cheese dog. Star Wars–themed desserts include Blue Milk Panna Cotta and Tie Fighter with Caramel Corn. Indoor and outdoor seating.

Min and Bill's Dockside Diner

QUALITY Fair **VALUE** C **PORTION** Small–medium **LOCATION** Echo Lake
READER RESPONSES 81% 19% **DINING PLAN** Yes

Slow-roasted beef with mashed potatoes, corn, and carrots; chili-cheese hot dog with chips; macaroni and cheese with pulled pork; sushi veggie roll with edamame salad; chocolate cake for dessert. Kids' meal is a turkey sandwich with carrots and cookie.

PizzeRizzo *(closed until spring 2017)*

QUALITY Good **VALUE** B+ **PORTION** Medium **LOCATION** Muppet Courtyard
READER RESPONSES 76% 24% **DINING PLAN** Yes

Cheese, pepperoni, and vegetarian pizzas; meatball subs; salads; cookies and cupcakes; child's meatball sub or cheese pizza. Pizza Planet closed in late 2015 to undergo an extensive refurbishment, featuring a new Muppets theme, and will reopen as PizzeRizzo in spring 2017.

Starring Rolls Cafe

QUALITY Good **VALUE** B **PORTION** Small–medium **LOCATION** Sunset Boulevard
READER RESPONSES 93% 7% **DINING PLAN** Yes

Breakfast croissants and bagels, deli sandwiches, soup, desserts, coffee. Slowest counter service in Studios.

Sunset Ranch Market

QUALITY Fair **VALUE** B– **PORTION** Medium–large **LOCATION** Sunset Boulevard
READER RESPONSES 80% 20% **DINING PLAN** Yes

Several restaurants in one location: smoked turkey legs and beer at Toluca Legs; pizzas, salads, and banana parfait at Catalina Eddie's; cheeseburgers, soups, fried green tomato sandwich, and child's turkey sandwich or chicken nuggets at Rosie's; and barbecue chicken and ribs, hot dogs, and Fairfax salad (with barbecue pork, bacon, and tomato-corn salsa) at Fairfax Fare.

Disney's Hollywood Studios Special Treats Menu

Ursula Special

This is one mean sandwich! Cooked to order (we like ours a little more well done than the one in the picture), the Ursula Special is the best deal on eight legs anywhere. Move over buffalo wings! *$5.25*

Toy Story Treat

This frozen treat is just the ticket to revive a wilting Mouseketeer! Alternating lemon, lime, and raspberry flavors are tucked neatly into a cup modeled on Woody's vest and shirt ensemble. A milk chocolate cowboy hat provides a little caffeine boost to help you get back on the trail. *$5.95*

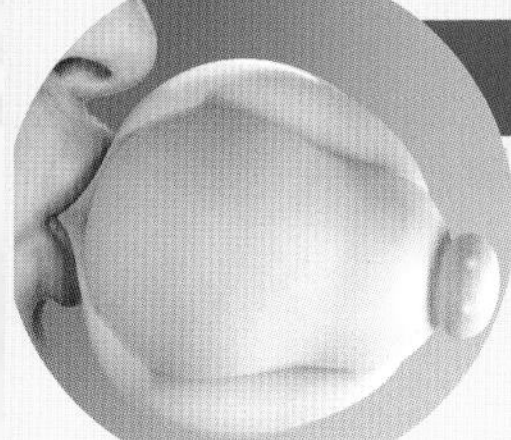

Baymax Bubble Blow

Enjoy your own Baymax with this bubble gum. Consistent, controlled blowing will result in a perfect Baymax bubble every time. Blow too hard and his head will be too big. Not blowing hard enough will result in a pea head and a big butt. For burst bubbles, try Bubbles Troubles heavy-duty gum remover. ....*Gum: $1.50; Remover: $3.00*

Hannah Montana Banana

Health-conscious eaters will love this fruity dessert showcasing a natural-blond banana dancing in a simple cherry, cranberry, and beebleberry distilled reduction. Certified by doctors as a complete potassium replenishment product. *$7.95*

PART 9

THE WATER PARKS

Beach

The two Disney World water parks—the mixed smooth- and surf-water Typhoon Lagoon, home to the country's most elaborate water coaster (Crush 'n' Gusher) and a huge inland surf pool; and the 66-acre big bear, Blizzard Beach, with the 120-foot free-fall speed slide—aren't only for kids. In fact, the idea of skiing barefoot at 60 miles an hour down 120 feet of water may redefine forever the thrill of victory and the agony of the feet. And both parks have a wide variety of attractions and their own fully developed Disney-quality themes, only without character breakfasts.

Individual water-park tickets are a little less expensive than admission at the four big parks—about $60 for adults, with a few dollars off for annual-pass holders—but hefty enough that you should be sure you want to spend the money instead of hanging out at your hotel pool complex.

You should also do a little advance weather research before planning your water-park outing. The water parks are obviously susceptible to closing for inclement weather, so you might do better to wait and add on a Water Park Fun and More option to your ticket once you arrive; you can do this at any Guest Services counter, your hotel, or any of the theme parks. If you do decide to go for just one day, you can buy water-park tickets at any Guest Services location resort-wide or at the ticket booths at the water park. Be aware that the water-park booths can get overwhelmed with overheated guests.

Also consider that the water parks are so popular, especially in the hottest season, that they reach capacity fairly frequently and are then closed to the public; even if you are staying at a resort and have guaranteed access, it means a huge crowd of people splashing and yelling.

Both parks are regularly refurbished, although on a rotating schedule and usually out of season, so if the water parks are among your primary destinations, you may want to check out their status before booking your trip. Call ☎ 407-939-5277 or go to the water-park websites at disneyworld.disney.go.com/destinations to see their calendars.

Although the watery thrill rides get most of the press, both water parks have quieter, nonstrenuous attractions as well, such as the chairlift at Blizzard Beach or Castaway Creek at Typhoon Lagoon, so the less robust need not write these parks off entirely. But if you suffer from high blood pressure, circulation problems, heart disease, or obesity, or are taking certain medications, you should avoid going on very hot days.

▶ **UNOFFICIAL TIP** Picnic areas are scattered around the park, as are pleasant places for sunbathing.

PLANNING YOUR VISIT TO THE DISNEY WATER PARKS

Generally speaking, the regulations and limitations placed on water visits have to do with space—that is, saving it for your fellow swimmers—and safety.

- You can't bring in your own flotation devices, but you can borrow an inner tube or a life vest (for the vest, you'll have to leave a credit card or driver's license behind as security deposit).
- You can rent a towel for $2 and rent a locker ($10 for regular, $15 for large).
- Only one cooler is allowed per group, but no glass containers or alcoholic beverages may be brought in. (Both water parks have picnic areas.)
- If you drive, the parking is included. There's also free bus transportation, though on the way back to your hotel, your wet self may have to withstand the attentions of your fellow travelers.
- Oh, and we're not kidding when we say you need to consider your bathing costume. Are you going to sunbathe, or slide? Float the tube or brave the flume? Wear something too flimsy, and you're going to give "decorative" a whole new meaning. Summit Plummet is famous among Disney cast members for the number of bathing-suit tops that come down without their owners (or vice versa), but Slush Gusher and Humunga Kowabunga are just as bad; and men, especially those wearing low-riders, jammers, or drawstring shorts, are not immune from exposures of their own. If you're not positive that your suit is up to the test, consult with an experienced cast member; you can always take a few minutes to buy something else to wear in the gift shops. (By the way, bathing suits with exposed metal, buckles, studding, chains, and so on are prohibited on all the rides, but why would you want to risk a branding burn, anyway?)
- Sunscreen and sunglasses are a must; it's not just the light itself but also its reflection off the water and concrete. Don't forget lip protection. And wear water socks rather than flip-flops; these are places to preserve body *and* sole.
- There is usually ample seating at the water parks, but some of it is quite a distance from both the entrance and the main water areas. Cabanas and preferred umbrella seats are available for a substantial upcharge. Call ☎ 407-939-7529 for pricing and reservations.

TYPHOON LAGOON
© Stefan Zwanzger/thethemeparkguy.com

 Typhoon Lagoon is a theme park in its own right, with a surf pool, a 420-foot-long aquatic roller coaster, flume rides, tube slides, body slides, and a 360,000-gallon tank where you can snorkel with the sharks. Don't think that you can do this in half a day; as at the four main parks, the thrill rides back up pretty quickly. If the park is open late, you could aim to get here about the time the morning people (and presumably the worn-out little ones) will be headed out, and then stay into the cool of the evening.

The "story" behind the park is that it used to be a pleasant tropical resort that was upended by, in quick order, a typhoon, an earthquake, and a volcanic eruption. The entrance passage to Typhoon Lagoon is a misty forest and a ramshackle "town" of concession stands. The last disaster left a hapless shrimp boat, the *Miss Tilly* (of home port Safen Sound—get it?), marooned 100 feet in the air atop Mount Mayday, where it periodically blows water out of its stack like a beached whale. (Here's a tip for sunbathers pursuing an even tan: The smokestack goes off every 30 minutes—time to turn over.)

© Alice Wojtaszek

One of the most popular attractions is the **surf pool**; its machine-produced "tsunamis" throw up ridable waves close to a 6-foot curl every 90 seconds or so, thanks to huge water tanks that fill, discharge, and refill. The pool gets pretty full of surfers of all (and unhappily, little) ability, but it's certainly impressive. These waves are higher than a lot of people ever see at the ocean, so do not wear jewelry, cameras, or any of those "decorative" swimsuits. You may also want to consider a trip to the man spa: One of our all-time favorite letters was from a teenage girl who commented:

> **The surf pool was nice except that I kept landing on really hairy fat guys whenever the big waves came.**

▶ **UNOFFICIAL TIP** A final warning: The surf pool has a knack for loosening watchbands, stripping jewelry, and sucking stuff out of your pockets. Don't take anything out there except your swimsuit (and hang on to that).

Can't surf—yet? In summer, early-morning surfing lessons are available for $165. Lessons occur before the park opens, and no park playtime is included, but surfboards are provided. Call ☎ 407-939-7529.

Among the big thriller rides is **Crush 'n' Gusher**, the "decor" of which is supposedly the rusted-out and partially collapsed remains of a fruit-packing plant, which the jungle has started taking over since the typhoon. It's a 400-plus-foot flume slide (actually, three of them, slightly different in length and fervor) with inflatable-raft "cars" that twist and turn like a roller coaster—and run uphill—thanks to powerful water jets.

Crush 'n' Gusher

© Stefan Zwanzger/thethemeparkguy.com

Humunga Kowabunga is Space Mountain with water, a five-story drop in the dark at about 30 feet per second. It's a little like being buried at sea in a casket, lying on your back with your arms folded. This is everybody's choice source for a record-breaking wedgie. You have been warned.

The three "falls" raft rides at Typhoon Lagoon come in Goldilocks style: father bear, mother bear, and baby bear, though all three are approved for all ages. **Mayday Falls** is a tube ride for solos that is relatively scary, running through tunnels and waterfalls in big sweeping curves; **Gangplank Falls** is a 300-foot waterslide employing the larger four-person rafts. **Keelhaul Falls** is the calmest of the tube rides, although if you get a little weird in caves, you might want to skip even this one.

Storm Slides is sort of Humunga Kowabunga light, with a three-story drop and twisting, on-your-back body slides though waterfalls, geysers, and caves to a bottom pool, only in this case you aren't in a vehicle.

The 360,000-gallon snorkeling tank called **Shark Reef** is a fairly low-key but fun attraction, stocked with smallish and nonthreatening hammerhead and leopard sharks, stingrays, and flocks of tropical fish. All the equipment—snorkeling mask, fins, and optional life jacket are provided at no charge. (A brief introductory lesson is free as well.) If you really want to dive in, you can rent a supplied air tank from Hammerhead Fred's Dive Shop. But plan to do this early in the day, as it's a popular draw.

▶ **UNOFFICIAL TIP** Try Shark Reef in the mornings—afternoons can get crowded, and you may be ushered out of the pool more quickly than in the early hours.

Shark Reef

The calmest areas here are the Sandy White Beach and Castaway Creek. Although **Sandy White Beach** has no age limits, and sometimes parents have to impose a time-out here to avert a total breakdown, its low-key character means that fewer youngsters wind up here, or at least few stay for long. It has lounge chairs, palm trees, and even hammocks. **Castaway Creek** is a sort of throwback to the old River Country days, a 2,000-foot flowing "river" that encircles the rest of the park and serves as easy transportation (there are five places to get on and off). Cruising around on your tube is a wonderful way to see the elaborate scenery.

In addition, there are plenty of areas at the foot of rides worth viewing just for the fun of it, and the Shark Reef tank can be admired through viewing portholes in the wall of the tanker, similar to the view at The Seas in Epcot.

A family raft ride with an elevated flume is rumored to open in summer 2017, west of Crush 'n' Gusher. It's the first new ride in more than a decade for the park.

BLIZZARD BEACH

Blizzard Beach, Disney World's bigger (66 acres) and slightly bolder (bigger thrills) water park also has a full-blown Disney storyboard "history," though one with a logic only a Floridian could love.

It seems that during an unusual cold snap that dumped a freak blanket of ice over the area, a real-estate developer had the smart idea of making lemonade from lemons by opening a ski resort, complete with a little chalet and ski lifts. But of course the climate eventually reverted, and the entire resort went into meltdown, leaving the stranded alpine village, ski lift, bobsled runs (turned into waterslides), pools of melted ice, and of course the mountain. What's a Disney World theme park without a mountain?

This particular peak, Mount Gushmore, tops out at about 90 feet, and the big thrillers—Summit Plummet, Slush Gusher, and Teamboat Springs—all come down along it. Altogether Blizzard Beach boasts 17 waterslides of various forms.

The infamous **Summit Plummet**, which measures about 350 feet, starts off with a 120-foot free fall at a 66-degree angle, and it generates sliding speeds of close to 60 miles per hour. (The "chicken" slide, Blizzard Beach's version of Mission Space's green team, is only 90 feet long.) This is one of those rides that requires very serious elastic or Spandex—see our warnings about Crush 'n' Gusher earlier—and those with very sensitive backsides, or sunburns, should think twice. In addition, older visitors or those with back or neck problems should avoid Summit Plummet; many people complain of being shaken up and bruised, especially on the backside, which is undoubtedly part of the fun for kids but not, perhaps, for the rest of us.

Summit Plummet

▶ UNOFFICIAL TIP If you're going primarily for the slides, you'll have about 2 hours in the early morning to enjoy them before the wait becomes intolerable.

From the air Blizzard Beach looks like a plastic set on a model railroad layout.

Slush Gusher is just about as unnerving (and undressing) as Summit Plummet, but not quite as teeth-rattling in the jarring sense; its 90-foot double-hump slide is like the biggest and wettest camel you ever fell off.

Teamboat Springs is the group ride here, a rousing 1,200-foot-long white-water flume ride something like Kali River Rapids. The hint for this one is the more weight, the more speed, so make friends in line.

▶ **UNOFFICIAL TIP** The more people you load into the raft on Teamboat Springs, the faster it goes. If you have only a couple in it, the slide is kind of a snore.

Teamboat Springs

Downhill Double Dipper could, we suppose, qualify as a romantic encounter, since two people go down side-by-side 230-foot tube slides, but it might not elicit exactly the sort of screaming you had in mind—even if part of it is in the dark, and those walls of water can be shockers. Each of you is given an inner tube, and the two gates open simultaneously as if you were racing down, which in a way you are: top speed is about 25 miles an hour.

The Blizzard Beach equivalent of Castaway Creek is **Cross Country Creek**, a 45-minute solo-raft circuit of the park, this one with seven portals and some small surprises (such as dripping "icicles" and a house that spouts water from its chimney).

Check Out the View

For those who remember the old Skyway in the Magic Kingdom—and even those who don't—the ski resort–style, 120-foot chairlift at Blizzard Beach is a must even if you don't feel up to screaming down Summit Plummet. The view is a stunner, and you can spend as much time as you want at the observation deck; there's even a gondola for wheelchair users. Just be prepared to wait in line. On the other hand, if you just want to get up there to go down the fast way, take the stairs.

Other attractions include **Snow Stormers**, a pseudo–ski slalom course with riding mats that resemble toboggans; **Toboggan Racers**, which is sort of Snow Stormers light (and gets more kids); and **Melt-Away Bay**, a mild wave pool. There are also some very kid-oriented areas you're not likely to spend much time in, unless you're being paid for babysitting.

Blizzard Beach fills early during hotter months. To stake out a nice spot and to enjoy the slides without long waits, arrive at least 35 minutes before the official opening time.

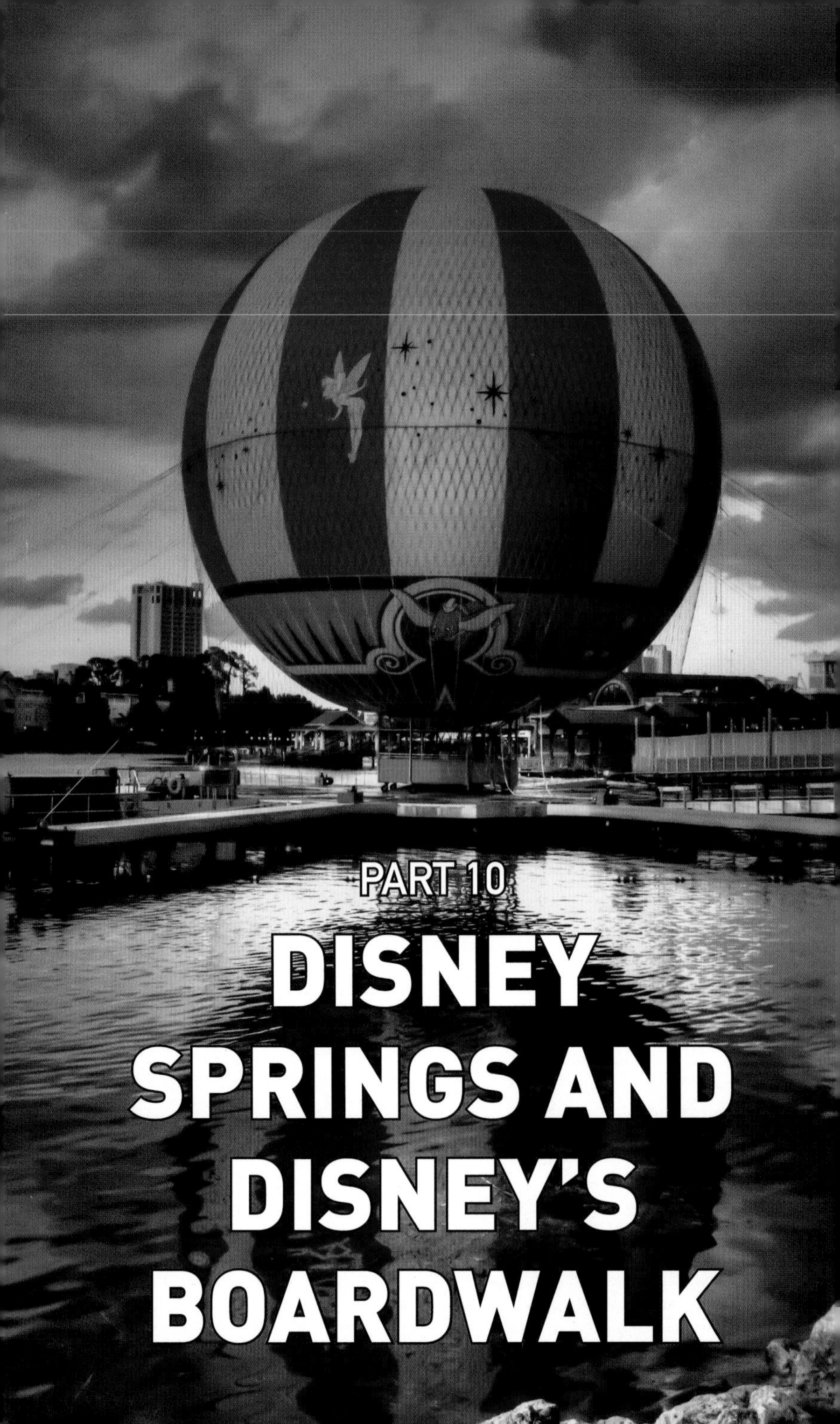

PART 10

DISNEY SPRINGS AND DISNEY'S BOARDWALK

DISNEY SPRINGS

Following an expansion and retheming, the former Downtown Disney area was renamed Disney Springs in 2015. Disney Springs is a shopping, dining, and entertainment area stretching along the banks of Village Lake. There is no admission fee to explore Disney Springs, and it's often open later than the theme parks; if you want nightlife, this is one of the key places to find it.

The rethemed area comes with a new-and-improved Disney-invented story line. The reimagination was done with the assumed story that there was a lovely natural spring in the area that attracted settlers. As the new "town" grew, the development followed the historical time line of the development of Florida. The architecture, landscaping, costuming, and such gets progressively newer as you expand from the center of the Springs.

The central area, formerly Pleasure Island, is now known as **The Landing** and abuts a new area called **Town Center.** To the east of Town Center and The Landing is **The Marketplace,** which has an expanded World of Disney store. To the west is the aptly named **West Side,** anchored at the far end by Cirque du Soleil's ***La Nouba*** tent. These areas are now served by a network of bridges and water taxis (making it easier to bypass some areas on the way to others), multistory parking garages, and a direct exit off the highway.

Disney Springs has doubled the number of shopping and dining venues previously available, from 75 at Downtown Disney to 150 at Disney Springs.

Disney Springs is within walking distance of the Saratoga Springs Resort, as well as several of the Buena Vista Drive hotels, notably the Hilton Orlando Lake Buena Vista and Wyndham Lake Buena Vista. Free bus or boat service is available from all the Disney-owned resorts but not from the theme parks. If you'd like to use Disney's free transportation system to get from a theme park to Disney Springs, you'll have to use a two-step process: first taking transportation to a resort and then transferring to a Disney Springs bus or boat.

The Marketplace

The Marketplace is the oldest part of Disney Springs. It offers interactive fountains, a couple of playgrounds, and a lakeside amphitheater, but it's primarily a shopping and dining venue.

Marketplace Shopping

Shopping has probably long since replaced baseball as America's national pastime, but only the Walt Disney Company could figure out a way to make it as entertaining as a theme park. The Marketplace is the single most complete souvenir mall in Disney World. The shops open at 9:30 a.m. and stay open until 11 p.m. on weekdays, 11:30 p.m. on weekends. (Times vary seasonally; check your resort's Times Guide or the My Disney Experience app for exact information.) The centerpiece of shopping is the 50,000-square-foot **World of Disney,** the largest store in the United States selling Disney-trademarked merchandise. (Its status as the largest Disney store in the world has been usurped by a new Disney Store in Shanghai, China.)

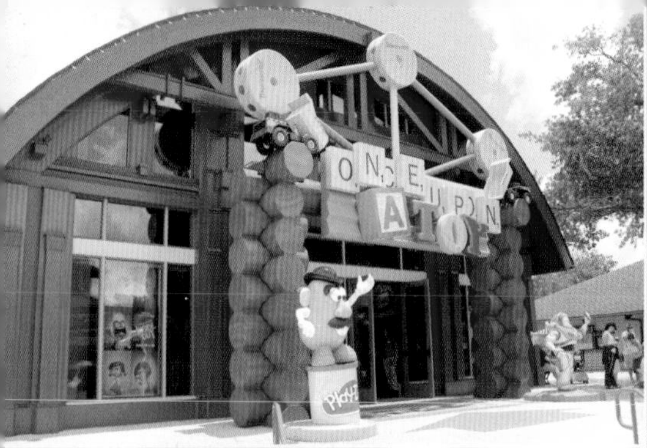
ONCE UPON

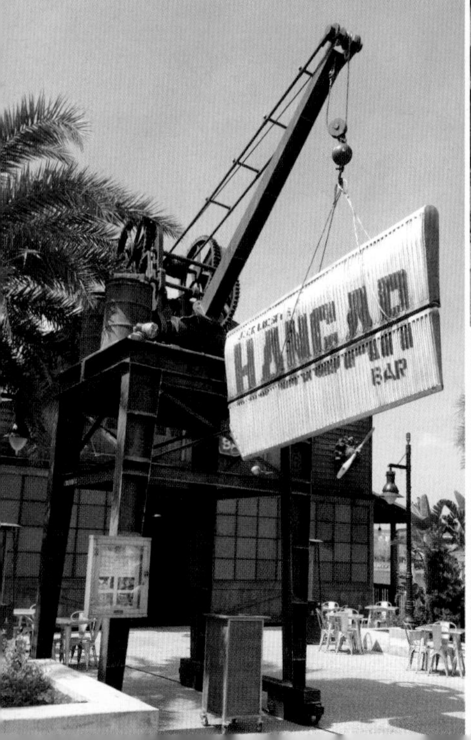

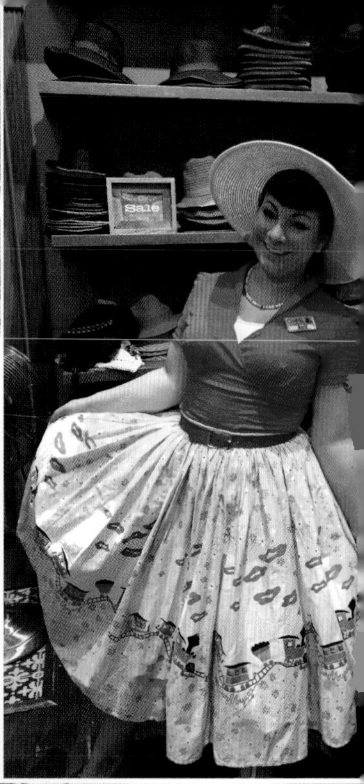
Sale

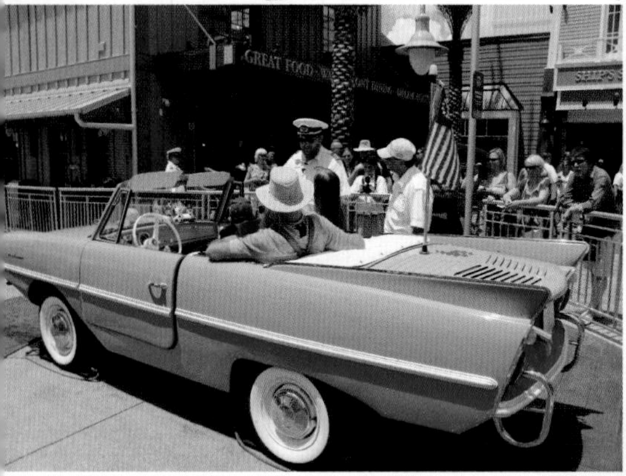
GREAT FOOD

HANGAR
BAR

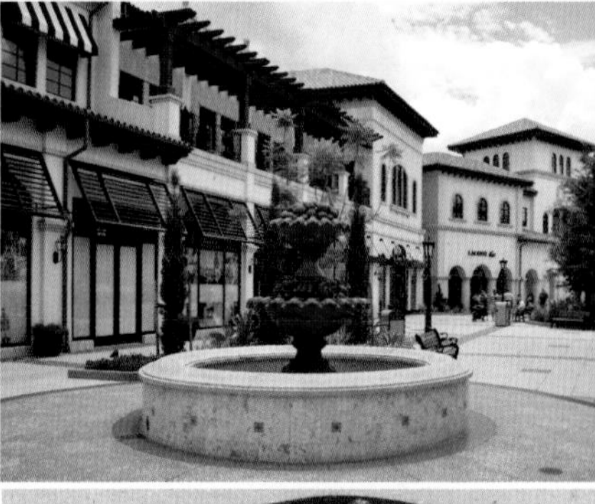

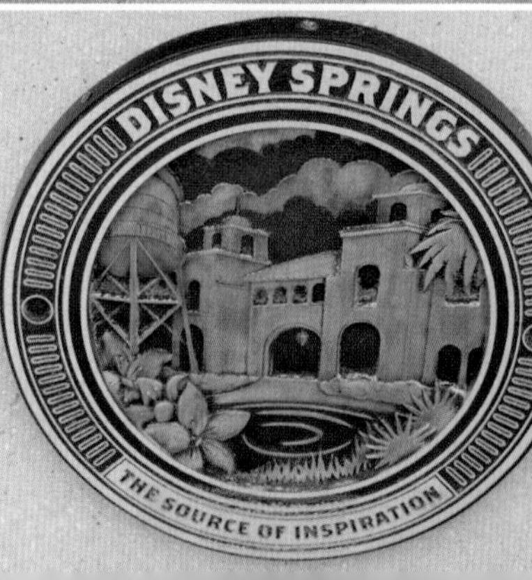

DISNEY SPRINGS
THE SOURCE OF INSPIRATION

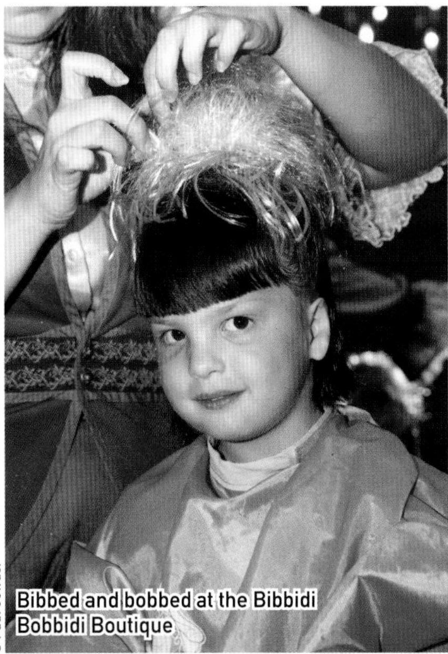
Bibbed and bobbed at the Bibbidi Bobbidi Boutique

© Paul Gowder

The **Bibbidi Bobbidi Boutique** princess makeover salon has moved out of the World of Disney store and into a new location at the rear of the Once Upon a Toy store nearby. Little ladies in need of a royal coif should head over there.

At Disney's **Design-a-Tee** you can create customized T-shirts, and **Mickey's Pantry** offers Disney home and kitchen products, including the Donald Duck Press (joke!). Another noteworthy retailer is the **LEGO Imagination Center,** showcasing a number of huge and unbelievable sculptures made entirely of LEGO "bricks." Spaceships, sea serpents, sleeping tourists, and dinosaurs are just a few of the sculptures on display. **Once Upon a Toy** is a toys, games, and collectibles superstore. Rounding out the selection are stores specializing in resort wear, athletic attire and gear, Christmas decorations, Disney art and collectibles, and handmade craft items.

Marketplace Dining

The Marketplace's sit-down restaurants—**Rainforest Cafe** and **T-Rex**—are profiled on pages 148 and 152, respectively.

Counter-service restaurants at the Marketplace include **Earl of Sandwich,** in our opinion the best sandwiches in Walt Disney World; **Wolfgang Puck Express Café,** serving tasty pizzas; **The Daily Poutine;** and **Ghirardelli Soda Fountain & Chocolate Shop.** A small **Starbucks** is next to World of Disney, along with a much larger location on the West Side.

The Landing

Virtually all traces of The Landing's former incarnation, Pleasure Island, have been removed. The area is now a hub for large restaurants: **The Boathouse, Morimoto Asia** (featuring pan-Asian cuisine), **Paradiso 37, Portobello Country Italian Trattoria, Raglan Road Irish Pub and Restaurant,** and **STK Orlando Steakhouse.** The former Fulton's Crabhouse has been rethemed as **Paddlefish,** a modern seafood venue. Small restaurants and food-related shops include the vegan and allergy-friendly bakery **Erin McKenna's, Cookes of Dublin, Tea Traders by Joffrey's, Vivoli il Gelato,** and **The Ganachery** chocolate shop. The cavernous **Jock Lindsey's Hangar Bar** (named for an establishment in the Indiana Jones films) is adjacent to a unique form of entertainment, the **Vintage Amphicars.** Guests may rent amphibious automobiles and take them for a spin in the river; the cost is $125 for up to three guests.

The Landing's remaining area is occupied by small stores, many of which will be familiar to mall shoppers. Among them: **Sunglass Hut, SANUK, The Art of Shaving,** and **Sound Lion.**

Town Center

The Town Center's theme, based on the expansion of a Florida town, has a 1920s Southern feel. The retail shops here are larger than the boutiques seen in The Landing, with familiar, international brands represented, such as **Johnston & Murphy, Lilly Pulitzer, Pandora** jewelry, **Tommy Bahama, Uggs, Uniqlo,** and **Zara.** The Town Center gateway and entry to Disney Springs features a signature water tower.

Town Center also includes a number of food spots, including **Sprinkles** cupcakes and **Amorette's Patisserie.** More substantial fare can be found at **Blaze Fast-Fire'd Pizza, D-Luxe Burger,** and **Frontera Cocina.**

West Side

Disney Springs West Side offers a range of entertainment, dining, and shopping. The **Crossroads,** the House of Blues restaurant, serves Cajun specialties, and **The Smokehouse,** attached to Crossroads, is a walk-up barbecue joint. There's also a popular gospel brunch at Crossroads on Sunday mornings, as well as live music in concert. Check houseofblues.com/orlando/#calendarsearch for schedule information. The Planet Hollywood location here was recently rethemed and renamed to **Planet Hollywood Observatory.** The old Earth-shaped exterior was given a brick veneer, and the interior is reminiscent of a turn-of-the-20th-century observatory. **Bongos Cuban Café** serves Cuban favorites, while **Wolfgang Puck Grand Cafe** features California flavors. The full-service restaurants are profiled in Part Four.

The West Side's **Food Truck Park** features gourmet truck fare from four franchises. **Namaste Café** serves Indian-inspired cuisine such as butter chicken and tandoori shrimp; **Fantasy Fare** has corn dogs, ham-and-cheese sandwiches, and noodle salads; **Superstar Catering** serves meatballs (turkey, lamb, and beef) in a variety of sandwiches; and the **World Showcase of Flavors** offers beef sliders, lobster rolls, and *pierogis*. Prices range from $8 to $12.

Other dining options on the West Side include a large **Starbucks** (which also offers wine and tapas-style bites in the evening!) and **Wetzel's Pretzels, Häagen-Dazs,** and similar snack stands.

West Side shopping is some of the most interesting in Disney World. For example, **Pop Gallery** sells high-end paintings and sculptures, **Super Hero Headquarters** and **Star Wars Galactic Outpost** are one-stop shops for all your geek accoutrement needs, and **United World Soccer** and **Fit2Run** provide serious sports gear. Get your ride on at **Harley-Davidson,** or find sweet treats at the **Candy Cauldron.**

In the entertainment department, **AMC Cineplex** is a 24-screen movie theater equipped with THX surround sound, stadium seating, and even several screens where they'll bring you dinner and adult beverages while you enjoy the film. **Splitsville,** an upscale bowling, billiards, and dining venue, occupies 45,000 square feet on two levels. Prices are high and reservations are a near imperative. If you feel like getting high (literally), try **Characters in Flight,** a tethered hot air balloon ride where you soar 400 feet over Disney Springs, with a view of nearly all of Walt Disney World. Try the

ride at night for a particularly lovely view. The weather-dependent ride (it's nonoperational even in moderate winds) lasts 8–10 minutes and costs $18 for adults (age 10 and up) and $12 for kids (ages 3–9). The West Side is also home to Cirque du Soleil's ***La Nouba,*** an amazing production with a cast of more than 70 performers and musicians (more on that below).

DisneyQuest

The giant indoor arcade, **DisneyQuest,** will be closing in 2016 or 2017. While not surprising—much of the technology was woefully outdated—the DisneyQuest closure does leave a hole for active indoor entertainment at Disney Springs. DisneyQuest had been a boon for spouses and siblings who wanted something else to do while other family members spent a few hours shopping. Splitsville bowling does not have the turnover or capacity to handle all the non-shoppers. The movie theater is still an option, but guests sometimes need a place where kids can move around a bit.

Cirque du Soleil's *La Nouba*

© Disney

Easily the most impressive attraction on the West Side, and the one that not coincidentally sits at the end of the street like a real-life Cinderella Castle, is the handsome theatrical palace that is a permanent showplace for **Cirque du Soleil** (☎ 407-939-7600; cirquedusoleil.com/la-nouba), the Montreal-based acrobatic troupe that has revolutionized the concept of modern circus entertainment.

The theater is designed to suggest both a castle and an old-fashioned tent, with multiple peaks under which technicians have created a fantastic array of rigging, sound and light equipment, hooks, and hideaways. Inside, its steeply raked seating makes for (nearly) perfect views of every act; the built-in trampolines, elevated stage sections, orchestra balconies, and multilevel trapezes return tumbling to high theater.

This Cirque show is called *La Nouba*, which refers to the party spirit or, depending on your age, "get down," and has a cast of more than 70 acrobats and musicians. (It may seem odd to Cirque novices that a Walt Disney attraction has no animal acts, but that's a Cirque tradition.) The Cirque style of music, usually wordless or sung in a language all its own, is immediately recognizable, as is the sinuous and vivid costume design (which makes the souvenir shop a magnet for fans).

Even with its quite-serious ticket prices—ranging from about $63 to $150—it is worth every penny. *La Nouba*, in the old Disney phrase, is an e-ticket ride. Anyone who has ever seen a performance by one of the Cirque companies or its alumni spin-offs, such as Cirque Eloise, knows that it is gripping, thrilling, mysterious, enigmatic, funny, exhilarating, and altogether addictive. There are visual and emotional references to classical theater, movies, memories, dreams, and the confluence of desire and fear. This is one place where even the most child-averse vacationers need have no qualms; children are as spellbound as adults.

DISNEY'S BOARDWALK

The BoardWalk is a little like a costume party where the hosts hope you'll dance, but have left the championship fight on the big-screen TV in the rec room just in case you won't. Unlike Disney Springs, which is an entirely commercial complex, the BoardWalk is part resort hotel, part entertainment zone. The BoardWalk Inn and Villas is built over and behind the entertainment and shopping strip, and the theme is the Atlantic City and Long Island resorts of the 1930s.

Children are allowed almost everywhere at Disney World, even in bars and lounges. This barkeep finds it easier to manage the parents:

There are two nightclubs for those age 21 and older, plus **ESPN Club,** open to all ages though heavily bar- and sports TV–oriented, especially later in the evening. The main entertainment venue on the BoardWalk is an elaborate big band–era dance hall called **Atlantic Dance Hall,** which plays the martini-lounge nostalgia theme to the hilt with a ceiling glittering with mirror balls, marble bars, a bandstand, a grand staircase, a balcony to retire to between jitterbugs, and lake-view terraces to take in the fireworks. There's no cover charge at Atlantic Dance, no live music, and sometimes no patrons either. The music is heavily 1980s and '90s.

For the dance-challenged in the party, the BoardWalk has a comedy-and-music bar called **Jellyrolls,** a sort of dueling banjos on ivory, with two pianos, two players, and a lot of shouted encouragement. (Although dancing is not the main concept, people often do get down.) The music tends to the classic-rock variety, but that means that the patrons are sometimes lured into singing along. (Because Jellyrolls attracts some local residents, it occasionally seems like karaoke night at the VFW.) It's a 21-and-up venue.

For the nonmartini crowd, **Big River Grille & Brewing Works** can be a draw, but the bar itself is quite small—unfortunate for those who like to talk brewing with the staff. You can sample at least a half dozen microbrews crafted on the World premises in the huge copper vats visible from the bar. All are preservative-free, with four standards available all the time and others that change seasonally. There may be bigger beers served in the World, and there may be more exotic beers too, but there's something about a beer brewed on the Mouse's turf that makes it seem, well, a bit magical.

Though ESPN Club and Big River Grille & Brewing Works offer gut-busting fare, the culinary show pony of the Boardwalk is the **Flying Fish** with a Coney Island theme and a decidedly adult range of fresh seafood preparations dressed in trendy frills. **Trattoria al Forno** rounds out the offerings with Italian classics such as fresh pizza, lasagna, and ravioli. For breakfast, it serves American favorites and American favorites with an Italian twist.

© Steve Burns/Burnsland.com

PART 11

RECREATION

You would be hard-pressed to come up with any sort of (nonextreme) recreational activity that is not available somewhere in Walt Disney World, with the possible exception of bungee jumping and the super slalom. Otherwise, the World is your playground: golf, tennis, bowling, croquet, swimming, boating, fishing, waterskiing, weight lifting, trail riding, rock climbing, running, volleyball, basketball, horseback riding, biking, surfing, and SCUBA diving.

There are no official skateboard or in-line skating areas at Disney, but none are necessary; there are sidewalks, parking lots, roads, and, though we hate to point it out, stairways everywhere. Other activities available in the World include ballooning (of a sort), parasailing, and gliding (simulated but exhilarating).

In addition, if you or your team are into baseball (at any level), lacrosse, track and field, cricket, rugby, martial arts, field hockey, cheerleading drills, gymnastics, soccer, wrestling, or even foot bag (among other sports!), look into the numerous events at the various ESPN Wide World of Sports venues. Who knows? Perhaps Disney magic can bring out the inner Olympian in you. In any case, the spectating is spectacular.

▶ **UNOFFICIAL TIP** If you plan to include the more traditional sports in your vacation, you should make reservations or tee times as early as you can.

DISNEY RESORT RECREATION

	FITNESS CENTER	WATER SPORTS	MARINA	BEACH	TENNIS	BIKING
All-Star Resorts	—	—	—	—	—	—
Animal Kingdom Lodge & Villas	★	—	—	—	★*	—
Art of Animation Resort	—	—	—	—	—	—
Bay Lake Tower	★	★	★	★	★	—
BoardWalk Inn & Villas	★	—	★	—	★	★
Caribbean Beach Resort	—	—	—	★	—	★
Contemporary Resort	★	★	★	★	★	—
Coronado Springs Resort	★	—	—	★	—	★
Dolphin	★	★	★	★	★	—
Fort Wilderness Resort	—	★	★	★	—	★
Grand Floridian Resort & Spa	★	★	★	★	—	—
Old Key West Resort	★	—	★	—	★	★
Polynesian Village, Villas, & Bungalows	—	★	★	★	—	★
Pop Century Resort	—	—	—	—	—	—
Port Orleans Resort	—	—	—	—	—	★
Saratoga Springs Resort & Spa–Treehouse Villas	★	—	—	—	★	★
Shades of Green	★	—	—	—	—	—
Swan	★	—	★	★	★	—
Wilderness Lodge & Villas	★	★	★	★	—	★
Yacht & Beach Club Resorts	★	★	★	★	★	—

**Kidani Village only*

IT'S MORE FUN WHEN YOU'RE WET: WATER SPORTS

© Disney

Water comes in a lot of forms in Walt Disney World—Bay Lake and Seven Seas Lagoon, Buena Vista Lagoon, the Fort Wilderness waterways, the Sassagoula River, Barefoot Bay, Crescent Lake, and so on—and not surprisingly, boating comes in nearly every variety imaginable too, from Jet Skis and Sea Raycers to mini speedboats and WaveRunners to 20-foot pontoons for larger parties. There are also canopy boats, rowboats, pedal boats, sailboats, canoes, and kayaks. Not every resort offers watercraft, nor do all the resorts with marinas offer the same watercraft, but you're welcome to visit and rent boats no matter where you're staying.

The most concentrated site of water sports, if you plan to spend a lot of time playing, is at the Contemporary Resort, which offers parasailing, wakeboarding, waterskiing, WaveRunners, canopy boats, and pontoons. For more information, call ☎ 407-WDW-PLAY. *Note:* You can make a reservation for most activities 3 months in advance, but you must cancel at least 24 hours ahead of time.

Boating

For those who would rather be chauffeured than steer themselves, you can book charter boats and excursions in advance, either for private parties, fireworks viewing, fishing (catch and release only), or picnic lunches. Ask about these activities at the BoardWalk, Yacht & Beach Club, Wilderness Lodge, Contemporary, Bay Lake Tower, Polynesian Village, and Grand Floridian hotels.

The most luxurious water ride in Walt Disney World is the ***Grand 1,*** a 52-foot yacht that cruises around Bay Lake and Seven Seas Lagoon from the Grand Floridian. An hour's cruise will set you back more than $500, but the watercraft has its own kitchen with a microwave, four TVs, air-conditioning, and room for 13 guests. And if you schedule it right, maybe you can catch the Magic Kingdom fireworks while onboard. Call ☎ 407-824-2473 to schedule a reservation.

Fishing

Bay Lake was originally stocked with 70,000 largemouth bass that have been cheerfully spawning ever since (many are in the 8- to 10-pound range), and you can arrange a bass-fishing expedition on pontoons that leave from most places with a marina, and putter along Bay Lake and Seven Seas Lagoon for 2 or 4 hours. All these excursions—strictly catch and release—include an experienced guide, rod and reel (if you don't have your own), tackle and bait, and nonalcoholic beverages. Rates for 2-hour trips are $270 for parties of up to five; 4-hour trips are $455. (Hiring a tournament-style boat is a little more expensive.) All equipment is provided, but no coolers (or food or beverages) can be brought aboard. Reservations can be made up to 180 days in advance but must be made a day ahead. Call ☎ 407-939-2277.

Swimming

As for swimming—hello? There isn't a hotel on the place without its own white-sand beach, mini water park, or variety of pools, lap pools, hot tubs, whirlpools, fountains, waterfalls, geysers. The "real" water of Bay Lake and Seven Seas Lagoons isn't for swimming. Those white-sand beaches are for dry-land activities only.

Alligators can be found in almost all bodies of water in Florida, including those at Walt Disney World. Though alligator-related deaths are very rare, both adults and especially children can be attacked while swimming, wading, or sitting near the water's edge. Alligators are most active when feeding in the late afternoon and at dark. If you happen to see an alligator, give it a wide berth (they can run faster than you). Do not feed them, as that can lead to them becoming habituated to humans.

HOTEL POOL RATING

1. Yacht & Beach Club Resorts	★★★★★ (shared complex)
2. Animal Kingdom Villas (Kidani Village)	★★★★½
3. Grand Floridian Resort & Spa & Villas	★★★★½
4. Saratoga Springs Resort & Spa—Treehouse Villas	★★★★½
5. Wilderness Lodge & Villas	★★★★½
6. Animal Kingdom Lodge & Villas (Jambo House)	★★★★
7. Bay Lake Tower	★★★★
8. Caribbean Beach Resort	★★★★
9. Coronado Springs Resort	★★★★
10. Dolphin	★★★★
11. Polynesian Village, Villas, & Bungalows	★★★★
12. Port Orleans Resort	★★★★
13. Swan	★★★★
14. BoardWalk Inn & Villas	★★★½
15. Contemporary Resort	★★★½
16. All-Star Resorts	★★★
17. Art of Animation Resort	★★★
18. Fort Wilderness Resort & Campground	★★★
19. Old Key West Resort	★★★
20. Pop Century Resort	★★★
21. Shades of Green	★★★

Waterskiing

Waterskiing can be arranged for $165 per hour, which covers the boat, a driver-instructor, up to five friends who can ride along, and skis if you don't have your own, along with mini surfboards and kneeboards; make reservations at least 24 hours in advance at ☎ 407-939-0754, and meet at the Contemporary Resort marina office.

BACK ON DRY LAND

Tennis

You can rent a tennis racket, tog up in brand-name or souvenir sportswear, and even buy shoes to suit the surface in the respective pro shops. In fact, you can rent a pro as well. If you want to go back home with a new drop shot, this is definitely the place. For $90 an hour, you can take tennis lessons from a tennis pro at Animal Kingdom Lodge, Bay Lake Tower, Boardwalk Inn, Saratoga Springs, or Yacht & Beach Club Resorts. Lessons can be booked 180 days in advance, and it's probably a good idea to do so. For lesson reservations or video analysis, call ☎ 321-228-1146. (Ask which facilities have racket rentals.)

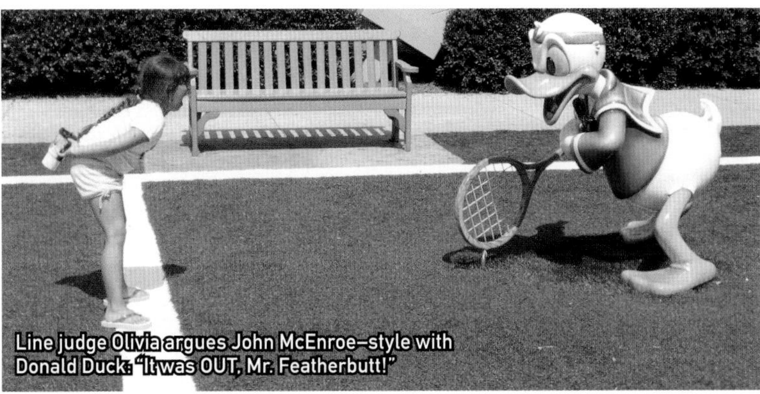

Line judge Olivia argues John McEnroe–style with Donald Duck: "It was OUT, Mr. Featherbutt!"

Saratoga Springs has two clay courts located near the Carriage House lobby. Bay Lake Tower and BoardWalk Inn have two hard courts each. Old Key West, Yacht & Beach Club, Kidani Village at Animal Kingdom Lodge, and the Swan and Dolphin have hard, rubberized surface courts, most of them lighted for evening play; inquire when making reservations. These courts are available for free to resort guests on a first-come, first-serve basis; they are open 8 a.m.–10 p.m. Equipment is available for rent; Disney Vacation Club members can borrow equipment for free, except at the Swan and Dolphin.

Horseback Riding

Let's be frank: nowhere in Walt Disney World are you going to get into any serious galloping or cross-country event. Nevertheless, you can take a guided trail ride (at a very gentle pace) or a more scenic half-hour carriage ride at Fort Wilderness for $45–$64. The holiday sleigh ride through the backwoods of Wilderness Lodge is quite romantic (though it costs about $80). You can also pick up your carriage at Port Orleans Riverside. Reservations can be made 180 days in advance but must be cancelled at least 24 hours before your scheduled time in order to get a refund; call ☎ 407-WDW-PLAY.

Golf

In late 2011 Arnold Palmer Golf Management inked a 20-year deal with Disney to operate and manage all of the Disney World courses. Golf legend Arnold Palmer and his design team added innovative features to several of the courses, including a full renovation of Disney's Palm to become a Palmer-designed course. The courses have to stand up to more than 250,000 rounds of golf every year, along with nearly 400 tournaments. Greens fees on these courses are about $45–$125 for resort guests, including electric carts (except at Oak Trail) and practice balls. The golf carts, incidentally, are everything you'd expect from Disney and one of the high-tech wonders of the World: They come equipped with GPS technology and full-color monitors so that at each hole you can see computer-generated three-dimensional images of the fairways, greens, and hazards and pick up professional tips and, in some cases, tournament scoreboard information.

If all this is way beyond your game, private lessons from PGA and LPGA Tour pros are available for $75 per 45-minute session. A bucket of balls is $7. You can rent really good clubs for about $50 and shoes for $10. If you seriously plan to play golf at Walt Disney World, stay at one of the resort hotels. Resort guests can book tee times up to 90 days in advance, while day guests can only call 60 days in advance (credit card number required). Resort guests also get discounted greens fees, charging privileges, and overnight shipping of clubs from one course to another. Even better, you can avoid the hassle of driving or hauling your clubs around on a Disney bus; if you're staying at a resort hotel, round-trip transportation to a Disney course is free (you pay the cabbie with hotel vouchers).

Remember that high golf season is in a way the opposite of high water-park season; that is, rates are lower May–January and higher in the spring. If you're just a regular vacationing duffer, you can also cut costs by signing up for early or twilight tee times, which may slash rates by half. Fees for replaying the same course on the same day (if space is available) are half the full rate.

Also note that golf courses are one place where Mickey T-shirts are not appreciated. Proper golf attire is required, meaning a collared shirt for men, Bermuda-length shorts (nothing torn), and spikeless shoes.

Walt Disney World Golf Course Profiles

To find information about or to book tee times at any of the courses, call ☎ 407-WDW-GOLF or visit golfwdw.com.

Palm Golf Course Completely renovated in 2013 by Arnold Palmer, the new course has more-difficult bunkers (59 of them) and undulating greens. The greens play medium-fast to fast, so either go with a lot of spin and loft or try to bounce your shot on. Staff service is excellent. Nine of the holes have water hazards. Beware the alligator in the water at hole #9 (we're not kidding).

Magnolia Golf Course Another fine Joe Lee creation, Magnolia is Disney's longest course and features a whopping 97 bunkers, including the famous one in the shape of Mickey Mouse's head. But the layout is slightly less challenging than the Palm's. At more than 7,500 yards, this course may be the longest most guests ever have the opportunity to play.

Lake Buena Vista Golf Course There are several memorable holes here, but this layout is the only one at Disney with housing on it—a lot of housing—that detracts from the golf experience. Nonetheless, the Joe Lee–designed course itself is relatively pristine and was certified by Audubon International as a Cooperative Wildlife Sanctuary. The setting is geographically unique among the other layouts, tucked behind Saratoga Springs and Old Key West, and has a swampy feel reminiscent of the area's pre-Disney wetlands, with trees dripping Spanish moss. Narrow fairways and small greens emphasize accuracy over length.

Oak Trail Golf Course This Ron Garl nine-holer is a "real" course, not an executive par-3 like many nine-hole designs. Geared toward introducing children to the game, it also makes a good quick-fix or warm-up before a round, and the walking-only layout is the only such routing at Walt Disney World. Pull carts are available.

Tranquilo Golf Club at Four Seasons Orlando Opened in September 2014, the course—which is also a certified Audubon wildlife sanctuary—is shared by the Four Seasons Resort Orlando and Golden Oak, a Disney-owned luxury residential development. Tom Fazio, who designed the original 1992 course (then called Osprey Ridge), also supervised the redesign, which involved re-contouring the greens and renovating/adding bunkers. A new par-3 hole (#16) features deep bunkering and sand and minimal greens. The updated clubhouse has a pro shop and a restaurant called Plancha, serving casual Cuban American fare in a lakeside setting. The course is open to the public, not just Four Seasons guests and Golden Oak residents. Overall, it is more challenging than the other Disney courses, which typically feature wide fairways and are forgiving. Though Tranquilo is no longer an official Disney golf course, we've included it here due to its proximity to the World.

Miniature Golf

Disney World also has two 36-hole mini golf complexes for less ambitious types, or for those who are still wandering around at night looking for something to do after the fireworks. No doubt Disney designers would have preferred to call it Goofy Golf, but there are older such attractions in Florida than Disney World, and as the Disney corporation knows all too well, trademarks are serious things.

Fantasia Gardens This miniature golf complex, tucked behind the Dolphin hotel on Epcot Resorts Boulevard, is two courses in one, both 18 holes and quite prettily landscaped. The setups at Fantasia Gardens are designed to resemble, as you might guess, scenes from *Fantasia*, complete with the hefty hippos and ballerina ostriches,

a *Sorcerer's Apprentice*–style final hole with tipping pails and walking brooms, and so on. Not only that, but there are surfaces and laser beams that react to passing balls with music, special effects, and pop-up scenery. It's more of a game than a golf course.

Its sibling course, Fantasia Fairways, is more truly a miniature golf course—a traditional fairway course on a small scale, lavished with topiaries and fountains and with some impressive back scenery courtesy of Disney's Hollywood Studios.

Prices are about $14 per course, and each is open daily 10 a.m.–11 p.m., weather permitting. Got the munchies? There's a snack bar.

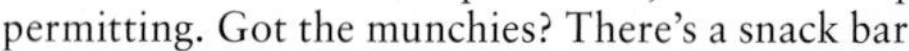

Winter Summerland This complex offers two 18-hole courses near Blizzard Beach: one round, called the Winter Course, is designed to evoke the holidays in Florida, complete with Santa and elves. The other, the Summer Course, has a surfboards-and–sand castles, "Gidget Goes to Disney World" theme. Hours and prices (and snack bar) are the same as for Fantasia Gardens; call ☎ 407-WDW-PLAY.

Biking and Running

Though biking may seem more appealing to those with several days to explore Disney World, or repeat visitors who'd like to see more of the nature side, it's a great way to see several of the prettiest resort areas. There are bicycles for rent, sometimes tandem bikes too, at Fort Wilderness, Wilderness Lodge, Port Orleans Riverside, Saratoga Springs, Old Key West, BoardWalk, Caribbean Beach, and Yacht & Beach Club resorts. Four-wheeled surreys, which are like covered bikes, are available across from the BoardWalk marina, Wilderness Lodge, Port Orleans Riverside, Old Key West, Caribbean Beach, Pop Century, and Art of Animation. The routes range in length from about a mile around the BoardWalk to 9 miles of path at Fort Wilderness. (Remember that most bike paths are also jogging and walking routes and, in some cases, might have golf cart traffic as well.)

Running is obviously popular in a place with so much scenery and sheer space; Disney World is the site of a popular marathon that takes place on a different course through the theme parks every January, plus half-marathons, triathlons, and assorted races throughout the year. If you're the sort of habitual runner who can't pass a week without a road race, check rundisney.com or call ☎ 407-939-4786. For less ambitious joggers, maps are available at each of the hotels that show the nearest trails and access points. Trails are usually no more than 3 miles long, but most are loops, so you can just go around again. The one between the Wilderness Lodge and Fort Wilderness has fitness stations as well.

The Unofficial Guide to Walt Disney World with Kids author Liliane Opsomer (right) and friend Laura Spencer

Working Out and Other Exercise

Among the most elaborate of the resorts' fitness facilities are those at Saratoga Springs, the Contemporary, Animal Kingdom Lodge, and the Grand Floridian, all of which adjoin spas. Guests at the Polynesian Village Resort have free access to the Grand Floridian facility. Wilderness Lodge has a fitness center but not a spa. Yacht Club and Beach Club share a fitness center where you can get spa services by advance arrangements; the BoardWalk Inn & Villas have a similar arrangement. Both the Swan and Dolphin hotels have fitness centers—the one in the Swan is slightly larger—and guests have access to the Mandara Spa in the Dolphin. Most of the clubs also have personal trainers available and, in some cases, nutritionists for diet advice; check with the specific fitness club.

All health clubs have age limits that require guests to be at least in their teens, and most clubs require even those guests to be with an adult. Some spas have child services, but spas tend to be quieter anyway.

HOTEL FITNESS CENTER RATING

1. Saratoga Springs Resort & Spa–Treehouse Villas	★★★★★
2. Grand Floridian Resort & Spa and Villas	★★★★½
3. Animal Kingdom Lodge & Villas	★★★★
4. BoardWalk Inn & Villas	★★★★
5. Yacht & Beach Club Resorts	★★★★ (shared facility)
6. Contemporary Resort–Bay Lake Tower	★★★½ (shared facility)
7. Coronado Springs Resort	★★★½
8. Wilderness Lodge & Villas	★★★½
9. Dolphin	★★★
10. Shades of Green	★★★
11. Swan	★★★
12. Old Key West Resort	★½

SPECTATOR SPORTS

ESPN Wide World of Sports

The Wide World of Sports includes a retro-ish 9,500-seat, six-luxury-suite lighted baseball stadium, where the Atlanta Braves train and play their home exhibition-season games. It also houses four major-league practice fields, 20 major-league pitcher's mounds, four softball fields, and eight batting tunnels. The 5,000-seat field house holds six basketball courts and a weight room and hosts dozens of competitions and clinics in fencing, wrestling, martial arts, badminton, racquetball, gymnastics, and even coaching and groundskeeping. There's an Olympic-quality track-and-field complex, and an Olympic-tested 250-meter velodrome was disassembled after the 1996 Atlanta Olympics and moved to Disney World. The complex has four convertible fields suitable for football, rugby, soccer, field hockey, lacrosse, and so on; 10 tennis courts, including a 2,000-seat stadium center court where the U.S. Men's Clay Court Championships are played; and five outdoor, sand volleyball courts.

To inquire about events here, call ☎ 407-541-5600. Many events do sell out, so you should try to call or visit espnwwos.com in advance.

© Disney

SPA PLEASURES

Luxury spas are big business, and as far as Disney is concerned, conspicuous consumers R Us, so the place is fairly rife with pampering possibilities—many of them (naturally) fantastic ones. Exotic scents and aromatherapy (citrus zest, ginger, and coconut milk), body wraps (mud, mineral, or seaweed), and hot stones are almost passé. These days, nearly every facial or body treatment description implies not merely ambience but spiritual healing. Some services at the Mandara Spa in the Dolphin are even rituals.

You can banish cellulite, encourage collagen production, erase sun damage, articulate your spinal column, and even soothe your overfed colon—not an impractical suggestion in these indulgent parts. But luxury spa services aren't cheap, here or anywhere else. Ask at your hotel lobby what services they have—most of the fitness centers also have whirlpools, saunas, or steam rooms; massages by appointment; and tanning booths—and decide how fragrant you need to be.

A couple of tips: if you have a preference for a male or female massage therapist, advise spa personnel when you call. Be sure to discuss any physical ailments or allergies with any therapist, whatever the service; it's a good idea to mention this when booking as well. And ask whether a gratuity has already been added to your bill and, if so, what percentage. That way, if you have a really good experience and want to leave a few dollars more, you won't be going overboard.

Four spas are on the Walt Disney World campus. The Senses Spas at **Saratoga Springs** (☎ 407-939-7727; tinyurl.com/saratogaspa) and the **Grand Floridian** (☎ 407-939-7727; tinyurl.com/gfspa) are in their own buildings; the **Mandara Spa** in the Walt Disney World Dolphin (☎ 407-934-4772; mandaraspa.com) is on the main lobby level. The fourth spa is in the **Buena Vista Palace** (☎ 407-827-3200; buenavistapalace.com/spa-en.html), which is one of the Disney Springs Resort Area hotels just across the highway from Disney Springs Marketplace. All are nearly equal in their quality of ingredients and variety of services. Personal service at the Grand Floridian and Saratoga Springs spas is a touch above the rest. The overall facilities at Saratoga Springs are fine; check out the machine that sucks all the water out of your bathing suit. The spa at the Grand Floridian is generally the most expensive; locker rooms are spare. Rates at the Buena Vista Palace are at the lower end of the scale.

INDEX

PHOTO CREDITS

Alija/iStockphoto.com: 44 top center. Ana Abejon/iStockphoto.com: 100 bottom. Amber Alexandria: 162. All AroundOrlando.net: 350. Theo Amditis: 346. Kara Bacon: 13; 229 top. Darren Baker/iStockphoto.com: 105 top. Nick Barese: 41 top; 125 top. Midhat Becar/iStockphoto.com: 100. Mike Billick: iii; 89 bottom; 247 center left; 282 top. Joshua Blake/iStockphoto.com: xii bottom right; xiii top; 81 top; 86 top; 113; 213 top; 254 top; 297 top; 331 top. bobbieo/iStockphoto.com: 124 bottom left. Brendan Bowen: 317 bottom. Tom Bricker: 1; 10; 11 top right; 16; 34; 46; 55; 59 bottom; 83 bottom left; 88; 91 top left; 108 bottom left; 109 top; 141; 173 bottom; 192 bottom; 201 bottom right; 208–209; 218; 249 top; 261; 299; 307 bottom. BeeBright/iStockphoto.com: 254 bottom. belchonock/iStockphoto.com: 331 center left. Derek Burgan: 163 top. Steve Byland/iStockphoto.com: 62 top. Brian Carey: 207 top right; 243 top. Dave Cass: 57; 193 top. Kirk Damato: 186 bottom. Phil Date /iStockphoto.com: 363. Leo DeCandia: 309–310. Samantha Decker: 79 top; 129 top; 153; 168 center; 173 top; 177 center right; 187 bottom; 188 bottom; 222 top; 240 center; 250 bottom; 252; 257 bottom right; 259 bottom; 280 top; 303 bottom. Mustafa Deliormanli/iStockphoto.com: 53. Franky De Meyer/iStockphoto.com: 21. Cory Disbrow: 12; 13 bottom; 37 top; 72; 80 bottom; 143; 165; 182 bottom; 184; 189 top; 193 bottom; 221 bottom left; 246 bottom; 249 bottom; 320 top; 323 top. DNY59/iStockphoto.com: 26. Dennis Dunkman: 260. Ron Duphily Jr.: 197 bottom left. Jaimie Duplass/iStockphoto.com: 22. Marina Dyakonova/iStockphoto.com: 103 top. elgol/iStockphoto.com: xiii center. Jon Fiedler: 19 top left; 258 bottom; 312 bottom; 323 bottom. Floortje/iStockphoto.com: 213 center right. FloridaStock/iStockphoto.com: 5 top. Lukasz Fus/iStockphoto.com: 297 center right. Luis Garcia: 156–157; 170 top; 177 center left; 223 bottom; 329 bottom. Tim Gerdes: 183 bottom. Giraphics/Shutterstock.com: 155 (border). GlobalP/iStockphoto.com: 81 bottom right. Brandon Glover: 348 center right. John Gomez/iStockphoto.com: xii top. Malanie Gorrasi: 56. Nicky Gordon/iStockphoto.com: 134. Gravicapa/iStockphoto.com: xiii bottom. Laney Griner/Getty Images: viii. Vanessa L. Guzan: 127 bottom; 131; 285 bottom left. Samantha Jo Hendricks: 98. Paul Hill/iStockphoto.com: 54. Brian Hogan/iStockphoto.com: 4 bottom. Iaartist/iStockphoto.com: 81 bottom left. ismagilov/iStockphoto.com: 44 bottom. Kris Jaus: 190 top left. jorgene/iStockphoto.com: 254 bottom. Jostaphot/iStockphoto.com: 60 top. Juanmonino/iStockphoto.com: 297 bottom. Randall Keller: 104. Vic Kesse: 125 bottom right. Brett Kiger: 169 top. Jerry Koch/iStockphoto.com: xii bottom. Irena Kofman/iStockphoto.com: 28. Mark Kostich/iStockphoto.com: 5 bottom. Leslie Krzan: 220 top. Jesse Kunerth/iStockphoto.com: 4 top. Reto Kurmann: 272 left. Diane Labombarbe/iStockphoto.com: 23. Laures/iStockphoto.com: 254 bottom. Sergey Lavrentev/iStockphoto.com: 254 bottom. Marine Le Bras: 314. Sean Locke/iStockphoto.com: 62. Daniel Loiselle/iStockphoto.com: xi bottom. Marc Lorenzo: 43 top; 70; 82; 298; 313. Diane Luba: 177 bottom. Ritzy McCarthy: 80 top right; 232 bottom. Brian McEntire /iStockphoto.com: 27. Don McLaughlin/3rd Sibling Photography: 125 bottom left. microgen/iStockphoto.com: 86 top right. Mlenny Photography/iStockphoto.com: 38. Ellen Moran/iStockphoto.com: 213 top left. Peter Morrey: 168 top. mrdoomits/iStockphoto.com: 352 top. MR1805/iStockphoto.com: 86 top left. Chad Oneil Myers: 125 top left and center right. Mystock88photo/Dreamstime.com: 86 bottom. Nastco/iStockphoto.com: 254 center. ND1939/iStockphoto.com: 113. nicolesy/iStockphoto.com: 254 bottom. Alex Nikada/iStockphoto.com: 43 bottom right. Andrew Nokes/iStockphoto.com: 254 center. Nomadsoul1/iStockphoto.com: 20. Greg Nutt: 242 bottom. Dave Oranchak: 269 right. Pahazzard/Wikimedia Commons/CC BY-SA 3.0: 163 bottom (bees; creativecommons.org/licenses/by-sa/3.0). Jay B. Parker: 19 top right; 227 center right; 236 top; 322 top. Marina Parshina/iStockphoto.com: 213 bottom. Matt Pasant: xviii; 17 center; 36 top; 83 top; 109 bottom; 178 bottom; 179 bottom left; 199; 227 top left; 229 bottom; 230 inset; 236 bottom; 305 center; 307 top; 319 (all images). Joe Penniston: 36 bottom; 108 top; 109 center; 176 top; 192 top; 200 top; 201 top; 202 bottom; 203 top; 259 top; 283 bottom; 304; 310; 311; 316 top left; 317 top left. PhotoCG/iStockphoto.com: 86 top left. Photo_Concepts/iStockphoto.com: 213 center right. pixhook/iStockphoto.com: x top. Matthew Pock/flickr.com /photos/fdrspock: 188 top. thepraetorian/iStockphoto.com: 127 top. Jeremy Randall: 357 top. Alan Rappaport: 128 top. RelaxFoto.de/iStockphoto.com: 81 top left. richliy/iStockphoto.com: 297 bottom. Steven Robertson /iStockphoto.com: 106 top. Bri Sabin: 133 inset. Thomas Damgaard Sabo: 18. Matthew Sanchez: 364. Bart Sadowski/iStockphoto.com: 86 top left. Doug Schneider/iStockphoto.com: 105 bottom. Serega/iStockphoto.com: xiii center. Eugene Sergeev/iStockphoto.com: 81 top right. Victoria Shingleton: 32 top. Mike Sperduto: 197 top left. Neil Staeck: 132 bottom. Don Sullivan: 196 bottom; 197 right; 205 top; 221 bottom right; 247 top left. Rob Sutton: 92 top right. Tashi-Delek/iStockphoto.com: 44 center bottom. tetmc/iStockphoto.com: 44 top. Annette Thompson: 293 bottom. Alex Timaios/iStockphoto.com: 8–9. Sergey Titov/iStockphoto.com: 190 top right; 234 top; 317 top right. Dragan Trifunovic/iStockphoto.com: 254 bottom. George Trovato: 103 bottom. Andrea Updyke: 85 top right. Diane Watkins: 224 bottom right; 273 top. Larry White Jr.: 194 bottom. Dane Wirtzfeld /iStockphoto.com: 175 top right; 178 top left; 202 top right; 233 top; 282 center; 308 top. Darren Wittko: 108 bottom right. Victor Zastolsky/iStockphoto.com: 81 bottom right.

COME CHECK US OUT!

Supplement your valuable guidebook with tips, news, and deals by visiting our websites:

theunofficialguides.com
touringplans.com

Also, while there, sign up for The Unofficial Guide newsletter for even more travel tips and special offers.

Join the conversation on social media:

#theUGseries

Other Unofficial Guides

Beyond Disney: The Unofficial Guide to SeaWorld, Universal Orlando, & the Best of Central Florida

The Disneyland Story: The Unofficial Guide to the Evolution of Walt Disney's Dream

Mini-Mickey: The Pocket-Sized Unofficial Guide to Walt Disney World

Universal vs. Disney: The Unofficial Guide to American Theme Parks' Greatest Rivalry

The Unofficial Guide to Disney Cruise Line

The Unofficial Guide to Disneyland

The Unofficial Guide to Las Vegas

The Unofficial Guide to Mall of America

The Unofficial Guide to Universal Orlando

The Unofficial Guide to Walt Disney World

The Unofficial Guide to Walt Disney World with Kids

The Unofficial Guide to Washington, D.C.